NOW ON THE BIG SCREEN

The Unofficial and Unauthorised Guide to *Doctor Who* at the Movies

NOW ON THE BIG SCREEN

The Unofficial and Unauthorised Guide to *Doctor Who* at the Movies

Charles Norton

First published in the UK in 2013 by Telos Publishing Ltd
5A Church Road, Shortlands, Bromley, Kent BR2 0HP,
United Kingdom

www.telos.co.uk

This edition 2015

Telos Publishing Ltd values feedback. Please e-mail us with any comments
you may have about this book to: feedback@telos.co.uk

ISBN: 978-1-84583-930-7

Now On The Big Screen: The Unofficial And Unauthorised Guide To Doctor Who
At The Movies © 2013, 2015 Charles Norton

Index by Ian Pritchard

The moral right of the author has been asserted.

British Library Cataloguing in Publication Data.
A catalogue record for this book is available from the British Library.

Acknowledgements

Special thanks for their help in the compilation of this book go to: David Thompson, Kevin Davies, Marcus Hearn, Brian Eastman, Dr Fiona Subotsky, Peter Litten, Diana Tyler, John Illsley, Jill Foster, Hannah Hatt, Rodney Matthews, Andrew Pixley, Martin Geraghty, Mark Ezra, Paul Magrs, Philip Hinchcliffe, Colin Higgs, Paul Tams, John Humphreys, Allan Cameron, Paul Catling, Ashley Morgan, Barbara Levy, Vic Simpson, Ian Wingrove, Gary Russell, Stevens and Willey Chartered Accountants, Ian Grutchfield, Edward Russell, Philip Fleming, Alex O'Connell, Martin Wiggins, Michael Stevens, Mary Collins, Jack Malvern, Mat Irvine, Richard Bignell, Alan Barnes, Mike Southon, Jayne Crimin, James Hoare, Fiona Liddell and the staff of the Britsh Board of Film Classification, Dick Fiddy and the staff of the British Film Institute Library, the staff of the British Library and my editors Stephen James Walker and David J Howe, and Ian Pritchard for the Index.
Apologies if I've forgotten anyone.

Contents

'Now you can see them in colour on the big screen, closer than ever before. So close, you can feel their fire. So thrilling, you must be there ...'

(*Dr. Who and the Daleks* – original theatrical trailer)

Introduction

In November 2011, David Yates, the director best known for his work on the *Harry Potter* franchise, told *Variety* magazine that he was developing a *Doctor Who* movie for BBC Worldwide.

A rash of speculation exploded across the internet and a lot of people got very excited very quickly.

However, there was one group of people who didn't get very excited at all – who actually didn't seem terribly fussed about the idea. And this was odd, because these were exactly the sort of people you'd have most expected to be excited. These singularly unexcited people were the *Doctor Who* fans.

For the average Saturday teatime viewer, when David Yates told the *LA Times* in December that he was 'developing *Doctor Who*,' the news seemed all rather thrilling. However, *Doctor Who* fans have long memories and they'd already been here before … many times.

Lots of *Doctor Who* films[1] have been proposed over the years, but few have ever succeeded in making it past the script stage. In the 1990s, there seemed to be a new film project entering development every few months. But, after many years of rumours and false hopes, fans have grown somewhat sceptical. Every time another project is announced, it is greeted with a flurry of tabloid headlines. However, tempered by bitter experience, publications like *Doctor Who Magazine* have sensibly lower expectations.

In fact, from the 1970s onwards, there has never *not* been a *Doctor Who* movie at some stage of development or pre-production. All of them have failed and most of them got a lot of people's hopes dashed along the way. Actually, it can be almost guaranteed that someone somewhere in the film industry is probably planning another attempt even as you read this.

Just how difficult can it be to make a film based on a much-loved television institution like *Doctor Who?* Well, as it turns out, very difficult indeed.

It all seemed so much easier when, over just a few short months in 1965, American producers Milton Subotsky and Max J Rosenberg were able

---

[1] This book considers a *Doctor Who* film to be a project designed for the cinema, based on the characters and concepts from the BBC's *Doctor Who* television series. Its discussion will largely confine itself to this definition, with only occasional deviations. This book is *not* about television stories that happen to have been shot on film, nor is it about amateur 'fan films' that happen to have been given unofficial screenings. Neither is it about films that are thematically similar to *Doctor Who*, but not directly based on it.

quickly to pull together the colourfully epic *Dr. Who and the Daleks* for an eager crowd of school-holiday cinemagoers. A sequel followed in 1966, just as easily.

Subotsky and Rosenberg's two *Doctor Who* films were bright, colourful and *very* '60s. The budgets weren't all that large and they didn't win any awards. However, they are still remembered as rather special. These two films did something nobody else has ever managed to do since – they took *Doctor Who* to the movies.

Decades have passed since the production of the last of those two films. Many have tried to produce sequels, re-makes or re-imaginings, but all have failed in one way or another.

In the meantime, the *Doctor Who* television series has come, gone, come again, gone again and then finally come back once more. There have been novels, comic strips, plays, radio episodes, LPs and internet webcasts based on it. However, in all this time, nobody has been able to repeat what those two Americans did from a shed at Shepperton Studios back in the booming summers of 1965 and 1966. Nobody else has ever quite succeeded in taking *Doctor Who* back to the cinema.

Of course, that doesn't mean they won't still keep on trying …

Charles Norton
March 2013

1
Adventures in Time and Shepperton
'Dr. Who and the Daleks'
(1964-1965)

MEN OF STEEL

Ridley Scott was busy.

In October 1963, a brief arrived at the BBC's design department for a new adventure series, then being recorded over at Lime Grove studios in West London. The series was called *Doctor Who* and the brief involved the design and construction of a new race of alien monsters called the Daleks.

What Ridley Scott would have made of the Daleks remains one of history's stranger might-have-beens. Scott was busy working on other shows[2], so the job of designing the Daleks was passed over to the man who had the drawing board next to him – Raymond P Cusick. Cusick's design for the Daleks would become one of the 20th Century's most enduring icons and would help catapult *Doctor Who* from moderately successful weekly TV show to national institution.

From their first appearance in December 1963, in a serial scripted by freelance writer Terry Nation, the Daleks were the new stars of *Doctor Who*, rapidly supplanting the Doctor and his friends in the nation's affections and clocking up more episodes than any other guest character. And in 1965, it was the Daleks (and not the Doctor) who first took *Doctor Who* to the cinema.

'Everyone was rushing around the corridors at Threshold House[3] saying: "Oh, there are going to be Dalek films. They're going to make Dalek soap and Dalek tea-towels,"' remembered Raymond Cusick. 'Everyone had visions of lots of money. I was quite friendly then with Terry Nation. We appeared on a very famous show on BBC2 called *Late Night Line-Up* and I remember asking him after the show, "Well, what about the films Terry?"

---

[2] It was possibly his work on either *Comedy Playhouse* or *Marriage Lines* that forced Scott to move away from *Doctor Who*.

[3] Threshold House was home to the *Doctor Who* production office. A comfortable walking distance between two of the programme's main recording studios at BBC Television Centre and Riverside Studios, it remained the series' base of operations until the early 1990s.

And he said, "Oh, leave it to me." I never saw him again.'[4]

DR WHO'S HOUSE OF HORRORS

Milton Subotsky was born in New York on 27 September 1921. He'd studied engineering in his youth, but his first love had always been the cinema. 'I always wanted to make films, ever since I was a kid,' he recalled. 'I used to save my lunch money and on Saturdays go and see three double features. When I got out of high school, at the age of 17, I wrote to every film company in the New York telephone book and one of them gave me a job as a general assistant.'[5]

Before the Second World War, Subotsky worked as a television producer in New York and Schenectady. After a war spent as a film editor for the US Signal Corps, he returned to television as a writer and producer.

It was around this time that Subotsky met Max J Rosenberg. Also born in New York, on 13 September 1914, law graduate Rosenberg was then working at one of America's biggest and most sucessful film distribution companies with his partner Joseph E Levine.

Rosenberg and Subotsky struck up an almost instant friendship, and in 1954 it was some of the former's cash that paid for Subotsky's own television documentary series –*Junior Science*.

Subotsky and Rosenberg's first film together was the teen-musical *Rock, Rock, Rock* (1956). The picture benefited from the vocal talents of Chuck Berry and Connie Francis, but it wasn't terribly well received by the critics, with *Variety* dismissing it as a mere 'pasted together quickie'.[6] Nevertheless, the film launched Subotsky and Rosenberg in the industry and a sequel appeared the following year. This was *Disc Jockey Jamboree*, calling on the equally impressive musical abilities of Fats Domino, Count Basie and Jerry Lee Lewis.

The budgets on these early films were extremely low – around $75,000 for a nine day shoot. As such, they had always had good profit margins, regardless of any critical maulings from the press.

'Max and Milton would budget a film and try to raise the money for it,' explained film director Freddie Francis. 'Eventually somebody would offer them about half or two thirds of what they needed and they would go ahead and begin production, then raise the rest as they went along.'[7]

Without a single written contract ever being signed between them, the

---

[4] From *Daleks – The Early Years* produced by John Nathan-Turner – BBC Video (1992)
[5] From *DWB (Dream Watch Bulletin)* – Issue 81 (September 1990) p.40
[6] From *The Times* (20 September 1991) p.53
[7] From *The Times* (21 June 2004)

Subotsky/Rosenberg alliance was based on friendship. With that in mind, they later christened their first production company Amicus Films (*amicus* being the Latin word for friend).

'I trusted my partner completely during our partnership because I hardly ever saw him,' explained Subotsky. 'I was busy making pictures and writing scripts and he was busy running around making deals.'[8]

In 1957, the UK government passed the Cinematograph Film Act, establishing a special fund to support film production in Britain. Known as the Eady Levy (named after Treasury official Wilfred Eady), the scheme redistributed a percentage of box-office receipts directly back to British production companies. It encouraged a massive expansion in UK-based film production. A number of overseas producers soon began setting up shop in the UK in order to exploit the money available through the new ruling. Among them were Rosenberg and Subotsky who, together with music publishers Franklin Boyd and Cyril Baker, registered Amicus Productions as a British company on 2 November 1961.

Amicus's 'studio without walls' worked out of a little wooden shed in the grounds of Shepperton Studios in Middlesex. From here, through a combination of frugal financial planning and escapist moviemaking, they would become one of Britain's most prolific production companies. The kind of musicals they'd been making in the States failed to garner similar interest in the UK and they turned to more macabre fare. They would, like their better-known rivals Hammer Studios, become primarily associated with horror pictures[9].

'Hammer was a business set-up,' said Freddie Francis in 1995. 'Had it dealt in garbage disposal, it would have been just as successful. Milton Subotsky from Amicus, on the other hand, was a real horror buff.'[10]

It was a horror film that saw Amicus score their first really big hit – 1964's[11] *Dr. Terror's House of Horrors*. The first of their 'portmanteau' films featuring a number of interlinked short stories, it was a huge success, helped in no small part by the large UK film distributor, Regal Films, which released the picture.

Formed in 1958, Regal (later British Lion) Films was based at the imposing Broadwalk House on London's Appold Street, and was headed up by managing director Joe Vegoda. Following the success of *Dr. Terror's*

---

[8] From *Amicus – The Studio That Dripped Blood* ed. Allan Bryce – Stray Cat Publishing (2000) p.150

[9] In fact, it was arguably Subotsky who first launched the horror boom in Britain, writing an early draft for Hammer Films' first gothic horror hit, *The Curse of Frankenstein*, in 1956.

[10] From the *Guardian* (13 February 2009)

[11] The film wasn't actually released in UK cinemas until the February 1965.

House of Horrors, Vegoda was keen to work with Amicus again and he saw a golden opportunity to do so in the BBC's flourishing *Doctor Who* television series.

'He said, "Let's do another film,"' remembered Subotsky. 'We thought about it and after a while we decided to do *Doctor Who*.'[12]

THE RIGHTS STUFF

In 1964, the BBC was gearing up production on a second Dalek television serial. With special television trailers and extensive publicity in the *Radio Times*, there was a Dalek-themed sense of occasion about *Doctor Who*'s new season. It was amidst all this activity that the *Doctor Who* production team were approached with a joint deal from Milton Subotsky, Max J Rosenberg and Joe Vegoda to make a Dalek feature film.

'[Vegoda] approached the BBC and series producer Verity Lambert to sort out the details,'[13] remembered Subotsky.

The intellectual copyrights to the *Doctor Who* brand, the character of the Doctor, the TARDIS and the supporting characters of Ian, Susan and Barbara were entirely owned by the BBC. However, the rights to individual storylines and characters developed by freelance scriptwriters remained with those scriptwriters themselves. If Vegoda wanted to make a *Doctor Who* movie, he would need only to get the agreement of the BBC. However, he and Amicus also wanted to include the Daleks. To get them, they'd need to speak to the scriptwriter who penned the original television scripts in which the creatures first appeared – their 'creator', Terry Nation.

The BBC had recently reached a formal agreement with Nation whereby the rights (and profits) to the Daleks would be divided up between themselves and the writer[14]. Under this arrangement, the BBC and Nation had joint ownership of both the idea and the design of the Daleks, rather than Nation owning only the idea and the BBC owning only the design. And it was according to this understanding that the deal for the first *Doctor Who* feature film was drawn up with Vegoda.

Film historian Marcus Hearn explains: 'The deals ... were done at a very strange time in the programme's history ... I think that they were making it up as they went along really. All sorts of things could have happened.'

Vegoda, Subotsky and Rosenberg eventually paid the BBC the princely sum of £500 for the exclusive rights to make a film that would be directly

---

[12] From *DWB (Dream Watch Bulletin)* – Issue 81 (September 1990) p.40

[13] From *Doctor Who Monthly* – Issue 84 (January 1984) p.21

[14] This deal was negotiated by Nation's then agent Beryl Vertue who, in a quirk of television history, would go on to become the mother-in-law of Steven Moffat – a writer and executive producer on the 21st Century *Doctor Who* television series.

adapted from Nation's original scripts for the BBC's first seven-part Dalek television serial. Nation would earn a small percentage of the eventual box-office takings on the picture.

Subotsky and Rosenberg would produce the Dalek feature from their base at Shepperton Studios, with Vegoda distributing it in the UK through Regal Films (just as he had done with *Dr. Terror's House of Horrors*). However, Vegoda was reluctant to have the *Doctor Who* film actually go out under the name of Amicus Productions. British Lion Films (who ran Shepperton Studios) were also wary of the Amicus brand. The hope was to produce a family-friendly film, particularly suited to younger audiences. However, the general feeling (certainly at British Lion) was that the Amicus name had too many associations with horror movies, making it an inappropriate tag for the project. Vegoda instead insisted that the movie be released under his own Aaru production label. Although essentially still an Amicus production, it was as an Aaru film that the movie was eventually billed.

The budget was set at a not entirely inconsiderable £180,000. To put this into perspective, Subotsky and Rosenberg's early pictures, like *City of the Dead* (1959), had been budgeted at only £45,000. Even the comparatively glossy *Dr. Terror's House of Horrors* had come in at just around £100,000. Hammer Studios would at this time generally be making films for around £120,000 per picture; and the *Doctor Who* television series was having to get by on roughly £2,000 per episode. Amicus's Dalek film would thus be the company's most expensive to date, comfortably nudging its way into the mid-budget mainstream of popular '60s cinema.

On 12 November 1964, the production was announced in the pages of *Kinematograph Weekly*. Meanwhile, over on BBC1, *Doctor Who*'s second television season had now begun, with the second Dalek story less than a fortnight away. It was as this second Dalek serial was being broadcast through December, that contracts between the filmmakers, Terry Nation and the BBC were finally signed to allow a motion picture to be made.

THE WRITE STUFF

The title of the new film was announced as *Dr. Who and the Daleks* on 4 January 1965. Vegoda went on to describe the film to the *Daily Cinema* as a colourful comedy film for the school summer holiday market.

With shooting pencilled in to start at Shepperton Studios by 1 March, attention had already turned to the film's screenplay.

There seems never to have been any real intention to use Terry Nation as a writer on the film. 'I went to a couple of meetings, I think, at the beginning,' recalled Nation. '[However] I was absorbed in doing something else.'[15] Instead, and apparently at Nation's suggestion, the television show's original story editor, David Whitaker, was briefly drafted in to flesh out some ideas for the movie.

Whitaker was one of the BBC staff members involved in the creation of the *Doctor Who* programme and was enthusiastic about the Daleks in particular. Later that year, he would collaborate with Nation on a Dalek stage play (*The Curse of the Daleks*) and the pair had already worked together on a series of short stories for Souvenir Publishing's *The Dalek Book* (1964). Whitaker was also working on a popular Dalek comic strip for *TV Century 21* comic and had recently novelised Nation's first Dalek television serial for Frederick Muller Ltd. Despite his keenness however, it wouldn't be Whitaker who got the film's eventual screenplay credit.

Writing was very important to Milton Subotsky and it was rare for him not to have a hand in an Amicus script. The *Dr. Who and the Daleks* movie was to be no exception and, working with Whitaker's suggestions, it was Subotsky who essentially wrote the film.

'The most important part of making a film is the script,' Subotsky said. 'It's not the actual shooting of the film. The technicians know their job. The cameraman knows his job. The director knows his job ... Whether or not a company is successful depends on what they choose to shoot and that's all there is to it.'[16]

Subotsky's views on the pre-eminence of the script perhaps go some way to explaining why he never directed any of the pictures he produced. It was a temptation that few producers over at Hammer Studios ever resisted.

Nation's original script was sent to Subotsky and he started to shape his film from there, producing a finished draft by the opening months of 1965. It ran to around 100 pages. 'I just read the script. In fact, I haven't seen those Dalek episodes at all,'[17] he explained. 'I was interested only in comedy and action, and making a film that would delight its audience and be fun. I did every piece of action I could think of and just enough plot to tie the action together. What I was after was a very fast-paced wham bam action movie with fun and comedy.'

In April 1965 he told *Kinematograph Weekly* that he found it 'impossible to do a script about mean people.'[18] 'Meanness means monsters to Subotsky,'[19] explained the journal's Derek Todd.

---

[15] From *Dalekmania* dir. Kevin Davies – Lumiere Video (1995)

[16] From *A History of Horror with Mark Gatiss* dir. John Das – BBC Four (18 October 2010)

[17] From *DWB (Dream Watch Bulletin)* – Issue 81 (September 1990) p.40

[18] From *Kinematograph Weekly* (April 1965)

[19] From *Kinematograph Weekly* (April 1965)

Subotsky's script stayed fairly true to the plot of the original television serial. However, it took sweeping liberties with the concept of the *Doctor Who* series itself. 'We have taken the first seven episodes of the TV serial and have re-written them into a screenplay,'[20] he later told the *Daily Mail*.

'I kept as close as possible to the original scripts in terms of structure,' Subotsky explained in a later interview, 'but cut it down in order to keep the action going. What I was after was action all the way with no pause for dialogue. The sole purpose of the dialogue was to push the action forward, so when I went through the original scripts I cut out big sections simply because they were just padding.'[21]

In the original television version of *Doctor Who*, the Doctor is an irascible and mysterious alien from an (initially unknown) planet – a stranger from another time and place. He is haunted by an unknown past, cut off without friends or protection. He is a refugee from his own world, unable to return home. He travels through time and space in a mysterious machine called the TARDIS, with his granddaughter Susan and two 1960s schoolteachers called Ian Chesterton and Barbara Wright. The TARDIS is bigger inside than it is outside. It is designed to disguise itself, like a chameleon, to blend in with its environment, but a malfunction has left it trapped in the shape of a 1960s London police public call box. Almost none of this background appears in Subotsky's screenplay.

Subotsky's film is instead about an amiable British scientist called Dr Who ('Who' appears to be his surname). The original UK cinema trailer would call him a 'brilliant science professor.'[22] Dr Who lives in London in a comfortable Victorian town-house, with his two granddaughters, Barbara and Susan (Susie). Barbara's boyfriend visits the Who family at their home and discovers that Dr Who has built a time machine in his back garden. The time machine still resembles a police box, but there's never any explanation as to why. The machine is referred to simply as TARDIS (rather than *the* TARDIS) and at no time does the film make any pretence of fitting in with any of the television show's established continuity.

The change of the central character's name from 'the Doctor' to 'Dr Who' is probably the most obvious of Subotsky's adjustments. However, it was perhaps not so surprising, considering that Terry Nation had identified the character as 'Doctor Who' in his original television scripts for the BBC (from which Subotsky was working).

Overall, the most substantive change Subotsky imposed was his overall child-proofing of the story, which drew it away from some of its more adult themes and brought it into line with the contemporary family output of

[20] From the *Daily Mail* (13 March 1965)
[21] From *DWB (Dream Watch Bulletin)* – Issue 81 (September 1990) p.41
[22] From *Dalekmania* dir. Kevin Davies – Lumiere Video (1995)

studios like Walt Disney and film producers like Charles Schneer.

The only entirely original parts of Subotsky's script (not to be based on elements of Nation's teleplay) are at the very start and very end of the film.

The movie sets up its new order with an opening scene at the Who family home. Barbara's bumbling boyfriend Ian visits her, bringing with him a box of her favourite soft-centred chocolates, which he promptly proceeds to sit on. Dr Who takes Ian out to the garden to show off his latest invention (TARDIS). Ian stumbles onto one of the controls and whisks them all off to the planet of the Daleks. From this point on, the film then fairly closely follows the central thrust of the television serial, with only minor deviations. The travellers discover the fascist Daleks and the pacifist Thals in the wake of a nuclear war. They help the Thals to defeat their cruel and mutated oppressors, and the Daleks are no more.

Originally, Subotsky ended his script with an elaborate prehistoric coda. The TARDIS travellers have defeated the Daleks and pile back into their ship. Dr Who sets the controls to return them to 1960s London. However, something goes wrong and they don't end up where they expected to. They materialise in a dense jungle. Venturing outside, they run into a group of ferocious cavemen. The film was then to end on a cliff-hanger with the cavemen bearing down on the time travellers, leaving the way open for a potential sequel. The scene remained a part of the script that was circulated to the cast and crew at least until early March 1965. However, for some unknown reason, none of it was ever filmed. At some stage, it was replaced with a significantly cheaper cliff-hanger, where TARDIS arrives in Britain during the Roman occupation – courtesy of some (not entirely convincing) stock-footage. The Roman scene didn't require the casting of any additional actors, nor the construction of a prehistoric forest set, and may have been created to save money by the film's eventual director, rather than by Subotsky himself.

THE CULT OF THE DIRECTOR

Subotsky was never terribly concerned about who directed his pictures, as long as he retained some control over the writing of the script and the editing of the film. The only occasions he ever fell out with a director came when they (perhaps understandably) attempted to take some of that control away from him.

'The direction is not that important,' said Subotsky. 'I think that the cult of the director only came into being because the critics have to attach some name to a film … They think the director is the man who makes the film, but he is not. I don't really think it's all that important who directs a picture …

You can always take a director off a film if things go completely wrong.'[23]

The person originally chosen to direct Subotsky's Dalek movie was Freddie Francis, and he was officially announced to the press early in January 1965.

Francis was well-liked by Subotsky. He'd started off his career in the camera department before working his way up to cinematographer on 1956's *A Hill in Korea*. By 1964 he had turned away from cinematography to work as a director on movies like Hammer's *Paranoiac* (1963) and the colourful *The Evil of Frankenstein* (1964). He had also directed *Dr. Terror's House of Horrors* – Amicus's first hit – and was currently working over at Shepperton on Subotsky's next picture, Robert Bloch's *The Skull*.

Francis later recalled: 'I was always presented with scripts that were about half as long as they should be, so I'd have to set about adding scenes, sometimes even as we were shooting.'[24]

Subotsky's intention was that Francis would start on the principal photography as soon as filming wrapped on *The Skull*, and the start date for *Dr. Who and the Daleks* was accordingly revised to 9 March.

With a director pencilled in, casting on the picture could begin in earnest, and certainly seems to have been well under way by January 1965, when a variety of Amicus's regular crew members were signed up to work on the new film.

DR WHO?

By 1965, William Hartnell had been playing the part of the Doctor in the *Doctor Who* television series for nearly two years. He would continue to do so until October 1966. Nobody else had ever played the lead in *Doctor Who* and there was no indication than anyone ever would. William Hartnell *was* the Doctor.

However, from the earliest days of pre-production on Amicus's *Dr. Who and the Daleks*, there was never any intention that Hartnell would be making the transition to the big screen. Nor, for that matter, would any other members of the principal television cast.

Even if Subotsky had wanted to use Hartnell in his movie, there wasn't

---

[23] From *Amicus – The Studio That Dripped Blood* ed. Allan Bryce – Stray Cat Publishing (2000) p.11
[24] From *The Times* (21 June 2004)

any guarantee he would have been available[25]; although there is no evidence that he was ever even asked.

'He would dearly have loved to play the Doctor [on film],' said Hartnell's wife Heather, 'but he just didn't have the time. The programme was then on for 48 weeks of the year, and when his four weeks of holiday came he certainly needed the break.'[26]

In looking for his movie Doctor, Subotsky's chief concern was to find an actor of some international standing. At the start of 1965, the only countries outside the UK to have broadcast *Doctor Who* on television were Australia[27] and Canada[28], with a small number of others picking up the series as 1965 progressed. Crucially, the programme didn't yet have any presence in the USA. *Dr. Who and the Daleks* would essentially be the first exposure that America would have to *Doctor Who*, and if Subotsky wanted to attract the interest of this lucrative market, he felt that an established transatlantic 'name' was essential.

News of Subotsky's plans had started to reach America as early as 3 January, with pieces in the *Chicago Tribune* and the *Cumberland Times* from Maris Ross of the UPI press agency. 'Britain is resounding to the footsteps of "things from outer-space …" And the United States could be next,'[29] teased Ross (clearly overlooking the fact that Daleks don't have feet).

THE BARON

The man Subotsky selected to take *Doctor Who* to America was Peter Cushing. Cushing's name had been a bankable one in the States ever since the 1957 release of Hammer's *The Curse of Frankenstein* (a film on which Subotsky had also worked). More recently, Cushing had taken top billing for Amicus in *Dr. Terror's House of Horrors* and was then working with them over at Shepperton on *The Skull*.

---

[25] Hartnell's contract with the BBC committed him to work on the television series' second production block from late July 1964 through to early August 1965. During that time, neither he nor any of the other regular cast would have had more than a few days when they were not needed either in the studio or on location. Hartnell wouldn't have been available to shoot any film of any kind until August and even then, he'd only have been available for less than four weeks (up until 1 September 1965).

[26] From *The Doctor Who File* by Peter Haining – W H Allen & Co (1986) p.33

[27] *Doctor Who* was first broadcast in Australia via the ABC network on 12 January 1965.

[28] *Doctor Who* was first broadcast in Canada via the CBC network on 23 January 1965. However, the series ran only until the spring and no further new *Doctor Who* episodes were broadcast on Canadian TV until 1976.

[29] From the *Chicago Tribune* (3 January 1965)

Peter Cushing was born in Surrey on 26 May 1913 and trained as an actor through night classes at the Guildhall School of Drama while working during the day as an assistant surveyor. From 1936 onwards he appeared in a number of stage roles; and in 1939 received his first film credit, in *The Man in the Iron Mask*. He later had a small part in the Laurel and Hardy movie *A Chump at Oxford* (1940). His early films were made in America, but Cushing's reputation was forged in Britain, to which he returned in 1942. Alongside Patrick Troughton and André Morell, he was part of the UK's first wave of leading television actors, making an impression in the Rudolph Cartier and Nigel Kneale productions of *Nineteen Eighty-Four* (1954) and *The Creature* (1955).

He played Sherlock Holmes for the first time in 1959's *The Hound of the Baskervilles*, later going on to portray the character for a record 18 times on film and television[30]. Soon becoming one of Hammer Studios' leading stars, he took the lead in six Frankenstein movies and five Dracula films.

By the mid-'60s, however, Cushing was finding himself increasingly typecast in horror pictures for companies like Hammer and Tigon. He viewed Subotsky's offer to play Dr Who as a chance to break the cycle. 'I have to admit,' he said, 'it got a bit tiresome when the neighbourhood kids all used to say, "My mum wouldn't like to meet you in a dark alley!" For … I'm really a very gentle person.'[31]

He accepted the role of Dr Who eagerly. He did however sympathise with William Hartnell. He remembered times when he too had been similarly recast. 'I had played Winston Smith in *Nineteen Eighty-Four* on television,' he recalled. 'It was probably the highlight of my television. I'd like to have done the film version, but they gave it to Edmond O'Brien. I still don't know why. Then the next thing is, I'm playing Dr Who while Bill Hartnell is doing it on TV. That's the way it goes. Down one minute and up the next.'[32]

Following Subotsky's logic, Cushing explained: 'The difficulty with playing Dr Who on the screen was that one couldn't expect everyone in the world to know about him and his TARDIS and the television series. So we decided to play him simply as a professor who invented this machine … I created my own character out of that idea, realising that a lot of people in Britain might be disappointed.'[33]

'Although I did not consider myself a fan of the programme,' explained Cushing, 'I did watch it when I agreed to take the part. I decided my Doctor

---

[30] Cushing's record for the most screen appearances as Holmes (between 1959 and 1984) was only broken by Jeremy Brett in 1986.

[31] From *Doctor Who – A Celebration* by Peter Haining – WH Allen & Co (1983) p.80

[32] From *Doctor Who – A Celebration* by Peter Haining – WH Allen & Co (1983) p.74

[33] From *Amicus – The Studio That Dripped Blood* ed. Allan Bryce – Stray Cat Publishing (2000) p.37

had to be a bit less eccentric and crabby and a bit more lively and amusing.'[34]

Peter Cushing was announced as the new movie's lead in January 1965, with a proposed June release date, tying in as a double-bill with Amicus's ultimately never-made *Adventure Island*.

Subotsky was happy with his leading man, saying: '[He is] very professional indeed. He is very inward, not very sociable, but very pleasant towards his fellow actors. He's a true pro ... Very formal. An excellent bloke to have around.'[35]

'It was a change from all the horror pictures,' the actor later commented, 'and made me popular with children, which I was very pleased about. I still believe that Dr Who, as a heroic figure, is one of the best parts any actor could play.'[36]

CLASSIFIED

With a cast-list beginning to come together and a version of the script now completed (by around February), Subotsky and Vegoda got in touch with the British Board of Film Censors (BBFC).

Any film intended for release in a British cinema had first to be awarded a certificate from the BBFC, denoting its suitability for different audiences. In 1965 there were three categories of certification – 'U', 'A' and 'X'. A film would be given a 'U' (or Universal) certificate only if the BBFC judged it suitable to be viewed by all possible audiences, including children. An 'A' (or Adult) film was one that (in certain local council areas, at least) could not be shown to anyone under the age of 16 unless they were accompanied by someone over that age. Finally, the 'X' certificate applied to films from which those under the age of 16 were barred altogether.

Certificates had been a part of British cinema in some form or other since 1912 (when there were only two categories), and studios were well used to working within the system. If a film contained material that was judged to be offensive by the BBFC, then that material would often be removed from the film, to save the production being classified as 'A' or 'X'. However, cutting a finished film could be problematic, sometimes disrupting the narrative or even requiring reshoots to restructure it. In order to minimise the expense involved in re-editing, production companies would often decide on the type of certificate they wanted to get in advance. They would then submit an early draft of the movie's screenplay to the BBFC for

---

[34] From *Doctor Who – 25 Glorious Years* by Peter Haining – WH Allen & Co (1988) p.106

[35] From *DWB (Dream Watch Bulletin)* – Issue 81 (September 1990) p.42

[36] From *Doctor Who – 25 Glorious Years* by Peter Haining – WH Allen & Co (1988) p.106

comment on any areas judged to be potentially unsuitable for a particular category. No film company was ever legally obliged to do this. However, it was fairly standard practice at the time. If a producer knew that a certain scene was likely to end up being cut, there was no point having it filmed it in the first place. The BBFC charged a fee for this service, but it could save a film company much more money in the long run.

Bearing in mind *Doctor Who*'s large established audience of children, Vegoda was naturally keen that his picture would go out in the UK in the 'U' category. Subotsky was similarly keen on making it a 'children's' picture. The only caveat to this was in possible overseas distribution. Vegoda was aware that audiences in places like America[37] and Japan might have an appetite for something a little stronger and more visceral than was permissible in the UK. As such, consideration was also given to the production of alternate versions of *Dr. Who and the Daleks* for certain overseas territories – something that had worked well for Hammer movies like *The Curse of Frankenstein* (1957) and *The Mummy* (1959).

A letter from Milton Subotsky (on his new Aaru headed notepaper) was duly sent to John Trevelyan, director of the BBFC, on 1 February 1965, together with a copy of his draft script. In his letter, Subotsky outlined his hopes to get a 'U' certificate and asked if Trevelyan could 'let us know as soon as possible if there are any changes you would like or if there is anything you would like us to be careful about in shooting the film.'

Trevelyan passed Subotsky's script over to one of the board's senior examiners, who was also then looking over scripts for Amicus's arch-rivals at Hammer Studios.

Later that week, the BBFC's examiner concluded her review of Subotsky's script. She passed a copy of her internal 'Examiner's Report' to Trevelyan on 4 February. In this, she commented that despite concerns about the Daleks, 'the Thals look like handsome human beings, so present no problems from our point of view.' She also correctly observed that as the script was left open-ended, all was clearly being made 'ready for the next adventure – which I am sure, will not be long in coming.'

The majority of the examiner's more pronounced criticisms of Subotsky's script related to the frequent incidence of screaming and the evident terror experienced by some of the film's main characters. In scene two, she singled out the occasion where: 'Barbara <u>screams</u> at a mouse[38]. My only objection to this is that there are too many screams.' On coming across a scene in which Ian screams, she noted simply, 'Must he?' The examiner also raised concerns over the film's (destined never to be seen) closing shots of 'ferocious

---

[37] The Motion Picture Association of America (MPAA) were particularly less likely to request cuts.

[38] This section was later cut (probably prior to filming).

cavemen' closing in on Dr Who and his friends (Scene 119, Page 97).

Trevelyan read through the examiner's comments and on 8 February posted[39] Subotsky's draft screenplay to Joe Vegoda with an accompanying letter. This letter ran through the BBFC's primary concerns about the movie and relayed a series of observations based both on the 4 February report and on Trevelyan's own feelings. It ran as follows:

Dear Joe,

We have now examined the scripts of DR. WHO AND THE DALEKS. It is difficult at this stage to know whether this material will turn out in a way that is suitable for the 'U' category or not, but we think that if shot with discretion it could be suitable. The fact that you are shooting in colour will probably help.

Our two main points of concern are related.

These are:-

1. In 'U' films we are always anxious not to have shots of people who are terrified, particularly close shots. The more that Dr. who [sic] and his party appear reasonably calm and collected in the face of all kinds of apparent dangers, the better from our point of view.

2. We are always worried about screams, for the 'U' category, and there are a great many in this script. In view of this you should take a lot of care with your soundtrack.

My comments on points of detail are as follows: -

Page 1 – Scene 2	The film opens with Barbara screaming. See my general comment.
Page 9 – Scene 6	Barbara screams again.
Page 10 – Scene 7	Here we have 'a hideous reptile-like creature – the sort that exist only in nightmares'. Great care will be needed and close shots should be avoided. I think you would also be wise to avoid

---

[39] This is actually a little odd, since Vegoda's office at Regal Films was less than 100 yards away from Trevelyan's desk at the BBFC. He could have delivered it to Vegoda by hand, but didn't for some reason.

any shot of the creature advancing into the camera, since we believe that this kind of shot is much more frightening for little children than shots of a creature moving across the screen from one side to the other. Ian screams in this scene; is this necessary?

Page 12 – Scene 7   Here we get a shock as the hand touches Susan who screams and starts to run. The hand grips her and she shrieks. We do not care for this and would advise you to alter it.

Page 19 – Scene 12   Here Ian yells, and finds that it is Dr. Who. See my previous comments.

Page 19 – Scene 14/15   This incident may well be troublesome, and I think you might well provide for cutting or indeed for some alternate scene. She should certainly not look too frightened and we would prefer to avoid screams.

Page 24 – Scene 20   Ian screams again as the Dalek fires at him and makes him collapse. All this should be shot with great discretion, and you should provide for cutting if necessary. The incident itself is alarming for young children.

Pages 30-32   This again is a difficult scene and
Scenes 28-29   you should provide for cutting. We would certainly not want much made of Susan's terror – certainly not close shots – and the quicker we come to realise that the furry feet belong to a quite nice-looking Thal, the better.

Page 35 – Scene 30   Care should be taken with the scene in which Susan is interrogated under a cone of bright light.

Page 37 – Scene 33   Ian wakes with a scream. See previous comments.

Page 48 – Scene 40   The strangling incident should be short and not unpleasant. We would certainly not want to see Ian's tongue pop out of his mouth.

Page 51 – Scene 40   It is difficult to visualise the 'large

	glistening green claw.' We hope it will be all right.
Page 58 – Scene 54	I suppose burning Daleks will be all right.
Page 65 – Scene 79	We are never very keen in 'U' films for people being killed by flame-guns; even if the picture goes into negative it may be difficult.
Page 76 – Scene 91	The shot of the eyes in the water may be really frightening. We would certainly not want a close shot.
Page 77 – Scene 92	Here we have a 'dreadful scream' from Elyon. See previous comments.
Page 85 – Scene 98	Antodus screams as he falls into the chasm. See previous comments.
Page 94 –Scene 116	The final fight should be shot with discretion and allowance should be made for cutting if necessary. There is a lot of flame, and even if it does not hit any human being it might be a bit much.
Page 97 – Scene 119	We would not want the caveman to look or sound really frightening.

I do appreciate the point that you made on the telephone, that a version for the 'U' category here will not be strong enough for the United States, and I hope that it will not be too difficult or expensive to provide alternate versions.

Yours:

John Trevelyan

Vegoda replied to Trevelyan's letter the following day, 9 February. He mentioned that he had already passed the observations onto Subotsky for further consideration and concluded: 'I do hope that during the shooting of the film you will take the opportunity of having lunch with me at the studios.'

As a consequence of the BBFC's comments, a number of elements in the script were either reworked or removed altogether, before it went into the studio. The opening section at the London residence of Dr Who lost a scene in which Barbara screamed at the sight of a mouse. This could also have been done to help sell the image of the character as intelligent and scientifically well-informed. The overall amount of screaming in the script was also reduced (particularly from Ian) and a strangling scene involving Ian was changed.

Possibly in a bid to stir up interest in the production, news of the BBFC's suggestions was leaked to the newspapers the following month – in somewhat inflated form. *The Daily Sketch* reported (not entirely accurately) on 5 March: 'Mr. Trevelyan, secretary of the British Board of Film Censors, has told American producer Milton Subotsky that he will have to cut three pages of script from his film *Dr. Who and the Daleks* before it will get a "U" certificate.'[40] The article continued with a quote from Subotsky stating: 'If the BBC TV serial of "Dr Who" [sic] was a film it would get an "X" certificate. Mr Trevelyan thinks it is horrible, just horrible, and he even asked for cuts in my script, which is a very light-hearted treatment.'[41]

Although the person responsible for leaking the BBFC information to the papers was never divulged at the time, it was, of course, Milton Subotsky himself.

PLANET OF THE DALEKS

Back over at Shepperton Studios, filming on Amicus's *The Skull* came to an end on 19 February, giving Peter Cushing a window of just over three weeks before shooting on *Dr. Who and the Daleks* was due to begin (again at Shepperton). Once *The Skull* entered the cutting room, director Freddie Francis finally had more time to devote to the Dalek project, and work had began in earnest on the construction of some of the movie's many elaborate sets over on Shepperton's expansive H-Stage.

At nearly 30,000 square feet, H-Stage was then the largest stage in Europe and was often flooded to be used as a giant water tank for seafaring pictures. The substantial floor space allowed for the construction of some massive jungle sets and gave the exterior of the Dalek city a sense of scale far beyond anything that had yet been seen in the television series.

'We had a set designer called Bill Constable who we used on all our pictures,' said Subotsky. 'He was very good and we worked very well with him. The petrified forest was very good. I thought that design was excellent, as was the hill going up to the city which opened up.'[42]

'They actually built the Dalek city far to the other end of the studio,' commented actress Roberta Tovey, 'as though we were actually seeing the Dalek city in the distance. It was all there for us.'[43]

'It's probably the world's first plastic set,' Subotsky (not entirely

---

[40] From the *Daily Sketch* (5 March 1965)
[41] From the *Daily Sketch* (5 March 1965)
[42] From *DWB (Dream Watch Bulletin)* – Issue 81 (September 1990) p.41
[43] From *Dalekmania* dir. Kevin Davies – Lumiere Video (1995)

accurately) told reporters at the time. 'It's all plastic, but it looks metallic. We used all sorts of new materials.'[44] In reality, the majority of the forest was made from plaster of Paris at the Shepperton plaster workshops.

Special effects artist Gerald Larn recalls: 'I remember the stage and what the set-dressers had done. This ... weird sort of upside-down foliage of some sort or another, scattered about the place that was a sort of green ... all on H-Stage.'

It was also around this time that work started on the construction of Dr Who's all-important time-machine – TARDIS. For the BBC series, the TARDIS interior had been designed by staff designer Peter Brachacki and constructed by an external contractor, Shawcraft Models (who also built the Dalek props). Brachacki's design made a feature of a multi-sided console with a transparent column at its centre. The walls had a recurring circular motif, reportedly inspired by the patterned ceiling of the scenery block at BBC Television Centre. The outer-shell of the TARDIS was a shortened (and not entirely accurate) wooden facsimile of a contemporary police box.

The movie would retain the police box idea but give the ship an entirely different interior layout, losing both the central console and the patterned wall motif.

'Bill Constable decided to design his own and I accepted his design,' said Subotsky. 'We wanted something that was very spacious inside.'[45]

The result is far less of a machine (as seen in the television show) and far more of a room. The overall effect is of a sprawling laboratory, full of cluttered equipment and experiments. There is no overarching layout to the space. On balance, the set is not a particularly memorable one.

The doors of the television TARDIS were always something of an oddity. Outside, the doors of the police box would open. There would be some degree of dark space and then a large pair of futuristic internal doors lay beyond. There was little indication of how the outer doors connected with the inner ones. The film neatly avoided this grey area by simply having the inner doors as a reverse of the outer ones. There was only one set of doors and no middle section. This idea would eventually find its way into the BBC's television series when the TARDIS interior was redesigned in 2005.

Another area in which the film differed from the designs of the television series was in the construction of the TARDIS's police box exterior.

The TARDIS of the television series was based on a 1929-type police public call box. These boxes were designed by Metropolitan Police surveyor Gilbert MacKenzie Trench and quickly became one of the most recognisable pieces of British street furniture. They were built from concrete, with a wooden door. Any member of the BBC design department in the 1960s

---

[44] From *Doctor Who Monthly* – Issue 84 (January 1984) p.22
[45] From *DWB (Dream Watch Bulletin)* – Issue 81 (September 1990) p.41

would probably have been familiar with the look of them. It is therefore surprising that in the entire history of *Doctor Who* on television, the BBC's production team have never yet managed to construct a faithful facsimile of a police box for use in the actual programme. At the time of writing, there have been half a dozen or so police box props used in the series and every one of them has been either too short, the wrong shape, the wrong colour or incorrectly proportioned. In addition, the outer doors have almost always opened inwards, whereas on a real police box, they open outwards.

The box constructed by Bill Constable and his team for *Dr. Who and the Daleks* was quite different. Constable's police box *was* the right size, the right shape, the right colour and even retained the correct St John's Ambulance logo on the door. It was an exact replica. The doors even open as they should.

On 26 February, the BBFC sent a representative down to Shepperton, where they had the opportunity to see all the newly-erected sets for themselves. They also got to speak to Freddie Francis and the film's production manager Ted Lloyd. The BBFC representative was reportedly impressed with the expansive studio sets, but still advised caution over a number of shots of screaming and frightened crowds.

Preparation for the film was now well under way. However, it was at this point that something seems to have gone wrong.

It is not altogether clear what happened or why, and nobody who might have known is still alive to ask. However, less than two weeks before filming was scheduled to begin, Freddie Francis was replaced as the director of *Dr. Who and the Daleks*.

A CHANGE OF DIRECTION

It seems highly unlikely that Subotsky would have forcibly removed Francis from the film. With less than a fortnight to go before studio work was due to start, there would have had to have been very serious reasons indeed to have justified such a move, and there is no evidence for this. Indeed, Subotsky was glad to have attracted the talents of the Oscar winning[46] Francis, and the pair would go on to work together again in the future – Francis later directed Amicus's *The Psychopath* (1966), *The Deadly Bees* (1967), *Torture Garden* (1967) and *Tales from the Crypt* (1972). They clearly hadn't fallen out to any great degree. However, for whatever reason, in early March 1965, Francis left the production.

Francis's replacement on the Dalek picture was Gordon Flemyng.

---

[46] Francis won an Academy Award for his black and white cinematography on 1960's *Sons and Lovers*. Many years later he won another Oscar for his cinematography on 1989's *Glory*.

Described by *The Times* as 'a tall, earnest Glaswegian,'[47] Flemyng had been born in the slums of Glasgow in March 1934. He'd got his break as a director around 1959 at Scottish Television (STV), where he also met his future wife, Fiona Jackson. He moved to Granada Television in 1960, to work on shows like *The Army Game*[48]. While still taking on directing jobs at ITV and Merton Park Studios, Flemyng first worked with Milton Subotsky on the 1963 film *Just For Fun* – one of the producer's early pop vehicles. The movie was described by the marketing people as the 'biggest teen musical on Earth.' Critics described it as 'the worst film made anywhere, ever.'[49]

Happily, Flemyng felt more comfortable with the escapism of *Dr. Who and the Daleks* than he had with musicals, and he embraced the new production with enthusiasm. Following what appears to have been a brief period of hand-over, with Flemyng trailing the departing Francis, Flemyng was fully installed as director on the picture by around March 1965.

'I take every film as it comes,' he later said of his approach to directing. 'It could be comedy, drama, musical. If it presents a challenge in production then I like it better.'[50]

THE FAMILY WHO

Still early in pre-production, Ann Bell was initially announced to be playing Barbara – Dr Who's eldest granddaughter and the film's top-billed actress. This followed her appearance as Ann Rogers in the second 'chapter' of *Dr. Terror's House of Horrors*.

Bell's career had grown out of her theatre work with the Old Vic in the late '50s and early '60s, including an appearance in John Fernald's 1960/1 production of *The Seagull*. Television work followed with episodes of the first season of *The Avengers* (1961) and *Out of This World* (1962). She had played the lead in a 1963 production of *Jane Eyre* and had appeared in a number of low-budget British films, with *Dr. Terror's House of Horrors* being the third of these.

Also to be carried over from the cast of *Dr. Terror's House of Horrors* was the multi-talented musical star Roy Castle. He had appeared in *Dr. Terror* as Biff Bailey, a doomed musician, in a part that had called on his talents as a trumpeter. (He'd been a very last-minute replacement for jazz clarinettist Acker Bilk.) Subotsky and Francis had been impressed with Castle and were quick to cast him as Ian Chesterton in *Dr. Who and the Daleks*.

---

[47] From *The Times* (29 October 1966)
[48] Although William Hartnell was one of the central cast in *The Army Game* in 1960, Flemyng didn't actually direct any episodes featuring him.
[49] From *The Times* (29 October 1966)
[50] From the (Glasgow) *Evening Citizen* (22 July 1966)

'They always said that I should be the guy for the next musical,'[51] Castle later told film historian Marcus Hearn with some puzzlement. 'I was the song and dance man, and yet my first two films were a horror movie and a science fiction picture.'[52]

Playing Dr Who's youngest granddaughter Susan (often referred to as Susie) was 11-year old child actress Roberta Tovey, who, despite her age, had already appeared in four films, with a fifth on the horizon.

'I remember Gordon Flemyng coming down to the stage school I was at – the Corona,' recalled Tovey. '[He saw] a whole bunch of girls that would be the age for the Susan he was looking for, and we all had a chat with him. And then, I got a call a few weeks later to go down to Shepperton Studios, to actually do a film test for the part. I had to go into a sort of library room and pick a book off the shelf and sit and read it aloud. It was one of Spike Milligan's poetry books, which at that age, I didn't understand a word of, but I think he really enjoyed that. And by the time I got home from Shepperton Studios, I'd got a call that I'd been cast as Susan.'[53]

'She was indeed very young but she coped wonderfully,' said Subotsky. 'I think children in general handle pictures very well … She was just perfect.'[54]

Unlike Roy Castle, Tovey was a viewer of the BBC's television version of *Doctor Who*. 'I had watched the TV series with William Hartnell,' she said. 'I knew what it was about and at the thought of actually doing it on film, I was really, really thrilled.'[55] She later commented: 'I was a fan of Carole Ann Ford's Susan, but I didn't try to copy her.'[56]

Among the rest of the cast were Barrie Ingham as Alydon, Michael Coles as Ganatus, Geoffrey Toone as Temmosus and Yvonne Antrobus as Dyoni.

'I was the Queen,' said Antrobus. 'I had a tribe of very tall women and I don't know why I was cast, because I was five foot three and the tribe were all models.'[57]

There was only one major cast change before shooting began, when Ann Bell was replaced by Jennie Linden as Barbara. Again, there's no obvious explanation for this replacement, which took place at some point before February 1965. However, it is possible that the switch was made while Freddie Francis was still on the production. Francis had worked with Jennie Linden before on her first film, *Nightmare* (1964), where she'd been a

---

[51] From *Doctor Who Magazine* – Issue 218 (26 October 1994) p.49

[52] From 'Death to the Daleks' (Special Features) – BBC DVD (2012)

[53] From *Dalekmania* dir. Kevin Davies – Lumiere Video (1995)

[54] From *DWB (Dream Watch Bulletin)* – Issue 81 (September 1990) p.42

[55] From *Dalekmania* dir. Kevin Davies – Lumiere Video (1995)

[56] From *Doctor Who Magazine* – Issue 353 (2 March 2005) p.30

[57] From *Dalekmania* dir. Kevin Davies – Lumiere Video (1995)

replacement for Julie Christie, and Francis may perhaps have cast her on the strength of that.

Linden's previous screen work had all been on television, with parts in *Emergency Ward 10* (1963), *The Avengers* (1964) and *Dr Finlay's Casebook* (1965). She had also recently been seen in the first episode of the BBC's new *Sherlock Holmes* series, alongside Douglas Wilmer as Holmes.

Although not overly familiar with the *Doctor Who* television series, Linden did confide to the *Sun* newspaper: 'I've got a secret method [to keep the Daleks under control]. But, I can assure you that fluttering the eyelids is useless.'[58]

Flemyng was apparently keen that Barbara would be a practical character, and it was at his suggestion that she be kitted out with a pair of hardwearing trousers and warm sweater – all the better to cope with the script's many action sequences.

TIN POT DICTATORS

Of course, regardless of the casting, the humans were never really going to be the stars of *Dr. Who and the Daleks*. The Daleks themselves were the chief attraction, and Subotsky was prepared to invest a healthy sum into bringing a new cinematic army of them to the screen.

Reports vary wildly as to exactly how much Amicus/Aaru spent on building their new Dalek props, but the figure would most likely have been between £2,800 and £4,500 – significantly more than the BBC had originally spent on their television Daleks in 1963.

With Raymond Cusick's original plans loaned to them by the BBC, the film's production team turned to the same external contractors who had originally built the Daleks for television – Shawcraft Models Ltd. A small independent props company, Shawcraft worked out of an unassuming 5,000 square foot industrial building at 69 Rockingham Road in Uxbridge.

'[They] made special props and effects for at least the first three years of *Doctor Who*,' remembered Cusick. '[They] operated from a couple of sheds just west of London airport.'[59]

Shawcraft built eight fully operable fibreglass Daleks for the film. Subotsky later remembered there being 25 to 30 on set. However, some of

---

[58] From the *Sun* (11 February 1965)
[59] From *Doctor Who – The Beginning* (*The Daleks* – Special Features) – BBC DVD (2006)

these were actually plaster dummies, built at Shepperton for crowd scenes[60].

Being made by the same company and to essentially the same design, the new Dalek props were unsurprisingly very similar to their television counterparts back at the BBC. Their raised fenders made them somewhat taller than those in the Daleks' first television story but approximately the same height as those with similar fenders in the second story, 'The Dalek Invasion of Earth'. They stood about 5' 6" tall (although the press were told 5' 8") and had a base of 4' 1" by 2' 9". One of the few constructional differences was that the box mountings for the arms were moulded into the fibreglass shell of the shoulders themselves rather than being added separately[61]. Other variations included the use of larger dome lights, and a pincer in place of the usual sucker cup arm attachment.

Keen to make the most of their vibrant Technicolor film stock, Aaru also had their Daleks painted somewhat more colourfully than those seen on television. Six rank-and-file Daleks had the same silver finish and blue hemispheres as their television counterparts, but with blue domes and fenders, and theirshoulder rings were painted gold. Two more senior Daleks were liveried in black – similar to the Dalek Supreme in 'The Dalek Invasion of Earth' – and red – a colour adopted for the Supreme Dalek in the much later television story 'The Stolen Earth'/'Journey's End' (2008) – with gold fenders rather than blue.

Thus the movie Daleks were essentially the same shape and size as those seen in 'The Dalek Invasion of Earth' – the creatures' most recent television appearance – and had colour schemes only moderately bolder than those featured in the BBC's own productions. However, to young cinemagoers, used to watching *Doctor Who* on a small black and white screen in their living rooms, they no doubt *seemed* much larger and (obviously) more colourful than ever before – an impression that the hyperbole of the movies' publicity did nothing to dispell. This misconception much later inspired the introduction of a far larger and more colourful rank of 'paradigm' Daleks in the television story 'Victory of the Daleks' in 2010

Of course, in other unavoidable ways, the movie Daleks were just the same as every other Dalek prop, as Flemyng remembered: 'They couldn't go up stairs and they couldn't travel on anything that wasn't smooth.'[62]

---

[60] Thirteen moulded plaster of Paris Daleks were built at a cost of about £100 apiece and included flashing lights and poseable limbs, although they had nobody inside them. You can spot these 'stunt' Daleks by looking for a distinctive 'zig-zag' detailing around their shoulder sections, next to the gun-boxes. They appear *en masse* in a scene where the Daleks start up a war-chant in their city.

[61] A flat top was added to the boxes to allow them to come out of these new moulds.

[62] From *Doctor Who – The Sixties* by David J Howe, Mark Stammers and Stephen James Walker – Virgin Publishing (1993) p.130

Earlier in the month, the BBFC had raised some concerns about the Dalek guns. In the television series, the effect of a Dalek firing its gun had been simply achieved by flicking the studio camera image from positive into negative. This effect continued to be used on the series, in some form, until 1988. However, Subotsky's original script had taken this idea and embellished upon it. The plan for the movie was to retain the negative image effect, but to add a jet of light or flame to it, blasting out of the Dalek gun. This would have been achieved using one of Shepperton's top-of-the-range optical printers. However, when John Trevelyan read the words 'flame' and 'gun' in close succession, it caused him to worry. His comment to Vegoda was: 'We are never very keen in "U" films for people being killed by flame-guns; even if the picture goes into negative.' 'John Trevelyan ... thought children were frightened of flames,'[63] a disappointed Flemyng told *Kinematograph Weekly* in April.

The problem of devising a less graphic alternative appears to have been left to Shepperton Studios' special effects department, led by Ted Samuels. Effects assistant Allan Bryce recalled: 'The Daleks were armed with something like an egg-beater. We had a Dalek in the department and we had to build it this egg-beater device with something that poked in and out at the end when it fired. The trouble was, everything we did, we didn't like. At one point we even used a modified egg-beater. Then somebody came up with the idea of using fire extinguishers. I can't remember exactly whose idea it was. I think it was probably the result of a brainstorming session in the special effects department.'[64]

The solution of having the Daleks fire jets of carbon dioxide from a fire extinguisher was both simple and cheap (always a winning combination in filmmaking). It also had the added bonus of allowing all of the Dalek gun effects to be achieved on the studio floor, thus cutting down on post-production costs. 'We used that simply because we couldn't afford to add a ray to the film and it wouldn't have been good enough to just have people fall down,' explained Flemyng.[65]

With a filming schedule bearing down on him, on 5 March production manager Ted Lloyd contacted the production office of the BBC television series, asking if they could provide or recommend eight of the show's own Dalek operators to work on the new film.

At the time, the BBC were themselves gearing up to begin production on their third full Dalek television serial. As such, some of their own Dalek operators were likely to be unavailable due to their commitments at the BBC.

---

[63] From *Kinematograph Weekly* (April 1965)
[64] From *Doctor Who Magazine* – Issue 197 (17 March 1993) p.21
[65] From *Doctor Who – The Sixties* by David J Howe, Mark Stammers and Stephen James Walker – Virgin Publishing (1993) p.130

(Initial filming dates for the BBC's production would run from 9 to 15 April and would clash with some of the work on the movie.)

Nevertheless, the BBC provided the names of some of their operators; and of these, Robert Jewell, Kevin Manser and Gerald Taylor were all duly contracted to work on the movie. All three men had worked on both of the BBC's previous Dalek serials and had just finished bringing life to a race of giant ants called Zarbi on *Doctor Who*'s February/March serial 'The Web Planet'. The three Dalek operators were joined by Len Saunders, who had recently worked as an extra on the previous *Doctor Who* serial, January/February's 'The Romans'.

The film's other four Dalek operators were supporting artists drawn from outside the BBC's pool: Bruno Castagnoli, Michael Dillon, Bryan Hands and Eric McKay. Robert Jewell would be the principal operator and help school the newcomers in the rigours of Dalek-wrangling. This also earned him an extra fee, much to the annoyance of some of his fellow operators.

'What we needed were fairly small but quite strong people,' explained Flemyng. 'It was actually quite tiring to move those things around all day.'[66]

'I think that they must have been very hot and uncomfortable,' commented Jennie Linden. 'In fact, I know they were.'[67]

THE NIGHTMARE BEGINS

Delayed following the eleventh hour change of director, filming on *Dr. Who and the Daleks* did not start as originally planned on 8 March. Instead, studio work actually began at Shepperton on 12 March (as reported in that month's *Films and Filming* magazine). Following the taking of some publicity shots outside H-Stage and on the studio backlot, the cameras finally started rolling on the very first *Doctor Who* movie.

With the conflicting criteria of both cost and spectacle in mind, the production used an Italian cost-cutting process called Techniscope[68] to get the most out of its Technicolor film stock. 'We did the film in Techniscope,' said Subotsky, 'which is when you take a 35mm frame and put two ... images on each frame, so your film costs are cut in half.'[69]

---

[66] From *Doctor Who – The Sixties* by David J Howe, Mark Stammers and Stephen James Walker – Virgin Publishing (1993) p.130

[67] From *More Than Thirty Years in the TARDIS* dir. Kevin Davies – BBC Video (1994)

[68] The process is also sometimes called 2-perf 35mm. This is because, whereas a normal 35mm frame will have four perforations running along the side of the film, Techniscope has only two perforations. The actual height of the frame itself is only half that of the industry standard – hence half the number of perforations down the side.

[69] From *DWB (Dream Watch Bulletin)* – Issue 81 (September 1990) p.41

The format was very popular with cost-conscious filmmakers at the time. It had helped bring Amicus's *Dr. Terror's House of Horrors* to the screen and had recently been used by Hammer Films on the previous year's *The Curse of the Mummy's Tomb*. It was also in use over at Pinewood Studios on *The Ipcress File*.

Among the first scenes to be shot were those in the alien forest on Skaro, in which the Doctor and his friends first spy the Dalek city in the distance. The sand on the set was later to give Roy Castle problems, when the grit stuck to his contact lenses, irritating his eyes.

To give the forest a feeling of disorientating and alien perspective, Flemyng experimented with anamorphic lenses[70] to distort the picture, to dramatic effect. He explained: 'I had gone into the viewing room to see the rushes from the previous day, but the person who had been in before me had been viewing his material through an anamorphic lens[71]. They had forgotten to take the anamorphic lens out of the projector and all my rushes had this strange, unearthly quality, with all the angles not quite right and the pictures looking wrong somehow. I decided that we could uses this effect in the film, so all the scenes in which we wanted the forest to look strange and alien, we filmed without the anamorphic lens on the camera, while the rest was filmed with the lens on. The distortion achieved was enough to give the film the alien look I was after.'[72]

SHINY HAPPY PEOPLE

The actors playing the Thals were first called onto set when shooting moved to the scenes of Barbara, Ian and the Thals journeying past the swamp to the Dalek city.

The Thals of the television series had essentially been little more than slightly Aryan-looking human beings, in low-cut jackets. They were intended to be good-looking, but in most other respects, appeared no different from the rest of the cast. For the film, however, Flemyng and his team tried something altogether more outlandish. The men were all a

---

[70] Anamorphic lenses are used to 'squash' an image, either horizontally or vertically. The process is routinely used when shooting in widescreen, where the picture is of a greater 'width' than the capacity of the film onto which it is being exposed. One anamorphic lens will squash an image of 35mm 'width' onto an area of only 16mm. A second projector lens will then stretch the finished image back to its original 'true-to-life' proportions for screening.

[71] Although the Techniscope process didn't use any anamorphic lenses on the camera, an anamorphic lens could be used to view completed footage with a projector. An adapted moviola might also be used.

[72] From *Doctor Who – The Sixties* by David J Howe, Mark Stammers and Stephen James Walker – Virgin Publishing (1993) p.129

minimum of six feet and the women five foot six. Many were models and all wore a combination of iridescent gold wigs and shiny blue eye-shadow.

'I would love to see it now in a cinema,' commented Barrie Ingham, who played the Thal leader, Alydon. 'These kind of John Wayne legs akimbo ... and you get what purports to be a chest with no hair on it. And then at the top of it is Jean Shrimpton.'[73]

'I thought the make-up was absolutely wonderful,' said Roberta Tovey. 'I'm sure they didn't enjoy doing it. I'm sure that they had to be there at the crack of dawn, before I even arrived, to get all this make-up on. There were these wonderful false eyelashes that they were wearing.'[74]

As Barrie Ingham explains, the garish look did however create friction with some of the 30 or so Thal extras: 'We did actually have a pretty ugly moment on set. All the guys who were playing the Thals, they were really tough, heavy guys ... They got the real Covent Garden porters. They got the guys who were really used to slinging around the apples and pears and that kind of thing. And they were tough guys, until the moment when they got into make-up. And they started putting this grey make-up on. And then they started putting these eyebrows on, like Jean Shrimpton. And then they started putting things on like Twiggy. Then the make-up ladies said, "Okay, before we make up your bodies ... we would like you to shave all the hairs off your arms and your chests." And they couldn't believe it, because this was absolutely a blow against their masculinity. It was like Samson and Delilah ... They had a meeting and they decided that the only way they'd do it ... was if they'd get more money. So they got about another pound a day. And they all went and shaved the hair off their chests. And it changed their personalities. They all became a little bit more subdued. It was as if they'd given something up and couldn't wait until the day they could grow their hair [back].'[75]

A TOUCH OF GLASS

Following the scenes by the edge of the swamp, filming next moved to sequences set inside the caves underneath the Dalek city, including Antodus's fall into the chasm, which had earlier caused such concern for John Trevelyan at the BBFC. Moving in some semblance of chronological order, shooting then continued with the group's emergence into the city set itself, before shifting back to cover the scene of the party's trek across the mountainside.

The mountainside set was actually quite small - just a few feet across

[73] From *Dalekmania* dir. Kevin Davies – Lumiere Video (1995)
[74] From *Dalekmania* dir. Kevin Davies – Lumiere Video (1995)
[75] From *Dalekmania* dir. Kevin Davies – Lumiere Video (1995)

and covering only of one side of a rocky slope. The rest of the mountain range and the vibrant vista beyond it were the work of Gerald Larn, a matte painter in the Shepperton effects department, who also worked on David Lean's *Doctor Zhivago* (then filming in Spain). 'I was a resident artist/designer at Shepperton from '64 'til '75,' he explains. 'I was on the staff of Shepperton Studios as their resident artist/designer.'

Working from the rushes, Larn created a vast oil-based painting of the Dalek planet, brushed directly onto a large sheet of glass. This was then combined with the 'live' studio film, in post-production. '[The matte painting] was essential,' he says. 'Many, many shots couldn't have been done other than with matte painting.

'We got the image on the film and …. made colour separations from [it] … and did all the technical work on that . Then we recomposed the film, with the bit that we needed to put the painting in blacked out with no exposure. That was then projected onto the glass, so that we knew the area that had got to be painted. Then the painting went on … I looked at that through a viewer and simply matched everything on the glass, in colour. None of them were foreground glasses – which is the term used for anything that's actually included or added to a set … It was all done in the optical printer …

'I can't remember being particularly pushed for time. The average time would have been two to three weeks at the most, I guess, to have something finished and filmed. Sometimes it would take longer, of course, [if] the Technicolor rushes were not good or something like that. There are all sorts of technical problems that can crop up … The work was brought in by Ted [Samuels, the effects supervisor] and he relied on me a great deal. Ted wasn't ignorant of the optical effects side of things, because his brother, George Samuels, had been, for quite some time, working under Percy Day in the '30s and '40s and had been a matte painter of some repute, while Ted himself was all the time working on floor effects.'

Most of Larn's work on the picture was based around footage filmed comparatively early on in the shoot, allowing as much time as possible for him to work on the painting. 'I can remember the painting [of the slopes and vista],' he says. 'I can remember the soft join I had to do between the original footage from H-Stage and the texture of it and all that. It was a sort of greeny colour. There were several shots I think, where this strange landscape was seen. More close-up shots; you didn't have to see vast distances.'

In addition to the planet landscape, Larn and Samuels also added to the chasm scene. 'You can … see a glistening river effect at the bottom of the gorge painting,' Larn noted later. 'We filmed some mirror-reflected light that was then burnt on at a low exposure to try to give some life to the shot.'[76]

Larn completed his work on the effects painting around the start of April. The only serious difficulties he'd encountered had been working around the peculiarities of the 'squashed' Techniscope rushes. 'You're always having to work on a squeezed image,' he says. 'Only when it's filmed in the optical room would we have used an anamorphic lens. That's when we see the marriage of the two unsqueezed ... It means that you've got a lot of visual imagery to retain when ... you go back to your painting in the studio ... You're thereafter looking at a squeezed image in a projector, which you're having to hold up to the eye all the time.'

CUSHING

With work on the small mountain set finished, the crew then returned to the forest, where the Thal encampment had been set up close to the TARDIS prop. This section of filming featured Barrie Ingham's first scene – in which his Alydon and Cushing's Dr Who discuss how to defeat the Daleks.

'We were both sitting by the fireside and just talking,' recalled Ingham. 'Just before the take, he, this vastly experienced film actor with all these credits behind him, said, "Gosh, I always feel so nervous. Don't you? Before the first scene of a film." And because he asked me that, I totally forgot my nerves and we had a lovely scene and I never had another nerve on the rest of the film.... That's the kind of guy he was. He did it quite deliberately to put me at my ease.'[77]

Many others remarked upon Cushing's professionalism and kindness during the shoot. 'Peter Cushing was Dr Who to me and he was like a grandfather to me,' said Roberta Tovey.[78]

'He was meticulous,' remarked assistant director Anthony Waye (later better known for his work on the Bond films). 'You can see it in the films, with his continuity. He was charming to us on the set. He was always even-tempered.'[79]

'It was a curious experience taking over Bill Hartnell's role while he was playing it on television,' said Cushing. 'Especially as I knew Bill and I know he would love to have played the Doctor on film.'[80]

'Peter Cushing was a great flower man,' recalled Tovey. 'He had come up with this idea about this flower, like a tulip, that Susan finds in the forest.

---

[76] From http://www.galeon.com/artinmovies/GeraldLarn/Gerald_Larn.html

[77] From *Dalekmania* dir. Kevin Davies – Lumiere Video (1995))

[78] From *More Than Thirty Years in the TARDIS* dir. Kevin Davies – BBC Video (1994)

[79] From 'Death to the Daleks' (*Special Features*) – BBC DVD (2012)

[80] From *Doctor Who – 25 Glorious Years* by Peter Haining – WH Allen & Co (1988) p.105

And he actually phoned up the horticultural society and actually found a name [Lillium Philadelphicum]. And he came to me and said, "Right, this is what we'll call it." I had to try to remember what I thought were a really long couple of words.'[81]

Tackling his work with consummate dedication, Cushing's quiet obsession to the detail of a character was something he brought to all his films, and it earned him the consistent respect of all those around him. However, he was also a very private man and, although always friendly, did not socialise much with the rest of the cast – often disappearing on long walks, during which he would learn his lines.

'After a shot, he would disappear off to his dressing room,' remembered Dalek operator Bryan Hands. 'He didn't really socialise, certainly not with the Dalek operators, but Roy Castle did.'[82]

ROY CASTLE BEATS TIME (TRAVEL)

Castle was an altogether more gregarious individual than Cushing. and despite his reservations about straying from his preferred song and dance image, he got on well with the other cast and crew. He was especially keen that his performance shouldn't be seen to draw too heavily from the Ian of the BBC television series, but should stand alone as something in its own right. 'I sat down with the producer and we worked it out between us,' he said. 'I wanted to bring my personality to it, rather than copy someone else's.'[83]

'I remember that some days he would bring his trumpet with him to practice,' said Tovey. 'The trouble was that he had the dressing-room down the corridor to me and, of course, when I wasn't on set, I had to be doing my schoolwork with my chaperone and tutor, Mrs Nelson. And Roy would start playing all these songs and I would be trying to concentrate on history and things like that. And you'd get carried away and start singing along to some of the tunes that you recognised. In the end, some days we'd give up and send a message down to him saying, "Can you play this one. We like that one."'[84]

'Roy and I got on really well,' added Barrie Ingham. '[He] was always such tremendous fun to work with – those little bright shining eyes. Such a talent and everything that anybody's ever said about him. No side, no star –

---

[81] From *Dalekmania* dir. Kevin Davies – Lumiere Video (1995))

[82] From 'Death to the Daleks' (*Special Features*) – BBC DVD (2012)

[83] From *Amicus – The Studio That Dripped Blood* ed. Allan Bryce – Stray Cat Publishing (2000) p.33

[84] From *Dalekmania* dir. Kevin Davies – Lumiere Video (1995))

just a wonderful person.'[85]

It was Castle who suggested many of the final film's more slapstick moments. These included his unscripted walking into the open TARDIS door near the end of the movie, and the improvising of Ian's frenetic attempts to take the TARDIS away from Roman Britain in the film's coda. The film gave little scope for Castle to show off his considerable abilities as a dancer, but behind the scenes, he and Cushing did perform a short dance routine for the benefit of a Welsh documentary crew, who were covering the studio filming.

There were, of course, numerous other occasions for back-stage fun too, on what was a mostly good-humoured production. 'One of the funniest things I can remember was really done as a joke,' said Subotsky. 'The leader of the Thals had just finished his lines urging the Thals to fight the Daleks, when Barrie Ingham … just for fun, put in the famous speech from *Henry V*. It wasn't until he got up to the end of this that the director woke up to what he was doing and shouted "Cut!" When everyone saw the rushes of this section they were in fits of laughter.'[86]

CITY OF THE DALEKS

Next to be shot were scenes on the imposing fibreglass slopes at the foot of the Dalek city.

'I had to climb down, and I think Gordon Flemyng saw the look of horror on my face,' said Roberta Tovey. 'It was quite slippery and made of fibreglass… The camera was to stand at the top and pan down with me. I think he saw me looking over the edge and he said, "Don't worry. I'll come down with you. I'll be just behind the camera and I'll catch you if you fall."'[87]

There was some more filming on the swamp and forest sets, before the crew then descended onto the full Dalek city itself.

Built at a cost of £12,500, the city sets covered an area of around 18,000 square feet and were one of the most expensive elements of the production. Making extensive use of Perspex and metallic-sprayed hardboard, the multi-coloured décor made the best of the movie's Technicolor stock, with every surface glinting a vivid copper or aluminium. Meanwhile, flat metallic floors and ramps had been designed to accommodate the Daleks' unfortunate aversion to stairs.[88]

---

[85] From *Dalekmania* dir. Kevin Davies – Lumiere Video (1995))

[86] From *DWB (Dream Watch Bulletin)* – Issue 81 (September 1990) p.41

[87] From *Dalekmania* dir. Kevin Davies – Lumiere Video (1995))

[88] The only flying Daleks in the '60s were in the pages of the *TV Century 21* comic strip.

'Bill Constable built sets that facilitated them as opposed to humans,' recalled Flemyng. 'For example, the doors in their city opened from the centre and were wide at the bottom, narrow at the top – Dalek shaped. The city was designed by Daleks for Daleks.'[89]

Among the first of the city sets to be used was the prison cell where the Doctor and his friends are taken soon after their arrival. These sections would have been shot early on, as material from these scenes was later needed to appear on Dalek security monitors on another set – where black and white rushes were back-projected onto small screens.

By far the biggest of the interior sets was the Dalek control room, a cavernous multi-coloured space, with a gigantic rotating computer console. Most of the scenes taking place here were tackled a little further into the shoot. The impressive set had cost £2,500, in addition to the hire costs of various special props and set-dressings. The set also included (inexplicably) a number of lava-lamps, which were still a fairly new invention at the time.[90] At the top of the set, small slide and ciné film projectors cast images of stock-footage onto miniature screens.

The city scenes also offered many of the cast and crew their first opportunity to work with the Daleks. There were apparently some frictions on the studio floor when the Daleks arrived. Operator Gerald Taylor reportedly had a disagreement with Flemyng when a take went wrong. The money men at Amicus/Regal had also been somewhat put out by their having to use the BBC's own Dalek actors, rather than standard extras, to man the Daleks.

'I had to be very helpful with the Daleks,' recalled Tovey. 'I had to make it look as though he was taking hold of my wrist, but at the same time, I had to sort of help him along, because their sight in there was limited. They couldn't see very much. So, you had to do it so that you were helping, but make it look as though you were really quite frightened.'[91]

An additional problem arose fairly early in the shoot, when Flemyng misunderstood the purpose of the lights on top of the Dalek casings. In the television series, these lights flashed in conjunction with the Dalek voices. The operators controlled the flashing with a switch from inside their casings (as best they could). At the BBC, the illusion was helped by the fact that the voice of the Daleks was being delivered on set by out-of-shot voice artists

---

[89] From *Doctor Who – The Sixties* by David J Howe, Mark Stammers and Stephen James Walker – Virgin Publishing (1993) p.130

[90] Dorset inventor Edward Craven-Walker created the first lava lamp in 1963 using a Tree Top orange squash bottle, although it didn't get a US patent until 1968 (filed in 1965). At the time of *Dr. Who and the Daleks*, the lamp must have seemed an impossibly exotic device, but it wouldn't remain so for very long, as they quickly became very popular indeed.

[91] From *Dalekmania* dir. Kevin Davies – Lumiere Video (1995)

Peter Hawkins[92] and David Graham[93]. As long as they were familiar with the script, the operators just had to listen to the voice artists and flash their lights in sympathy with the rhythm of the speech patterns.[94]

For the movie, however, neither Peter Hawkins nor David Graham were actually on set during the filming. Instead, the operators inside the casings learnt their dialogue and spoke the lines out loud from within their casings – to the occasional amusement of their fellow cast members. The voices were then overdubbed (and modulated) in post-production by Hawkins and Graham (who had been recommended by the BBC). This meant that they ended up having to match their performances to the lights, rather than the other way around.

With this in mind, a generous session of additional dialogue recording (ADR) was allotted to iron out any bumps. Or at least, that had been the plan. In practice, Flemyng failed to grasp the true purpose of the lights, assuming the bulbs were intended simply to flash on and off intermittently throughout the film without any connection to what the Daleks were saying. Subotsky was hardly ever on set and so failed to pick up on the mistake until he saw the first batch of Dalek rushes some way into filming.

'The director didn't pay any attention,' said Subotsky, 'and just had them flashing any old how. So when I got the first film in the cutting room, I had to rewrite a lot of the dialogue to fit the flashes.'[95]

The result of Subotsky's rewriting is that some of the Dalek dialogue in the finished film has a very odd and staccato delivery, with strangely extended and contracted sentences, designed to match the randomly flashing lights. It is to the credit of Hawkins and Graham that the results work as well as they do, lending an impressively grating gravitas to the creatures.

Nicholas Briggs, who would later take over as the voice of the Daleks for the BBC[96], has been particularly complimentary of the work Hawkins and Graham did on the picture, commenting: 'Arguably the movies have the best

---

[92] Peter Hawkins provided Dalek voices for all of the 1960s Dalek stories on television (and film) between 1963 and 1967. He also voiced the Cybermen in their first four TV stories, between 1966 and 1968.

[93] Best known as the voice of Parker in *Thunderbirds*, David Graham provided Dalek voices for all of their television stories between 1963 and 1966. Other work on the show included voicing the Mechanoids in 'The Chase' (1965) and playing (flesh and blood) characters in 'The Gunfighters' (1966) and 'City of Death' (1979).

[94] When *Doctor Who* returned to television after a long absence in 2005, the light flashing was taken away from the operators, but in most other respects the operation was unchanged.

[95] From *DWB (Dream Watch Bulletin)* – Issue 81 (September 1990) p.41

[96] Initially, Briggs' Dalek work was purely for the audio-only *Doctor Who* series. He took on the television series as well from 2004 onwards.

Dalek voices of all. Here Hawkins and Graham do us proud, harking back to their staccato delivery from the first Dalek story. The crowning glory is … the masses of reverberation added. There is a really icy metallic ring to every line.'[97] This polished performance is almost certainly down (at least in part) to this being the first time that Dalek voices were recorded exclusively in a dedicated sound studio.

Following completion of the bulk of the main Dalek control room scenes, recording then relocated to the cells where Dr Who and his friends disable a Dalek. At the end of the day, after principal shooting had concluded, Cushing returned to the set to give an eye-line for Tovey and make it easier for her to finish her shooting on the scene. This was the first time that Tovey had seen Cushing without his wig and false moustache.

DEATH TO THE DALEKS

The grand set-piece of the film was the destruction of the Dalek control room. This was left until quite late in the shoot. The bulk of the work was handled by Ted Samuels and the Shepperton effects department, with a combination of different techniques brought in to create a suitably epic explosion.

'A lot of that was actually done with rubber bands,' explained effects assistant Allan Bryce. 'We made eight copies of the big panels that rolled around, out of balsa wood and plaster. Behind them, we stretched a large rubber band that had wooden balls threaded onto it. We also planted fireworks and the little flashes onto the panels. The rubber band was stretched back onto a quick-release hook. When we wanted the control panels to explode we pushed a button that lit the fireworks and released the rubber band. The rubber band flew forward, hitting the back of the panel and knocking it out and breaking it up, while lots of little explosions went off. The process was useful because you could create a large explosion effect that people could practically stand on top of. You couldn't be too close though, because the rubber band actually came through and flew back. The great thing was that you knew exactly where the rubber band was going to come to, so you could stand quite near it. Not only that, but it was fairly quiet.'[98]

Although the explosion worked well on the single take in which it was filmed, Flemyng was reportedly annoyed that one of the Dalek operators had apparently neglected to switch off his casing's lights after the explosion – giving the impression that at least one of the Daleks was still left 'alive' following the blast.

---

[97] From *Doctor Who Magazine* – Issue 326 (5 February 2003) p.47
[98] From *Doctor Who Magazine* – Issue 197 (17 March 1993) p.21

There were many effects created by the Shepperton effects department, of which this was only the most complex. Others included the creation of a working lift mechanism in the Dalek city and the fitting of a fully functional flame cutter to one of the Dalek props.

The in-house Shepperton effects department was a resource available to any producer hiring the studio facilities. 'Wally Veevers was the man in charge,' explains matte artist Gerald Larn, who along with Bryce had been brought into the effects department by Veevers. 'Credits [for any and all effects] were given either to Shepperton Film Studios or to Wally Veevers, because …. he'd established his reputation as the head of department … People like me were uncredited on the films.'

'At the time of the Dalek films there were maybe four of us doing practical work and about six to eight people handling optical work,'[99] recalled Bryce. Later, the two effects disciplines would be more usually divided between visual effects and special effects – one production-based and the other post-production-based. However, in 1965 they were largely taken together, albeit often split into parallel teams

'There was a bit of rivalry between Ted Samuels and our special effects cameraman, Peter Harman,' recalls Larn. 'Peter always felt that the optical effects people should predominate over people who were involved in just floor effects and mechanical things and bangs and things like that. And that's what Ted Samuels was. He was floor effects, Nevertheless, he'd been there for an awfully long time, so [when Wally Veevers later left the department] he was given the mantle [of head of department] by the establishment at Shepperton, rather than Peter Harman, which irked Peter quite a bit.'

'Ted Samuels and his brother Joseph had already been there for many years,' said Bryce. 'I worked on a lot of Amicus films including *The Skull, Dr. Terror's House of Horrors* and *Tales from the Crypt*. Amicus always used the same personnel on a film, in so far as they used the Shepperton department … Sometimes things were quiet, but occasionally it got so busy we were working on several productions simultaneously.'[100]

WRAPPING UP

Around the start of April 1965, the Amicus/Regal publicity machine began to swing into action. A number of prospective merchandisers and toy manufacturers were asked to come to Shepperton Studios to get a feel for the forthcoming film and hopefully to express an interest in some of the merchandising rights. The ploy seems to have worked, and on 5 April a total

[99] From *Doctor Who Magazine* – Issue 197 (17 March 1993) p.20
[100] From *Doctor Who Magazine* – Issue 197 (17 March 1993) p.20

of 42 pieces of individual film merchandise were announced to be going into production to coincide with the release of the picture (with many more to follow). It was also announced that a special Dalek city set was to tour the country's department stores, along with accompanying props.

With articles appearing in the *Daily Worker* (3 April) and *Kinematograph Weekly* (8 April), interest in the new movie was beginning to percolate down to the public, and with filming almost completed, a provisional release date was set for August.

Towards the end of the shoot, most of the scenes involving the film's large cast of extras had now been shot, leaving Flemyng to concentrate almost exclusively on material featuring the core cast of Cushing, Linden, Castle and Tovey.

This material focused on the opening scenes set in Dr Who's townhouse. At the start of this first section of the picture, Dr Who, Barbara and Susan are seen sitting in their living room. Barbara is reading *The Science of Science: Society in the Technological Age*, edited by Maurice Goldsmith and Alan Mackay and published in 1964 by Souvenir Press, while Susan is reading *Physics for the Enquiring Mind – The Methods, Nature and Philosophy of Physical Science* by Eric M Rogers and published in 1960 by Princeton University Press. Both were fairly heavyweight science books of the time. Dr Who meanwhile reads a copy of *The Eagle and Boy's World* comic. It was the latest issue, dated 20 March 1965 (Vol 16 No. 12)[101] and had been purchased from a local newsagent specially for that day's filming.

Recording on Bill Constable's TARDIS interior followed, during which Tovey struggled with her dialogue explaining the nature of the ship's dimensional transcendentalism. The Dalek control room set, renovated after its punishment at the hands of the effects boys, then was used for the recording of a final two set-ups.

On 12 April, the same BBFC representative who had earlier seen the construction of the film's sets with Freddie Francis, now returned to the studios and watched about 45 minutes of unfinished footage from the movie in order to give his professional opinion on the material. This time, the representative reported back that he didn't feel there would be any great problems in granting Subotsky his desired 'U' certificate.

Another visitor to the studio during these final few days of shooting was BBC broadcaster Lyn Fairhurst, who recorded some interviews with Flemyng, Cushing and Castle for inclusion in an edition of the BBC Light Programme's *Movie-Go-Round* radio show entitled 'The Daleks Invade Shepperton'. The programme was broadcast on 9 May, with a special introduction from a Dalek.

---

[101] That week's issue featured the adventures of both Dan Dare and Heros the Spartan (just in case you were wondering).

Subotsky rarely spent much time on the sets of any of his films, preferring to encounter them first in the cutting-room. It was instead mostly left to Joe Vegoda to represent the company's interests on the studio days, and this had already contributed to problems with the Daleks' light flashes (see above). However, as shooting began drawing to a close in mid-April, Subotsky had at least got a good excuse for being away from the studio floor on one day. On 13 April 1965, he married his fiancée Fiona McCarthy.

Following a few additional shots elsewhere on the Dalek city set (a lift scene, for example), shooting on the film was finally brought to a close with the filming of a handful of model shots, created by the special effects team.

The final day of principal photography was 23 April – an overrun of about a week from the initially planned schedule. The movie wrapped just in time for Dalek operators Jewell, Manser and Taylor to be released from their filmic commitments to start work on rehearsals for the BBC's next Dalek television serial, 'The Chase', on which pre-filming had started on 9 April. Also shortly to be released from their commitments on the film were Dalek voice artists Hawkins and Graham, who likewise joined the BBC's next Dalek serial. Among Linden's and Castle's final commitments was a last brief photo-shoot, shortly after principal photography, in which the pair were pictured reading about the Daleks' latest exploits in the pages of that week's *TV Century 21*[102] comic strip.

Roberta Tovey in particular has fond memories of her final days on the movie. 'We had a deal going on the side of the filming. If I did a shot in one take, [Gordon Flemyng] would give me a shilling. So, we went through the whole of filming, and every time I did a take in one, he said, "I owe you another shilling." I wasn't really sure about this at the time, or whether it was just something he was saying to me. But, on the last day of filming, we'd finished and he called me over and said, "I've got something for you." I said, "Oh?" And he gave me this little bag and it said, "To one-take Tovey. Love Gordon." And inside were 21 shillings[103]. So, I must have done 21 takes for him.'[104]

Following completion of the film, each member of the core cast was also presented with a toy clockwork Dalek (manufactured by Cowan de Groot), as a keepsake of their time with the Daleks.

With shooting on the feature film concluded, the main eight Dalek casings that had been constructed for it were now made available to the BBC (for a fee). The BBC took up Aaru's offer and paid for three of the Dalek props to be used in future *Doctor Who* television productions. These

---

[102] Castle and Linden were photographed reading Issue 14 of the comic, dated 24 April.

[103] Worth about £13.50 in modern money.

[104] From *Dalekmania* dir. Kevin Davies – Lumiere Video (1995)

three props were soon pressed into service at the corporation's Riverside Studios on 14 May during the studio recording for episode three of 'The Chase'. The film props are easily spotted in the final broadcast, due both to their distinctive paint jobs and to the fact that they had all had their fenders and bases removed. The movie props were also used in the studio recording for episode five of the same serial on the afternoon of 28 May, although they are harder to spot in the finished product.

Actually, the BBC's new Dalek serial would narrowly beat the first Dalek movie to the screen, being broadcast between 22 May and 26 June. As one was just finishing its run on television, the other entered the cinema. As such, although viewers wouldn't have realised it at the time, the first screen exposure of the newly-constructed Dalek props wasn't at the cinema at all, but in the television series.

Another cross-pollination between the television and film variants of *Doctor Who* came a few months later, in September 1965, when Barrie Ingham moved from playing a blue-skinned alien in *Dr. Who and the Daleks* to portraying a Greek Prince in the *Doctor Who* television serial 'The Myth Makers'.

POST PRODUCTION

Post-production and editing on the movie began before shooting wrapped. Extensive overdubbing was undertaken for all the Dalek voices and for some of the other actors too, including all of Yvonne Antrobus's dialogue. Gerald Larn had to have his matte paintings delivered to the optical printer, and other optical effects had to be created as well. The music also needed dubbing, together with sound effects.

The editing process was the facet of filming that interested Subotsky most. 'I look at the rushes every day from the point of view of editing,' he explained. 'If I don't feel that [the director] covered a scene well enough I will ask him to take the extra shots that I need ... Editing is the thing that really interests me ... In the cutting room you can do anything you like with it.'[105]

Flemyng seemed fairly happy with Subotsky's hands-on approach to editing. However, some of his other directors were rather less than enamoured with it. Gordon Hessler, who worked for Subotsky in 1986, said: 'Subotsky would argue for frame upon frame upon frame. It was very tedious.'[106]

---

[105] From *Amicus – The Studio That Dripped Blood* ed. Allan Bryce – Stray Cat Publishing (2000) p.11-12
[106] From *Amicus – The Studio That Dripped Blood* ed. Allan Bryce – Stray Cat Publishing (2000) p.60

Various special optical effects were made for *Dr. Who and The Daleks*, under the supervision of Shepperton's effects cameraman, Peter Harman.

'It was an interesting finesse that we could produce in our optical room,' recalls Gerald Larn. 'The optical printer's a remarkable piece of equipment.' It was the optical printer that (nor entirely successfully) composited the footage of a Roman army at the film's conclusion.

However, chief among the optical work was the creation of the film's opening title sequence, made using lights and coloured strips of translucent plastic[107].

Originally there seem to have been some hopes that this new psychedelic sequence would be paired with a recording of the BBC's original title music to open the picture. The already famous *Doctor Who* theme had been written in 1963 by Ron Grainer. It had been realised as a groundbreaking piece of entirely synthesised electronic music by Delia Derbyshire and the BBC's Radiophonic Workshop in its studios at Maida Vale. Remarkably the BBC didn't actually own the copyright to the music itself however (and at the time of writing, still don't). The rights were instead lodged with the Warner Chappell record label. And, although Aaru duly approached the company, an agreement was never reached for the music's inclusion in the film. 'We couldn't get it because they were asking far too much money,' explained Subotsky.'[108]

Joe Vegoda ultimately chose composer Malcolm Lockyer to score the incidental and title music for *Dr. Who and the Daleks*. A total of 36 minutes of sweeping orchestral arrangements were recorded by Lockyer and his musicians, overlaid with additional stock electronic elements from *Thunderbirds* composer Barry Gray.

'I didn't like the music,' commented Subotsky. 'It was too heavy. I wanted a more action packed score ... Joseph Vegoda had a publishing company and he wanted his company to publish the music, so he commissioned the composer.'[109]

DALEKS – INVASION CANNES 1965 AD

As one batch of film Daleks was menacing William Hartnell's Doctor in a Hammersmith TV studio, another was on its way across the English Channel to France. On 17 May, a total of 12 Dalek props (a combination of

---

[107] Many years later, Subotsky commented that he would have liked to have used the original series' title sequence, but the BBC asked for too much money. This seems very odd as the BBC's TV titles had (at this point) only ever been filmed in black and white.

[108] From *DWB (Dream Watch Bulletin)* – Issue 81 (September 1990) p.40

[109] From *DWB (Dream Watch Bulletin)* – Issue 81 (September 1990) p.40

fibreglass casings and plaster 'dummies') were taken to the prestigious Cannes Film Festival, arriving early on 20 May. Among their ranks were the 'senior' red and black Daleks.

Daily Cinema reported on the 'Dalek Invasion of Cannes' on 2 June, with *Kinematograph Weekly* picking up the story the following day. Thanks to the Beatles' concurrent promotion of their second feature film, *Help!*, one newspaper even managed to snap a photograph of John Lennon standing with one of the film's Daleks, which certainly wouldn't have hurt publicity.

By now, the decision had been made to bring forward the film's first release date to June, when it would open at London's Studio One cinema on Oxford Street. On 11 June, details of the Studio One trade show were published, scheduled for 10.30 am on 30 June.

WHAT THE CENSOR SAW

A finished print of *Dr. Who and the Daleks* was officially received for censorship by the BBFC on 16 June, only a few weeks ahead of the planned trade show. The film was, at this stage, 82 minutes and 45 seconds long (7,422 feet). Approximately 17 seconds of material was subsequently cut from this version, prior to the film going on theatrical release. However, how much of this material was cut on the instruction of the censor and how much for other reasons is unknown, as no further paperwork still exists at the BBFC relating to *Doctor Who* at the cinema .

Some members of the cast and crew did, though, recall some of the specific cuts that were made (mostly on the apparent instruction of Subotsky).

For the scene in which Dr Who and his friends disable a Dalek and reveal the Dalek mutant inside, a special hand-puppet had been constructed by Ted Samuels' effects team. Although no photographs survive, the mutant was described in Subotsky's original scripts as 'a hideous reptile-like creature – the sort that exist only in nightmares'. It had already caused concern for John Trevelyan at the BBFC, when his examiner first read the script. 'We made a green, writhing, ukky thing for the inside of the Dalek,' explained effects assistant Allan Bryce. 'Somebody was underneath the creature with their hands inside it, making it writhe. I think it was the editor's decision to cut that, and as far as I can remember, it was the only thing that was cut. That was an example of the sort of thing you couldn't show in a "U" certificate film. Context is very important, and although the creature probably wouldn't have frightened children, it was eventually decided to show the horror as registering on the actor's face.'[110]

'We had a huge problem over whether or not we were going to actually

---

[110] From *Doctor Who Magazine* – Issue 197 (17 March 1993) p.21

show what was inside the Dalek,' Flemyng added. 'No one had ever shown what a Dalek looked like and we decided that it was basically a brain, an intelligence with no recognisable features. I remember going to talk to the censor about what I was going to show when I took the lid off this thing and how I might be able to get round not showing it. Because, what the censor was saying was, "You are not to show it. If you show something and it's a problem to us, we're going to cut it out, because this is a young person's film." Ultimately we decided it was a brain with one arm, because it had to have the means to operate the machine – firing the gun and steering – and we showed the claw hand on the end of the arm.'[111]

On the whole, it appears that Subotsky's early contact with John Trevelyan paid off, and his 'science fiction comedy' was eventually classified as suitable for younger audiences.

'We were quite definitely going for a "U" certificate and if hadn't received a "U" certificate it wouldn't have succeeded,'[112] said Flemyng.

Another scene, in which a tentacle reaches out of the swamp to claim one of the Thals (inspired by a similar scene in the original BBC serial), was also apparently cut, possibly even prior to reaching the BBFC, when Subotsky reportedly judged the tentacled creature to be too unconvincing and embarrassing.

The final print of *Dr. Who and the Daleks* was awarded a 'U' certificate by the BBFC as Aaru had hoped, and the film went into distribution with a final running time of 82 minutes 28 seconds (across eight spools).

A movie trailer was produced, with a voiceover from Cushing, speaking of a 'lost planet' of Daleks. 'Come with us into that strange new world,' intoned Cushing. 'We cannot guarantee your safety, but I can promise you unimagined thrills.'[113] Posters and lobby-cards meanwhile went under the tag-line: 'NOW ON THE BIG SCREEN IN **COLOUR!**'

WHAT THE PAPERS SAID

On 22 June, two days ahead of the movie's opening, the *Dr. Who and the Daleks* team held a special reception for the press. Attendance was healthy, possibly helped by the promise of a free Dalek toy for each of the journalists (probably the same type of clockwork model that had been earlier given to members of the cast).

Reviews were initially mixed, with only a slight bias toward the

---

[111] From *Doctor Who – The Sixties* by David J Howe, Mark Stammers and Stephen James Walker – Virgin Publishing (1993) p.130
[112] From *Doctor Who – The Sixties* by David J Howe, Mark Stammers and Stephen James Walker – Virgin Publishing (1993) p.130
[113] From *Dalekmania* dir. Kevin Davies – Lumiere Video (1995)

favourable. *Kinematograph Weekly* were happy to recognise the film as 'a sure fire popular money maker'[114] and recommended it to cinema owners. However, the *Daily Sketch* dismissed it as 'boring'[115]. *The Times* dammed it further, claiming it owed too much to H G Wells and saying, 'The technical advantages of the cinema over the television only show up the shoddiness of the sets and the dialogue, which is too feeble even to be funny.'[116]

Leonard Mosley of the *Daily Express* concurred, writing: 'The dotty doctor is played by Peter Cushing rather in the manner of a mad hatter looking for a lost tea party ... [The film] hits you in the eye like a squirt of fly-spray.' His view of the Daleks themselves was only marginally better: 'Their abrasive voices cut your eardrums. Their spiny protuberances spit smoky venom. They pretended to be dead at the end of the film, but I don't believe it.'[117]

Barry Norman, writing in the *Daily Mail*, only reluctantly admitted, '[It had] all the preposterous ingredients for box-office success ... If there is a door to be hurtled through, a box of chocolates to be sat on, a pratfall to be taken, Mr Castle hurtles, sits and takes, skidding through the film like a man on a banana skin.'[118]

It was left to the *People* newspaper to highlight more of the movie's good points, with a quote that also ended up on Aaru's posters. 'Kids will love it,' the paper reported. 'Their parents will find this gigantic schoolboy lark Dalektable.'[119]

The movie premiered on 24 June in London at Studio One, and this was the first time that many of the cast and crew actually got to see it in its finished state.

'I thought he was a little too gentle,' said Terry Nation of Peter Cushing's performance. 'I thought he was too kindly and too warm. The thing that Bill Hartnell had was ... this irascibility. He's a bad tempered old curmudgeonly figure and I'd like to have seen more of that in the character.'[120]

Perhaps most disappointed of all was Yvonne Antrobus, who got to watch back her performance as Dyoni for the first time. Initially, the character's voice had needed over-dubbing for only a few scenes, due to sound recording problems. However, when Antrobus was unavailable for that work, Subotsky felt forced to bring in another actress (identity unknown) to redub all of her original dialogue for the entire film, so that the

---

[114] From *Kinematograph Weekly* (24 June 1965)

[115] From the *Daily Sketch* (23 June 1965)

[116] From *Amicus – The Studio That Dripped Blood* ed. Allan Bryce – Stray Cat Publishing (2000) p.35

[117] From the *Daily Express* (June 1965)

[118] From *Dalekmania – Doctor Who at the Cinema* by Marcus Hearn (1995) p.7

[119] From the *People* (June 1965)

[120] From *Dalekmania* dir. Kevin Davies – Lumiere Video (1995)

voice would remain consistent throughout.

'I remember going to the first screening, which was at Oxford Circus,' Antrobus recalled. 'All I really remember about the actual screening is that it wasn't my voice coming out of my body. I knew it wasn't going to be, but it was still a very unpleasant experience watching it. I was already contracted to do something else and, because it was a small budget, they'd hired a sound studio for a short space of time and I wasn't available for any of that time. So, I couldn't do the post-syncing and they got somebody else to do it … I remember saying rather rudely afterwards to Gordon Flemyng, "Who's was that awful voice doing mine?" And he accosted, "Oh, I thought it was your awful voice," which I suppose I deserved.'[121]

The film's formal opening to the public came the following day – 25 June – with Studio One screening it four times a day on a double bill with Disney's short featurette *The Tattooed Police Horse*[122] (1964).

That day, F Maurice Speed argued in *What's On* magazine that *Dr. Who and the Daleks*: '… proves again , if any additional proof were needed, how much more entertaining is the large screen. Frankly, I find the TV pieces ludicrous beyond measure and aimed, one sometimes imagines, at morons: the same story on the screen, with a generally higher level script, greater production qualities, colour and a sense of healthy humour (the film I find is always chuckling at its own ridiculousness, while the TV serial seems to take itself seriously) allied to far better performances generally, makes the movie quite good clean and simple fun, which I'm sure the youngsters will lap up.'[123]

On the same day, the *Daily Cinema* were less enthusiastic, finding the 'script juvenile and the direction uninspired.'[124] Patrick Gibbs was only slightly more positive in his review for the *Daily Telegraph*: '"In colour and on the wide screen", proclaims the poster for *Dr. Who and the Daleks* (Studio One, U), no doubt to point to the advantages [over] the children's television serial from which it derives. On the other side of the balance-sheet, I might mention it lasts nearly an hour and a half against just under half an hour on TV, reminding us that some prescriptions are more effective in small doses … The way [Dr Who] overcomes his allies' tendency to pacifism and we are left with the idea that might is right … will perhaps upset those in ivory towers.'[125]

---

[121] From *Dalekmania* dir. Kevin Davies – Lumiere Video (1995)

[122] *The Tattooed Police Horse* was a 48 minute support feature, originally designed to accompany that year's *Emil and the Detectives*. It told the story of Roger, a well-bred stable horse frightened of loud noises, who is trained to win a race by an amiable Boston police chief. 'Branded an outcast among trotters, he became a high-steppin' member of the force'… which is nice.

[123] From *What's On* (25 June 1965)

[124] From the *Daily Cinema* (25 June 1965)

[125] From the *Daily Telegraph* (25 June 1965))

As if in response, the weekend brought with it yet more reviews, with Nina Hibbin picking up on the film's 'blimpish militarism'[126] in Saturday's *Daily Worker* – the comments presumably made from her own ivory tower.

At the opposite end of the political spectrum, Philip Oakes[127] concurred with Terry Nation's feelings in the following day's *Sunday Telegraph,* reporting: 'Peter Cushing's Doctor is a pale shadow of the TV grouch.'[128]

TV Century 21 had been happily getting behind publicity for the film for quite a while and first printed an image from it on 26 June 1965, on the cover of issue 23, with a photo of the Daleks in their control room. Meanwhile, the adventures of the Daleks also continued in comic strip form on the back page.

There was more good press that morning from the *Star*, where Ron Thompson reported: 'The sets are extremely well done, the dialogue and the cutting could be better, but young eyes will not worry unduly over these points.' But he too felt, 'Peter Cushing … is far less lovably grumpy than William Hartnell on TV … However, I predict, with very little fear of contradiction, that "Dr. Who and the Daleks" will be one of the most popular films of the year.'[129]

Ewan Ross echoed some of these sentiments in his weekly column for *Film Review* magazine: 'The Daleks march again. Best of the cast is little Roberta Tovey, playing Susan. She is charming, natural and fittingly cleverer and braver than any adult. Peter Cushing dithers and mumbles as the dotty old Doctor. Miss Linden looks lovely – and looks most of the time as if she can't understand how she got mixed up in this madness. Roy Castle makes Ian an excellent hero. The Daleks, glowing, spitting death in all directions, grinding out their "de-stroy-the-Thals" lines like robots with laryngitis, are as they ever were, one of the finest creations for children since Bambi. Should you take your children to see it? Have you any choice?'[130]

Meanwhile, fellow *Film Review* contributor Kevin McEgan commented: 'Most readers will have seen the Daleks on TV but the limitations of the small screen, with black and white presentation, can give little idea of the impact of the Daleks when seen on a big cinema screen and in breathtaking Technicolor.'[131]

Three days into the film's residency, Studio One were already reporting large queues outside the cinema. The film was enjoying the biggest opening

---

[126] From the *Daily Worker* (26 June 1965)

[127] Philip Oakes knew Terry Nation personally. In 1963, just before Nation joined *Doctor Who,* they had both been scriptwriters for the comic actor Tony Hancock

[128] From the *Daily Telegraph* (27 June 1965)

[129] From the *Star* (26 June 1965)

[130] From *Film Review* (June 1965)

[131] From *Film Review* (June 1965)

week British Lion Films had ever seen in their entire 46 year history. By the close of that first week, takings stood at £2,000.

'If you get a piece of a picture, that means you get a tiny percentage of the profits,' remembered Terry Nation. 'Film companies are notorious for being able to hide those profits for years and years and years and you never get anything. Well, the money came in so fast on that first Dalek picture, that they were in profit within the year and they actually had to pay me money, which was wonderful.'[132]

Second week takings were still healthy at £1,850. By the third week, they were down to £1,719 and by the fourth, £1,401. But, on the fifth week, as the school holidays began, takings rocketed to an unprecedented £2,159, outselling even the latest Peter Sellers vehicle, *Heavens Above!*. Record takings were also soon reported in Hastings, Worthing and Hove. Week six was still high at £1,500. £1,082 clocked in for week seven and even week eight brought in a not inconsiderable £951. By any standards, British Lion had much to be pleased about.

With the first Dalek film such a rapid success, Nation's hopes were high for the future of his creations, and he soon told both the *Daily Mail* and *The Observer* of his intention to set up an American-backed Dalek television show (which ultimately never happened).

PUBLICITY

'Dalekmania', as some papers termed it, had now reached its peak. And the people at Amicus and Regal knew it. In July, a special campaign book was produced for the press, containing an 18-page merchandising section (prepared by the BBC television series' own favoured merchandiser, Walter Tuckwell), as well as a free copy of *TV Century 21* comic. Including a series of black and white (colouring-in) line drawings for children and a recipe for Dalek chocolate cake (courtesy of Cadbury's), the campaign book also detailed some of the characters and concepts in the film.

'Looking like truncated cones, the Daleks are gruesome creatures who have to live in metal shells because of excessive radiation,' it explained. 'His personal armament includes a flame gun [not strictly true] which can either destroy or cripple. Probably because of their environment, which has tended to warp their natures, the Daleks are a malevolent race ... We have only four human beings in our story. The first is Dr Who (Peter Cushing), a brilliant experimental scientist ... TARDIS ... was invented by Dr Who ... If there appears to be a lot "inside" in so small an "outside", you must remember that this is a very fantastic invention!'[133]

---

[132] From *Dalekmania* dir. Kevin Davies – Lumiere Video (1995)
[133] From *Dr. Who and the Daleks – Campaign Book* (June 1965)

Promotion for the film continued when Joe Vegoda was interviewed for BBC South's *A Quick Look Round* on 26 July.

31 July saw the start of a grand promotional tour for the movie, in which sets and props from the production were taken around the country to cities where the film was playing. The first stop was at the Exhibition Hall in Manchester, where the exhibition opened at 10 am that day (a Saturday) and was reported by the *Manchester Evening News*. Its intentionally juvenile nature was demonstrated by a noticeboard 'signed by Dr Who' that exclaimed with atypical responsibility: 'All citizens of Dalek City must speak the truth and promise not to tell fibs, help Mummy and Daddy, help their sisters and brothers, take care crossing the road, help old people crossing the road, be kind to animals, do a good turn for somebody every day.'[134]

Around late July, *Dr. Who and the Daleks* was also featured in an edition of *Movie Magazine*, a film programme for ITV's TWW network. The episode in question was presented by the father-and-son team of Bruce and Peter Lewis and picked up on their recent set visit to Shepperton Studios. The spot included behind-the-scenes footage from the Dalek control room set and was rounded off with a preview clip from the film (narrated by Roy Castle).

Movie Magazine also ran a competition for children to send in their Dalek drawings. The 23 September edition of the *TV Weekly* listings magazine revealed that this had brought in 30,000 entries. Reportedly the TWW office was completely overwhelmed and the studio's scenery dock had to be used to store the sack-loads of drawings, including at least one hardboard painting and a rendering of an unlikely-sounding 'Beatles-style Dalek'.

Also around this time, an eight page section of photographs helped publicise the film in the 1965 *Dalek World Annual*.

Continuing their close relationship with *TV Century 21*, British Lion sponsored a special promotion that ran in issue 28 of the comic, published on 31 July – the same day the exhibition tour started. Following a full-colour photograph from the film on the magazine's cover, there was a wealth of content promoting the movie inside. A half-page advertisement for the film ran on page 10, together with a Woolworths advert for Dalek pin-badges (that would set you back 1s 3d each). There was a full-page plot synopsis overleaf, together with ten images from the film. Page 12 then went on to advertise the latest Louis Marx battery-operated Dalek toys.

Strangest of all, page 13 recorded an occasion when Lady Penelope and Parker[135] from Gerry and Sylvia Anderson's *Thunderbirds* series, had met up with some of the Dalek movie's stars. 'Come along Parker,' says Lady Penelope. 'Put on your best bib and tucker. We're going to have lunch with

---

[134] From *Doctor Who Magazine* – Issue 353 (2 March 2005) p.33

[135] Parker, as previously noted, was voiced for television by David Graham, who also provided voices for the Daleks in the movie.

the Daleks.' She continues: 'You all know Roy Castle – that versatile and very talented man who has been called Britain's Sammy Davis Jnr ... Doctor Who was not able to come along (probably busy inventing something to defeat the Daleks once and for all ... Little Roberta didn't look in the least scared when I saw her, but I think she had a few sleepless nights when she was acting with the Daleks, and Roy Castle openly admitted he was more scared of them than he was in his horror film [*Dr. Terror's House of Horrors*].'[136]

In the bottom right-hand corner of the page, Cadbury's demonstrated their support by showing readers how to make their own chocolate Daleks, with the same recipe that had earlier appeared in the film's campaign book. Apparently, the cakes were 'quite easy to make, delightful to look at and delicious to eat.'[137] A list of related merchandise followed on page 18. Then page 19 showed two stills from the film, with ten slight differences between the pictures, which readers had to spot.

To top it off, the featured competition that week could win you a 'real' Dalek. A special photo (taken back in July) to launch the competition showed two of the plaster 'dummy' Daleks that were (apparently) up for grabs. One of these was won by Keith Stark of South Woodford. However the Dalek casings won by Anthony Barber and Terrence Worrel were actually fully-functional principal props (repainted red for Barber and black for Worrel).

As the promotion continued, 2 August even saw a Dalek on top of a floral float at the Jersey Battle of the Flowers[138], alongside advertising boards to publicise the film.

Local paper the *Evening Star and Dispatch* reported on the arrival of the Dalek movie tour in Birmingham on 3 August – where six Daleks invaded the board room of Lewis's department store for a photo-call. The paper invited its readers to see for themselves the metal warmongers, who would be in residence for a little over two weeks. Roberta Tovey visited both Manchester and Birmingham around this time (coinciding with her twelfth birthday), and opened Lewis's fifth floor Dalek city at 11.30 am on 5 August. The Daleks were there to meet her (including the original red Dalek prop from the film).

The *Daily Mail* brought its customary level of doom to bear on 5 August, with Christopher Wood's article entitled 'When a Child in the Dark Comes Face fo Face With the Monsters of Dr Who', in which parents were warned: 'Despite its "U" certificate [the film] is criticised as entertainment for

---

[136] From *TV Century 21* – Issue 28 (31st July 1965) p.13
[137] From *TV Century 21* – Issue 28 (31st July 1965) p.13
[138] An annual event, first set up to celebrate the coronation of Edward VII on 9 August 1902

children by Harley Street psychiatrist Dr Ellis Stungo. He said last night: "These horrible things are enough to upset a stable child, let alone one who is not so well balanced. Even adults are likely to be disturbed by them. These relentless monsters with absolutely no feelings, bent on destruction, are bound to give children nightmares. In these days of space travel, when nothing is impossible, these things could have a highly detrimental effect on a child's mind." Mr Charles Selvage, manager of Studio One, said: "We cater for family audiences, but a lot of the films we think would be nice for children are not tough enough for them. This is one of them."'[139]

The next day found the *Berkshire Chronicle* rather less bleakly dubbing the film a 'riot of pseudo-scientific invention. [It] has all the appeal that the television serial had – with the added advantage of colour. The all-metal city of the Daleks, with its fascinating "scientific" trimmings and its electronically operated doors, emerges as a marvel of ingenuity.'[140]

August's edition of the *Everywoman* also commented on the new film, with an article that belatedly recycled the earlier minor controversy over the script's passage through the BBFC. It reported (not entirely accurately): 'The beetle-brow of the censor, Mr John Trevelyan, beetled blackly when he heard that the Daleks in the film were going to be equipped with flame-throwing devices … So the producer went to the other extreme and ordered that the film Daleks should be armed with fire extinguishers! The Daleks' main weapon … will now be foam.'[141]

The national tour reached Selfridges in London on 9 August, for a three-week residency. A new Dalek city set was built specially for the event by Shawcraft. At least one of the five Daleks on display was one of the 'dummies' and was missing its eye-stalk. Three of the props were given away as prizes in a competition compered by Birmingham pop group the Applejacks.

The same day, Daleks also arrived in Liverpool, with the *Liverpool Echo* running another competition to win a real Dalek, with commercially available Dalek 'play suits' as runner-up prizes. Liverpool's Dalek display was similar but not identical to Manchester's and comprised a corridor set and control room in their own branch of Lewis's. The display closed on 20 August, marking the end of the tour. However, Dalek props would continue to promote the film in a variety of settings in the months that followed. One, for example, appeared to promote a screening in Darlington on 9 September.

By now, even the film's detractors were lending it some begrudging recognition. Critic Alexander Walker commented: 'I am not at all surprised that the Daleks are so popular. I am only a bit depressed. For Terry Nation's

---

[139] From the *Daily Mail* (5 August 1965)
[140] From the *Berkshire Chronicle* (6 August 1965)
[141] From *Everywoman* (August 1965)

armour-jointed serial on BBC television, now mutated into a wide-screen Technicolor movie, embodies everything I shrink back from in daily life. Call me a prophet of doom for the under-twelves if you wish, but I find the whole set-up infinitely sinister. Space ships in other science fiction fantasies have often been cosy old crates. But the Doctor's flying laboratory is camouflaged as one of those chilly mini-dungeons you find on street corners, namely a Metropolitan Police call box. No wonder it ushers us straight into a police state. The Daleks probably appeal most to people who live out of tins. They strike me as the final glorification of the jukebox that has had servile TV panels pronouncing judgement on its "Hit or Miss" utterances and now rounds angrily on the humans belching fire and steam. Daleks talk in a hyphenated infant's primer way, which betrays a low level of literacy for all their technological know-how.'[142]

'A slice of sci-fi for beginners' was how *Variety* described the picture on 10 August, noting that 'a few more thrills and a rather more edged script would have made Dr Who a shade more acceptable,' but nonetheless conceding, 'Gordon Flemyng has played his direction straight [and] Peter Cushing plays Dr Who with amiable gravity.'[143]

The August *Films and Filming* magazine commented that the producers had: '... wisely chosen to cod it as far as possible without overtly burlesquing it and thus alienating its prospective audience of schoolchildren home for the summer holidays. In choosing Peter Cushing to take over the part of the Doctor they were batting on a safe wicket. Gone is his Hammer image of the macabre and villainous suavity: he is William Hartnell to the life ... Gone is Dr Who's vaguely arresting extra-worldliness. He is now unambiguously of the earthly, firmly anchored to a Victorian villa like H G Wells' SF heroes ... All this may cause Dr Who purists some slight distress, but I suspect that it was all done to avoid a lengthy preamble ... In a film like this we have to set aside pedantic hair-splitting. For Junior it is all good fun and will pass 90 minutes of the school holidays happily enough ... and Dalek lovers will have a field-day.'[144]

Also during August, Souvenir Press and Panther Books expanded their existing range of *Doctor Who* titles with the addition of the *Paint and Draw the Film of Dr. Who and the Daleks* book. The same publishers followed up with *The Dalek Pocketbook and Space-Traveller's Guide*, with material written by Terry Nation, on 7 October.

A more tangential tie-in was the launch of the young Roberta Tovey on a less-than-spectacular music career via a single on the Polydor label on 13 August (though some sources give July as the release month). With music

---

[142] From *Doctor Who – A Celebration* by Peter Haining – WH Allen & Co (1983). p.76
[143] From *Variety* (10 August 1965)
[144] From *Films and Filming* (August 1965) p.28

provided by the film's composer Malcolm Lockyer, the *Who*-themed 'Who's Who' and its B-side 'Not So Old' and are now little-remembered slices of '60s pop. Columbia also released on the same day a re-recorded single of Lockyer's film theme tune under the title 'The Eccentric Dr Who', with more re-recorded film music appearing as 'Daleks & Thals' on the B-side. Another film-related release from the previous month was a strange incidental dance track from Polydor called 'Dance of the Daleks' by Jack Dorsey and his orchestra.

DALEKS IN MANHATTAN

Dr. Who and the Daleks went on general release on 22 August, shortly after the end of its run at Studio One (where it was replaced by a re-release of *The Magnificent Seven*). In Birmingham, the ABC circuit took the film from 29 August. A month later and it was still doing excellent business around the country, with 100 additional prints ordered at the end of September in readiness for the Christmas market. Buoyed with enthusiasm for the film, one screening in Belfast even went so far as to have a 'Dalek Dance' tie-in on 29 September, arranged in conjunction with the local Mecca bingo hall. Even the box-office poison of *Coast of Skeletons*[145] as a supporting feature failed to slow the film's steady rise through the charts.

By the end of 1965, *Kinematograph Weekly* were reporting the Dalek film to have been one of the UK's top 20 most profitable pictures of the year. However, UK audiences had been only part of the plan for Aaru and, with the home market having now given it a warm reception, plans for the movie's American launch were soon well under way. As early as 10 August, *Variety* speculated, 'It will be interesting to see how the film stands up to stiffer Yank "sci fi" competition.'[146]

Vegoda had hoped to look after the Stateside distribution of the movie himself and intended to give the picture a big push for American audiences, even suggesting an alternate (more visceral) edit specifically tailored for their tastes. However, his funds weren't unlimited, and he was eventually outbid on the American rights by rival companies Crown International and the Walter Reade Organisation, headed up by Walter Reade Jr[147].

Oddly, considering their keenness to bid for it, Reade Jr and his group actually had very little confidence or interest in the film. *Doctor Who* had never been screened on US television and the new feature was essentially

---

[145] Another Techniscope feature. Richard Todd played Harry Sanders in this poorly-received 1964 Edgar Wallace adaptation, a sequel to the much more successful and better-known 1963 adaptation of *Sanders of the River*.
[146] From *Variety* (10 August 1965)
[147] Not to be confused with his father – the famous American theatre impresario.

treated just as a cut-price kid's filler, on which territory it was never going to compete with the might of Walt Disney. American posters billed the picture as 'The wildest space adventure on … or off the Earth!' but there was little other publicity for the screenings. Consequently, very few Americans ever went to see it.

One of the few US tie-ins was a short comic-strip adaptation, released as a one-off comic-book around Christmas 1966 by the Dell Publishing Company. It cost 12 cents and came with crudely block-coloured artwork by Dick Giordano.

'We … look[ed] like we were space-people in our Maidenform bras,' said Barrie Ingham on seeing his character's bulging chest muscles in the comic. 'And I must say that I look like I'm in more need of a bra than anybody else.'[148]

It appears that when working on his comic-strip rendition Giordano must have had access to an early copy of Subotsky's original draft screenplay as well as a print of the film, as the strip features Subotsky's original 'cave man' ending. This is now the only known record of the proposed prehistoric coda, as the draft screenplay itself has since been lost.

Perhaps the single oddest piece of publicity connected to the Stateside release (and there wasn't a lot of competition) came from America's *Famous Monsters of Filmland* magazine – a publication, famed for the punning, jokey style of its editor, Forrest J Ackerman. In issue 44, cover dated May 1967, a six page feature commented: 'Altho they are jello-fellows, the Daleks are anything but jolly. They are capable of instantly decoding any language but have one of their own which is unbreakable. Only two words in the Dalekian language[149] are currently known to human beings: *zyquivilly* … which is the equivalent of our "goodby", "farewell", "so long", "let's split" or "really gotta go now". And *clyffl*, most easily pronounced if you have a cold with a sniffle, meaning, "I understand you, but I do not agree with you". Understood?'[150]

---

[148] From *Dalekmania* dir. Kevin Davies – Lumiere Video (1995)
[149] The Dalekian words in this section were in fact borrowed from Panther Books' *Dalek Pocketbook and Space Traveller's Guide*.
[150] From *Famous Monsters of Filmland* – Issue 44 (May 1967))

Dr. Who and the Daleks
By
Milton Subotsky and David Whitaker[151]
From a story by Terry Nation

PLOT SYNOPSIS

Barbara is sitting in the living room of the comfortable townhouse[152] she shares with her grandfather (Dr Who) and little sister Susie. Ian Chesterton arrives to take Barbara out for the night. While Barbara dashes upstairs to get changed[153], the accident-prone Ian is shown into the front room, where he nearly sits down on a very fragile super-ionised electro-kinetic pre-oscillator. Dr Who only just manages to stop him before he can destroy the delicate apparatus.

The oscillator is a vital component in Dr Who's latest invention – a time-space machine that he has built in his back-garden. He calls his new creation TARDIS. It has seemingly been constructed inside a standard London police telephone box. However, once inside, Ian discovers that there is a much larger room than the shell of a police box could accommodate.

Dr Who and Susie have been working on TARDIS for many years. In theory, all Dr Who has to do is set the controls for the time and place he wants to visit and his machine will take them there.

---

[151] David Whitaker went uncredited on the opening credits of the film – possibly due to the fact that the film's final screenplay was mostly the work of Milton Subotsky.

[152] We never get a clear enough look at the house to find out where it is, but it appears to be a modest Victorian townhouse. It has a brass doorknocker and a walled back garden. The presence of a tin bath by the backdoor suggests that the house doesn't have a bathroom.

[153] It's never stated where Ian and Barbara were going on their date, but the film starts off with Barbara wearing a small red skirt and a blouse. She then races upstairs to change into an altogether more utilitarian combination of blue jumper, pink slacks and flat shoes. Wherever they were going, it seems that Barbara felt it required her to wear something more practical – which is fortunate, as it turns out.

At that moment, Barbara enters the machine and throws her arms around Ian. This sends Ian off balance and he stumbles backwards against a heavy lever. Dr Who is horrified and tells Ian that his stumbling has inadvertently 'transferred us in time and space and I haven't even set the controls. We could be anywhere in the universe and at any time.'[154]

Ian doesn't believe him at first. He opens the doors, expecting to step back out into Dr Who's garden. However, they are no longer in England. Outside, Ian discovers a completely different world. They truly have travelled through time and space and now find themselves on an unknown planet – barren and desolate. They navigate their way through a 'petrified' jungle, where even the trees and animals have been turned into rocky fossils.

Far off in the distance, the travellers see a large futuristic city gleaming on the horizon. Although Ian and Barbara want to return home, Dr Who is keen to investigate further (as is Susie).

Returning to TARDIS, Dr Who fakes a malfunction, saying that there's been leak in one of the ship's fluid links. The vital component needs to be refilled with mercury. Dr Who concludes that they will have to venture into the city, to look for some more mercury to repair TARDIS.

Outside, the party find a small box of glass vials has been left by the door of TARDIS. The vials look like they contain some form of medication and Dr Who has the box placed back in the ship for safe-keeping.

Arriving at the grand entrance to the city, the group split up to explore. The inside of the city is a vast maze of colourful space-age corridors and cavernous chambers, humming with futuristic equipment. Dr Who finds something that he believes to be a Geiger counter. Reading off it, he realises that the planet's surface is highly radioactive. The weaknesses that they have all been feeling may be the early signs of radiation sickness. Realising the terrible danger they are all in, Dr Who admits to his deception over the fluid link.

At that moment, they are suddenly surrounded by a phalanx of strange tank-like machine creatures gliding toward them across the floor of the chamber – the Daleks. Ian tries to make a break for it, but runs directly into one of the Daleks, which blasts him with a built-in gun. Ian's legs buckle underneath him and he falls to the ground, temporarily paralysed. The Daleks search Dr Who and find the (fully functioning) TARDIS fluid link inside his waistcoat pocket. They take it away for inspection, before confining the travellers to a cell.

Following a long nuclear war with a race called the Thals – natives of the same planet – the Daleks have been forced into bulky permanent life-support machines and cannot go out of the city, they explain.

---

[154] From *Dr. Who and the Daleks* dir. Gordon Flemyng – Aaru/Amicus Productions (1965)

Alone in their cell (but secretly monitored by the Daleks), Dr Who and his friends deduce that the box that they found on the ground outside TARDIS must have contained anti-radiation drugs.

The Daleks know of only one anti-radiation drug. It was developed by the Thals and they are eager to get a sample of it for themselves. Cured of their afflictions, they would then be able to leave their city and swarm over the planet exterminating all. The Daleks offer to allow their human captives to go outside and collect the vials left outside TARDIS. They will also allow the humans to use some of the drugs to cure their own sickness. However, the Daleks will permit only one of the travellers to leave. The others will stay as hostages. Despite Ian's protestations, the only one of the group who is still strong enough to walk is Susie.

Susie leaves the city on her own, trekking through the darkened forest, terrified of the bizarre noises that ring through the night. She finally reaches TARDIS and goes inside. However, she leaves the door unlocked and when she turns she finds someone standing in the doorway in front of her.

Happily, the intruder is friendly. It is Alydon – leader of the Thals. He is tall and blond with pale, bluish skin. It was Alydon who earlier left the vials outside for them. He now gives Susie a second set of the drugs, just in case the Daleks break their promise to share them. He also gives her his plastic cape, so that she may more easily hide the drugs about her person.

The Daleks later summon Susie back to their control room and persuade her to write a letter to the Thals on their behalf. They dictate the message to Susie, who writes quickly with a pen that has been provided. The message tells the Thals that the Daleks desire only an end to the many years of war. In order to reach a peaceful understanding, they promise to leave food in their control room as an act of good faith. It is, of course, a trap, with the Daleks using the girl only to make their offer of peace seem more credible[155].

The TARDIS crew quickly discovers the Daleks' true plan to ambush and kill the Thals as soon as they appear in the city. When a Dalek next comes with food and water for the prisoners, Dr Who and his companions swing into action. They jam open the door and blind the Dalek by smearing its eye with food. They immobilise its gun with a piece of the security camera wrenched from the wall. They then push the Dalek forward onto Susie's plastic cape, insulating it from the metal floor so that it can no longer draw

---

[155] This part of the script doesn't really make a great deal of sense. The letter doesn't contain any of Susie's own words. It's dictated to her by the Daleks. She even uses a Dalek pen. Forcing Susie to write the letter on their behalf does mean that the final message will be in the girl's own handwriting. However, the Thals have never seen her handwriting before. The Daleks might as well have just written the note themselves. What do they gain from getting Susie to do it? Maybe Dalek handwriting (suckerwriting?) is too distinctive to fool the Thals?

power from beneath. Without electricity, the Dalek's systems shut down and it becomes inert. While the girls keep watch, Dr Who and Ian open up the Dalek's top and scoop out the hideous creature from inside using the plastic cape[156].

Ian then gets inside the empty Dalek casing and seats himself at the controls. With Ian posing as a Dalek guard, the party pretend to be prisoner and escort. Dalek-Ian is allowed to follow his friends down the corridor and over to the lift area.

The adventurers make it as far as the area outside lift shaft seven before the Daleks realise the deception. The travellers summon the lift to make their escape. However, the exit hatch on Ian's Dalek has become stuck and they can't get him out of the casing. The group is forced to leave him behind still trapped in the Dalek, while they flee up the lift shaft. The Daleks burst through a door and fire their guns into Ian's casing, leaving it charred and blackened. However, when the Daleks open it up, they find it empty. Ian has gone – escaped in the lift just seconds before. He rejoins his friends on the floor above.

The four run down a corridor, just in time to see the Thals congregating outside the city. They shout out a warning to them, but it's too late to save Temmosus – a Thal elder – who is gunned down by the Daleks. The others flee back into the forest with Dr Who and his friends close behind.

Back in their city, some of the Daleks are used as guinea-pigs to test the efficacy of the Thal anti-radiation drugs. However, the results are not good. Dalek biochemistry is totally incompatible with the Thal medicines, and the test subjects react very badly. The Daleks conclude that if they cannot share in the Thals' freedom, then they will destroy them instead. They plan to explode a gigantic neutron bomb. It will increase the radiation on the planet many times, to a point where only the Daleks (in their protective casings) will be able to survive. The Thals will be wiped out.

Dr Who and his friends travel with the Thals to a camp that has been erected in the forest, where they persuade the otherwise pacifist Alydon to take the fight to the Daleks, before the Daleks have a chance to make the first move.

Alydon, Susie and Dr Who lead the assault on the front of the city. They use a series of small hand-held mirrors to reflect light back at the Dalek scanners, confusing their equipment and giving the impression of a greater number of Thals. However, the ploy is only temporarily successful. The Daleks cause a chasm to open up in front of the city, which many of the Thals fall into. The rest retreat back to the forest, while Dr Who and Susie are

---

[156] We see very little of the Dalek creature in the finished film. There were originally plans for something more gruesome, but the more graphic glimpses were cut prior to the film's release, for fear of disturbing younger cinemagoers.

recaptured by the Daleks.

Ian, Barbara, and three of the Thals – Ganatus, Antodus and Elyon – meanwhile make up their own party, to find a way into the city over the mountains and through a network of caves. They eventually reach a cliff-edge with a seemingly bottomless gorge beneath. They have to jump across this gorge in order to get any further into the caves. However, Antodus doesn't take enough of a run-up and plunges into the chasm. He is left dangling at the end of a rope, with the others desperately struggling to pull him up. Realising that his weight is pulling Ian over the edge, Antodus produces a knife and cuts the rope that is holding him. The Thal tumbles away into the chasm. However, just in time, he manages to get a hold of the rock face and is able to climb back up to safety.

Inside the main Dalek control room, Dr Who begs the Daleks not to detonate their bomb, but his appeals are ignored and the countdown is started at 100 rels[157]. Meanwhile, Ian, Barbara, Ganatus and Antodus have found an opening that comes up into the Dalek city, and they force a metal gate apart in order to gain entry.

Attacking the Daleks and their control room, the combined efforts of the Thals and the humans rescue Dr Who and Susie, with only seconds to go before the bomb is activated.

Dr Who calls out to Ian to stop the countdown before it is too late. Ian deliberately alerts the Daleks to his presence and then dives to the floor as they all simultaneously fire their guns in his direction. The Dalek guns blast into the control-panels behind Ian and the countdown freezes with only three rels left. The control room is quiet now. All the Daleks are dead, killed when their control panel exploded.

The TARDIS crew then depart in their ship, on the way back home to 20th Century Earth. However, something goes wrong with TARDIS's destination settings and when Ian opens the door he finds a group of giant Roman soldiers marching towards them outside[158].

---

[157] Roughly equivalent to 100 seconds.

[158] Due to an unfortunate mismatch with some stock footage, the film of the Roman soldiers that is played in when Ian opens the door gives the impression that the Roman soldiers are much larger than they should be; they seem to be over ten feet tall.

2
Masters of Earth
'Daleks – Invasion Earth: 2150 AD'
(1965-1966)

SECOND COMING

Milton Subotsky was never terribly keen on movie sequels. Hammer Films – his arch nemesis – lived off the idea, with an army of Frankenstein, Dracula and Mummy sequels, following one after the other (frequently starring Peter Cushing), but Amicus was a subtly different studio. 'Hammer seem happy to make the same film over and over again,' said Subotsky, keen to be seen taking the higher ground. 'I'm always looking for something different.'[159]

However, the spectacular success of *Dr. Who and the Daleks* meant that even Subotsky had to concede this might have to be an exception. It seems that Joe Vegoda first suggested the idea of a second film long before the first had even opened. The sensational box-office made the idea almost inevitable.

As early as the spring of 1965, Subotsky had been clearly talked round to the idea. As Roberta Tovey recalled: 'Just before we had finished shooting the first *Dr. Who and the Daleks*, Milton Subotsky came to see me in my dressing room and asked me if I would do another film with Dr Who. He said to me that he'd been to see Peter Cushing and he asked him, would he do another movie. And Peter is supposed to have turned round and said to him, "I will do another movie, if Roberta would be in it as well."'[160]

'It was no surprise to me to learn that the first *Doctor Who* film came into the Top 20 box office hits,' said Peter Cushing in 1983. 'That's why they made the sequel, *Daleks – Invasion Earth 2150 AD*. And why they spent almost twice as much money on it.'[161]

'I think people very quickly realised they'd got a moneymaker on their hands,' explained Gordon Flemyng, 'and the second film was made in a hurry to cash in on it before it stopped.'[162].

Initially, it seems that there may have been some thought given to using

---

[159] From the *Guardian* (13 February 2009)
[160] From *Dalekmania* dir. Kevin Davies – Lumiere Video (1995)
[161] From *Doctor Who – A Celebration* by Peter Haining – WH Allen & Co (1983) p.76
[162] From *Doctor Who – The Sixties* by David J Howe, Mark Stammers and Stephen James Walker – Virgin Publishing (1993) p.131

the script of Terry Nation's second *Doctor Who* television serial, 'The Keys of Marinus' (1964), as the basis for Aaru's second *Doctor Who* picture. (The possibility of developing an entirely original storyline doesn't seem to have been considered.) 'The Keys of Marinus' was only the fifth *Doctor Who* serial produced for television and had been broadcast between 11 April and 16 May 1964. Across six episodes, it had told of the Doctor's quest across the planet Marinus in search of four lost computer keys. The script certainly contained plenty of scope for cinematic expansion, with its sprawling space-age travelogue and unusual planetary vistas. However, what a film version might have been like is something nobody ever got to find out: it was reasoned that the greatest selling-point of the first film had been the Daleks, so the Dalek-less 'The Keys of Marinus' was quickly dismissed (although the idea of a *Doctor Who* quest movie would recur in numerous other forms over the next quarter of a century).

With the BBC's first Dalek serial having been adapted for their first movie, this left Aaru with only two other full Dalek television serials to chose from[163] to form the basis for their next film: 'The Dalek Invasion of Earth', transmitted in 1964, and 'The Chase', transmitted in 1965, both written by Terry Nation. Aaru chose the former.

But despite the riotous success of their first Dalek picture, Milton Subotsky still had reservations about embarking on a sequel at all. 'I didn't think it would be [as successful],' he said. 'In fact, I suggested that we didn't make it ... The selling point of the original film was that it was in colour and on the big screen. By the time of the second film we had done all this, so really it was just another film. I suppose the title *Daleks – Invasion Earth* was as good a selling point as any, but apart from that there was no great selling point.'[164]

Ultimately, the second Dalek film would be the only true movie sequel that Subotsky ever made.

Happily for Dalek fans, Joe Vegoda at Regal Films[165] and his partner Max J Rosenberg seem to have shared few of Subotsky's reservations, and development on a second Dalek film was proudly announced in the pages of *Kinematograph Weekly* on 16 December 1965.

---

[163] Another Dalek serial, 'The Daleks' Master Plan', was then in production at the BBC. However, work had only just begun on this and some of the scripts for the later episodes hadn't even been fully written yet. The BBC had also transmitted a single standalone Dalek episode, 'Mission to the Unknown', in October 1965, but this was less than 25 minutes long and didn't feature the Doctor or the TARDIS, so doesn't seem to have been ever considered for a cinema remake.

[164] From *DWB (Dream Watch Bulletin)* – Issue 81 (September 1990) p.41

[165] Regal Films was soon to vanish as a company in its own right and was being amalgamated into the larger British Lion film company (which also owned Shepperton Studios, where the Dalek films were made).

The title of the projected sequel (tellingly not featuring the *Doctor Who* name at all) was, at this stage, *The Daleks Invade Earth*.

THE DALEKS INVADE EARTH

The BBC's 1964 television production of 'The Dalek Invasion of Earth' had probably been the most ambitious *Doctor Who* story yet made for the series. The central cast all got a rare chance to stretch their legs away from the studio with some impressive location filming around London, and the return of the Daleks was heavily promoted on television and on the front cover of the BBC's listings magazine, *Radio Times*.

The serial finds the Doctor and his companions arriving in the desolate war-torn London of the 22nd Century. The planet has been invaded by Daleks, who plan to hollow out the Earth's core in order to use the planet as a giant pilotable spaceship. The Doctor teams up with an underground resistance movement and travels to Bedfordshire in order to destroy the Dalek base. Overcoming hordes of Robomen – surgically and electronically augmented zombie humans, who work as servants for the Daleks – the Doctor and his friends eventually win through. However, at the story's conclusion, the Doctor leaves his granddaughter behind to marry one of the victorious rebels and build a new world on Earth.

As with the first film, Subotsky took on the job of creating the movie screenplay himself, working from Terry Nation's original scripts. There was again some contribution from David Whitaker, who had acted as story editor on the original television serial back in 1964.

'I was so interested in visual action,' said Subotsky, 'what we did was have the whole plot on a chart. Dr Who took 20 seconds to explain what they were going to do and then – bang! – you were into two reels of action showing them doing it.'[166]

Nation's serial had featured the characters Ian and Barbara. However, it became clear fairly early on that neither Roy Castle nor Jennie Linden would be returning for *The Daleks Invade Earth*. Castle was then on more comfortable and familiar territory with a cabaret tour and Linden was increasingly moving away from the kind of pictures Rosenberg and Subotsky were making.[167] With this in mind, Subotsky shed Ian and Barbara altogether and developed two new companions to accompany Dr Who.

---

[166] From *Dalekmania – Doctor Who at the Cinema* by Marcus Hearn – Lumiere (1995) p.8

[167] Linden was just a few years away from her BAFTA nominated role in Ken Russell's 1969 film adaptation of *Women in Love*. She also auditioned for *The Lion in Winter* (1968), but was reportedly vetoed by Katharine Hepburn, who feared Linden might upstage her.

2: MASTERS OF EARTH

Barbara was replaced by Louise. No background (nor surname) was ever given to the character, beyond that Dr Who was her uncle. However, her similarity to Jennie Linden's Barbara suggests that she may have been a comparatively late substitution.

Ian's replacement was given a slightly more detailed backstory. He was PC Tom Campbell, a special constable with K Division of the Metropolitan Police. Fit and resourceful, he was actually more similar to the original Ian Chesterton character of the *Doctor Who* television series than Roy Castle had ever been. However, Tom Campbell's surname was actually taken from another character altogether: in Nation's original 1964 teleplay, the resistance fighter that Susan fell in love with was a Londoner called David Campbell.

Subotsky had decided very early on that he wished to retain Susan for his second film. He'd been impressed with Roberta Tovey's performance in *Dr. Who and the Daleks* and she'd been among the first to be approached about a second picture. However, as Tovey was only 12 years old, it was naturally felt to be inappropriate to give her a love-interest, and the lusty David Campbell was toned down accordingly.

Another casualty of Subotsky's restructuring was the character Larry Madison. He'd befriended Ian in the original television serial, but had most of his dialogue given to Louise for the film version.

Later tweaks and rewrites to Subotsky's script were fairly minimal this time around. In the original script, when Dr Who and David leave the rebels' bunker to head off to Bedfordshire, they run straight into a trio of Daleks standing on the tube platform outside. This was altered during shooting, and the final film has them encountering the Daleks in a passageway. There were other similarly minor changes instigated during production, but none as substantive as the first film's elimination of its concluding cavemen scene.

Gordon Flemyng was glad to come back on board as director for a second Dalek film, having recently finished producing a West End show for Peter O'Toole called *Ride A Cock Horse*. 'I chose the picture for two good reasons,' said Flemyng. 'One – it was offered. Two – I like entertainment pictures. I'm not saying that the message pictures are not good, because they are. The industry is full of very clever people who are doing message pictures and they've every right to do them. By the same token, I've every right to do entertainment pictures. I don't take them any less seriously and I don't think anyone else should.'[168]

---

[168] From *A Whole Scene Going* prod. Elizabeth Cowley – BBC Television (16 March 1966)

CASTING OFF

Alongside Tovey, Peter Cushing had also been approached very early on about the possibility of a second Dalek picture. Following a summer break, he had been playing Sir Hector Benbow in a revival of Ben Travers' play *Thark*, directed by Ray Cooney, which ran from August at the Yvonne Arnaud Theatre in Guildford. During that time, he'd also appeared in an episode of BBC2's *30 Minute Theatre*, transmitted on 4 November. And on 22 November work started at Pinewood Studios on his next feature film, *Island of Terror* – a low-budget horror, produced by Tom Blakeley's short-lived Planet Films Ltd. With his run in *Thark* coming to an end around Christmas, Cushing was happy to make himself available for shooting on a second *Doctor Who* film, lined up to begin in January 1966.

Tovey was also keen to return as Susie/Susan. She had recently appeared in an episode of the BBC spy drama *The Mask of Janus*, transmitted in September, and had also landed a part in *Operation Third Form,* a family movie for the Children's Film Foundation, released the following year.

Tom Campbell was to be played Bernard Cribbins. By 1965, Cribbins was already a very well-known face (and voice) in the UK. He'd enjoyed two top ten records[169] and had his own BBC1 comedy show, *Cribbins*. In fact, a *Doctor Who* spoof had been included in an episode of *Cribbins* broadcast the previous year, with that episode, recorded on 6 February, also featuring Peter Cushing.

Cribbins' extensive list of film credits included: *The Wrong Arm of the Law* (1963), *Carry on Jack* (1963), *Crooks in Cloisters* (1963) and *Carry on Spying* (1964). He'd also recently acted alongside Peter Cushing in Hammer Studios' glossy adaptation of Rider Haggard's *She* (1965). Gordon Flemyng last worked with Cribbins when he directed him in the 'Don't Send My Boy to Prison' episode of *The Army Game* in 1960[170].

The role of Louise went to Jill Curzon, who was then probably best known for playing the character Norma in the successful sitcom *Hugh and I* (1962-1963), alongside Hugh Lloyd. Her previous movie work included a part in the Morecambe and Wise vehicle *The Intelligence Men* (1965).

'I remember my agent calling me,' said Curzon. 'I remember going to see Milton Subotsky, who was a little bit awe-inspiring really. I mean, he was American and I hadn't met many of them at that time in my career. He seemed to like me, but he was very austere and I didn't really know what he thought. And then I met Gordon Flemyng, who was delightful, and then I

---

[169] In 1962, Cribbins' 'Hole in the Ground' single had got to number nine in the hit parade and the better-known 'Right Said Fred' had reached number ten; but his 'Gossip Calypso', released the same year, had stalled at number 25.
[170] Episode 20 of the programme's fourth series, broadcast on 12 February 1960.

knew I had the part.'[171]

'There was no love interest but you've got to have a bit of glamour,'[172] she later remarked of her character in the film.

Also cast in the picture was Ray Brooks, who had just scored a notable hit, co-starring with Rita Tushingham in that year's *The Knack ... and How to Get It* for director Richard Lester. He'd also been a semi-regular member of the cast of Granada Television's *Coronation Street*, playing Norman Phillips (manager of the viaduct sporting club) between December 1963 and October 1964. Brooks would be playing the character David (no surname) in the new Dalek movie – a somewhat less obviously virile version of Susan's David Campbell love-interest from Nation's original 1964 teleplay.

Playing Wyler (originally Tyler) in the film was Andrew Keir. Later to be better known for twice playing Nigel Kneale's Professor Bernard Quatermass[173], Keir was, at this point in his career, probably most readily associated with his performance as Prince John in television's *Ivanhoe* (1958-1959) alongside Roger Moore. He'd also had minor parts in big-budget films like *Cleopatra* (1963) and *Lord Jim* (1965) and had only recently completed work on *Dracula: Prince of Darkness*, the first of a number of pictures for Hammer Studios.

The main cast for the new film was rounded off with Philip Madoc playing a black-marketeer, Brockley. The actor was to later become well-known for his various and numerous guest-appearances in *Doctor Who* on television (not to mention *Dad's Army* and *The Life and Times of David Lloyd George*).

SHOOTING

'[It] was much more ambitious – much bigger in scope,' said Allan Bryce, who was again to work on special effects for the film from the in-house workshops at Shepperton. 'This was a general tendency in the business; each James Bond film had to be bigger and better than the previous one, so we needed to make the second Dalek film more impressive.'[174]

In fact, the new Dalek film would be the biggest picture Amicus had ever been involved with. Subotsky and Rosenberg had never worked with such a large budget before. And although British Lion were prepared to put up some of the funding, they wouldn't finance it all.

In something of an unlikely partnership, part of the increased budget was

---

[171] From *Dalekmania* dir. Kevin Davies – Lumiere Video (1995)

[172] From *Doctor Who Magazine – Spring Special* (February 1996)

[173] In the 1967 film adaptation of *Quatermass and the Pit* and the 1996 BBC radio drama *The Quatermass Memoirs*.

[174] From *Doctor Who Magazine* – Issue 197 (17 March 1993) p.21

eventually raised through an unusual sponsorship deal. Breakfast cereal producers Quaker Oats Ltd agreed to put up some of the money, in return for which Aaru would advertise Sugar Puffs in a variety of subtle(ish) ways throughout the film, with boxes of the cereal appearing fairly prominently in shot during a number of key moments. Quaker Oats would also promote the film on packets of Sugar Puffs and advertise special film tie-in competitions.

As before, the new picture was to be shot in Technicolor (to make it as impressive as possible) and in Techniscope (to make it as cheap as possible). On 31 January 1966, just two days after the broadcast of William Hartnell's final Dalek episode[175] on BBC1, shooting started. The new production would work across a number of stages at Shepperton Studios, including H-Stage (where Andrew Keir had worked on *Lord Jim* the year before) and also B-Stage. The film would use much the same crew as *Dr. Who and the Daleks*. With the first film having been such a success, interest in the sequel was fairly immediate, and *Kinematograph Weekly* soon picked up on the start of filming for their 2 February edition.

A small number of the cast had other commitments that would cross over with their work. Ray Brooks, for example took on a role in an episode of *Dixon of Dock Green*[176] back at the BBC. However, these cross-overs would not generally interfere with, work on the film

Bernard Cribbins also signed on to play a part in the James Bond comedy *Casino Royale* around this time. This wouldn't interfere with his *Doctor Who* work, thanks to Aaru's earlier filming dates and the fact that his Bond role was minimal. However, since *Casino Royale* had already started shooting at Shepperton Studios a few weeks earlier, the cast and crew of the Dalek film were certainly aware of a James Bond movie being made over on the expansive A-Stage[177].

'We were in Studio B down at Shepperton and next door to us was Studio A, and the two doors were side by side,' remembered Jill Curzon. 'In Studio A, they were shooting *Casino Royale* with Ursula Andress and David Niven and a horde of beautiful girls. It was rather fun, because I was the only girl going into Studio B. I was the only one in that door and all the rest were in the other door. So I felt quite exclusive about that. But at lunchtime, we had great fun. Bernie Cribbins would go off fishing and the rest of us would sit with Ursula Andress and all the beautiful girls and we got to

---

[175] 'The Destruction of Time' by Terry Nation and Dennis Spooner – transmitted on 29 January 1966.

[176] Brooks played Ken Hardy in the nineteenth episode of the programme's twelfth series. The episode was called 'The Heister' and was transmitted on 5 February 1966.

[177] A-Stage was 18,000 square feet, whereas the Dalek film's B-Stage was only 12,000 square feet.

know all of them very well indeed. I think Bernard missed out on a few things there. But he seemed to enjoy his fishing better.'[178]

Cushing's costume for this second film was very similar to that which he had worn in *Dr. Who and the Daleks,* although the cravat and trousers were different. He now also wore a pale blue scarf and gloves (reportedly to set off his blue eyes). Cribbins wore a version of a standard Metropolitan Police officer's uniform of the time, while Curzon was particularly pleased with her tweed ensemble, designed to emphasise her character as a practical and intelligent member of Dr Who's crew.

'I did a lot of bikini shots and glamour poses for various magazines and newspapers,' recalled Curzon. 'But when I came to this role, they'd designed a beautiful costume for me – a sort of female Sherlock Holmes, with a beautiful lapel ... in green satin and lovely tweed with wing arms, plus culottes, which was really ahead of its time, with nice short legs and these boots, which were fabulous. I think that they were frightfully expensive and I kept them for years. They had two double zippers up the front. They were really beautiful.'[179]

Filming appears to have begun on the smaller sets first, over on B-Stage. Scenes on the entirely new TARDIS set were certainly tackled early on.

Unlike the first Dalek film, *Daleks Invade Earth 2150 AD* (as it was soon known) would also include a large amount of exterior shooting, portraying both the war-torn streets of London and the surrounding Bedfordshire countryside. In reality, the vast majority of this material was achieved on the Shepperton Studios backlot, only a matter of yards away from the studio complex itself. However, the illusion was well concealed.

The first of the backlot filming appears to have been concerned with the film's pre-title sequence and closing scene, in which first a 1966 jeweller's shop is burgled and then later (by the wonders of time travel) the robbery is foiled by Cribbins' Special Constable Campbell.

Over on H-Stage, a 150 foot section of the Dalek saucer had been erected on a street set, with a long ramp down which the Daleks could emerge. 'When we built the saucer on the set (which was gigantic),' recalled Subotsky, 'it was built on H-Stage at Shepperton, which is ... a silent stage, which was good because we didn't need sound.'[180]

The set made full use of the large studio space, which had also been so important to the spectacle of the first film. 'What you see on the screen is what we saw in the studio,' recalled Subotsky. 'H-Stage at Shepperton ... really is *huge.* It's the same size as two city blocks. You can build absolutely anything on there. They built the forest for the 1980 *Flash Gordon* film on

---

[178] From *Dalekmania* dir. Kevin Davies – Lumiere Video (1995)
[179] From *Dalekmania* dir. Kevin Davies – Lumiere Video (1995)
[180] From *DWB (Dream Watch Bulletin)* – Issue 81 (September 1990) p.42

there and I remember that I used it on a film called *Danger Root*, where we flooded [it] and had boats going up and down it. The entire harbour for the film *Lord Jim* was built on there.'[181]

The set was a massive job for the set builders, led by construction manager Bill Waldron. However, the task was not perhaps *quite* as massive as it appeared on screen. As with the first film, Gerald Larn had been brought in to artificially extend the appearance of the set with a large matte painting in Shepperton's special 'optical-room'. 'I had to visualise and paint the crashed flying saucer matte very early in the production of the film,' he recalled. 'At that point the flying saucer model (later to be filmed on our effects stage) had not yet been made. The only saucer reference I had to work from was a selection of scale drawings being prepared for the construction of the model. I can remember it being a tricky operation trying to design the craft from those drawings and at the same time ensure the saucer sat convincingly on the circular underbelly built on the set. It ended up being a series of compromises with which I was never entirely satisfied … There was quite a lot of matte work involved in the other shots, adding and topping up ruined buildings.'[182]

With a more complex set of locations (and exteriors) than had been used first time around, Larn was also on set more for the second picture. 'Very often I was out there,' he says. 'I was responsible for more or less second unit directing the shot, because all sorts of tricky things had to be avoided. If there was going to be a matte painting, then you had to make sure that none of the action actually went through where the matte line was going to be and so on and so on … Very often, one was acting in an advisory capacity, just to be sure. That was the nature of the art director's or production designer's job – to be sure that if a matte shot of some sort was required, then … there wouldn't any problem with the finished footage.'

These scenes around the Dalek saucer ramp were also among the first to feature the Dalek casings themselves, which were somewhat different from the props used in the first movie.

RESURRECTION OF THE DALEKS

By 1966, Shawcraft Models Ltd had been building props for the BBC's *Doctor Who* series for over two years[183] and had become particularly proficient in the manufacture of Daleks. After their sterling work on *Dr. Who and the Daleks*, there was never any question that they'd also be providing Dalek

---

[181] From *DWB (Dream Watch Bulletin)* – Issue 81 (September 1990) p.42
[182] From http://www.galeon.com/artinmovies/GeraldLarn/Gerald_Larn.html
[183] Other 'non-Dalek' *Doctor Who* serials, on which Shawcraft worked included: 'The Rescue' (1965), 'The Web Planet' (1965) and 'The Macra Terror' (1967).

props for Aaru's follow-up picture. However, not all of this second wave of movie Daleks were entirely original creations.

On 21 December 1965, the Daleks had made their theatrical debut in David Whitaker and Terry Nation's *The Curse of the Daleks* – a two act play that opened at London's Wyndham Theatre. This had not featured the Doctor, but had made use of quite a number of Daleks.

The ever-dependable Shawcraft had been commissioned to provide these Dalek props. However, the play did not have a particularly large budget and the show's producer, John Gale, was keen to make economies where he could. It seems that, with the second Dalek film also going into production at the same time, a deal was struck between the producers of the stage play and the producers of the movie, whereby the costs of building a new set of Daleks would be shared between them. The Daleks would be used first on the stage, and when the play came to the end of its run, they would then be refurbished before going on to appear on the set of the film. As such, Aaru were credited as the owners of the Dalek props in the theatre programme for *The Curse of the Daleks*.

The co-financing deal saw the new batch of Daleks constructed somewhere around November/December 1965. Altogether, five were built taken from moulds that had been created for the first Dalek film earlier in 1965, but dressed to resemble more closely the BBC's then current design for the television Daleks. The props also featured a number of unusual 'arm' attachments and accessories, originally designed for the play, but which can also be glimpsed occasionally in certain parts of the finished film.

Once the play had finished, the five props were sent back to Shawcraft in Uxbridge, where manager Bill Roberts and his team repainted and retooled them ready for the new movie. Four additional ones were also made at this time. Aaru made use of these nine principal 'hero' props in the film. However, only four of the nine were used with any degree of prominence. The other five were rarely seen at all and appear only in a small number of crowd scenes in the finished film. In addition to this, three more fibreglass Daleks were built for special effects shots – making 12 Daleks in total. They were an impressive sight.

In 1965, the Daleks' original designer, Raymond Cusick, had slightly altered the BBC's own Dalek casings by having a row of thin perspex slats added to the shoulder section of each of them. His idea was that these solar panels generated the power the Daleks needed to move about freely outside their city. The development was carried over onto the new Aaru production, with slats (now metal) added both to the five existing theatre props and to the four additional movie ones.

Meanwhile, raised light housings and wider skirt buffers were retained from the first movie. And the overall paint scheme of the rank-and-file Daleks was also tweaked to match that of their BBC counterparts, although some were later repainted in different colours to denote various ranks in the Dalek chain of command (one red and one black, as in the first film, and one gold – a colour scheme that would be adopted for the Dalek leader in the later television story 'Day of the Daleks' (1972)).

Although Peter Hawkins would carry on providing the post-dubbed Dalek voices, the operation of the Dalek props was handled differently on the second film. Gordon Flemyng had resented the idea of having to use specially-trained BBC Dalek operators for the first movie, as he'd felt the jobs could have just as easily gone to lower-paid extras.

Flemyng had, however, got on well with 'lead' Dalek operator Robert Jewell. Much to the annoyance of the BBC's other operators (particularly Kevin Manser), Flemyng therefore decided that only Jewell would be rehired to work on his new Dalek film. The other regular operators would not be used at all. Instead, Jewell would (as with the first film) earn himself an additional fee in exchange for training a group of film extras to operate the Dalek casings.

Strangely, Aaru hired only six extras to work alongside Jewell. Consequently, only seven of the Dalek props could ever be manned at any given time. Just a tiny number of shots in the finished film actually feature more than seven Daleks. In these instances, at least one of the props was just an empty (and immobile) shell.

To make directing them easier, Flemyng would give each prop a name (like Bob or Bill), which he could shout out to the operator on set. Not that this made working with the often unintentionally comical Daleks any easier for some of the cast. 'I got into trouble 'cause of the Daleks: I kept laughing when these little voices were coming out of them,'[184] recalled Bernard Cribbins.

'We were on set doing a scene with the Daleks for the very first time,' Cribbins said on another occasion. 'They were on the ramp in the spaceship, and Peter [Cushing] and I had just been introduced to the Daleks. And the Dalek operator in the machine, Bob Jewell, was Australian.[185]

'When he uttered the immortal words, "You'll be exterminated", he did it in this light Australian accent. I couldn't help myself. I started laughing, Peter started laughing and we got a terrible bollocking from … Gordon Flemyng. He was a Glaswegian … and he was barking, "Come on you Cribbins, you bastard, get on with the show". We just got very silly about it because this fearsome creature was speaking in an Aussie accent. It was just wrong. It should have been in *Neighbours* not inside a Dalek.'[186]

Despite the filmmakers' best efforts, the lack of experienced operators

---

[184] From *Doctor Who Magazine* – Issue 390 (9 January 2008)
[185] From a talk at the National Film Theatre (16 January 2010)
[186] From the *Daily Record* (24 December 2009)

shows in the finished film, with the Daleks generally being less agile than in their first picture, something that was compounded by the more rugged terrain of 22nd Century London.

'We couldn't go very far because we couldn't make the Daleks work,' explained Flemyng. 'They wouldn't run on anything other than a smooth surface. On the backlot at Shepperton we could put down camera tracking for them to run on and prepare the set accordingly. In the film, if you see a Dalek moving through rubble, the rubble is either in the foreground or the background. Hopefully the audience doesn't realise this and the trick works.'[187]

MISADVENTURES IN TIME AND SPACE

The new, less experienced Dalek operators were more accident prone than their predecessors. During one scene, a Dalek was meant to roll down the central ramp and lose control. However, all did not go to plan[188]. 'He was meant to overturn and fall over, which he did,' recalled Jill Curzon, who was on set that day. 'But he caught fire. It caught a spark or something at the bottom of the ramp, and it was really frightening. We all dashed up. They had to cut the scene, because the flames came up, but they got the guy out. He wasn't burnt, thank god. They had to get him out very quickly, because you couldn't breathe in there with the fire.'[189]

Other on-set accidents were equally serious. The most notable was when stunt co-ordinator Eddie Powell ended up in hospital following a fall. Powell had been working on a scene in which one of the Dalek prisoners tries to escape over a ruined building. He recalled: 'I ran over the rubble and up the side of the building. Then I had to run along the joists, and one of the joists had been rigged so that, on a special effects guy tripping it, it would collapse and I would go into a fall. The trouble was that he was supposed to trip it just as my foot was on it, so that I could position myself for the fall to go into a roll to land on my back. What happened was, he tripped it too soon. I went through the air with one foot down and landed on my foot on the awning first, which twisted my ankle and busted something there, and then I went straight on through the awning, onto the pavement. In the film, you'll notice that I'm favouring my right leg – keeping it out of the way to get me into the position they wanted me in, for the Daleks to come forward and blast me to death. But because I couldn't keep still with the pain, they cut there and sent me off to hospital, where they put my foot in plaster. I

---

[187] From *Doctor Who – The Sixties* by David J Howe, Mark Stammers and Stephen James Walker – Virgin Publishing (1993) p.131
[188] The scene happens at about 25 minutes into the finished film.
[189] From *Dalekmania* dir. Kevin Davies – Lumiere Video (1995)

came back on crutches, and in the afternoon they put me in the same position – where I could keep perfectly still now – but kept my plaster-laden foot out of the way – and they shot me dead.'

You can see the unedited entirety of Powell's accident about 18 minutes into the finished film. Powell's memory is actually a little imperfect: it was only the shot of his lifeless body lying on the floor *after* his extermination that he filmed on his return from the hospital. His plaster-cast leg was kept out of frame for this single brief shot, although the cast is plainly visible in a publicity still, later used on one of the movie's lobby cards.

'After my accident on the set, I was about to be taken off to hospital,' continued Powell, 'when Gerry Crampton, one of the stuntmen – and they're always very eager to step in when they can – told the director that he would take over and look after things for him. And I must say, Gordon was very fair. He said: "Don't you worry. Eddie Powell's coming back." So, that cheered me up quite a bit. And when I came back from hospital, on crutches that is, I think I must have been the only stuntman ever that carried on doing the stunt co-ordinating on crutches.'[190]

The film's bad luck continued. It was also around this time that Peter Cushing became ill, leaving the picture altogether for a protracted period of time. The knock-on effect on filming schedules was obvious. 'I was quite ill during much of the shooting and they had to work around me a good deal,'[191] remembered Cushing.

'He became ill and his doctor said he couldn't work,' recalled Subotsky. 'What we did was to film every single scene that didn't include Peter Cushing. [We would then] pack-strike the set – which means you take it down and put it into storage [so that it can be] put up again quite quickly [later on]. So what we did was to shoot a scene with everyone but Peter, pack that bit away (because we needed the studio space) and put it up again when Peter came back. But we only needed to show behind him … I have no idea what was wrong with him. The insurance company paid £30,000 for the extra days' filming that we had to have. What I did was to keep the costs for the insurance company as low as possible so, in effect, they paid for Peter's illness.'[192]

By an odd coincidence, in the BBC's original 'The Dalek Invasion of Earth' serial, William Hartnell too had occasion to be absent from the studio due to illness: he had suffered a minor accident on set and was entirely absent for the serial's fourth (of six) studio sessions. He had to be doubled by another

---

[190] From *Dalekmania* dir. Kevin Davies – Lumiere Video (1995)
[191] From *Doctor Who – 25 Glorious Years* by Peter Haining – WH Allen & Co (1988) p.106
[192] From *DWB (Dream Watch Bulletin)* – Issue 81 (September 1990) p.42

2: MASTERS OF EARTH

actor, with the script rewritten accordingly[193]. Something of a cursed storyline perhaps.

A HOLIDAY FOR THE DOCTOR

In the final film, Cushing's absence is concealed fairly well, with Flemyng very carefully dropping in close-ups of him (recorded later) into already completed footage. Changes to the script were minimal, and as far as possible filming continued on schedule during the actor's absence. Among the scenes filmed during this period were those around a cottage on the backlot with Tovey, and scenes inside the Dalek ship where Cribbins' Tom attempts to hide himself among the Robomen.

It was also at this time that the crew filmed the bulk of the material featuring Jill Curzon and Bernard Cribbins. '[Bernard] was great fun to work with,' Curzon later commented. 'I did more scenes with him than anybody else and we had a lot of fun. Very shy, very sweet guy – good sense of humour.'[194]

Among the most unusual of their scenes together was their ride down a Dalek waste-disposal shoot[195] – a working suction pipe, with fans ducting air down out of the back of the set. 'One of the most enjoyable scenes in the whole thing was going down the waste-shoot out of the spaceship,' said Curzon. 'It was incredible … but quite frightening. I didn't know how much the vacuum was going to sort of tear our hair apart and that sort of thing. It wasn't a huge drop, but it was quite hard. When you get there, you roll over. You've got to make sure you roll rather than trip and break your ankle.'[196]

The scenes involving a rebel attack on the exterior of the Dalek saucer were also completed largely without the involvement of Cushing. This section is perhaps most notable (and unintentionally comical) for its treatment of Andrew Keir's character, Wyler. During the attack, Wyler is shot first in the head by a Dalek gun (about 27 minutes into the finished film). However, unlike those around him, he doesn't seem to notice the blast and just runs off. Then a few minutes later, a Roboman shoots him again. Once more the blast causes no apparent ill-effects, but does sufficiently annoy Wyler for him to throw a brick at the aforementioned Roboman. A few moments later, a Dalek blasts Wyler one final time. Naturally, he doesn't notice and makes his escape, although by this time he has at least developed

---

[193] As a consequence of this, William Hartnell doesn't actually appear at all in the story's fourth episode ('The End of Tomorrow').
[194] From *Dalekmania* dir. Kevin Davies – Lumiere Video (1995)
[195] The disposal shoot makes its first appearance about 38 minutes into the finished picture.
[196] From *Dalekmania* dir. Kevin Davies – Lumiere Video (1995)

a limp in his right leg – oddly enough, one of the few parts of his body not actually to have been fired at.

DALEKS – INVASION EARTH: 1966AD

Coverage of the Shepperton filming reached the press quickly. An image of the filming of the rebels' attack on the Dalek saucer appeared on 18 February in the *Daily Cinema*, advertising the movie to cinema proprietors. On 26 February, *Titbits* then did its bit to champion gender equality with a story written by David Hunn and headed 'Deadeye Jill is a match for the men' – an article commenting on the fact that Jill Curzon was a former winner of the British Ladies' Clay Pigeon Shooting Championship. Curzon was reported to have been following shooting as a hobby alongside her husband and fellow actor, the appropriately named Derek Partridge[197]. A photo accompanying the piece showed Curzon in a spotted bikini, holding a toy Dalek and standing next to one of the adapted Dalek props from *The Curse of the Daleks*.

Following some shots taken in woodland on the backlot, filming then returned indoors for scenes set inside a rebel 'bunker'. It was during this filming that the Sugar Puffs product placement was first seen. Boxes of the cereal (packaging circa 1966AD) were arranged amongst the rebels' supplies and on a shelf in Dortmun's office. Neither of these fleeting cameos is really prominent enough to register much. However, when filming returned to the backlot, the placements were a lot harder to miss. Large Sugar Puff advertising posters pasted up on the walls outside TARDIS's landing site and inside a mocked-up London Underground station asserted proudly: 'Everyone loves Sugar Puffs – The honeyest cereal of them all!'

From the perspective of set dressing, the disused Underground station is, in fact, one of the film's more noteworthy sets. Alongside the Sugar Puffs billboard there are also some (very 1960s looking) advertising hoardings for Del Monte Pineapples. Another accidental piece of product placement saw a poster for Player's Cigarettes feature during the film's opening sequence.[198]

---

[197] With a varied career, Derek Partridge started as an actor in the UK in programmes that included *Dixon of Dock Green* (1962) and in films such as *Thunderball* (1965). He later moved to America, to work on shows that included *Star Trek* (1968) and *Dallas* (1986).

[198] Another of the posters on the walls of the disused underground station advertises a wrestling match between Tony Mancelli and Johnny (Henry) Yearsley. Mancelli and Yearsley were popular post-war heavyweight wrestlers, who hit the peaks of their respective careers in the 1950s. Mancelli retired from wrestling in the 1960s. 1966 would have been one of the last times the two men shared a ring together. It is more than a little anachronistic that they would both still be billed on a poster around 180 years later.

To be fair, perhaps the idea of the Sugar Puffs and Del Monte brands surviving into the year 2150 isn't all that fanciful. However, with all the sets, costumes and vehicles in the finished film essentially undisguised examples of Earth in the year 1966., it does perhaps beg the question if certain production departments were made aware of the 200-years-in-the-future setting at all. If Daleks had invaded London in the year 1966, one imagines that this would be very much how it might have looked. The 2150 dating, however, is harder to reconcile.

The Underground station itself is perhaps a little more prescient in its design. A sign on the wall cheerfully proclaims it to be 'Embankment'. The real Embankment station, opened in March 1906, had changed its name to Charing Cross in 1915. At the time the film was made, it was still called Charing Cross. There was no Embankment station. However, clearly the filmmakers knew something the audience didn't, because in September 1976 the station was renamed Embankment again.

THE CHASE

A further example of the second Dalek film's anachronistically 1960s vision of the 22nd Century came with the scene in which Susan and Wyler escape from the capital in a stolen van, only to be chased by a Dalek saucer.

The van that the pair escape in was a Morris J-Type[199] delivery van; a model that had been introduced in 1949 and remained in production until 1961. At the time of filming it was still a common enough sight on Britain's roads, but a number of organisations had already begun replacing their J-Type fleets, and so it was with relative ease that the production team were able to find two identical(ish) ones for filming. The vehicle has since gone on to become very rare and is now much sought-after by enthusiasts. The idea that one would be found unattended on the streets of 2150 London seems odd, to say the least. Unlike in the original television serial on which the film was based, the anachronism is never explained however.[200]

For the filming of the van chase sequence, the pair of red Morris J-Type vans was supplied to the production team by an outside firm. The two vehicles were both former delivery vans for Palmer and Harvey[201]. The main driving work for the film was undertaken by a van with the registration plate 693 WML. The second vehicle, the registration plate of which is not fully

---

[199] A Morris J-Type would later go on to appear in the 2006 *Doctor Who* television story 'The Idiot's Lantern', starring David Tennant.

[200] In the BBC's 'The Dalek Invasion of Earth' serial, the antiquated 1960s transport was explained to have been seized from a transport museum.

[201] A British wholesale business founded in 1925, specialising in tobacco and sweets. By 1965 it was a very big firm indeed, with a large fleet of delivery vehicles.

visible but appears to begin 6387 (inconsistent with the format of standard UK registration numbers), was used for a scene in which the van explodes after being fired upon by the Daleks.

To achieve the impression of an impressively scattered explosion, the body of the second van had large panels cut out of its side by the effects crew. These panels were then taped back into position, and when the explosive charges were detonated, the panels flew out, exposing the fiery innards of the poor J-Type. In fact, this second van was not a complete, roadworthy vehicle to start with, but just a shell, with most of the interior and engine bay having been ripped out for scrap (probably before the crew even got their hands on it).

Both vans used in the film would have been manufactured around 1959-60, with the blown-up one being the older of the two. There's no record of what happened to 693 WML after filming, and at the time of writing, it is no longer still registered as being on the road. The other vehicle was presumably damaged beyond repair during the filming of the explosion.

The van chase was an elaborate set-piece for the film, shot across a number of days on the Shepperton backlot. It was completed largely as planned, although Keir did injure his wrist at the point where Wyler was seen to punch out the van's windscreen with a house brick. For the bulk of the driving work, stuntman Eddie Powell (prior to his on-set accident) doubled for Keir behind the wheel of the van, with Keir only returning to the screen after the van has stopped. However, no stunt double was provided for Roberta Tovey, who sat on the passenger seat throughout the complicated shoot.

'We were driving along, bumping along,' recalled Tovey, 'and he was going quite fast. One of the Dalek airships was supposed to have spotted us and was chasing us along. And I remember at the time being quite terrified that I was going to get thrown out of this van any moment.'[202].

'It was a very sort of muddy road that I had to go along and I knew that I had to hit it at speed, if I was to make it look anything at all,' said Powell. 'So, I had the feeling that it was going to be sliding all over the place, which it did, but I managed to control it.'[203]

'I had to sit in the van the whole time,' added Tovey. 'We were trundling along at about 90 miles an hour, and we had to do the shot where the van actually gets attacked by one of the flying saucers, and we again only had one take to do that. We drove into the scene, with the van all wired with explosives, and had to jump out and run, and they ignited the detonators and blew the van up. And we did all of that for real. There were no stunts in that.'[204]

[202] From *More Than Thirty Years in the TARDIS* dir. Kevin Davies – BBC Video (1994)
[203] From *Dalekmania* dir. Kevin Davies – Lumiere Video (1995)
[204] From *Dalekmania* dir. Kevin Davies – Lumiere Video (1995)

HE'S BACK, AND IT'S ABOUT TIME TOO

Feeling sufficiently recovered from his illness, Peter Cushing returned to Shepperton to resume his work on the film just as shooting shifted focus to scenes near the Dalek mining operation in Bedfordshire and at the woodland cottage of a Dalek collaborator. These outdoor scenes were, of course, mounted on the backlot, with a specially built frontage for the cottage erected close to the Littleton Park footbridge. Situated in the grounds of Shepperton Studios, the Littleton Park area sits in a patch of picturesque woodland by the River Ash. It was often used for filming on all manner of Shepperton-based productions (and still is).[205]

The exterior of the great Dalek mine itself was also constructed not far from the studio complex, with an impressive open-cast facility created by Bill Waldron and his construction crew in a dip in the countryside. Gerald Larn also supplemented the footage in the opticals room. It was these mine scenes that called for the greatest mobilisation of the film's extensive cast of extras. Meanwhile, the interior of the mine, with its maze of darkened tunnels and drill-shafts, was realised on one of the main stages at Shepperton.

With Cushing back on set, the opportunity was now also taken to remount parts of those scenes that he had missed while away, particularly his rescue from a Roboman chamber on the Dalek saucer.

Further exterior work at this point also included filming on H-Stage's TARDIS landing-site in the rubble of invaded London. The skyline, created as a painted backdrop, featured both Saint Paul's Cathedral and the recently completed Post Office Tower[206], which had opened only a few months before, in October 1965.

Most daring of the material recorded here was a scene in which Tom Campbell (Cribbins) falls out of the upper storey of a derelict warehouse. Both Cribbins and Cushing were doubled by stuntmen for the set-piece. The scene (about 10 minutes into the finished film) involved Campbell hanging several feet above the ground, holding onto a door-handle, while Dr Who attempts to pull him in.

'Jackie Cooper ... was doubling Cribbins for the actual stunt,' remembered Eddie Powell. 'All he actually had was a strap around his wrist – a very tight strap. Nowadays you could possibly have a full harness on

---

[205] It was through Shepperton's less-than-tropical River Ash that Humphrey Bogart waded in *The African Queen* (1951). And it was in the surrounding woods where Kevin Costner's Robin Hood built his camp in *Robin Hood: Prince of Thieves* (1991).
[206] The new Post Office Tower was also to feature prominently in a forthcoming *Doctor Who* television story, 'The War Machines', which was then being written by Ian Stuart Black.

underneath, [with a wire that] goes up through the [sleeve] … and you [would be] as safe as houses. But he felt very confident to do it with that wrist-strap.'[207]

MINERS STRIKE

Filming on the climax of the movie began back indoors on the multi-level Dalek control room set. The set decoration was by Oscar-winning American art director Maurice Pelling[208], who had previously worked on Andrew Keir's biggest ever picture, *Cleopatra*[209] (1963).

It was during the filming of these control room scenes that the Black Dalek prop was damaged, stuntman Joe Powell (brother of Eddie) dislodging its pincer attachment during a fall. By the wonders of ill-judged continuity, in the finished movie, the claw magically reappears in the very next scene, without explanation.

The attack on the Daleks by the miners and the Robomen and the subsequent destruction of the Dalek mine was a complex sequence and probably the portion of the film that taxed Ted Samuels' visual effects team the most. 'I remember that those scenes were complex and difficult,' said Flemyng. 'Difficult, because we had limited facilities. We couldn't keep reshooting until we were totally happy. There were a number of model shots that we could afford to do a couple of times but after that we had to fake it. Although the film had a relatively bigger budget than the first, it was mostly eaten up by the sheer number of effects and the location work.'[210]

Among the shots where Flemyng did 'fake it' was one of a Dalek being crushed by a magnetic wave. The prop was a hollow, flexible model that could be deflated and compressed repeatedly, without the need to damage any of the expensive fibreglass 'hero' casings.

Another cheat was that the Dalek seen exploding behind a wall, and the black and red Daleks that fall down the mine shaft later, were all repainted and redressed commercial Dalek toys manufactured by Hertz Plastic Moulders. They were only seven inches tall and were bought in specially from a nearby branch of Woolworths.

Overall, the modelwork on the second Dalek film was considerably more extensive than on the first. The most important aspect was probably the

---

[207] From *Dalekmania* dir. Kevin Davies – Lumiere Video (1995)

[208] Clearly the BBC were impressed with Pelling's work on the Dalek film, as a few months later the rel counter from his the Dalek control room set found its way into the BBC's own studios, appearing as a prop in the *Doctor Who* television series, in episode three of 'The War Machines'.

[209] For which Pelling won his Academy Award.

[210] From *Doctor Who – The Sixties* by David J Howe, Mark Stammers and Stephen James Walker – Virgin Publishing (1993) p.132

construction of a working flying saucer for the Daleks to travel in. With in-built electric motor and lights (run from a battery), this (mostly) solid wooden model was flown around on wires in a number of shots and has become one of the most enduringly recognisable design concepts of the Dalek film series.

'The Daleks' flying saucer was, I think, designed by [art director] George Provis and was about three feet in diameter,' recalled effects assistant Allan Bryce. 'It was shot both against the sky and against the backdrop, suspended from a tower crane. When it first appeared over the bombed street in London, it actually flew over the stage. We brought it in, in such a way that we were messing the perspective up, so it actually looked as though it was further away. We also did that for the end sequence, just before it crashed. That was done over a model landscape at the special effects stage at Shepperton.'[211]

The optical printer was used for some shots of the Dalek saucer – including its very first appearance. The saucer was also matted into the van-chase sequence, although not entirely successfully. Its landings in Sloane Square and at the mine were model shots.

The saucer model had a fairly eventful afterlife once filming ended. It seems to have stayed in the Shepperton Studios effects workshop for some time. Then, in 1969, it found itself being used to represent an entirely different alien spaceship in the low-budget British science fiction movie *The Body Stealers*, produced by Tony Tenser for Tigon Films and featuring Sean Connery's younger brother Neil.

In the 1970s, when Shepperton Studios was being lined up for sale, various props and models were fished out of storage for a well-publicised auction. The event was covered by an episode of *John Craven's Newsround*, which included footage of the top being lifted from the Dalek saucer to expose its inner mechanisms. The saucer was bought at the auction by Zoran Perisic, a leading special effects artist who would be behind the celebrated optical effects on three of Warner Brothers' successful *Superman* films (1978-1987). Quite why he wanted it is unknown, but he remained the model's owner for some little time.

By 1980, the saucer had by some unknown route become the property of a London astronomical society, who initially had it stored in the basement at Alexandra Palace. There was a fire at Alexandra Palace in 1980, but the saucer escaped the flames, as it was, at the time, being looked after at the home of a society member. That member was Mat Irvine, who by coincidence was then working as a visual effects designer on the *Doctor Who* television series.

The saucer was, however, in a pretty poor state of repair by the early '80s;

---

[211] From *Doctor Who Magazine* – Issue 197 (17 March 1993) p.21

and nobody seems to know what happened to it following its last reported sighting in late 1983. Mat Irvine no longer recalls its fate, although there's every possibility that it is still out there somewhere.

JOURNEY'S END

On Tuesday 8 March, it was made known that Aaru wished to conclude filming on their new Dalek film by the end of that week (11 March). The idea was to have *Daleks Invade Earth 2150 AD* edited and fully completed by 30 June. However, Cushing's time away from the set had meant that the production was running behind schedule. Thanks to the insurance company, Aaru weren't out of pocket, but they were now forced to look a little further into the summer for their release date. Among the final sections of principal photography on the picture were some pick-ups for Cushing's scenes in the woods with Philip Madoc's Brockley and then his descent into the sewers following the raid on the Dalek ship. At around this time, Cribbins also filmed the material of Tom in the mineshaft beneath Dalek control. Meanwhile, Dortmun's death scene, outside a fictional pub called the Watford Arms, was achieved with a dummy thrown under some rubble and overdubbed with the cries of actor Godfrey Quigley.

Unlike on the *Doctor Who* television series, where the bulk of a given story's location filming would be generally shot first, before it entered the electronic studio, most of the non-Shepperton-based location work on the second Dalek movie was left until very late in production. It was, in fact, some of the very last principal photography on the film.

Following the example of the original television production, this location work took place in London. The memorable shot of a Dalek rising from the waters of the Thames (for no adequately explained reason) was filmed close to a jetty near Saint Mary's Church on Battersea Church Road. The skyline was later augmented back at Shepperton with a matte painting of a ruined Battersea Power Station, courtesy of Gerald Larn.

'We laid tracks down into the water when the tide was out and positioned a weighted Dalek on them, attached to a line,' explained Flemyng. 'We then waited for the tide to come in and pulled the Dalek out of the water using the line.'[212]

Scenes inside an abandoned warehouse were also (mostly) achieved at a location away from Shepperton. The crew descended on the Bendy Toys Factory on Ashford Road in Middlesex to get shots of Cushing and Cribbins walking about an empty storehouse. In the final film, boxes of rubbery Bugs Bunny toys, which the owners of the warehouse manufactured, can be seen

---

[212] From *Doctor Who – The Sixties* by David J Howe, Mark Stammers and Stephen James Walker – Virgin Publishing (1993) p.131

in boxes stacked up on the floor.

With all of the location scenes finished, the actors' work on the film was almost over (barring some sessions in the sound studio) and principal photography wrapped on 22 March – a little over a week later than hoped for. With his commitments on the project all but over, Cushing then gave an interview to William Hall of the *Evening News* later that week, on 25 March.

The hopes of the cast and crew were high that they would be returning to film a third *Doctor Who* picture before the end of the following year. However, it was not to be.

Although nobody knew it at the time, the last frame of the cinema's last *Doctor Who* movie had just been shot.

POST PRODUCTION

Subotsky, who always relished the opportunity to get his latest film into the cutting-room, was unimpressed with how certain things had turned out on his second Dalek picture.

'The second film was largely made in the cutting room,' he said. 'It didn't work until we got it there and *made* it work.'[213]

The arrestingly colourful title sequence for the new film was another attempt to recreate the ethereal atmosphere of the BBC's television series titles, only cheaply and in colour. Filmed at high-speed, the sequence was even more basic than it had been for the first film. 'That was very simple and done in the effects studio,' remembered Subotsky. 'It was nothing more than a series of paints and oils going down a drain – a simple and cheap effect.'[214]

On the audio side, under the supervision of sound editor John Poyner, a number of sound effects were reused from the first Dalek film, including those of the Dalek doors. Various sections of dialogue were also over-dubbed for a cleaner result (including Eddie Powell's painful stunt sequence outside the saucer).

Primarily a silent stage, Shepperton's H-Stage was less than ideal for sound recording and, as with the first movie, this led to extensive dubbing on the new Dalek picture. Inexplicably, one of the casualties of this was the voice of Sheila Steafel's character, which was completely replaced in post-production. (An unusual move considering how well known the actress was in Britain at the time.)

Subotsky had been disappointed with Malcolm Lockyer's score for *Dr. Who and the Daleks* and the composer was not carried over onto the sequel. Instead, Scottish Jazz artist and occasional Benny Goodman collaborator Bill McGuffie was called upon to create the movie's 50 minutes of incidental

---

[213] From *DWB (Dream Watch Bulletin)* – Issue 81 (September 1990) p.42
[214] From *DWB (Dream Watch Bulletin)* – Issue 81 (September 1990) p.43

music. He had been musical associate on the last of the Bob Hope and Bing Crosby *Road* movies, *The Road to Hong Kong* (1962), and had not long finished scoring another Bernard Cribbins film, *Cup Fever* (1965). In 1953 and 1954 he'd won polls for his piano playing in the recently launched *National Musical Express*. A less austere score than the first Dalek picture, McGuffie's up-beat jazz-influences found greater favour with Subotsky. As with the first film, the incidental music was also supplemented by electronic additions from Barry Gray.

Under the new (and final) title *Daleks – Invasion Earth: 2150 AD*, Aaru's second Dalek film was quickly submitted to the BBFC for classification, where it gained its desired 'U' certificate on 10 June 1966, allowing the film to be released in time for the lucrative summer market.

PUBLICITY

Promotion for the film was, if anything, even more intensive than it had been the first time round. *Dr. Who and the Daleks* had proven itself a popular cinema commodity and investors were keen to repeat its success and make back some of the sequel's inflated budget.

Despite a noticeable fading of the Dalekmania boom of 1964/5, press attention was still healthy for a second film, with articles appearing in publications as diverse as *The Times* and *Film and Television Technician*.

Lewis's department stores also continued to support the franchise, following the success of the previous year's Dalek exhibitions. As early as 10 February (while the new film was still being shot), the third floor of Lewis's Liverpool branch was proudly showing off a special Dalek display. From 26 March to 23 April, the Hanley store in Stoke on Trent hosted an exhibition of some rather worse-for-wear movie props on its second floor.

Meanwhile, on 30 March, delegates from a Soviet Culture Mission from the USSR met with some Daleks over at Shepperton. They were shown around by the studio's managing director, Andy Walker, who commented: 'You just try, through an interpreter, explaining what a Dalek is to a foreign guest who has never seen one and you will know what it is to feel a proper Charlie.'[215]

Television coverage was healthy too. On 16 March, Gordon Flemyng appeared as an interviewee on an edition of the BBC's *A Whole Scene Going*, which also showed its viewers some behind-the-scenes footage from the studio floor (captured during filming on the Dalek control room set). On 10 April, independent television caught up, with a similar report from Westward Television's *The Film Makers* series. Extracts from the film also

---

[215] From *Dalekmania – Doctor Who at the Cinema* by Marcus Hearn – Lumiere (1995) p.10

appeared as part of Granada Television's *Cinema* programme with Michael Scott.

On 29 July, with the film now in cinemas, the BBC even went somewhat against its charter when it broadcast the new film's trailer as part of *Junior Points of View*. The BBC also transmitted around 30 minutes of soundtrack from the film as part of the Light Programme's *Movietime* radio show, presented by Gordon Gow[216].

In May, the *Boy's Own* printed some on-set photos from the production (taken at Shepperton by Richard Grenville); and in the States, the *Psychotronic Film Book* (13 May 1966) even ran a photograph of a Dalek on the streets of New York. British Lion's publicity people meanwhile described 2150 as 'the year when even strong men shivered.'[217]

Back in his native Glasgow, Gordon Flemyng gave an interview to the *Evening Citizen* newspaper in July. 'I am not kidding,' he said. 'It frightens the daylights out of me to think that one day creatures from outer space may pay us a visit.'[218]

The *Kentish Mercury* even had an exclusive 'interview' with a Dalek in person. 'We-have-no-use-for-girls-like-Roberta-Tovey-and-Jill-Curzon,' said the Dalek. 'We-exterminate-your-sort-of-strapping-heroes-like-Ray-Brooks ... Personally-I-am-getting-fed-up-with-films-about-Earthmen-and-if-I-see-another-one-in-which-one-of-our-flying-saucers-is-made-to-look-as-though-it-is-held-up-by-strings-I-shall-burn-up-the-screen-with-my-ray-gun.' Er. Quite.

TV Century 21 comic also continued its general support for all things Dalek (albeit belatedly) in their eighty-seventh issue, published on 17 September, when a Dalek film once again graced the magazine's front cover.

However, most extensive of all the film's publicity was the aforementioned tie-in with Sugar Puffs, which *TV Century 21* also did their best to link in with.

Quaker Oats' promotions kicked off with a series of television spots before the main campaign itself began with adverts emblazoned on packets of Sugar Puffs. Sugar Puffs consumers were even given the chance to win one of three real Dalek props from the film, with 500 battery-operated miniature Daleks (manufactured by Louis Marx Toys)a lso up for grabs.

Future television director and *Doctor Who* fan Kevin Davies remembers: 'I didn't like Sugar Puffs as a kid. Mum tried buying them and I hated them. I didn't like the texture. Not sure I'd be that fond of them now, but I was quite jealous of my friends a few doors down – a few Irish lads – that had the

---

[216] This programme was recorded in studio B13 at Broadcasting House and reached wireless sets on 18 November.
[217] From *Doctor Who Monthly* – Issue 84 (January 1984) p.33
[218] From the (Glasgow) *Evening Citizen* (22 July 1966)

"Win a Dalek" thing on their breakfast table. I was a bit jealous of that and thought, "Gosh, what an exciting thing to win."'

The promotion on the sides and backs of all new Sugar Puffs boxes (alongside a full-colour still of the red Dalek in the robotising room) read as follows:

> Enter the exciting Sugar Puffs Dalek contest and you could be one of the lucky winners of a life size Dalek from the latest film Daleks Invasion Earth 2150 AD. You can actually get inside and make the Dalek move anywhere you want! Operate the 'Human Detector' [otherwise known as a sink-plunger] and the deadly Dalek ray. There are three Daleks to be won, and for 500 runners up, there are battery operated toy model Daleks manufactured by Louis Marx Ltd.

Below is a list of qualities for fighting Daleks. Pick the six you think most useful, then put them in order of importance.

> A. Be able to imitate a Dalek voice.
> B. Have a protective suit against Dalek ray guns.
> C. Carry emergency food and water pills for a week.
> D. Know how to do first-aid.
> E. Be able to travel anywhere in space.
> F. Have a knowledge of electronics.
> G. Carry a radio to contact Earth from space.
> H. Have a resistance to brain-washing.
> I. Know how to operate the Tardis [sic].
> J. Be as clever as Doctor Who.
> K. Know how to tell other people what to do.
> L. Never panic when in danger.

Presumably there was no single 'right' answer to this question, although 'B' would probably have rendered most of the other options pretty redundant.

By late July, the cost of British Lion's publicity campaign was reported to have reached £50,000.

RELEASE

On 24 June, the week after being granted certification from the BBFC, the producers organised a trade show for their new picture. This took place at 10.30 am on 5 July at Studio One on London's Oxford Street (as with *Dr. Who and the Daleks* before it.)

On 11 and 12 July, the film's Sugar Puff sponsors were also given their own individual thank yous when a series of 'Dalek Special Screenings' were hosted on behalf of Quaker Oats at the Film and Arts Theatre at 6 Hanover Square, specifically for those working in the grocery business.

The movie officially opened at Studio One on 22 July, on a double-bill with the Western *Indian Paint*, starring Johnny Crawford as a Native American who tames a pony.

On 8 July, the *Daily Cinema* was one of the first to pass judgement on the new Dalek film, commenting that it had, 'a lot more polish and style than its predecessor … Just the job for the holiday season!'[219]

'Sure-fire family fare,' predicted *Kinematograph Weekly* on 21 July.

Alexander Walker also shared the upbeat tone in his review for the London *Evening Standard*, saying: 'Actually it's all much more inventive than the first Dalek film. The sets are quite an eyeful, so are the special effects, and director Gordon Flemyng can teach Disney a lot about packing in the action.'[220] Appropriately enough, the film had actually replaced a brace of Disney movies at Studio One (*Lt Robin Crusoe USN*[221] and *Run, Appaloosa, Run*[222]).

However, as before, other critics were less generous. David Robinson wrote in the *Financial Times*: 'The script is dim, the direction sloppy, the acting variable to execrable and the editing loose enough to mislay whatever dramatic excitement there might otherwise have been … I find the Daleks – cross little dustbins that they are – quite the most unattractive figures in science fiction … A film of unusually low standards.'[223]

Ann Pacey concurred in the *Sun*, reporting: 'It all looks a bit tatty and hastily churned out.'[224]

On 23 July, Nina Hibbin wrote in the *Morning Star*: 'The year is 2150, but it looks like … leftovers from an old film about the Blitz.'[225]

The Times was equally scathing, having commented a couple of days earlier that 'the second cinematic excursion of the Daleks shows little advance on the first … Even the strings which hold up the flying saucer in which the Daleks land are clearly visible – and the cast, headed by the long-suffering, much ill-used Peter Cushing, seem able, unsurprisingly, to drum up no conviction whatever in anything they are called on to do. Grownups

---

[219] From the *Daily Cinema* (8 July 1966)

[220] From the *Evening Standard* (20 July 1966)

[221] Dick Van Dyke starred as a marooned US Navy pilot, living on an island with a girl called Wednesday and a chimp from outer-space.

[222] Another film about a Native American and a horse. This one was only 47 minutes long.

[223] From the *Financial Times* (22 July 1966)

[224] From the *Sun* (21 July 1966)

[225] From the *Morning Star* (23 July 1966)

may enjoy it, but most children have more sense.'[226]

Of course, this is not to say that there was nobody in the daily newspapers writing in defence of the film. Cecil Wilson came to its aid in the *Daily Mail* with: 'Oh, the joy of seeing the Daleks thumped again … There used to be a fairground sideshow called "Breaking up the Happy Home" in which for a small fee you could hurl wooden balls at a kitchen dresser just to see how much crockery you could smash. You did it with a free conscience because it was not a real kitchen anyway, and I find the same uninhibited destructive appeal about these Dalek films. From the moment Dr Who is pitchforked by a time and space machine into a stark future and sees their flying saucer land in what he calls "the vicinity of Sloane Square", I cannot wait for him to annihilate these metal monsters … Mingled with the pleasure of seeing [them] perish is the chilling thought that they will be back before long, to glide and grunt their way through another Dalek picture.'[227]

A correspondent in the letters page of *Film Review* agreed, enthusing: 'Although the Daleks' chief adversary is not mentioned in the title of this futuristic film, Dr Who is as prominent as ever in this cinema-size helping of their latest destructive onslaught.'[228]

THE FINAL END

After three days, takings at Studio One clocked in at £1,200. By the end of the opening week the movie had brought in £1,843, a little bit down on the returns for the first film. The second week it took £1,810 – almost the same as the first movie. Overall, the takings for the second picture weren't bad. However, they weren't too good either, and by comparison, the first film had brought in a much better return for a significantly smaller outlay.

As the nation celebrated the victory of Bobby Moore and his team at the 1966 World Cup, 5 August was set for the new film's general release. *Indian Paint* was used as the supporting feature in most cinemas, although others opted for *Hide and Seek*[229] (1964) or *Queen of the Pirates*[230] (1960). To promote the new release, further press shows took place on 8 August, giving journalists another opportunity to take a shot at the film and its merits (or perceived lack of them).

Film Review took the chance to run an extensive feature on the picture in

---

[226] From *The Times* (21 July 1966)

[227] From the *Daily Mail* (July 1966)

[228] From *Film Review – Letters Page* (July 1966)

[229] A tongue-in-cheek cold-war spy thriller from the director of *Zulu*, starring Ian Carmichael.

[230] An Italian-language film, made with West German backing, this told a lurid story of 16th Century Mediterranean piracy. The film is more properly known as *La Venere dei Pirati*.

their August issue, with a double-page spread of photographs and further comments in their letters section. The magazine described the feature as 'even more lavish than its predecessor.'[231] Correspondents on the letters page, were more mixed in their assessments however. M Fisher from Kentish Town in London condemned the movie, saying: 'What is an actor like Peter Cushing doing in a film of this calibre? It is pitiful ... The acting in the film was more corny than a cob and the film sets were not authentic. The only thing I liked about the monstrosity was the music. Apart from that – ouch!'[232] It was left to J Miles from Southfields in London to come to film's defence, calling it, 'a great film in every detail. The robot-men [sic] acted very well throughout and their costumes were excellent. To me this was the film of the month.'[233]

'If this is what London will look like in 2150 AD, I can only say that it looks very old-fashioned: positively 1966,' wrote David Rider in August's *Films and Filmmaking*. 'I cannot really believe that hideous Battersea Power Station will stand in 2150,[234]' he continued. 'Given this basic inconsistency the film is good, undemanding entertainment, particularly suited to the younger cinemagoers ... They will miss William Hartnell as Dr Who, although Peter Cushing makes an acceptable substitute ... Equally enchanting is Bernard Cribbins ... There is one beautifully judged scene when, disguised as a brain-washed Roboman, Cribbins joins seven other zombies in a nourishing meal of coloured pills ... Short and to the point, it's a deliciously funny sequence.'[235]

The film's reception remained just as confusingly mixed for the rest of its run. However, whereas the lukewarm critics of the first film were soon brushed off in light of a brisk box-office, the second film wasn't so lucky. The British public had only just witnessed 12 consecutive weeks of Dalek episodes on television[236] and it seems that their appetite for the fascist pepperpots had been thoroughly sated (at least for the time being). After just four weeks, *Daleks – Invasion Earth: 2150 AD* was dropped from the bill at Studio One and replaced on 19 August with the proven box-office charms of

---

[231] From *Film Review* (August 1966)

[232] From *Film Review* (August 1966)

[233] From *Film Review* (August 1966)

[234] Actually, the film's vision of the future may not be so far out of line in this particular respect. Battersea Power Station was declared to be a heritage site in 1980 and given Grade II listed status (since upgraded to Grade II* listed status). Legally, the building cannot be knocked down by anyone, and any owner has an obligation to maintain it. It shows every sign of still being around up to and beyond the year 2150.

[235] From *Films and Filming* (August 1966) p.7

[236] The BBC had not long concluded broadcast of the epic 'The Daleks' Master Plan' – the last Dalek story to feature William Hartnell.

the musical *My Fair Lady* (1964), which did something to replenish the cinema's coffers, taking £3,033 in its first week. The day of the Daleks had passed. It seemed that the future belonged to Rex Harrison.

Tie-in merchandise for the second film was accordingly limited.Fontana Records registered an interest with Denham Recording Studios in issuing Bill McGuffie's incidental score on a 33 rpm LP[237], but in the end only a 45 rpm single appeared, on the Philips label, in February 1967. Entitled 'Fugue for Thought', this was a reworked section of music from the very start of the film, incorporating part of Bach's 'Tocata and Fugue'.

The film did however continue to pay for itself in the regions. August saw it do particularly stout business in Taunton, Yeovil, Plymouth and Accrington – mostly on the ABC circuit. By 22 August, the film was also doing well in Minehead, Chelmsford and on the island of Guernsey.

The *South London Advertiser* did its bit to promote the run of a film it saw as 'rather empty but good fun for the kids.'[238] The *Yorkshire Evening Post* meanwhile was rather more generous, calling it 'the hit of the hols'[239] (which, sadly, it wasn't).

The Dalekmania bubble of the previous year had now finally burst. The craze was all but over and there was little left for Aaru to cash in on.

In 1966, America's ABC television started showing its new comic-book adventure series *Batman*, starring Adam West as the titular caped crusader. Snapped up by ITV for its UK transmission, episodes aired from 21 May onwards. The series became ridiculously popular ridiculously quickly – just as the Daleks had in 1964. As Dalekmania ebbed away, Batmanmania replaced it. For many children, the Daleks were fast forgotten, to be replaced by the altogether healthier story of an older man's relationship with a teenage boy and their mutual love of brightly coloured tights.

DALEKS NOT IN MANHATTAN

However, if the second movie's UK box office had been unspectacular, its American box office was practically non-existent.

Max J Rosenberg described the picture's American distribution as 'a bloody mess. Joe Levine wasn't interested, Avco-Embassy never wanted it. It was Walter Reade who bought it and Reade's company went belly up, so I

---

[237] McGuffie's music did eventually feature on an LP. Released on 16 April 2011 in strictly limited numbers, the first *Doctor Who* vinyl disc to appear in a very long time, this was a compilation of music from both Dalek movies. The first film's music was on side A and the second film's on side B. The same material had already been issued on a CD on 5 October 2009 by the Silva Screen label (see Chapter Three).

[238] From the *South London Advertiser* (12 August 1966)

[239] From the *Yorkshire Evening Post* (20 August 1966)

don't think it ever got a decent theatrical run.'[240]

The timing certainly was unfortunate, as Walter Reade Junior's company did indeed go through a very bad time in the mid-'60s. In 1961 Reade had perhaps unwisely acquired a company called Sterling Television. Later the company also posted a major financial loss due to its speculation on art house films. *Daleks – Invasion Earth: 2150 AD* drowned somewhere in the middle of all this. Reade's misfortunes hit Rosenberg and Subotsky hard all round, as they'd just released another Peter Cushing picture, *The Skull*, through the same distributor, and that also suffered in the States.

Rosenberg hadn't been particularly enamoured with the second film anyway, and with the poor box office on both sides of the Atlantic, plans for a possible third Dalek film[241] were indefinitely shelved. Joe Vegoda seems to have had little appetite to finance a third offering, and Amicus were certainly incapable of raising the cash for such a production on their own. *Daleks – Invasion Earth: 2150 AD* is (at the time of writing) the last film directly based on *Doctor Who* actually to reach the cinemas.

It is perhaps a pity that Subotsky and Rosenberg did not persevere, as most fans and critics alike now agree the second picture to be considerably better than the first. It's certainly aged better. 'Looking back, I think the second one moved wonderfully,' said Subotsky in 1990. 'If you look at it now it looks as good as any picture made today.'[242]

AFTERMATH

Following her experiences with the Daleks, Jill Curzon didn't continue to pursue her acting career for very much longer. In 1967, she appeared in an episode of the BBC's *Adam Adamant Lives!*[243] (produced by *Doctor Who*'s first producer, Verity Lambert). However, a few years later she moved onto other things and her last television credit was an episode of ITV's *The Champions*[244] in 1969.

Roberta Tovey appeared on a number of occasions in the Wendy Craig comedy *Not in Front of the Children* (1967-1968) and in the period adventure series *The Black Arrow* (1972-1975). Her later career then took in an episode of

---

[240] From *Amicus – The Studio That Dripped Blood* ed. Allan Bryce – Stray Cat Publishing (2000) p.39

[241] The third may possibly have been based on the scripts for Terry Nation's fourth *Doctor Who* television serial, 'The Chase.' However, there's no evidence to suggest this idea went very far.

[242] From *DWB (Dream Watch Bulletin)* – Issue 81 (September 1990) p.42

[243] Curzon appeared in the tenth episode of the programme's second (and final) series, 'The Deadly Bullet'.

[244] Curzon appeared in the twenty-fourth episode of the opening series, 'Project Zero'.

Casualty (1986) and four episodes of Mollie Sugden's *My Husband and I* (1987).

Soon after the Dalek film wrapped, Ray Brooks started work on Jeremy Sandford's memorable *Cathy Come Home* for BBC1 – a world away from the comfortable certainties of *Doctor Who*. He played a London van driver who married the eponymous Cathy. With Ken Loach's (for the time) atypically gritty direction for a television play, it is among the medium's best remembered dramas. However, it probably isn't Brooks' most well-known part. That honour probably belongs to his role as narrator on the BBC's idiosyncratic children's series *Mr Benn*, which started in 1971. Only 13 episodes of this *Watch With Mother* animation were ever made, all written by the show's creator David McKee, but it was enough to earn it a place in the affections of generations of children. Brooks' other acting jobs have included parts in *Big Deal* (1984-1986) and *EastEnders* (2005-2007)

Immediately after *Daleks – Invasion Earth: 2150 AD* had wrapped, Bernard Cribbins crossed over to the adjacent stage at Shepperton to make his aforementioned appearance in the James Bond spoof *Casino Royale*. His *Cribbins* programme was soon revived by Thames Television, where it featured appearances from fellow Dalek co-star Sheila Steafel. In 1972 he appeared in Alfred Hitchcock's *Frenzy* and in 1975 gave a memorable performance in *Fawlty Towers*[245].

However, like Brooks, it was to children that Cribbins was to become best known. In December 1966 he joined the roster of storytellers on the BBC children's show *Jackanory*, and over the next few decades he'd host more episodes than anyone else – 39 in all – the last in 1991. In 1970 he played Albert Perks in the children's film *The Railway Children*, and between 1973 and 1975 he charmed another generation with his narration for *The Wombles*. His other credits on television, stage, film and radio are too numerous to mention, but by the start of the 21st Century he'd become that most indefinable of things – a national treasure. He even returned to *Doctor Who*. Soon after appearing in one of Big Finish's *Doctor Who* audio dramas, 'Horror of Glam Rock', broadcast on BBC Radio 7 and released on CD in January 2007, he found himself cast in the television series too.

In 2007, he was given a cameo part in that year's Christmas Special episode, 'Voyage of the Damned'. The production team enjoyed working with him so much that when the opportunity arose, they made his character a semi-regular. He played Wilfred Mott, grandfather of the Doctor's new companion, Donna Noble (Catherine Tate), and appeared in six[246] of the following year's episodes, before returning to see off David Tennant's

---

[245] Cribbins played Mr Hutchinson in the episode 'The Hotel Inspectors'.
[246] In 2008, Cribbins appeared in: 'Partners in Crime', 'The Sontaran Stratagem' (a two-part story), 'Turn Left' and 'Journey's End' (another two-parter).

Doctor in the actor's two-part swansong, 'The End of Time', broadcast over Christmas 2009.

'Mr Cushing was a totally different Doctor,' said Cribbins in 2008. 'He was a waffly old professor, very stereotyped, and then you've got David, who's on springs all the time, he's wonderful. I think I'd have to say that David's my favourite Doctor of all of them. I think Tom Baker – sorry, Tom – runs him a close second, but I think David's the guv'nor, for me.'[247]

---

[247] From *The One Show* (26 June 2008).

Daleks – Invasion Earth: 2150 Ad
By
Milton Subotsky and David Whitaker[248]
From a story by Terry Nation

PLOT SYNOPSIS

It is late at night and police constable Tom Campbell is on his beat. He looks in wistfully through the brightly-lit windows of an empty travel agent's.

Close by, a man is sitting nervously behind the wheel of a car parked outside a jeweller's shop. Tom hasn't noticed the man or his car, but the man has noticed Tom. Before he can turn round, Tom is violently struck on the back of the head and collapses to the ground. A moment later, the frontage of the jeweller's shop explodes in a cloud of shattered glass. Two burglars run out through the smoke. The man in the car revs up the engine and the two men jump in. Tom is just able to stagger to his feet as the vehicle speeds off into the night.

As Tom runs after the departing car, still dazed from his injuries, he spots a nearby police box and places a shaky hand on its door. The door opens and Tom collapses inside. The police box isn't a police box at all; it is TARDIS, and inside stand Dr Who, his niece Louise and his granddaughter Susan.

Helping the injured constable up from the floor, Dr Who and the two girls observe the commotion on the street outside. Quite a crowd has now gathered. One of the onlookers has already noticed the police box and is heading towards it. Dr Who decides to leave before anyone else makes an accidental entrance.

The controls are set and TARDIS vanishes from the pavement, leaving the passer-by clawing at the empty space left behind.

When Tom regains consciousness, he is keen to report the break-in to his superiors. He asks to use the phone. However Dr Who explains this might

---

[248] David Whitaker went uncredited on the opening credits of the film – possibly due to the fact that the film's final screenplay was mostly the work of Milton Subotsky.

be difficult. When Tom stumbled into TARDIS, Dr Who had been about to set off on a trip to London in the year 2150. They have now arrived at their destination. Refusing to believe that he is now in a time machine, Tom opens the doors and walks outside.

Outside, it is no longer night-time. The police box isn't standing where it was when he first entered it. They are indeed in London, in the year 2150. The city is deserted and decayed. Buildings are ruined. Rubble is strewn all around.

As Dr Who and Louise explore the local area, Susan accidentally dislodges an iron girder and causes a pile of rubble and debris to rain down from the upper storey of a ruined building. The travellers dive for cover. But when the dust has cleared they discover the doors to TARDIS have become jammed shut[249] by fallen girders.

While Louise stays behind to nurse Susan's twisted ankle, Dr Who and Tom head off to search through an adjacent warehouse for something to shift the girders blocking TARDIS. Walking through the dusty corridors of the empty warehouse they find the body of a dead man, wearing a plastic suit and a strange futuristic helmet. The helmet has a built-in miniature radio receiver of a highly advanced design. In one of the shadowy corners of the warehouse, the two men are observed by an unseen stranger.

Meanwhile, back at the landing site, Louise hears the sound of persistent gunfire somewhere off in the distance. She goes to check on Susan, but can't find her. As she searches through the ruins, a man's hand clamps over her face. The man tells her that he knows where Susan is. The man drags Louise off in the direction of a battered Underground station.

Continuing to explore the upstairs rooms of the warehouse, Tom falls from a hole in the side of the building, but manages to save himself by holding onto a broken door. As the two men look down to the street below, they too hear the sound of gunfire.

Leaving the warehouse, Dr Who and Tom see a massive flying saucer pass overhead. It disappears over the horizon, seeming to land somewhere around Sloane Square.

Louise discovers that the strange man who pulled her away from TARDIS is called Wyler. He takes her to Susan, as he had promised. The girls meet up at a disused London tube station. The station is the secret base of a group of rebel humans, fighting an alien invasion of Earth. Their leader is a wheelchair-bound munitions expert called Dortmun, who is planning to launch an attack on London's alien invaders with a batch of specially made grenades.

Returning to the inaccessible TARDIS, Dr Who and Tom start looking for

---

[249] Sadly that's what you get when the doors to your time machine open outwards. Something the *Doctor Who* television series never had to worry about.

the missing girls. There's no sign of them. However, in shouting out the girls' names they attract the attention of some heavily armed men. The men are all dressed in the same strange clothing that we earlier saw on the dead man at the warehouse. These are Robomen. Dr Who and Tom make a run for it. However, as they reach the banks of the Thames, they are suddenly confronted by a Dalek emerging from beneath the waters.

Back in the rebel stronghold at the tube station, the survivors of London listen to a Dalek radio broadcast ordering all those still alive to surrender to their Dalek invaders immediately. Dortmun explains something of the recent history of the Daleks' invasion to Louise and Susan. The oddest part of the invasion strategy has been the setting up of a gigantic mining facility in Bedfordshire. Dortmun doesn't know what the Daleks are doing there, but it involves a lot of slave labour.

Dr Who and Tom have been grouped together with a number of other Dalek prisoners being marched toward the Dalek spaceship. One of their fellow captives tries to make a break for it, but is killed by one of the Daleks.

Once inside the Dalek ship, the prisoners are all locked away in small cells. However, Dr Who and Tom manage to escape from their cell by tripping the door mechanism. Unfortunately their delight at being free is short-lived. They find out that their cell door had been deliberately designed for escape. The Daleks reasoned that only the brightest of prisoners would be able to escape, and the fact that Dr Who and Tom are among this group has earned them a place in the robotising programme. They will now have their memories and personalities wiped and be brainwashed to become Robomen – the technologically-augmented slaves of the Daleks.

However, as the men are put into the processing machine, a series of explosions ring out. The Dalek spaceship is under attack by the rebels using bombs provided by Dortmun. There is a pitched battle as the Daleks (largely successfully) attempt to fend off the human assault. During the confusion, Dr Who and Tom are rescued from the processing area. However, they lose one another in the crowds. Dr Who leaves with the retreating rebels, while Tom hides away in a storeroom on the Dalek ship.

Dr Who is chased from the ship by a squad of Daleks, but finally gives them the slip by heading down into the sewers.

Back at the rebel base, Dortmun, Wyler and Susan decide to make their way to the countryside near Watford, where they can regroup. Susan leaves a message chalked on the back of a door, telling her grandfather where she has gone. However, when Dr Who returns to the base, he fails to notice Susan's message and leaves on foot for the gigantic Dalek mining operation in Bedfordshire.

Tom has stolen a Roboman uniform so that he might move about the Dalek ship unnoticed. He finds Louise, who has also hidden herself aboard in the aftermath of the rebel attack.

Susan, Wyler and Dortmun find an old van in a disused garage and hope to use it to escape from London. However, their way is barred by a phalanx of Daleks across the road. Dortmun tries to blow up the Daleks with some of his home-made explosives, but he's killed in the process.

Hoping to make use of the ensuing confusion, Wyler and Susan drive off. As they motor on through the outskirts of London, they spot a Dalek ship overhead. The ship opens fire on their van, causing it to explode. However, Susan and Wyler manage to jump out just in time and hide in the woods.

The ship containing Tom and Louise eventually makes a landing at the mining works in Bedfordshire. Escaping down a wastepipe, they run off toward the mine-workings. One of the slave-workers agrees to hide them in a tool shed and bring them some food as soon as he can.

Wyler and Susan are captured by the Daleks when two collaborators tell the Daleks where they are hiding. The Daleks take Wyler and the girl to their HQ at the mine.

Dr Who has now also reached Bedfordshire. He is accosted by a black marketeer, Brockley, who says he can get him into the mine. They stay in hiding overnight and go into the mine with the early shift in the morning. When they get to the mine, they are taken to the same tool shed where Louise and Tom are hiding. There, one of the miners explains exactly what it is the Daleks are doing in Bedfordshire. They plan to extract the metallic core of the Earth, so that they can then pilot the planet like a giant spaceship. They have found a fracture in the Earth's crust and have set up an explosive device to go through the fracture. This will cause the planet's metallic core to burst out and plunge toward the Sun.

Dr Who studies a plan of the mine workings and discovers that there is a disused shaft adjacent to the Daleks' own. He suggests that if they could find a way of forcing entry to the abandoned shaft, it might give them an opportunity to divert the explosive device before it passes through the Earth's crust. By chance, the mine sits above a massive confluence of magnetic forces, and if they were able to divert the Daleks' bomb into this, the magnetism so released would be powerful enough to suck the invaders into the core of the Earth.

In the Dalek HQ, on the brow of a hill overlooking the mine, the Daleks are making their final pre-release checks. Their explosive device is moved into position and sits poised above the shaft, ready to be dropped.

Inside the shaft, Tom uses some loose planking from the walls to try to deflect the passage of the bomb.

Meanwhile, Dr Who has been betrayed by Brockley and is recaptured by the Daleks. He is reunited with Susan and Wyler and taken to Dalek control. Looking down into the Dalek shaft, he spies Tom a few feet below.

Hoping to cause a diversion, Dr Who spots a microphone on the wall. He suddenly grabs hold of it and uses it to order the Robomen to attack the

Daleks. The Robomen obey. The rebellion is only short-lived and the Daleks soon win. However, the distraction has provided Tom with enough time to finish the construction of his wooden bomb deflector in the shaft beneath.

The Daleks release their bomb and wait for it to explode in 23 rels' time. However, Tom's interference has the desired effect. The bomb is diverted and explodes above the magnetic confluence, causing the Daleks to be sucked down into the mine workings. The control room explodes and the mine is soon ablaze as the liberated slave-workers run for cover. The Daleks try to take off in their spaceship but the magnetic forces are too great and their saucer crashes into the mine workings in a ball of flames. The invasion is over.

Back in TARDIS, Dr Who sets course for the 20th Century. They take Tom back to the street where they first met, only a few seconds before he left. This time around, Tom is there in time to foil the robbery. He drives off, confident of a promotion to Chief Inspector.

3
Remembrance of the Daleks

Peter Cushing never did meet the Daleks again in any further *Doctor Who* movies. However, despite the Aaru franchise stalling after its second entry, those movies have cast a surprisingly long shadow. And *Daleks – Invasion Earth: 2150 AD* was not quite the last that we would see – or hear – of Peter Cushing's eccentric scientist Dr Who.

THE RADIO PILOT

In 1966, with the prospects for the second Dalek film still predicted to be good, an independent radio drama company called Stanmark Productions turned its attention to the idea of translating *Doctor Who* to radio[250].

Stanmark, run by a former pirate radio DJ called Doug Stanley[251], were mostly concerned with producing radio dramas for the international market. A company called Television International Enterprises (TIE)[252], which also distributed *Doctor Who* television episodes to some overseas markets for BBC Enterprises, helped Stanmark sell its programmes to stations as far flung as the Caribbean and Africa.

Stanmark's proposal was that they would record 52 *Doctor Who* radio episodes of roughly 20 minutes each. These would be syndicated in various overseas territories including Australia, New Zealand and Canada. Stanmark also hoped the programmes would be purchased by the BBC for broadcast on their Light Programme.

Stanmark collaborated on the proposal with another company called Watermill Productions, run by television producer Richard Bates, who had worked on ITV's *The Avengers* as a story editor between 1962 and 1964.

Surprisingly, their first choice to play the radio Doctor was neither William Hartnell nor Peter Cushing, but (of all people) horror legend Boris

---

[250] A Dalek radio series had been earlier suggested to the BBC, and rejected, in December 1965.

[251] Stanley ran the company alongside R W F Rice and secretary, A Kane.

[252] TIE was owned by Sir David Stirling, who founded the SAS. Stirling sometimes used TIE as a front for more clandestine international work that he undertook for the British government and MI6, trading in arms and helping to put down revolutions and military coups. Not that the arms-dealing appeared on any of their sales brochures.

Karloff. With an already long career behind him, Karloff had first found fame in Universal's 1931 film *Frankenstein*, and he had been a staple of a certain kind of gothic cinema ever since. In the '60s, he'd been taking on an increasing amount of television work. In 1962 he had hosted ITV's science-fiction anthology series *Out of this World*, recording an in-vision introduction to each of its 13 episodes, and in 1966 he was working on a variety of shows for American television, including *The Wild Wild West* and *The Girl From UNCLE*. Arguably even more surprising than Karloff being asked to play the lead in Stanmark's radio show was the fact that he was actually interested in taking the part. Unfortunately, just before a pilot episode was set to be recorded, Karloff fell ill and had to stay in America.

The producer's next choice to play the Doctor was Peter Cushing. Cushing had the international standing that William Hartnell lacked, and his part in the two Dalek movies made him the obvious candidate. The fact that publicity for the second Dalek film was then at its height didn't hurt his chances either.

To write the script for their new radio pilot, Bates called on an old colleague from *The Avengers*, Malcolm Hulke. In the late 1960s and early 1970s, Hulke would become one of *Doctor Who*'s most prolific television scriptwriters, working on a total of 47 television episodes between 1967 and 1974. However, that was still in the future and the radio pilot would be Hulke's first recorded script for the show, following numerous failed submissions to the *Doctor Who* production office.

Hulke's script told the story of an otherworldly English schoolgirl who turned out to be the Doctor's granddaughter, Susan. The Doctor's TARDIS, disguised as a police public call box, is in a park when a schoolfriend of Susan's, named Mike, stumbles inside and all three journey to 18th Century America.

Cushing recorded the 23-minute pilot episode, titled 'Journey Into Time', in summer 1966. The recording was shortly after submitted to the BBC for their feedback, along with a copy of the script. The response was not overly generous.

On 21 September, H Rooney Pelletier, the BBC's newly appointed General Manager of Radio Enterprises, forwarded a recording of the episode across to his colleague Martin Esslin, the Head of Sound Drama. Esslin replied in a memo later that week, stating that,although the pilot was 'quite well produced,' it was nevertheless 'extremely feeble and it certainly isn't anything I would recommend for broadcast in any of the spots for which I am responsible.'[253]

On 4 October, after further discussions, G Del Strother, Head of Pproductions at BBC Television Enterprises, outlined his feelings that

[253] From *Doctor Who Magazine* – Issue 349 (10 November 2004) p.26

Stanmark could be granted exclusive production and distribution rights for their radio series, to be recorded over the next two years and distributed over the next seven. However, they would not be allowed to distribute or broadcast any of it in Britain. Pelletier concurred with the decision not to allow the series to be broadcast on the BBC.

The series was still being advertised in January 1967 and was promoted in the *World Radio and Television Handbook* as 'the amazing DR WHO available for the first time on radio as a 25-minute serial.'[254]

The series linked in much better with the two Dalek films than it did with the television show, featuring as it did Cushing's Dr Who and a younger Susan. A photograph of Cushing from the second Dalek film was also used to promote the project.

On 7 February, Doug Stanley wrote to a *Doctor Who* fan that, 'it is hoped that the series … will shortly be carried by one of the British radio stations.'[255] However, Stanley's optimism proved to be misplaced. The project foundered and no further episodes were recorded. The pilot was never broadcast in Britain – nor anywhere else it seems. Today, the radio pilot is the only episode of *Doctor Who* ever recorded for which no recording of any kind is known to survive anywhere. A copy of the script was rediscovered at the BBC Written Archives Centre in 2011 by researcher Richard Bignell and remains the only record of the episode. Bignell later documented the full history of the radio show in his magazine of *Doctor Who* research, *Nothing At The End Of The Lane*, in 2011.

After a moderately successful few years, Stanmark went into liquidation on 7 November 1972 – the same year that the Dalek movies themselves went through something of a small renaissance, courtesy of the BBC.

NOW ON THE SMALL SCREEN … IN BLACK AND WHITE

Throughout the late '60s, the Dalek movies remained relatively popular with Saturday morning 'minor's matinee' audiences and other children's cinema clubs. This kept both pictures on the cinema screens, albeit sporadically, until the early 1970s. However, by 1972, audiences had all but tailed off and the movies' distributors put the television rights out to tender.

For obvious reasons, the BBC were very interested; and they successfully won the exclusive UK television rights (for a limited period). At 7.05 pm on 1 July 1972 – a Saturday – *Dr. Who and the Daleks* was transmitted as part of BBC1's *High Adventure* family movie strand. For an audience still awaiting the far-off start of the next *Doctor Who* television season (not due until December), it injected a much-wanted dash of colour into their lives – even

---

[254] From *The Frame* – Issue 10 (May 1989) p.18
[255] From *The Frame* – Issue 10 (May 1989) p.19

though most UK viewers would have still been watching on black and white television sets. The film pulled in an impressive 9.9 million viewers – the highest *Doctor Who*-related viewing figure that year.

The following month, the BBC broadcast *Daleks – Invasion Earth: 2150 AD* in the same slot[256]. It pulled in an even bigger audience of 10.7 million viewers – the highest *Doctor Who*-related figure since 1965.

On 27 June 1974, the second film returned to BBC1 when strike action caused a number of other shows to be dropped. The first film also got an unplanned repeat showing that year, when it was parachuted in to replace rained-off cricket coverage on 26 August. These '70s screenings brought a whole new generation of fans to the films.

'I didn't actually find them until that summer when they were on in about '72,' remembers director Kevin Davies. 'My Dad took me to see the Daleks in Selfridges in '65 – I've got that as a deeply ingrained childhood memory – but I never went to see the films. So when they came on telly that was a big revelation. I love [the second film] in particular … and I grew to love the first one later. I think I probably OD'd on the second one … I recorded [the soundtrack] off the telly one summertime in around '73 or '74 and …. drew my own comic strip based on the film.'

However, not all *Doctor Who* fans were converted to the Dalek films' charms. Scriptwriter Robert Shearman, who was later charged with resurrecting the Daleks for television in 'Dalek' (2005), has been less than generous in his views on Tovey's character in particular, describing her as, 'smug and humourless and far too bloody clever for her own good. Not so much an unearthly child as an ungodly one.'[257]

Both movies continued to be shown on BBC1 and BBC2 every now and then until May 1987, when much of the BBC's management fell out of love with *Doctor Who*.

The television rights to the films were next acquired by Channel 4 around 1994, and they remained a regular feature of its schedules for some years thereafter.[258] Following a 30 December 1997 broadcast of the first film, a commercial was aired for the BBC's new *Destiny of the Doctors* computer game – one the BBC's very first television commercials.

In 2005, the first film was back over on the BBC, as part of a line-up of programmes heralding the long-awaited return of *Doctor Who* as a television

---

[256] The film was slightly edited, to remove one supposedly graphic shot of a whip gripping a man's throat.

[257] From *Doctor Who Magazine* – Issue 300 (7 February 2001) p.25

[258] For some mysterious reason, each of the Channel 4 showings of *Daleks – Invasion Earth: 2150 AD* had the pre-credits scene and the title sequence swapped round in the edit, so that the film starts with the opening credits and then the pre-credits scene.

series.

Both films have since had numerous other UK television screenings, most recently (at the time of writing) on Channel 5. They have also over the years had occasional airings on non-terrestrial television networks, including BSB and UKTV.

HOME CINEMA

In 1977, the Dalek films became the first ever pieces of *Doctor Who* that you could actually go out and buy to watch in your own home, when they were both issued commercially on the Super 8 cine-film format by Walton Films Ltd. They came in a variety of different versions (edited, unedited, black and white, colour, silent and sound), the multiple reels of which were packaged in boxes featuring redrawn and simplified versions of the respective movies' original posters.

Higher-quality 16mm prints of the films were available to hire for events, too. Both were shown (in black and white) at the first ever *Doctor Who* convention, held by the *Doctor Who* Appreciation Society (DWAS) in a church hall in Battersea, London on 6 August 1977.

Then in 1982, the movies became the first *Doctor Who* home video releases, via the Thorn EMI label (on both VHS and Betamax formats) – pre-dating the start of the BBC's own range of *Doctor Who* videos by nearly a year. They have since been re-released many times on both VHS and DVD[259].

In May 2013 current rights holder, Studio Canal, also reissued them on the high definition Blu-Ray format. Advance promotion for this included the films being given a number of back-to-back cinema screenings, including one by the British Film Institute.[260]

DOCTOR WHO AND THE CAVE-MONSTERS

In the years following the release of their two Dalek pictures, Amicus predominantly concentrated on horror films, with such sensitive titles as *Torture Garden* (1968), *Scream and Scream Again* (1970), *The House that Dripped Blood* (1971), *And Now the Screaming Starts* (1973) and *Vault of Horror* (1973). All surprisingly starry productions, they were a mixed bag in terms of quality – sometimes much better than anyone had any right to expect, sometimes a lot worse. However, they were all firmly designed to be 'adult' pictures – a long way from the child-friendly fantasies of *Doctor Who*.

---

[259] Both films were first included in the *Doctor Who and the Daleks* DVD set from Studio Canal in 2001 (reissued many times since).

[260] A similar one-off back-to-back screening had taken place some years earlier, on 18 June 1994, at The Screen cinema in Walton-on-Thames.

Following the spectacularly successful release of their 1975 film *The Land that Time Forgot*, Amicus began to return to more escapist adventure fare in the second half of the 1970s. The British horror boom had begun to wane thanks to altogether more visceral offerings from America, and even titans like Hammer Studios had started to go bust. However, thanks to films like *The Land that Time Forgot*, Amicus managed to stay in business rather longer than many of its contemporaries, even enjoying a brief renaissance.

One of the most interesting of Amicus's offerings from this period (at least for *Doctor Who* fans) was 1976's *At the Earth's Core*, very loosely based on a story by Edgar Rice Burroughs. Like *The Land that Time Forgot*, it was directed by former film editor Kevin Connor and starred American action man Doug McClure in the lead. It also starred Peter Cushing playing an oddly familiar character.

The movie tells of an eccentric and doddery English inventor who has built a machine to travel to the centre of the Earth. The inventor's name is Dr Abner Perry. However, only twice is he distinctly identified as such. Throughout the rest of the movie, he is referred to only as 'Doctor' or 'Doc'.

The Doctor and his travelling companion discover that at the very centre of the planet Earth is a strange, brightly-coloured underground world, where primitive humans live under the oppressive tyranny of a race of telepathic dinosaurs. Naturally, the Doctor and his friend overthrow the evil tyrants and get back into their travel machine to return home.

In other words the plot is, essentially, much the same as that of *Dr. Who and the Daleks*, only with dinosaurs in place of Daleks. *At the Earth's Core* also sees Cushing present a virtual carbon copy of his earlier Dr Who persona, complete with an almost identical costume. The film was even later issued to cinemas on a double-bill with *Dr. Who and the Daleks*.

In fact, *At the Earth's Core* is so similar to the Dalek pictures that it can arguably be viewed as a continuation. One advocate of this theory is *Doctor Who* author Paul Magrs, who comments: '*At the Earth's Core* was for me kind of a third *Doctor Who* film ... because of Cushing's performance being similar to his version of the Doctor. I think that it might even have been conscious on his part.'

At the Earth's Core is, in retrospect, a peculiarly difficult film to pigeon-hole. At the time, it was a notional sequel to *The Land that Time Forgot*. However, it isn't really a sequel in its execution. It contains none of the same characters or concepts from that film and only one of the same actors. It was really left to 1978's *The People that Time Forgot* to be that sequel. Instead, *At the Earth's Core* works so much more obviously as a sequel to (and partial retread of) the Dalek films, and *Dr. Who and the Daleks* in particular.

Except, Amicus didn't really do sequels. They made their two Dalek films in the '60s and their two *Time Forgot* films in the '70s. And somewhere in the middle of that sits *At the Earth's Core* – halfway between being a *Doctor*

Who sequel and a *Time Forgot* film. Probably closer to the former, but never entirely either.

THE PARTING OF THE WAYS

At the Earth's Core is also significant for another reason. It was Subotsky's last movie for Amicus. The 20-year partnership between Subotsky and Rosenberg was dissolved during the picture's pre-production.

Frictions had existed between the pair for years. However, it had never got in the way of their filmmaking. 'That was always the case,' remembers Vic Simpson, construction manager on *At the Earth's Core*[261]. 'Milton Subotsky used to deal with all the scripts. Max was the money man. So, there was often friction over budgets and one thing and another, as you can understand. One is the guy who's religiously into the scripts and god knows what and just doesn't care about budget, and the other one, Max, is concerned about the budget all the time, being the money man.'

'We only heard about it as a bit of tittle-tattle and gossip,' recalls Gerald Larn, who at that time was still working in the effects department at Shepperton. 'We never directly encountered any of the fallout from their relationship.'

However, by early summer 1975, things seem to have changed, and as Amicus itself was enjoying one of its greatest successes with *The Land that Time Forgot*, the Subotsky/Rosenberg partnership finally split apart.

At the Earth's Core was the last Amicus film that Subotsky had any involvement in. He later told *Filmfax* magazine: 'We signed an agreement in June 1975 and I withdrew from the company. I just wanted to get away. It was terrible. There was a lawsuit that dragged on for five years.'[262]

'Thinking back, Amicus was an innocent company run by an odd couple,'[263] concluded Rosenberg.

With Subotsky's departure, Amicus was left in the hands of Rosenberg (at least until March 1976) and fellow board members Justin M Golenbock (lawyer[264]), Peter B de Berenger, Arthur Cleaver (accountant), John Dark (producer) and Maurice Carter (production designer).

Away from the partnership, both Subotsky and Rosenberg would continue to make films, but it was the beginning of the end for Amicus as a

---

[261] Simpson had also previously worked for Amicus on *From Beyond the Grave* and *The Land that Time Forgot*.

[262] From *Amicus – The Studio That Dripped Blood* ed. Allan Bryce – Stray Cat Publishing (2000) p.150

[263] From *Amicus – The Studio That Dripped Blood* ed. Allan Bryce – Stray Cat Publishing (2000) p.150

[264] Golenbock was senior partner and co-founder of the Manhattan law firm Golenbock & Barell.

production company. No longer based at their old Shepperton premises and with new producers taking on the running of the business, by 1976 Amicus was no longer the same company that had made the Dalek pictures in the 1960s. The British film industry as a whole was struggling to compete with bigger-budget American offerings, and with *Star Wars* about to be released in 1977, the company's future was sadly all too clear.

In 1977, Rosenberg also decided to leave the business he had co-founded. Amicus had formally ceased trading by the end of the following June. Rosenberg recalled: 'I heard John Dark say on the phone, "Why do we need the old man?" So I decided to quit there and then.'[265]

Amicus's last film production[266] (with AIP) was *The People that Time Forgot*. Although not a disaster, neither was it a great success. It probably wouldn't have saved Amicus even had its founders not bailed out. 'In the words of T S Eliot, the company ended up not with a bang but a whimper,'[267] said Rosenberg.

DOCTOR WHO'S GREATEST ADVENTURE

Following the collapse of Amicus, Milton Subotsky made only three further films as a producer (although he did clock up some additional co-producer and television credits). Soon after *At the Earth's Core* had wrapped, he was briefly reunited with Peter Cushing for 1977's commercially dismal *The Uncanny*. He followed this with the even less successful but starrier *Dominique* (1979) and *The Monster Club* (1981).

'He had a lot of projects in the '80s that didn't really come to anything,' recalls his wife, Fiona Subotsky. Among these many projects was a proposed return to *Doctor Who*.

Subotsky contacted BBC Enterprises around September 1984 to discuss the possible production of a third official *Doctor Who* film, this time based on an original story he'd written. The script apparently had the surprising provisional title *The Lossiemouth Affair*, although *Doctor Who's Greatest Adventure* seems to have been Subotsky's preference later on. The proposal doesn't seem to have had any links to his previous *Doctor Who* pictures, and there doesn't appear to have been any thought of approaching Peter Cushing to reprise his role from the '60s.

Subotsky's intent was to start production in February 1985 – presumably

---

[265] From *Amicus – The Studio That Dripped Blood* ed. Allan Bryce – Stray Cat Publishing (2000) p.150

[266] The Amicus brand was resurrected for film production many decades later, but was essentially set up as a new company, with no connection to the old outfit.

[267] From *Amicus – The Studio That Dripped Blood* ed. Allan Bryce – Stray Cat Publishing (2000) p.150

under the auspices of his own Sword & Sorcery Productions, which he'd set up with producer Andrew Donally around 1977/78. 'This one is a big, big film,' he suggested. 'I would think upwards of £15 million'[268] (actually a fairly conservative sum by the standards of the mid-'80s). 'I already had a screenplay written for a third ... after *Daleks – Invasion Earth: 2150 AD*,' he added. 'It's a giant monsters film and I call it *Doctor Who's Greatest Adventure*. It's got two Doctors in it, one old and one a younger one. I would use Jon Pertwee or Tom Baker for the older Doctor and anyone good enough could play the younger one. I included two Doctors because the problem is so big, it needs two Time Lords to solve it. It's a very good script.'[269]

Subotsky's suggestions regarding the casting of one of the BBC's own actors as the Doctor were certainly an interesting departure from his approach to the earlier films – perhaps suggestive of a picture more closely tied to the continuity of the television series. As he stated, Subotsky had a fondness for the Doctors of both Jon Pertwee and Tom Baker. However, he had little time for those of Peter Davison, Colin Baker or Sylvester McCoy (although he did like McCoy as an actor in general). He had in fact already worked with Pertwee on Amicus's *The House that Dripped Blood* in 1970, and Tom Baker had appeared in his *The Vault of* Horror in 1973. Baker may have had reservations about being involved in a *Doctor Who* movie, only a year after he turned down the BBC's offer of a cameo part in 1983's 'The Five Doctors' on television, but Pertwee might well have taken up Subotsky's offer to be involved.

Sadly, we'll never know, as ultimately the BBC did not grant Subotsky the rights. This was possibly due in part to ongoing negotiations with another production company concerning the making of a different *Doctor Who* film (see Chapter Seven). However, Subotsky's proposal never really stood a chance. The movie world had changed hugely since those first two Dalek pictures. Filmmakers like George Lucas and Steven Spielberg had created a market for hugely expensive blockbuster adventure films that only the biggest and most powerful studios could afford to make.

Added to this, in 1984 the British government under Margaret Thatcher, reviewed the Eady Levy, which had been supporting the nation's film industry since 1950. They didn't like the way that it sought to control the market and protect an industry from the effects of the international economy. The fund gave filmmakers the security to carry on making British films in Britain for British audiences, but it also stopped cinema chains from becoming the massively profitable mega-businesses that the government wanted to encourage them to be. In 1985, the Eady Levy was terminated. As a result, big cinema chains got a lot richer while smaller ones went to the

---

[268] From *DWB (Dream Watch Bulletin)* – Issue 81 (September 1990) p.43
[269] From *DWB (Dream Watch Bulletin)* – Issue 81 (September 1990) p.43

wall, and the British film industry was almost completely killed off overnight.

Even if Subotsky *had* got permission from the BBC to make his film, it is hard to see where the money to make it would have come from, in a climate where big-budget American pictures were fast becoming the only thing on offer in British cinemas.

'The *Doctor Who* films,' considers film historian Marcus Hearn. 'were what I would categorise as mid-budget films ... Although many people now look at them and think that they were low-budget films, they actually weren't ... They weren't blockbusters either. They were something in between the two. That market existed –for the mid-budget double-bill family film – until the late '70s, I think. And Subotsky was still active in that market up until the late '70s ... I think that it's pretty much possible that he could have made another film at any point during that era. From the '80s onwards, the whole landscape of films changed. ...From that point, there was a massive change in what people expected from action-adventure films and in what studios were prepared to commission as well. A film like *Dr. Who and the Daleks*, which could never have been a high-budget film because its potential market wasn't big enough, became very difficult to produce. You could in 1964/65 prepare *Dr. Who and the Daleks* as a mid-budget film and confidently expect to make your money back on the British market alone. Whereas from the late '70s onwards, you couldn't.'

Subotsky never made his last *Doctor Who* picture, and only *At the Earth's Core* can give us any idea what it might have looked like. He later had better luck when buying the rights to some of horror writer Stephen King's stories. His last film credit was as a nominal co-producer on *The Lawnmower Man* (1992). The film was very successful, but Subotsky didn't live to see it. He died in London on 27 June 1991, aged 69.

Max J Rosenberg had perhaps the more successful career of the two men following the break-up of their partnership. He stayed very active in the industry for much of the rest of his life. Probably his most notable later credit was as an uncredited executive producer on 1982's *Cat People* remake starring Natassja Kinski and Malcolm McDowell. Rosenberg died on 14 June 2004, aged 89.

Even the script for Subotsky's final *Doctor Who* film now seems to be lost. The BBC don't appear to have retained a copy (assuming one was ever even sent to them) and the Subotsky family don't recall recently seeing it either.

'Milton didn't actually leave much useful paperwork,' explains Fiona Subotsky. 'I don't know that anyone was thinking "archive". Milton basically didn't keep things in terms of memorabilia (which people are interested in these days). We've got practically nothing. It's quite extraordinary. That was his approach to it.'

MISSION OF DOOM

In 1986, 20 years after *Daleks – Invasion Earth: 2150 AD* had first hit UK cinemas, it was finally announced that there was going to be a sequel.

The new 'third Dalek film' gained pride of place in the pages of *Movie Maker* magazine, where it was described as a direct follow-on to Subotsky's Cushing films and 'the third of a trilogy'.[270] The film was titled *Mission of Doom*.

Of course, it never made it to the cinema. And, in reality, it had never been intended to. *Movie Maker* were actually covering the production of an amateur 'fan film' made by a group of young filmmakers from the DWAS (*Doctor Who* Appreciation Society).

Two decades since anyone had successfully mounted a *Doctor Who*-based feature for the cinema, *Mission of Doom* was an eye-wateringly ambitious and surprisingly professional attempt to make a follow-up to Aaru's Dalek films, with no stars, no BBC approval and practically no money. The project was largely the work of aspiring producer Paul Tams and model-maker Julian Vince.

'I said to Julian right from the start,' recalls Tams, 'if we were going to do something, it had to look professional. I didn't want any more running around Wimbledon Common with cardboard police boxes and people dressed up in bedspreads. I wanted it to look like it was a proper movie.'

'Really, it was, in essence, supposed to be the third Dalek film,' said Vince. 'Gradually, as I got further and further into it, I decided to make the thing bigger and better; and I think, at one point, I even built about 20 Daleks ... I wanted to go that little bit better than they had in the films. Keep that spectacle, but try and improve on it, if it was possible.'[271]

Tams told *Movie Maker* magazine: 'We see no reason why ... this film should be any different as far as production values are concerned from the two *Doctor Who* films made by Milton Subotsky.'[272]

Making the best of their cartridges of vibrant Kodachrome film stock, the movie's extensive model work was shot at the Epsom School of Art, where Vince was a student.

'I was working for Rank Films in Wardour Street at the time and used some of the facilities there to get some of the stuff done,' recalls Tams. 'We had a control console and Julian had built the TARDIS interior wall and doors, and we had this whole set on display at a *Doctor Who* convention –

---

[270] From *Doctor Who – 25 Glorious Years* by Peter Haining – WH Allen & Co (1988) p.109

[271] From *Dalekmania* dir. Kevin Davies – Lumiere Video (1995)

[272] From *Doctor Who – 25 Glorious Years* by Peter Haining – WH Allen & Co (1988) p.109

one of those PanoptiCon[273] things ... There's a photograph of Colin Baker standing next to the costume I designed at this control console.'

Like so many fan productions, *Mission of Doom* was never completed, although one of the characters (the Korven) was eventually worked into a *Doctor Who* spin-off series, *K-9*, that Tams co-devised for television in 2009[274].

It is perhaps surprising how many industry professionals started out in *Doctor Who* fan films in the late '70s and early '80. One of those involved was Kevin Davies. He worked with Tams on a fan film called *The Image Makers* in 1978. During shooting for the production, Tams recalls that a small tree-stump was set alight on the corner of Wimbledon Common. The fire aroused the attention of local resident Barry Foster (then best known as television's *Van Der Valk*). With the irate Foster heading toward the filmmakers, Davies quickly did his best to extinguish the fire by unzipping his trousers and urinating on the burning tree stump[275].

Over 15 years later, it was this Kevin Davies who found himself on location in London with a professional film crew, directing a much-awaited official documentary feature all about Aaru's two Dalek movies. The year was 1995.

ARCHIVE OF THE DALEKS

The rights to Aaru's two Dalek films were originally owned by the British Lion Film Corporation (sometimes known as Lion International). However, British Lion was taken over by EMI in 1976, around the time of *At the Earth's Core*. Its vast archive of assets was then subsequently sold on to the Israeli-founded Cannon Corporation. In turn, the archive next went to Weintraub Entertainment, before ending up with the Movie Acquisitions Corporation, later renamed Lumiere Pictures. By the mid-1990s both Dalek films (together with all associated properties) were owned by Lumiere and its expanding empire.

The physical films themselves were actually housed in a vault at Pinewood studios and had been for some time. As the assets were sold from company to company, the prints, papers and posters stayed where they were, under the patient administration of John Herron, keeper of the Pinewood archives. However, the intellectual copyright to the films was a different matter, and in

---

[273] The first PanoptiCon convention was organised by DWAS in the late 1970s, soon going on to become something of a fan institution.

[274] Following over a decade's worth of development and pre-production, Paul Tams and writer Bob Baker successfully brought to television a 26-part Australian-made adventure series based around the robot dog character K-9 from *Doctor Who*.

[275] Although Davies still recalls the incident, he believes he only *pretended* to urinate on the tree stump and that the fire quickly died down of its own accord. However, it's still a good story.

1995, one Lumiere employee started developing some grand plans for the Dalek properties.

Colin Higgs was at the time one of those working from Lumiere's London office in Wardour Street. He had high hopes for the Dalek material under his supervision. However, he had a problem. 'Lumiere Pictures … owned a huge archive,' he recalls. '[However] something close to five or six hundred of their best movies had been sub-licensed to Warner Bros. So what we were faced with was a catalogue that, on paper, looked great, but, in fact, every time you went to go and say, "I'd like to release *that* on video", you found that it had been sub-licensed. Included in this were the two Dalek movies. Frustratingly, they were good sellers for Warner, but the only way we could do anything ourselves was to use the clips, trailers, merchandise and all the promotional material that was stored down at Pinewood.'

With Lumiere thus unable to release the Dalek films themselves, but still able to use all the materials connected to them, Higgs saw that the opportunity might exist to use the growing home video market to support an entirely new Dalek production. 'It was one of the few subjects we had,' he says, 'where … it would probably sell almost as well as the actual features themselves.'

At that time, video tie-in tapes related to *Doctor Who* were becoming quite popular – most of them produced outside of the BBC by fan-run enterprises including Reeltime Pictures and BBV (see Appendix A). By 1995, Kevin Davies had already directed two of these videos.

THE DEATH OF DR WHO

In 1993, *Doctor Who* was 30 years old. To mark the occasion, the team behind the BBC's *Late Show* was charged with the making of a special anniversary documentary. The result was *30 Years in the TARDIS*, an elaborate and expansive look at the series, put together with great ambition by Davies, whose most celebrated previous credit at this point had been working on the animated sequences for the television adaptation of Douglas Adams' *The Hitchhikers' Guide to the Galaxy*.

Davies wasn't entirely satisfied with the finished edit of *30 Years in the TARDIS*, which was transmitted by the BBC on 29 November 1993. However, he soon got the opportunity to revisit the material for the even more ambitious *More Than 30 Years in the TARDIS*, released by BBC Video the following year. This dazzlingly creative and innovative feature mixed documentary sections with newly-shot dramatic sequences starring Jon Pertwee, Colin Baker, Sylvester McCoy, Elisabeth Sladen, Nicholas Courtney, Nicola Bryant and

Sophie Aldred.[276].

Sitting amidst its 87 minute running time was a lengthy section on Amicus's Dalek movies, which reunited Jennie Linden and Roberta Tovey on a special replica of the set from *Dr. Who and the Daleks* erected in the studios at BBC Television Centre in November 1993. However, although the Dalek films were allotted a significant chunk of material in the finished programme, there were still some cast members who didn't take part. The ailing Roy Castle was among them. Although he took no active part in the shooting, he was in the vicinity during studio recording on 9 November, as Davies remembers:

'He had been through [recent treatment for] cancer, and we'd just heard that he'd recovered. So we were all kind of tiptoeing around the edges of it a bit, but when we found out that [his show] *Record Breakers* was in the next studio to us and [effects designer] Mike Tucker knew an assistant floor manager working on that show ... well, he got the word to him, and in the tea break he popped in ... mooching around with Roberta Tovey and Jennie Linden, whom he hadn't seen in all those years.'

It is particularly sad that Castle never recorded anything for the *Doctor Who* documentary. On 26 November 1993, just a few days before the programme's broadcast, he announced that his cancer, which had been in remission, had returned. Although he still managed to undertake a high profile national tour to raise money for charity, his health deteriorated rapidly, and he died on 2 September 1994, just two days after his sixty-second birthday and shortly after the release of *More Than 30 Years in the TARDIS* on video.

Dr Who himself, Peter Cushing, was also absent from Davies' programme. He had remained active over the previous decade, despite having been diagnosed with prostate cancer in 1982. However, his work commitments were scaled back. He had played Sherlock Holmes for one final time in 1984 and had a prominent part in the *Biggles* movie in 1986. Rumour has it that he was even offered a role in the *Doctor Who* television series in 1983, although if so, he did not take it[277].

On 26 May 1993, as Davies was starting to plan his *Doctor Who* anniversary show, a surprisingly energetic Cushing celebrated his eightieth birthday at a special party at his home in Whitstable. Those attending included fellow actors Michael Gough, Paul Eddington, Ernie Wise, Timothy West and Don Henderson.

---

[276] A future *Doctor Who* luminary, actor and writer Mark Gatiss, also featured in the tribute, as one of a number of Dalek operators used in a sequence shot on Westminster Bridge. He's inside the short Dalek near the back (waving his plunger).

[277] The suggestion is that Cushing was offered the part of Borusa, president of the Time Lords in the 1983 story 'Arc of Infinity'. The character was eventually played by Leonard Sachs.

3: REMEMBRANCE OF THE DALEKS

In 1994, Cushing worked as a narrator on the television documentary *Flesh and Blood, The Hammer Heritage of Horror*. It was broadcast on 6 August. The following week, Davies and his team were editing *More Than 30 Years in the TARDIS* at BBC Television Centre when they heard the news that the actor had died. It was 11 August 1994. Cushing was 81 years old.

Admired for his quietly meticulous professionalism and loved dearly by almost everyone he'd ever worked with, the great man soon received many effusive tributes. 'One of the nicest men you could possibly meet,'[278] said John Mills, who had played Dr Watson alongside Cushing's Sherlock Holmes ten years earlier. 'This modest, quiet man, is perhaps the most underrated of British screen actors,' Cushing fan Mark Gatiss later said. 'In a very English way, beneath that perfectly composed mask, lay obsession, fanaticism and a deeply suppressed passion.'[279]

With its impressive replica sets and costumes (many the work of Julian Vince), *More Than 30 Years in the TARDIS* featured probably the most extensive coverage that Cushing's two *Doctor Who* pictures had received since the '60s, both having previously fallen somewhat out of favour with fans. In part, this acted as a timely tribute to both Castle and Cushing and their lesser-known contribution to the *Doctor Who* story.

'They are among my favourite roles,' said Peter Cushing in 1983. 'Especially because they brought me popularity with younger children … They just loved the Doctor. After all, it is one of the most heroic and successful parts an actor could play. That's, no doubt, one of the main reasons why the series has had such a long run on television. I shall always be grateful for having been a small part of such a success story.'[280]

FARBROTHER WHERE ART THOU

The release of *More Than 30 Years in the TARDIS* was soon brought to the attention of Colin Higgs at Lumiere, who was still planning his special Dalek production. Higgs recalls that it was magazine editor/writer Marcus Hearn who first mentioned it to him: 'Marcus was editor of the *Hammer Horror* magazine. He and I worked quite closely together because I was releasing films like *Dracula: Prince of Darkness* and *I Monster*[281] and those sort of things.'

Following Hearn's suggestion, Higgs approached Davies to both produce and direct a Dalek programme for him in the spring of 1995. The budget

---

[278] From *ITN Nine O'Clock News* – ITV (11 August 1994)
[279] From *A History of Horror with Mark Gatiss* dir. John Das – BBC Four (18 October 2010)
[280] *Doctor Who – A Celebration* by Peter Haining – WH Allen & Co (1983) p.80
[281] Actually, *I Monster* was an Amicus film, not a Hammer one. It was written by Milton Subotsky.

would sit somewhere around £20,000 – a comparatively generous sum for the time.

Higgs was planning to release the feature as a stand-alone straight-to-video production on 24 July, and a completion date of 26 June was set. This left Davies little time – about five weeks – to put it together, but he was keen to tackle the project, treating it almost as a sister film to his earlier work for the BBC. However, there was a problem. Davies had never worked as a producer before, only as a director. Higgs had assumed that he would effectively take on both jobs, being in overall charge of the entire production, but the responsibility wasn't something Davies was prepared to shoulder alone.

'I made a very bad decision,' says Davies candidly. 'I was offered … the money immediately to go and make the film … Just fielding the whole cash issue was a bit of a difficult thing. So, I said, "I'd rather somebody else produced it and I'll just direct it."'

With time pressing, Higgs got in touch with independent video outfit Amity Productions, run by Ashley Morgan and Colin Webb, and asked them to help him. 'We were already doing other work for Lumiere,' explains Morgan. 'I think that, at the same time, we were producing a programme about Christopher Lee.'[282]

Under the new arrangement, Amity would act as producers on the Dalek video, now titled *Dalekmania*, with Davies hired by them to work purely as a director. 'The contract ended up as an Amity contract instead of a Kevin Davies contract,' confirms Higgs. Morgan and Webb hired freelancer John Farbrother to effectively act as Amity's production manager and (officially) producer on the new project.

'[Amity] were really into doing films about tanks and World War Two stuff,' remembers Davies. 'I should have just bitten the bullet and done [*Dalekmania*] myself. But, at the time, I think I'd been signing on and I was worried about ten grand suddenly arriving in my account. It was going to be half up front and half on delivery. I wasn't VAT registered or anything like that. I think it was all going to be a bit scary. So, I decided that I'd rather have someone else produce it and just pay me to direct. I'm not a businessman.'

Unlike Davies and many of those working on the show, John Farbrother was not particularly a *Doctor Who* fan. 'Prior to getting into the film and video industry, he was actually in the Army, and he's now gone back to working with the Army,' says Morgan. 'He had a lot to do with logistics, I think. He was incredibly brilliant at organising things. So he had the ideal skills for being a production manager.'

When Farbrother joined the production, Kevin Davies quickly regretted his

---

[282] Another of Colin Higgs' straight-to-video releases, this was *The Many Faces of Christopher Lee* – a 60 minute interview-based feature, with Ashley Morgan as producer and John Farbrother as her production manager. It was released in 1996.

decision not to produce. He says: 'I didn't get on with that producer ... I kind of resented the idea in the end because, of course, he was trying to assert his authority over it, and I'd abdicated the authority, which I should never have done ... I was wary. I felt like I was going into battle with one arm tied behind my back.'

RECOLLECTION OF THE DALEKS

Dalekmania, like Davies' earlier *Doctor Who* project, would fuse drama and documentary together. The documentary sections would be made up of reminiscences from members of the cast and crew of the original Dalek films. The framing narrative for those sections however would be a little drama in its own right. The plot, such as it was, would see a young boy being taken to a 1960s cinema with his sister to see the latest Dalek film, but once he gets there, beginning to question whether the events on the screen are as fictional as they seem or whether the Daleks have not indeed invaded Earth.

The first day of recording[283] was on 25 May. This was to be spent interviewing Jill Curzon in London at Arundel House, in the offices of Marvel Comics' *Doctor Who Magazine*. Curzon had flown over from Spain to visit her daughter and was not often in the UK, which is why the interview was arranged right at the start of the shoot, to make use of her availability.

Davies meanwhile continued his work to try to get other members of the films' former cast and crew to participate in his project. With only a small budget, it wasn't easy. Of the actors approached, Geoffrey Toone, Philip Madoc, Jennie Linden (who'd already appeared in Davies' BBC production), Andrew Keir and Ray Brooks all ultimately declined to take part. Those who *did* agree included Roberta Tovey, Barrie Ingham, Yvonne Antrobus and Eddie Powell.

Bernard Cribbins, co star of *Daleks – Invasion Earth: 2150 AD*, was also high on Davies' wish-list of participants, but fell through. 'His agent [James Sharkey] was very off-hand,' recalls Davies. 'He really didn't want to know. We were offering a few hundred quid I think ... We just wanted him for an hour, just to reminisce. Even nowadays people don't get more than a few hundred quid, if they're lucky. But his agent was very kind of, "Come back when you can talk thousands." Maybe I did offer a thousand. I remember him saying, "Five times that and maybe we can start talking ..." Five grand is what he wanted – just for an interview with Cribbins ... I really seriously doubt that Cribbins ever heard. It was totally down to the agent.'

Davies was also keen to get in touch with the movies' original director,

---

[283] As with the *30 Years* documentary before it, *Dalekmania* was shot and edited entirely on Beta SP videotape, with archive sequences dropped in from 35mm film transfers.

Gordon Flemyng. 'Flemyng was the one we kept faxing,' says Marcus Hearn, who worked with Davies on the project. 'Kevin was faxing Gordon Flemyng endlessly and getting no response … This was the era before the internet, and everyone was sitting around wondering what Gordon was up to. I remembered having seen an episode of *Minder* that he'd directed – a very good episode, where Arthur Daley is selling dodgy satellite dishes, ends up having to fit one himself and gets stuck on top of the roof. That was directed by Flemyng just before we did *Dalekmania*, so I thought he was obviously still around and still working. But he didn't reply to any of Kevin's faxes.'

As it turned out, Flemyng had not been responding because he was seriously ill. He'd very recently been working as producer/director on a Yorkshire Television series called *Ellington*, starring Christopher Ellison and Sean Chapman, which was very much in the same mould as *Minder*. Following a pilot, Flemyng directed the first episode of the series proper. However, he didn't live to see it broadcast. He died on 12 July 1995, less than a month after the final edit of *Dalekmania* was completed. He was 61 years old.

Ahead of the main body of shooting, Davies visited the Lumiere vaults at Pinewood on 31 May and 1 June and spent those two days going through the archives' holdings, transferring various film clips to videotape for inclusion in the final edit. 'It was lovely,' says Davies. 'The Lumiere archive, as it was then, was a wonderful place to go and visit.'

Davies was aided by the vault's archivist, John Herron. 'John would know everything,' recalls Colin Higgs. 'If you went to him and said that there was a fashion shoot to promote series four of *The Avengers*, he'd go straight to the negs. He knew exactly where.'

'[He] was a lovely guy,' says Davies. 'World-weary; he'd seen it all. He'd just watched the logo change on the doors. He'd been head of this place forever. Kept hoping that somebody was going to make him redundant.'

Among the stills, posters and overseas trailers (re-dubbed for audiences in Italy, France and America), Davies was also pleased to unearth spools containing many of the films' original raw music tracks. They were found just in time, as it turned out. 'We got the original 35mm mag-tracks of the orchestral recordings of the music,' Davies confirms. 'They'd never been played – not since the old days. We ran them and they were leaving brown powder all over the Steenbeck. They smelt of vinegar[284]. They were really

---

[284] The music was stored on acetate safety film. This was safer than storing it on cheaper nitrate film stock (which can become flammable over time). However, acetate safety film has its own problems and can suffer from film-base degradation, or vinegar syndrome. This is where the film-base chemically deteriorates over time. The celluloid shrinks, becomes brittle and emits an acrid vinegary smell as acid builds up in it. Once it starts, the life of the afflicted film is likely to be very short, as the emulsion eventually buckles and breaks down completely.

getting old. So we had them all backed up onto DAT[285]. Mark Ayres [working on the production's sound and music] arranged for it all to be done ... Mark had always wanted to put them out on CD, but the problem was that the paperwork for the copyright ownership of the music was never clear, so it was unclearable. Nobody knew who owned it. It was a really difficult process ... It was only a couple of years back – a long, long while afterwards – when Silva Screen[286] finally bit the bullet and tackled it and put out a CD of the Dalek movie music ... When it came to it, I think Silva Screen tried to master the music elsewhere with someone else, and it was terrible apparently; there were all sorts of problems with it. Thank goodness that, in the end, they turned to Mark, who had kept his DAT recordings in pristine condition.'

The day after the final session at Pinewood, Davies' crew descended on a small independent studio on Union Street in London, run by Robin Lee[287]. While there, the crew recorded interviews with both Barry Ingham and Yvonne Antrobus.

Work on the production was progressing well, but was not without the odd ripple. One such ripple emanated from the agents of Dalek scribe Terry Nation. In mid June, the production team received a fax from Roger Latham at the BBC's intellectual property group. The fax said simply: 'I attach a fairly self-explanatory letter from Emma Derrel, a representative of Roger Hancock Ltd, the agents to Terry Nation. As explained to you, copyright of the Daleks is jointly owned by the BBC and Terry Nation, and I am therefore unable to grant permission for you to use the Daleks in your feature film.'

The attached letter from Derrel reinforced the point, stating:

Dear Roger:

Thank you for your letter of 9th June, in respect of the above. Having read through the proposal and subsequently discussed the project with Roger Hancock, I'm afraid that, in this instance, I am unable to grant permission for the use of Daleks.

PLAYING DALEKS

Recording started on the production's drama sequences on 11 June, with location work at the Muswell Hill Odeon. 'The North London Cinema Club

---

[285] Digital audio tape – a high-end professional audio tape format that comes in very small cassettes.

[286] An audio label specialising in the issuing of film and TV music on CD and LP. They'd already released a number of *Doctor Who* albums (including some of Mark Ayres' own scores for the TV series).

[287] The studio had played host to a number of *Doctor Who* related spin-off tapes before, mostly for the small Reeltime Pictures video company.

was based there and it was all pretty much like it was in the 1930s,' says Davies.

The old cinema was used for sequences in which the small boy and his sister go to see the Dalek films on the big screen. The boy was played by Josh Maguire, who had taken on a very similar part in the dramatic sequences of *More Than 30 Years in the TARDIS*. His sister was played by Natalie Jarrett and their mother by Anastasia Mulrooney. The cinema manager was played by Michael Wisher, a regular guest actor in the *Doctor Who* television series, best known for playing the original Davros in 1975. All were in attendance on this first day, as were Steve Arnott, Toby Aspin and Dave Hicks playing a platoon of Robomen in authentic costumes (mostly provided by Julian Vince).

'That was the fun stuff,' says Davies. 'Dressing up and getting Robomen marching up and down and the little boy and his sister going to the cinema and all that. That's all the fun stuff ... I had a chance to play Daleks.'

There were two Dalek props in use that day. One appeared in a sequence inside the cinema itself (as a static prop), while the other one (operated by Mick Hall) was used in a more expansive ambush scene outside the building. 'We didn't do much with the Dalek,' recalls Davies. 'We had it twitching its sticks a bit. It didn't move much. We thought we could get away with it.' Both sequences seemed innocuous enough, but would later cause problems in the edit.

On 17 June, recording continued with some fairly elaborate effects work. Despite the fact that it was in no way a BBC production, this work was done on the BBC's own Visual Effects Model Stage at 240 Western Avenue in Acton. 'It was just for hire, because Producer Choice[288] was all going on at that time,' recalls Davies.

Among the effects sequences shot here were all those involving a complex working replica of the Dalek saucer ship last seen in *Daleks – Invasion Earth: 2150 AD*. This new Dalek saucer had been built by model-maker Dave Brian, who was paid £300 for the loan of the model for one day's shooting, after which it would be returned to him. In fact, Brian provided the prop only on condition that it would not leave his side at any point. 'Where the saucer goes,

---

[288] Producer Choice was a controversial BBC initiative whereby BBC resources and facilities were all given a hireable price tag for the first time. Within the BBC, this meant that producers had to pay for the facilities and resources they used, rather than having them on tap. It meant that a lot of BBC producers could no longer afford to use the BBC's own facilities and were forced to find cheaper alternatives outside. Many departments and facilities were forced to close as a result. It also meant that independent companies (like Lumiere) could for the first time hire BBC resources for their own use. The BBC staff who lived through it largely saw the project as a disaster, with stories of staff members being forced to do things like buying a CD from the local HMV because their budget would not stretch to the higher cost of borrowing it from the BBC's own music library.

I go,' his original contract stated.

Brian had also recently done some model building for the 1994 *Doctor Who* spin-off video drama *Shakedown*, which had featured the Sontarans and had similarly been directed by Davies (See Appendix A).

'We only needed [the model saucer] for a few shots,' says Davies. 'It wasn't [filmed with] a motion-control camera, sadly. It was just us passing it [over the camera]. It was locked-off rigid on a pole, with a little wire coming out of the back, hidden by a bit of blue card. The camera moved underneath it and that was it. Just had it fly over. I would have loved to have done more.'

INVISIBLE DALEKS

The effects shoot fell on the final day of recording on *Dalekmania*. The production had been turned around on a seemingly impossible schedule and was now ready to be edited.

Following a single day's respite, Davies headed into the editing suite at Amity video in Surrey with a sheaf of handwritten notes outlining his 'paper edit'. He arrived on 19 June and stayed until the 23 June. 'I went and stayed there for a week while we did the edit,' he confirms. 'They put me up in a local hotel.'

Among the material to be included in the edit was footage, previously unseen by the public, from Paul Tams' and Julian Vince's *Mission of Doom* film, which Tams had transferred from Super 8 film onto Umatic video for Davies's use. Terry Nation was not interviewed for the programme but did appear courtesy of some interview tapes that had been passed on to Davies from David Jackson at BBC Enterprises in 1992[289].

By far the most pronounced problem to arise during the edit related to the fax message the team had received from Terry Nation's agent just ahead of the drama shoot.

Although plenty of Robomen would appear in the production, Davies had used only two full Dalek props in the dramatic sections. Aware of the copyright issues, he had no intention of attempting anything as extensive as the army of Daleks he'd mobilised across Westminster Bridge for the BBC's anniversary programme back in 1993. 'If you're doing a factual piece about the Daleks, they can't touch you,' explains Davies. 'The only

---

[289] The copyright of these tapes is actually somewhat uncertain. Davies believed them to have been shot by KRMA Denver Television in America (who were duly paid a fee for permission to use the material). However, it has since emerged that KRMA were not the actual owners of the footage at all and shouldn't really have taken the money. Today, nobody seems to know who shot the Nation interview or when. The tapes were cleared out of the office of producer John Nathan-Turner in 1992 when he left his employment at BBC Enterprises. One theory is that the interview may have been shot for an aborted BBC Enterprises project in 1991.

problem is if you start to pass it off as a new piece of drama.' In other words, the inclusion of an inert Dalek prop was acceptable as it didn't fulfil any narrative function as a Dalek and did not act as a Dalek. It was merely a prop, rather than a fictional character. Anyway, static Dalek props had indeed been posted outside cinemas back in the '60s to promote the movies, so Davies could quite legitimately stage a similar scene in his feature, as a kind of historical reconstruction.

However, the Dalek that Davies had appearing outside the cinema to menace the two children was a different matter altogether. This *was* a Dalek and it *did* act as such. Davies had no permission from either Nation or the BBC to allow for that, only a firm fax message forbidding it. When Colin Higgs and John Farbrother saw the footage, as Higgs recalls: 'We went, "Oh no, the Dalek moved!"' The offending portion of the image containing the Dalek was duly removed in post-production with the best technology that the small video company could manage in 1995. In the finished programme, only the Dalek's claw arm is (accidentally) visible in front of a Roboman's chest. 'What you'll see in the final programme is that we've masked the Dalek out,' Davies confirms. 'There's one bit where there's a bit of a shadow across it. We tried to make it as if we were filming under one of those archways ... just a curve of black to cover the Dalek up.'

A final sound dub was worked on by Mark Ayres using music from the scores of the original Dalek films, and the finished 60 minute edit was delivered to Lumiere on the deadline date of 26 June, ready for its release in the shops the following month. A specially numbered limited edition version was later brought out in an oversized 17 inch by 9 inch box set, along with a pair of replica film posters, six replica lobby cards and a specially written booklet by Marcus Hearn. The feature also later appeared alongside the two movies themselves in the *Doctor Who and the Daleks* DVD box set from Studio Canal in 2001, and since reissued many times.

DALEKMANIA-MANIA

Dalekmania helped to rekindle an interest in the Dalek movies in the mid-'90s, following a period during which they had not been so popular. That year a *Doctor Who Magazine* special appeared, containing an all-new comic strip adventure for Cushing's Dr Who titled 'The Daleks Vs The Martians'.

'I think that Colin Higgs deserves significant credit for *Dalekmania*,' says Marcus Hearn. 'This was a good four or five years before DVD really made an impact on the British market and here was a producer prepared to actually go out on a limb and commission what was effectively a DVD special feature, four or five years before such things actually existed ... To actually commit any money at all to a stand-alone video was, I thought, quite a brave thing to do.'

Following the production, Kevin Davies helmed episodes of *Space Island One* (1998) for Sky One. He returned to ambitious television-based documentaries in 2006 with *This Man is the One*, a feature about the BBC's *Adam Adamant Lives* series, and *Andromeda Memories*, about the BBC's *Andromeda* serials, commissioned for inclusion on their respective DVD releases.

Colin Higgs later went to work for DD Video on the DVD releases of series such as *The Saint*, and then for Sony Pictures on releases of the Hammer Studios back catalogue (among many other titles).

Dalekmania was the only *Doctor Who* production Lumiere ever made – although that wasn't for want of trying (See Chapter Eight). Lumiere Pictures was later renamed UGC (DA). Later still, the company's archive, including all three Dalek titles, was acquired by Studio Canal. The sign on the door of John Herron's archive at Pinewood changed again, as the assets were sold and resold. Herron was eventually asked to retire, and all his fellow archive staff lost their jobs. Studio Canal initially replaced them with a satellite team headed by an archive manager based in London. However, at the time of writing, there is now no longer any dedicated archivist at Pinewood looking after the Studio Canal vaults.

THE POWER OF THE DALEKS

Both of Aaru's Dalek pictures (together with *Dalekmania*) continue to occupy a special place in the affections of many *Doctor Who* fans, and not just because of their unique position in the history of the franchise. They also have something special about them – a certain innocent magic that no amount of adult cynicism can ever entirely dispel.

'A lot of people forget that there have been two movies,' Roberta Tovey told Kevin Davies in 1993. 'They seem to remember all the *Doctor Who*s [on television], which it was originally made for, but it's nice that there are quite a few fans out there who remember [the films].'[290]

Marcus Hearn is personally more sympathetic toward the first of the two pictures, but feels that both have their own very particular charms. He recalls: 'Recently, a friend of mine was quite ill and had a week off work, and I said to him, "Well, what did you do?" And he said: "I went and made myself a bowl of soup. I curled up on the sofa under the blanket and watched *Dr. Who and the Daleks*." I thought to myself at that point, "Yeah, that's what they are. They're comfort food – certainly for fans of a certain age."'

---

[290] From *More Than Thirty Years in the TARDIS* dir. Kevin Davies – BBC Video (1994)

4
It came from Tibet
'The Intelligence'
(1967-1971)

THE ABOMINABLE SNOWMEN

Following the release of that final Peter Cushing film in 1966, there have been numerous ambitious but ultimately unrealised proposals for further *Doctor Who*-related movie projects. As with the Cushing pictures, the catalyst for the next of these wasn't to be the Doctor, but one of his monsters. It was the late 1960s and the idea came from one of the television series' own scriptwriters – a man called Mervyn Haisman.

Beginning his career as an actor in the 1940s, Mervyn Haisman studied at RADA (alongside Roger Moore). After a spell of national service in post-war Germany[291], he formed his own theatre company in Devon, which then promptly went bust

There followed an unsatisfying decade working in insurance, before Haisman got his first credit as a television scriptwriter on an episode of the BBC's Scottish medical series *Dr Finlay's Casebook*[292]. Haisman was friends with the programme's producer, Gerry Glaister, and it gave him his first break in the business.

In 1963, Haisman met up with fellow actor Henry Lincoln[293] when they were both appearing in an episode of the police drama *No Hiding Place*[294].

---

[291] By coincidence, Haisman's national service found him back alongside Roger Moore (who was now a commissioned officer).

[292] Haisman wrote the ninth episode of the programme's fifth series. The episode was called 'The Forgotten Enemy' and was transmitted on 26 February 1967. It is sadly one of many episodes of the series for which no recordings are any longer known to exist in the BBC's archives.

[293] Lincoln acted under the name Henry Soskin. It was as such that he appeared in dramas including ITC's *The Saint*, with (once again) Roger Moore.

[294] Haisman played Robinson and Lincoln played Harvey in the eleventh episode of the programme's fifth series. The episode was called 'Scaremonger' and was transmitted on 10 September 1963. Again, no recordings of this episode are any longer known to exist.

Lincoln was also an aspiring writer and had recently scripted an episode of *Emergency Ward 10* for ATV. With both men's writing careers seemingly on the cusp, they decided to go into a writing partnership together.

Through his acting work, Lincoln had struck up a friendship with Patrick Troughton, with whom he had appeared in an episode of *No Hiding Place* in 1959[295]. In 1966 Troughton had just taken over the lead role from William Hartnell in *Doctor Who*. Work had already begun on the Troughton's first run of episodes when he and Lincoln had a chance meeting.

'Pat ran into Henry in the street in Kew, where they both lived,' remembered Haisman. 'Henry asked how he was getting on, and Pat said, "Well, I'm a bit pissed off with mucking about in space, frankly. Why don't they do something a bit more earthly? Why don't you come up with an idea for us?"'[296] Accordingly, Haisman and Lincoln decided to collaborate on a script submission for *Doctor Who*'s forthcoming fifth television season.

The idea that they came up with was for a story set in Tibet, revolving around the legend of the Yeti – a race of mythical ape-men fabled to stalk the slopes of the Himalayas. The BBC's head of serials, Shaun Sutton, liked their idea and the BBC duly commissioned the pair to write a story based on the outline.

There had been stories about the Yeti before. Hergé had written about them in 1958's *Tintin in Tibet* and the subject had also been covered in Nigel Kneale's television drama *The Creature* in 1955 – which was, in turn, later re-filmed for the cinema as *The Abominable Snowman* (1957). Haisman and Lincoln's version of the Yeti myth however was a little different from what had gone before.

In their story, an explorer called Professor Travers (played by Jack Watling) is searching the mountains of Tibet in the hope of tracking down a specimen of the mythical beast. He thinks he may have struck lucky when he finds a local monastery being menaced by a race of shaggy-haired giant monsters. However, all is not as it seems. The creatures attacking the monastery are not flesh and blood but are robots, controlled by the power of an alien entity known only as the Great Intelligence.

The tale was to be provisionally titled 'Dr Who and the Abominable Snowman', although, by the time the six-part serial reached BBC1 in September 1967, this had been tweaked to 'The Abominable Snowmen'. The most extensive location-shoot in *Doctor Who*'s history (to that point)

---

[295] Lincoln (under the name Henry Soskin) and Troughton appeared in the fifth episode of the first series of *No Hiding Place*. The episode was called 'The Stalag Story' and was broadcast on 14 October 1959. Again, no recordings of this episode are known to exist. The episode was written by Malcolm Hulke, who would write for *Doctor Who* on a number of occasions between 1967 and 1974.

[296] From *Doctor Who Magazine* – Issue 268 (26 August 1998) p.27

followed, with the mountains of North Wales doubling up as a decidedly snowless Tibet[297].

The production team liked the story so much that, while it was still being shot, they commissioned the two writers to develop a sequel. A few months later, a second Yeti story, 'The Web of Fear', was broadcast to even greater acclaim, and Haisman and Lincoln were quickly established among the production team's most favoured scriptwriters. Their unnervingly cute Yeti robots were part of a wave of popular new monsters that arrived that year, lining up alongside the Macra, the Cybermats and the Ice Warriors.

In 1968, following the success of the two Yeti storylines, Haisman and Lincoln were commissioned to work on a third *Doctor Who* story – a six-parter under the working title 'The Beautiful People'. Unfortunately, the show's producer Peter Bryant and script editor Derrick Sherwin didn't like the direction the story was going in, feeling that it featured satire at the expense of action A large part of the story was radically rewritten by Sherwin and assistant script editor Terrance Dicks, being cut from six episodes to five in the process. Haisman and Lincoln were unhappy with the finished scripts, which acquired the new title 'The Dominators'. Feeling it no longer represented the work as they had written it, they asked for their names to be removed from the credits and replaced with the pseudonym, Norman Ashby. Later, the BBC compounded matters when it began licensing merchandise featuring a race of robots called Quarks that Haisman and Lincoln had created for the story, without their consent.

As a consequence of all this bad blood, a proposal for a third Yeti script was shelved and the writers vowed never to work on *Doctor Who* again.[298]

BY THE BOOK

'For a long time after the scripts were written, we kept thinking "The Abominable Snowmen" would make a bloody good book,' recalled Haisman. 'At first we didn't think we could use it, but then it struck us that the only things the BBC owned were the Doctor, Jamie, Victoria and the TARDIS. Everything else was ours. If we forgot the TARDIS and had different characters, we were okay.'[299]

Haisman's plan for a Yeti novel was to retain the basic story and supporting characters of his and Lincoln's original teleplay, but to remove

---

[297] The following year, director Gerald Thomas and producer Peter Rogers also recreated the Himalayas in South Wales when filming *Carry On… Up the Khyber* for the Rank Corporation.

[298] Haisman later qualified that he would consider returning once Sherwin had left the show.

[299] From *Doctor Who Magazine* – Issue 268 (26 August 1998) p.28

any elements that were the property of the BBC. The regular characters of the Doctor and his companions (Jamie and Victoria) could thus not be used. However, other supporting characters, like Professor Travers and the Yeti, were owned entirely by Haisman and Lincoln, and they could do what they wanted with them.

'My wife [Vina Haisman] said she would write [the novel],' recalled Haisman, who by this time had now ended his writing partnership with Lincoln. 'She took the scripts and did a superb job, a wonderful book.'[300]

The new novel was written entirely by the Haismans, without any involvement from Lincoln, who remembers nothing of the project. The book discarded the television title and became simply *The Yeti*. The plot was however virtually identical to that of the television serial, even reusing large chunks of the original dialogue, although the removal of the BBC owned elements had led to the Haismans creating some new characters to fill the narrative void.

The Doctor's part in the story was largely taken up by a new creation called Professor Murray. The Professor was in turn accompanied by his two sons, John and Paul. There were other changes too. Although the character of Travers was retained from the BBC television episodes, he was no longer *Professor* Travers but now a military type called Major Travers (probably to avoid clashing with *Professor* Murray). Most of the other characters from the television serial remained intact.

In the early '70s, soon after the book was finished, Mervyn Haisman submitted his novel to Diana Tyler and Michael Bakewell at the recently-formed Michael Bakewell Associates (MBA) literary agency. Bakewell had formerly been Head of Plays at the BBC and Haisman had known him there. He was hopeful that the agent would be able to find a publisher for him and his new novel. However, MBA didn't take the Yeti story any further and neither were there any publishing deals forthcoming via Haisman's own agent, Barbara Levy. Much to the Haismans' disappointment, the Yeti book remained unpublished.

WALT DISNEY

The idea of making a film of the story didn't come about until after the novel had been written.

'Vina's version sat there for a long time,' recalled Haisman, 'until I heard through a director friend of mine that Disney was on the look-out.'[301]

Once the producer of exclusively animated films, Disney had diversified into live-action pictures in the 1950s. Within a decade, live-action production

---

[300] From *Doctor Who Magazine* – Issue 268 (26 August 1998) p.28
[301] From *Doctor Who Magazine* – Issue 268 (26 August 1998) p.28

was accounting for the majority of the studio's output. Live-action movies were quicker and cheaper to produce than the cartoon epics that had made the company famous, and studio head Donn Tatum[302] was always searching for the next child-friendly adventure story. Haisman wondered if his Yeti idea might work for them.

Disney had expressed a brief interest in making a *Doctor Who* film before. As early as July 1964, they had approached the BBC about the cinematic rights to the series when considering filming a version of the recently broadcast historical story 'Marco Polo'. Although that idea seems never to have been pursued further, it is easy to see how a series like *Doctor Who* would appeal to a company like Disney. The show had a strong following among children, but was not so juvenile as to deter older audiences as well. Its labelling as a 'family programme' suited Disney well.

The two Dalek movies had shown that children would be attracted to films based on characters and concepts from the programme, and it isn't difficult to see Haisman drawing parallels between himself and Terry Nation. Nation's Daleks had also made the transfer to film after only two television stories.

Haisman soon started work on a full screenplay for his putative Yeti film. He called it *The Intelligence*. Some of the changes that had been made for the novel were carried over into the script, but there were also some new additions.

The most noticeable alteration was another change of lead character. The novel had removed the Doctor as the story's hero and replaced him with Professor Murray. The screenplay took a different approach and replaced the hero with a character who wasn't even of Haisman's own devising – Sir Arthur Conan Doyle's Professor Challenger.

THE LOST WORLD

Professor George Edward Challenger had been created by Conan Doyle for his 1912 novel *The Lost World*. The character appeared in a further four stories between 1913 and 1929, and his fame increased substantially with the release of a film adaptation of *The Lost World* in 1925.

Doyle's Challenger was an explorer, an adventurer and an inventor – in many ways, the ideal Doctor-substitute and a good fit for Haisman's Yeti screenplay. Haisman kept his depiction of Challenger fairly faithful to the character as sketched out by Doyle in his books, but added sections of backstory that were entirely of his own devising. These included a change to Challenger's family.

In the Haismans' novel, the Professor Murray character had been

---

[302] Between 1968 and 1980, Disney was largely under the jurisdiction of Tatum

accompanied by his two sons, and for the new film treatment, the two children were to remain, but as Challenger's instead, with Paul becoming a female Paula. In his books, Doyle had also given Challenger a daughter, - Enid, who featured prominently in the third Challenger novel, *The Land of Mist* (1925)[303]. However, she wasn't to appear in Haisman's film. Challenger's new children, 16 year-old John and 15 year-old Paula, were, according to the screenplay, both to have 'spent most of their lives in the USA with their mother. Their outlook and accents are firmly American.'

The insertion of the two American children seems to have been an attempt to catch the eye of Disney, although considering Disney's fascination with all things British and European, the ploy may not have been necessary. The introduction of the screenplay's only female character, although perhaps a laudable attempt to address gender balance, also backfires, as Paula is given virtually nothing to do in the story except be protected by her father and brother and left indoors while the men go out to do manly things with guns and sharp pointy things.

Haisman stayed rather truer to Doyle in his use of Challenger himself. His screenplay describes the Professor as 'in his late fifties, but the years have treated him well. His bushy beard is flecked with grey, his tanned face lined, but the body is still as tough as ever … The voice still booms and he can be just as irascible, tetchy and quirky as he used to be.'

The description fits comfortably with that found in Doyle's books, which saw Challenger as 'a cave-man in a lounge suit. He had the face and beard of an Assyrian bull; the former florid, the latter so black as almost to have a suspicion of blue … This and a bellowing, roaring, rumbling voice.'[304]

Providing further continuity, Haisman set *The Intelligence* in 1923, which would have seen Challenger at the height of his powers and popularity, with the events of the film taking place in between the second Challenger novel, *The Poison Belt* (1913), and the third, *The Land of Mist*. Not that there was very much in the screenplay that tied in with Doyle's works.

Despite the absence of the Doctor and his TARDIS, the screenplay for *The Intelligence* followed that of the BBC's 'The Abominable Snowmen' serial very closely. In fact, the adaptation retained considerably more of the television original than either of the two Dalek films had done in the '60s.

A substantial section of material out on the mountains was cut from what had been the script for the BBC serial's fourth episode. However, apart from this, a good 75% or more of the Haisman and Lincoln teleplay was almost exactly transcribed into the film script. Only the first dozen or so pages were

[303] Possibly coincidentally, a character called Paula had also been inserted into the 1925 film adaptation of *The Lost World*.
[304] *The Lost World and Other Stories* by Sir Arthur Conan Doyle – Wordsworth Classics (1995) p.13

entirely original.

There are few new characters. The most noticeable is Challenger's native guide, Khedru, who is apparently killed by a Yeti early on in the film. A few of the monks also get their names changed, and the television serial's Thonmi becomes the slightly easier to pronounce Thomni for the film. Travers is again *Major* Travers, in order to avoid a clash with Professor Challenger.

The resultant movie would, without doubt, have been a very long film, at least by the standards of Walt Disney. The screenplay runs to 130 pages, which, at an industry standard of one minute per page, would have made it over two hours long. However, Challenger was still a bankable character in the wake of a 1960 cinema version of *The Lost World*, and Haisman was confident of his chances.

DOCTOR PWY

Haisman did have some filmmaking experience. In 1968, he and Lincoln had been called in by Tigon Films to write a low-budget British picture called *Curse of the Crimson Altar* for producer Lewis M Heywood. This was (loosely) inspired by an H P Lovecraft short story called *The Dreams in the Witch House*, although the movie version was largely Haisman and Lincoln's own creation. Originally written under the rather less lurid working title of *The Reincarnation*, it was directed by Vernon Sewell[305] and starred Boris Karloff (in one of his last roles), Christopher Lee and Mark Eden. It also (for reasons that are never adequately explained) featured a bright-green-painted Barbara Steele. As with Amicus's later *At the Earth's Core*, the film was distributed by AIP.

Ultimately, both Haisman and Lincoln were fairly unhappy with the finished result on *Curse of the Crimson Altar*. Its somewhat perfunctory nudity and condescending approach to '60s 'youth' led Haisman to describe it as 'a turgid horror … We wanted to take our names off it, but unfortunately they stayed.'[306]

In April 1970, the film was released in America as *The Crimson Cult*, where the presence of the late Boris Karloff (who'd died in February 1969) was used to attract audiences. The quaint (almost televisual) charms of the film failed to catch on in the US. However, having one of his films in

---

[305] The movie was filmed at the oft-used movie location of Grim's Dyke House in Northwest London. The former home of W S Gilbert, the house had only a few months earlier been used by the BBC to film the *Doctor Who* story 'Evil of the Daleks'. It had also featured in Hammer's *Journey to the Unknown* television series that same year.

[306] From *Doctor Who Magazine* – Issue 268 (26 August 1998) p.30

American circulation certainly didn't hurt Haisman's chances with Walt Disney for *The Intelligence*, the script of which was submitted to the company soon after.

'They loved it,' recalled Haisman, 'but unfortunately it was a time when Disney was going through one of their lowest financial ebbs.'[307]

It is true that the '70s were not the best of times for Disney live-action movies. Since the 1930s, the company had grown year on year in both reputation and scale. The '70s, however, had seen things plateau somewhat. For a time, Disney's live-action fare had been outperforming its more traditional animated pictures, but that trend had now been reversed.

Although Disney continued to produce a number of live-action pictures throughout the decade, they generally failed to replicate the success that they had enjoyed in the 1960s. Films like *Escape to Witch Mountain* (1975) and *Freaky Friday* (1976) were popular, but also exceptions to the rule.

Remembering how a cost-conscious BBC had recreated the wastes of Tibet in the mountains of North Wales, Haisman made the suggestion that Disney might also be able to spare their budget by doing the same. This would certainly have made shooting easier than it would have been in Tibet, although quite how much money it would have saved an American company like Disney is perhaps debatable. There was certainly a precedent for them working in the UK. Their very first live-action picture, *Treasure Island*, was filmed in Britain in 1950, and movies like *The Story of Robin Hood and His Merrie Men* (1952) and *The Sword and the Rose* (1953) quickly followed. However, in the mid 1950s, following the construction of a set of new film stages at Disney's HQ in Burbank, California, their live-action output had become increasingly based in America.

By the '70s, the heyday of Disney Anglo-American pictures was far behind it, and even films like the London-set *Bedknobs and Broomsticks* (1971) were largely shot in California. If *The Intelligence* had mounted a location shoot in Wales, it need not necessarily have saved the company all that much money, as the cast and crew would still have had to have been flown over from America and back again, with all of the transportation and accommodation costs that would involve. Unless Haisman could have suggested a way of mounting the production entirely in California, it is hard to see how any real economies could have been made.

'They just couldn't afford it,' Haisman concluded. 'It came to no avail. The story's sat there ever since.'[308]

Even if Disney had been prepared to get behind the film, there would still, without doubt, have been further challenges in bringing Haisman's movie to the screen. The screenplay would almost certainly have needed to

---

[307] From *Doctor Who Magazine* – Issue 268 (26 August 1998) p.28
[308] From *Doctor Who Magazine* – Issue 268 (26 August 1998) p.28

be edited to bring it down to a more palatable duration. And there were also problems with using Professor Challenger.

To make a film featuring Professor Challenger today presents few problems as all five of Doyle's Challenger stories are now comfortably out of copyright. Doyle died in 1930 and his estate largely lost any claim on his stories in the 1980s.[309] However, in the early 1970s, when Haisman was working on *The Intelligence*, this was not the case. Although the law can sometimes be open to interpretation, some of the Challenger stories would have remained in copyright until at least 1980 (and possibly longer in America). Haisman simply had no permission from the Doyle estate to use the character. To be fair, he probably wasn't aware that he needed it. There's no evidence to suggest that *The Intelligence* ever sufficiently progressed into pre-production for the issue to be properly examined. However, if it had, it would have become clear just how potentially problematic and expensive the use of the Challenger character could have been. Perhaps if Disney had demonstrated greater interest in the project, we would have seen the return of Professor Murray, the hero of the aborted Yeti novel. As it is, we shall probably never know.

ON TARGET

The only afterlife that the Yeti spin-off was ever to have came not long after the collapse of the Disney project.

In 1974, both Haisman and Lincoln were contacted by W H Allen and Co, whose Target Books imprint had recently launched a range of *Doctor Who* novels, based on adventures from the BBC's television series. The authors were asked for their permission to allow 'The Abominable Snowmen' to be adapted for the range.

The resultant book would be closely based on their original scripts (retaining the Doctor and the TARDIS etc), however, there was a catch. Haisman and Lincoln would not be allowed to write the book themselves. W H Allen instead insisted on giving it to another writer – Terrance Dicks, who had been involved in the rewriting of their final (problematic) *Doctor Who* television script a few years before.

Perhaps with this in mind, Haisman and Lincoln were reluctant to take up W H Allen's offer. Haisman reported back to the publishers that he and his wife had in fact just written a book, and asked if they'd be interested in a

---

[309] More recently, this situation has changed slightly. On 31 January 2011, the Conan Doyle estate filed a trademark on the character of Professor Challenger. This was formally registered on 27 March 2012. Although the stories and the characters remain out of copyright, the tradmark does now make Challenger's use difficult without the estate's consent.

reworked version. However, W H Allen insisted that any novelisation would have to be written by one of their own writers – namely Dicks.

'It was 500 quid or something for the rights,' recalled Haisman, 'and Henry and I agonised over it. Bless her heart, it was my wife, Vina, who told us to go ahead and let the adaptation be done – we needed the money. So Terry Dicks did it, and did a first class job.'[310]

One of the few changes that Dicks made for the book was the altering of some of the Tibetan monks' names, including that of Thonmi to Thomni – mirroring one of Haisman's own alterations in his script for *The Intelligence*.

Target Books brought out its new novelisation (their seventh *Doctor Who* book) as *Doctor Who and The Abominable Snowmen* in paperback on 21 November 1974, with a cover painting by Chris Achilleos and internal illustrations by Alan Willow.

EVIL OF THE DALEKS

'The Abominable Snowmen' wasn't the last Patrick Troughton *Doctor Who* story to be suggested for a big-screen remake. In 1985, Troughton himself had begun thinking about the possibility of appearing in a film alongside his regular *Doctor Who* co-star Frazer Hines. Troughton and Hines had clocked up an unprecedented three-year stretch in *Doctor Who* in the late 1960s (making Hines the longest running companion in the show's history) and had only recently returned for 1985's 'The Two Doctors'. Troughton's hope was to use the script of the 1967 television serial 'The Evil of the Daleks' as the basis for a new *Doctor Who* film.

'I wouldn't mind appearing in *Doctor Who* again,' said Troughton. 'It would be nice to remake "The Evil of the Daleks", which was a classic, as a full-length feature film. It probably wouldn't break all box office records, but in this day of videos I am sure there would be a ready market.'[311]

Sadly, Troughton died not long after (in 1987) and the film of 'The Evil of the Daleks' never progressed past Troughton's early thoughts.

DOWNTIME

Haisman would write no further *Doctor Who*-related scripts after the collapse of the Disney project. However, the characters that he and Henry Lincoln developed for the programme in the 1960s continued to endure. Most notably, Alistair Gordon Lethbridge-Stewart (from their 'The Web of Fear' serial in 1968), would go on to become one of *Doctor Who*'s best loved recurring characters. The Yeti would get a brief cameo on television in the

---

[310] From *Doctor Who Magazine* – Issue 268 (26 August 1998) p.28
[311] From *The Doctor Who File* by Peter Haining – W H Allen & Co (1986) p.102

1983 episode 'The Five Doctors'. And in 1995, the Yeti, the Great Intelligence and Professor Travers (again played by Jack Watling) would even get to feature in their own direct to video movie, *Downtime* (see Appendix A).

In the '70s and early '80s, Haisman worked as writer and script editor on a number of television projects. Most prominently, between 1976 and 1979 he was script editor of the BBC's hit costume-drama *The Onedin Line*, for which he also wrote some episodes. In 1982 and 1984 he also scripted BBC 2's *Jane*, a series based on a *Daily Mail* comic strip. It was this that finally took him back to the cinema, when the show later spun off into a film, *Jane and the Lost City* (1987), which he scripted.

Towards the end of his life, Haisman retired to Valencia in Spain. He died there in October 2010. His final on-screen credit came on a 2008 episode of the *Doctor Who* spin-off *The Sarah Jane Adventures*[312], in which his Lethbridge-Stewart character also made his final appearance[313].

Later, in December 2012, the BBC aired an unexpected prequel to 'The Abominable Snowmen', with that year's annual *Doctor Who* Christmas episode, 'The Snowmen', showing the origins of the Great Intelligence, how it came to be on Earth, and its first attempt to take over the world, through its possession of a man named Dr Simeon. The show starred Matt Smith as the Doctor, with Sir Ian McKellen as the voice of the Great Intelligence. Richard E Grant played Dr Simeon, who would continue the Great Intelligence storyline with appearances in two further episodes that season: 'The Bells of Saint John' (2013) and 'The Name of the Doctor' (2013).

---

[312] This was, in fact, the first time that Mervyn Haisman and Henry Lincoln were ever credited on television as the creators of Lethbridge-Stewart. Previous episodes that used the character never listed any 'created by' credit at all.
[313] Actor Nicholas Courtney died on 22 February 2011.

The Intelligence
By
Mervyn (and Vina)[314] Haisman
From a story by Mervyn Haisman
and Henry Lincoln

PLOT SYNOPSIS

It is 1923. Professor George Edward Challenger is journeying to Tibet with his two teenage children, John and Paula. He is making his way to the Detsen monastery – a secluded place of worship, perched high in the Tibetan mountains.

Night is drawing in fast as the party decide to set up camp. Paula and John struggle to put up a tent, as Challenger and a Sherpa called Khedru descend down the slope carrying some equipment. Some distance from the camp, John half-glimpses a shadowy shape moving around somewhere in an outcrop above him. However, before John can get any closer to it, the shape is gone. Khedru is deeply troubled by the boy's story and refuses to go any further.

A little later, John and the Professor are talking by the fireside when they hear the piercing scream of a man cut through the night air. A few moments later, there is a second scream – shorter than the first, but just as near. Challenger and the boy leap up to investigate, but Khedru stands in their way with his rifle. He refuses to allow them to leave the camp and insists that the screams were merely the sounds of a distant animal. Challenger is suspicious of his guide. However, in order to defuse the situation, he agrees to go along with Khedru's story and remain in the camp until morning.

The following morning, Paula and John awake to find the camp deserted. The fire has gone out and neither Khedru nor the Professor are anywhere to be seen. Paula finds a note from their father, tied to a tent-rope. It reads: 'Khedru has deserted us. Gone to monastery for help. Stay put.'

Challenger is striding down the mountainside toward the Detsen

---

[314] Mervyn Haisman's wife Vina was not credited on the script that was submitted to Disney.

monastery when he stumbles across another campsite, sheltering under an overhanging rock[315]. The camp has been seemingly abandoned. An empty knapsack lies next to the dead body of a Sherpa. Written on the side of the bag is the name 'Major Travers'. Nearby, a giant footprint has been left in the snow. Challenger picks up the knapsack and takes it with him.

When he finally reaches Detsen, he finds the great doors to the monastery have been left unlocked. They creak open and the Professor enters with caution. Suddenly he is surrounded by monks, who slam the door shut behind him.

Travers is at the monastery and accuses Challenger of the murder of his guide at the wrecked camp. As evidence, he points to the knapsack that Challenger is still carrying. He had believed the attack to have been carried out by a wild animal. However, when he sees Challenger's fur coat he changes his mind and suggests that this may have simply made Challenger *look* like an animal. Khrisong, leader of the monks, explains that there have been four other recent deaths in the local area and that Challenger's sudden appearance casts him as the prime suspect.

Meanwhile, out on the mountain slopes, John and Paula have ignored Challenger's instructions and left their campsite to follow their father. On their way down, they come across a strange opening in the rock. Paula believes it to be just a cave. However, John isn't so sure. There's a wooden infrastructure of beams and supports inside, which leads him to suggest it might be man-made. They go inside to investigate.

The mysterious cave is very dark. As they go deeper into the blackness, the two teenagers hear something behind them – 'the sound of heavy feet approaching … Something big growing even louder.' John drags his sister down with him behind a large rock, hiding from the unknown creature that has just entered the cave. After some time, the sounds suddenly stop. John peers over the top of his rock and sees a strange figure. It is eight feet tall, 'almost filling the cave entrance, silhouetted against the light … A huge hairy creature. A Yeti[316]. Motionless. Its back towards us – this monstrous, terrifying animal stands guard. Escape is impossible.'[317]

Back at the Detsen monastery, one of the younger monks, Thomni, goes to visit the Professor in his cell. Challenger explains to the young man that he last visited the monastery 20 years ago. He is disappointed to see that

---

[315] From this point on, the movie's screenplay essentially mirrors the script of the BBC's 1967 *Doctor Who* serial 'The Abominable Snowmen'. All of the scenes prior to this point are original and were created solely for the film. All of the scenes after this point are (to some extent) based on sections of the original television serial.

[316] It is roughly at this point in the narrative that the first episode of the original television serial ended and the second episode began.

[317] From Haisman's original screenplay.

Tibet is still every bit as backward as it was then. The two men talk a little about the history of the Detsen order. Challenger is particularly keen to talk about the great attack of 1823, when a holy bell was stolen from the monastery[318]. Legend foretells that one day, the holy bell will be returned.

Suddenly, Khrisong bursts in and has Challenger dragged out of his cell. However, as the Professor is hauled away he manages to whisper something to Thomni. He tells him to have a look under his straw mattress. When Challenger and his guards have gone, Thomni looks under the straw and finds something he wasn't expecting. It is the holy bell, finally returned to the monastery.

In the mountains, John and Paula are feeling their way through the darkness. They come to a smooth, rounded chamber, flooded with a bright blue light. In the middle of the room stands a pile of metal spheres, stacked in a neatly arranged pyramid. The spheres are about four inches in diameter and encircled by a thin misty vapour. John takes one of the spheres and puts it in his pocket. However, at that moment, the Yeti from the entrance suddenly lumbers into view. John picks up a piece of loose timber and uses it to dislodge one of the roof supports. The rocks creak overhead before finally the ceiling caves in, burying the Yeti under a mountain of rock and rubble. They assume the creature to be dead. However, as John goes over to investigate, the pile of rocks erupts open and the Yeti stands up, brushing aside the tons of fallen stone. John and Paula run off down the passageway and back onto the slopes outside.

Meanwhile, back at the monastery, Thomni has gone to visit the Abbot in his chamber. He has brought the bell with him and explains how he came by it. The Abbot takes Thomni in to see the head of the Detsen order, their leader – the great Padmasambhava[319].

The two men enter Padmasambhava's throne-room and Thomni places the bell at the Guru's feet. However, he cannot clearly see Padmasambhava. The man's face is obscured by curtains of thin fabric that give the figure behind them a ghostly appearance. Padmasambhava addresses the nervous Thomni directly, telling him in a weak hypnotic voice: 'Thomni, you will go to Khrisong. Tell him the Abbot orders the release of the Professor. Remember, these words were spoken by the Abbot. You will forget that you have entered this room or heard my voice.' Thomni leaves in a trance.

---

[318] In the original television version of this story, the year of the bell's disappearance was 1630. By changing the year to 1823, Haisman makes it exactly 100 years from the bell vanishing to the Professor returning it.

[319] Padmasambhava was a genuine historical figure. An Indian guru, he is said to have founded Buddhism in Tibet and Bhutan in around the 8th Century. He is also known as Guru Rinpoche. Statues of him can be found all over Asia and to his followers he is almost as significant a figure as Buddha himself. The character also appeared in the BBC's 1967 television serial.

Out on the mountainside, John and Paula are still out of breath from their run-in with the Yeti when the stumble upon Travers coming the other way up the mountain. The teenagers explain to Travers that they are going to the monastery to meet up with their father. They also tell Travers of the Yeti. Excited at the news of the creature, Travers agrees to escort them to the monastery in exchange for directions to the cave.

At the gates to the monastery, Khrisong has arranged for Professor Challenger to be tied up outside and left as bait for the Yeti. It is Khrisong's belief that Challenger is somehow controlling the Yeti and using them to do his bidding. If the Yeti leave Challenger unharmed, he will see it as proof that the Professor is in league with the monsters.

As Khrisong and his warrior monks sit in wait, the Yeti are sighted approaching the monastery. A few moments later, Travers appears with Challenger's two children. Seeing their father tied to the front of the building, John and Paula rush forward to his aid. As the children approach, Khrisong issues the order for them to be tied up along with their father.

Thomni then arrives with orders from the Abbot (and Padmasambhava) to release Challenger. Travers also pleads on behalf of the Professor, having now been convinced by John and Paula of his innocence.

Reluctantly, Khrisong has Professor Challenger released from his bonds. The Challengers are given something to eat and the Professor examines the sphere his son collected from the cave.

Later, when a group of Yeti are sighted just outside the monastery walls, Challenger picks up Paula and carries her away to safety, leaving John to help the monks prepare for an attack.

Challenger returns just in time to help his son and the monks to capture one of the Yeti in a net. After much thrashing around and roaring, the creature finally falls silent and apparently dead. As they haul the inert Yeti into the monastery, they fail to notice another of the steel spheres lying on the ground close to where the creature fell. The sphere begins to glow with a bluish light and rolls across the ground. There is a strange bleeping sound as it goes.

Inside, the 'dead' Yeti is laid out on a refectory table, ready to be examined by Travers and Challenger. Challenger makes a startling discovery. 'The creature is no Yeti,' he exclaims. 'It's a robot!' Tapping the Yeti's arm, he reveals a metal body beneath the fur.

The Professor finds a metal flap in the robot's torso and prises it open with his knife. He exposes an empty metal cavity inside – roughly spherical. John quickly realises that the cavity must have originally housed a metal sphere like the one he took from the cave. He also theorises that perhaps the sphere fell out of the robot in their struggle with it. It could still be lying outside. As Khrisong leaves, he hears a strange bleeping sound drifting down one of the corridors, but he cannot place it. The sound actually emanates from the sphere John brought back from the cave. Something has brought it to life and it is signalling to someone (or something)[320].

The Challengers and the remaining monks secure the inert Yeti using chains and a Buddhist 'spirit trap'. They then go out into the courtyard to search for the Yeti sphere that John brought back from the cave. They cannot find it. They notice that Major Travers has also disappeared and wonder if he perhaps took the sphere with him. Keen to get a hold of one of the spheres, Challenger suggests that they look outside. Khrisong reluctantly agrees to have the gates opened and he goes out into the night to search further. After some time, he finds a sphere, still lodged in the net they used to trap the Yeti. He picks it up. However, a pair of Yeti emerge from the darkness and bear down on him. One of the creatures tears the sphere away from him. The two Yeti then lumber off into the night.

The Professor theorises that the force controlling the Yeti robots is probably doing so by means of some kind of radio transmission. Perhaps if he could intercept this he may be able to trace the source. By happy coincidence, the Professor happens to have been recently working on an invention that can trace radio waves. However, he left it back at his campsite on the mountain[321]. John duly sets off with his father to collect the device.

Meanwhile, unseen and unnoticed, John's Yeti sphere continues to roll slowly and purposefully around the corridors of the monastery. It appears to be looking for something.

Travers is watching a group of Yeti congregate on the mountainside. He goes a little closer, hoping for a better look. However, as he does so, two more Yeti move in front of him, blocking off his escape.

Back at the monastery, the Abbot is in conference with Padmasambhava in his chamber. The veils of fabric around the Guru's throne are parted and, for the first time, Padmasambhava is clearly visible. He 'is a hundred and twenty-five years old. The face is lined and shrunken, the deep-set eyes, hooded. The very thin, wispy, white hair falls to below his shoulders, covering the faded and completely unadorned saffron gown that hangs from his emaciated body.' In front of Padmasambhava is something resembling a chessboard. However, in the place of chess pieces, there are instead a set of miniature Yeti figurines. Padmasambhava moves the Yeti models around the board and thus controls the movements of their life-size equivalents outside. He instructs the Abbot to go out onto the mountainside. Three Yeti will be waiting for him there and will escort him to a cave.

Padmasambhava reaches over to a small table at his side and picks up a little silver pyramid. He gives the strange object to the Abbot. As he does so,

---

[320] It is roughly at this point in the narrative that the second episode of the original television serial ended and the third episode began.

[321] In the original TV serial, the invention had been left behind in the TARDIS.

he is observed by Paula, who has been hiding behind a tapestry.

Hearing Thomni calling after her, Paula goes into a meeting room where the inactive Yeti is chained up. Hearing Thomni outside and keen to avoid trouble, she sits herself down in a chair and pretends to be asleep.

As she sits with her eyes closed, something stirs behind her. There's a clicking noise followed by a low hum. Paula opens her eyes. 'The Yeti sharply turn[s] in her direction. Suddenly its eyes[322] spring open and it emits a terrifying roar.' The creature snaps its chains and moves toward the girl.[323]

Thomni bursts in, attempting to ward off the Yeti with a chair, but to no avail. The Yeti leaves, with a dazed and bloodied Thomni staggering after it.

Pandemonium breaks out in the courtyard as the Yeti makes for the gate. It resists all attempts to halt it. Paula makes a dash forward and opens the gate ahead of the creature, allowing it to walk out back onto the mountainside. Travers is still hemmed in by the Yeti when he sees the Abbot arrive carrying the mysterious silver pyramid and escorted by a trio of Yeti. The four figures enter the cave, depositing the pyramid on top of the mound of spheres that Paula and John discovered earlier. When they have gone, Travers ventures inside to see for himself. The construction starts to glow. Then there is an explosion of energy. A steady flow of black and green slime starts to ooze from within the pyramid, covering the spheres and the floor of the cave.

Nearby, Challenger has collected his radio gadget from the campsite and is using it to try to trace the source of the Yeti's control signals. The Professor notices something strange in the readings. It suggests that the Yeti's signals come from the inner sanctum of the monastery itself.[324]

It is some time before father and son return to the monastery. However, when they do, they come carrying an unconscious Travers between them. They explain: 'We found him on the mountain. He had a look of terror in his eyes.'

A group of Yeti force their way into the courtyard, and a lone guard is powerless to stop them as they set about destroying the monastery. They have already brought down a section of the roof before help can be called. Khrisong orders everyone to barricade themselves into the meeting room. Challenger is eager to find his daughter. Thomni says that he believes she may have gone to visit Padmasambhava. Challenger is surprised at the mention of Padmasambhava's name. When the Professor last visited the

---

[322] The Yeti in the BBC's 'The Abominable Snowmen' serial didn't have any identifiable eyes at all. Just a dark patch of fur where a face would be.
[323] It is roughly at this point in the narrative that the third episode of the original television serial ended and the fourth episode began.
[324] In the original television serial, this material is not covered until much later in the narrative. This revelation comes in the second half of episode five.

monastery, 20 years ago, it was led by a Guru called Padmasambhava, but he was already elderly then. If he is still alive, he must be at least 125 years old now.

The monastery is now in chaos. One of the older monks is crushed to death under a falling statue. Overhead, the sky turns green and a wave of dark slime flows down the mountainside toward the monastery.[325]

Challenger has gone to the inner sanctum to meet Padmasambhava. His daughter is nowhere to be seen. The ancient Guru explains that he has been possessed by an outside entity, forcing him to act against his own will. The old man slumps forward, exhausted with the exertion – seemingly dead. Challenger turns and begins to leave the sanctum. However, when he has gone, the old man suddenly springs back into life again, once more possessed by the evil intelligence.

Back in the courtyard, Paula emerges carrying the holy bell. She too has now been possessed. She speaks not with her own voice, but with that of an old man – the deep, frail voice of Padmasambhava. 'I speak to you through the lips of this girl-child,' says the voice. 'Detsen must now be abandoned.' Khrisong is reluctant to obey and insists on speaking to Padmasambhava himself. However, as he turns to walk away, the Abbot comes up behind him and stabs Khrisong dead.[326]

Challenger wrests the sword from the Abbot's hand and knocks him out cold. He explains that he believes that the Abbot was acting under hypnosis. The same is true of Paula. Challenger brings her out of her trance, but she remembers nothing.

Outside the green slime continues to stream down the mountainside.[327] The monks evacuate the monastery. Paula and Travers go with them, leaving Thomni, John and the Professor to see off the menace in the inner sanctum. Entering the antechamber, Challenger and his friends are met by a blast of air that blows the tapestries from the wall. Oil lamps are wrenched from the wall and float around the room. Struggling against the effects of Padmasambhava's preternatural attacks, Challenger cautiously approaches the Guru's throne. John and Thomni rush in after and head for a bank of electrical equipment behind the throne. John sings to himself[328] in a bid to

---

[325] A version of this scene closed the fifth episode of the original television production of 'The Abominable Snowmen'. On television it occurred at a much later stage in the narrative than it does here.

[326] In the original television serial, Khrisong's murder takes place a little later in the narrative (early in the sixth episode).

[327] It is roughly at this point in the narrative that the fifth episode of the original television serial ended and the sixth (and final) episode began.

[328] The script has him sing 'I'm a Yankie-doodle-dandy' [sic]. Presumably, Haisman meant 'Yankee Doodle Boy', a song by George M Cohen, made famous by James Cagney.

resist Padmasambhava's attempts to hypnotise him. Thomni joins him in smashing up the machinery. As Thomni and John manage to smash some of the spheres that sit in a pyramid behind the throne, two Yeti stop dead outside. There are muffled explosions from their chests and they fall to the ground in a puff of smoke. Finally Challenger takes a sword and smashes the remaining spheres in the pyramid. There is a short rumble beneath their feet and then all is silent. 'All that remains of Padmasambhava is his crumpled robe. Gently it slides from the throne to the floor.'

Later, John, Paula and the Professor are back on the mountainside bidding their farewells to Major Travers. As they talk, they suddenly spot something moving high above them, in the rocks. It is a real Yeti. Travers hares after it in pursuit, while the Challenger family continues on their way back home.

5
Sympathy for the Devil
'Doctor Who Meets Scratchman'
(*aka 'Doctor Who and The Big Game'*)
(1974-1980)

WHEN HARRY MET TOM

Tom Baker and Ian Marter probably first met across a crowded table, shrouded in tobacco smoke, in the spring of 1974. It was the script read-through for the first story of *Doctor Who*'s new season. Baker and Marter were about to join the programme's cast as its two newest regulars. Baker would be playing the Doctor and Marter was to be his newest travelling companion, military surgeon Lieutenant Harry Sullivan.

Over the next year and a half, the pair would record 27 *Doctor Who* episodes together. And it was during the rehearsals for one of these at the BBC's Acton rehearsal rooms toward the end of 1974 that an interesting idea occurred to them.

'There were times when even Tom wasn't needed in rehearsals,' recalled Marter. 'He and I used to sometimes go and do *The Times* crossword puzzle. We never used to complete more than about three clues, because we could never do it. And one day, we were doing this and Tom suddenly said, "I'm fed up with this. Why don't we write a story to do on the series?" And he had a lovely idea for one.'[329]

Baker's idea was for the two men to write an almost surrealist fantasy of a story, involving Satan himself as the main villain. Although somewhat at odds with the programme's usual secularism, the idea wasn't entirely out of line with its increasingly gothic trappings in the mid 1970s.

'Tom sounded extremely confident. "Listen, I think we can write a script for ourselves," he told me,' explained Marter. 'I ... listened with mounting enthusiasm as Tom outlined his concept for a *Doctor Who* plot. It involved the Devil and some scarecrows and it sounded marvellous. I was hooked right from the start. At odd moments during the next few days we batted ideas to and fro, developing a storyline for a four-episode *Doctor Who* and

---

[329] From *Doctor Who Magazine* – Issue 379 (28 February 2007) p.15

jotting our thoughts down on the back of the script we were then rehearsing. When we had eventually worked out a rough plot, Tom took the idea to the production office. To our disappointment the reaction was not at all encouraging. So we went back to the drawing board more determined than ever to succeed.'[330]

'It was at the beginning of Tom's tenure as the Doctor, because Ian Marter was still there and they got on really well,' recalls *Doctor Who*'s then producer, Philip Hinchcliffe. 'Ian was quite interested in writing and I'm sure that, two chaps together, they got on really well, and I think that they thought, "Oh, let's do something here." But I don't ever remember anything with any real development.'

'The production office saw it and hated it,'[331] said Baker. 'The plot involved this malignant creature called the Scratchman – which is a name for the Devil – who loved causing trouble, revelling in chaos and destructions of all kinds and on all scales. It involved scarecrows coming to life; it was very frightening but had a lot of humour as well.'[332]

The idea was never actively considered for the programme and no scripts were ever commissioned by the production team. However, Baker and Marter didn't entirely give up on it either.

Tom Baker had another suggestion for Marter.

'Why don't we actually try and write a movie?' he said.[333]

THE DEVIL MAKES WORK

Marter and Baker both had some experience of acting in films. Marter had appeared with Elizabeth Taylor and Richard Burton in 1967's *Doctor Faustus*, and had more recently played a smaller part in 1971's *The Abominable Dr Phibes*, starring Vincent Price. Among Tom Baker's impressive list of film credits was a stand-out performance as Rasputin in *Nicholas and Alexandra* (1971) and an appearance in Amicus's *Vault of Horror* (1973). And it had been his performance as Koura the sorcerer in 1973's *The Golden Voyage of Sinbad* that had helped secure him the lead in *Doctor Who*. Despite their experiences in the film world, however, neither man had ever produced a picture before. Nonetheless undaunted, Baker still remained gushingly optimistic.

'The programme had recently started to figure prominently in the ratings and Tom and I agreed that the time was ripe for a new *Doctor Who*

[330] From *The Doctor Who File* by Peter Haining – W H Allen & Co (1986) p.152-153
[331] From *Doctor Who Magazine* – Issue 379 (28 February 2007) p.15
[332] From *Doctor Who Magazine* – Issue 92 (September 1984) p.24
[333] From *Doctor Who Magazine* – Issue 379 (28 February 2007) p.15

feature film,'[334] said Marter.

'Why don't we do one where the Doctor is actually played by the actor who is playing the Doctor on television at the time?'[335] asked Baker, with evident reference to the Peter Cushing films of the decade before.

'It seemed obvious to us that the actor currently playing the Doctor – Tom himself – should star in any film, rather than a big name totally unconnected to the television show,'[336] agreed Marter.

The pair (particularly Baker) were both kept very busy through their commitments to the *Doctor Who* television series, but remained enthused by their film idea and worked upon it at every available opportunity from about 1975 onwards.

The film went under the working title *Doctor Who Meets Scratchman*. 'We developed the story that Tom had already done,' continued Marter. 'He and I then started to work on it. And it was very much a kind of thing that we did in our spare time in rehearsals. We weren't going all-out to write a movie, we were just writing a bit when we had some time … We wrote a very rough screenplay for it, but it wasn't in any sense a final script – it was just a very extended scenario really.'

'The script was very frightening,' said Baker, 'but had lots of humour and I thought it would make a brilliant film.'[337]

'Tom and I met from time to time to adapt our scenario to cinematic terms,' added Marter. 'We wanted to keep the cast small – the Doctor, a male and a female associate and a villain called Scratchman plus a number of minor characters. Our monsters were to be scarecrows and a horde of quasi-cybernetic goblins in Scratchman's pay. We tried to keep the storyline tight, outlawing cheap devices wherever possible – like those familiar scenes where supposedly superintelligent villains armed with spectacular and frightening technology are nevertheless reduced to tying up their human victims or locking them in cupboards in order that later they can conveniently escape or be easily rescued by a hero.'[338]

Naturally, Marter had himself in mind as casting for the Doctor's male associate, fulfilling the same role he did on the television. Their initial plans would also have found Elisabeth Sladen reprising her television persona as the Doctor's female associate Sarah Jane Smith.

It wasn't a good time for British filmmaking. However, there had been a recent upturn in moderately successful big-screen versions of popular

[334] From *The Doctor Who File* by Peter Haining – W H Allen & Co (1986) p.153
[335] From *Doctor Who Magazine* – Issue 379 (28 February 2007) p.16
[336] From *The Doctor Who File* by Peter Haining – W H Allen & Co (1986) p.153
[337] From *The Doctor Who File* by Peter Haining – W H Allen & Co (1986) p.137
[338] From *The Doctor Who File* by Peter Haining – W H Allen & Co (1986) p.153

television series. In fact, film transfers of shows like *On the Buses*[339], *Love Thy Neighbour* and *Man About the House* had almost single-handedly kept Hammer Studios afloat through the early 1970s. There were also movie versions of *Steptoe and Son, Are You Being Served?, Dad's Army* and *Callan* from various other companies. A film of *Doctor Who* wasn't an entirely fanciful notion.

The major difference between the *Doctor Who* proposal and the other television films of the time, however, was scope. A film with a simple setting like *Steptoe and Son* could be achieved with a small number of sets and locations over a few weeks. A science fiction subject like *Doctor Who* was an altogether more ambitious proposition.

Recognising their own inexperience in the area, Baker and Marter soon resolved to bring on board someone to direct their movie. They chose Oscar winning[340] British film and television director James Hill.

ASKING FOR DIRECTIONS

Born in Yorkshire in 1919, Hill started in the film business as an assistant with the GPO Film Unit in 1937. Following a war service spent as a photographer for the RAF Film Unit, he started directing his own documentaries and children's pictures, such as *The Stolen Plans* (1952) and *The Home-Made Car* (1964). His first adult films started to appear in the 1960s and included *Trial and Error* with Peter Sellers (written by John Mortimer in 1962). The surprisingly opulent visuals of an otherwise low-key Sherlock Holmes film called *A Study in Terror* followed in 1965. However, Hill's biggest box-office success by far had been thanks to a lioness named Elsa. In 1966 he directed *Born Free*.

Following *Born Free*'s massive commercial and critical success, Hill scored a slighter hit with 1971's *Black Beauty*. When Baker and Marter approached him some five years later, he had begun to concentrate more on television work. His credits here included episodes of programmes such as *The Saint* (1963-1965) and *The Avengers/New Avengers* (1965-1976).

'Somehow the director James Hill became interested,' Baker recalled in his 1997 autobiography. 'The arrangement was that Ian and I would prepare the storyline for *Doctor Who Meets Scratchman* and write the dialogue, and that James would shape it into a screenplay.'[341]

---

[339] Hammer made three films based on the LWT series *On the Buses*: *On the Buses* (1971), *Mutiny on the Buses* (1972) and *Holiday on the Buses* (1973).
[340] Hill won an Oscar for his 1960 documentary *Giuseppina*.
[341] From *Who On Earth Is Tom Baker* by Tom Baker – Harper Collins (1997)

OLD HARRY'S GAME

On 26 September 1975, Ian Marter recorded his final episode as Harry Sullivan in *Doctor Who*. That evening he left studio TC3 at Television Centre for the last time, never to return to the programme.

His character had originally been created prior to Tom Baker being cast as the Doctor. It had been felt by out-going producer Barry Letts that if he ended up casting an older actor as the show's new lead[342], then the energy of a younger and more vigorous male in the TARDIS would help to carry the action. A similar logic had been behind the casting of various similar types opposite William Hartnell in the early 1960s. However, with the casting of Tom Baker – an actor quite capable of managing his own athletics and fisticuffs – this support eventually proved unnecessary. As such, the decision was taken that the Harry Sullivan character would be phased out. The dynamic between Elisabeth Sladen and Baker was felt to be working well, but Marter was (perhaps unfairly) seen as something of a spare part.

With more time now at his disposal, Marter took this opportunity to do further work on the film script. Soon after, he even joined Baker on an overseas holiday, hoping the isolation would enable them to really knuckle down to the task.

'I went to Italy for a few weeks,' said Baker. 'We decided that if Ian and I went on a little holiday together we could finish the script and have a good time together somewhere nice. So [my partner] Marianne and her daughter Harriet, with a little friend called Sophie Maloney, the daughter of director David Maloney, went off to a house near Sienna. For the first few days Ian and I worked hard at the script and tried to come up with some good stuff for James ... But the fleas got to Ian, Marianne and the two children.'[343]

The holiday was a bit of a disaster. There was even an incident where Baker nearly drowned in a swimming pool and had to be fished out by his friends. Needless to say, rather less writing was done than had been planned. Returning to London, the pair continued to try to squeeze some work in when and where they could. 'We worked as often as our separate commitments allowed at Tom's place or at James's delightful and eccentric house in Shepherd's Bush,'[344] explained Marter.

With Hill's assistance, a story was fleshed out featuring the ambiguously characterised Scratchman causing havoc in a small British village with the help of some animated scarecrows and a troop of Cybermen-like 'Cybors'.

---

[342] Prior to Tom Baker's name being put forward for the part, a number of other actors were under consideration to play the new Doctor. These included the comic actor Richard Hearne, then aged 66.
[343] From *Doctor Who Magazine* – Issue 379 (28 February 2007) p.16-18
[344] From *The Doctor Who File* by Peter Haining – W H Allen & Co (1986) p.154

'There were wonderful scenes of the ... [Cybors] coming out of the sea,'[345] recalled Baker.

'The trigger for Tom's plot was an amateur game of cricket played by the Doctor and his friends,' recalled Marter. 'Our climactic final scene neatly tied this up with another game of cricket, this time in celebration of their victory over evil. But was it a victory? Had Scratchman perished or had he escaped? We deliberately left the ending ambiguous so that if the film was a success, a sequel might be possible.'[346]

In fact, reading through the story now, the entire screenplay was ambiguous, not just the ending. Highly surreal, it had touches of Dali and art-house expressionism about some of its grander set-pieces. The plot wasn't entirely clear, at least in any traditional way. The evil Scratchman protagonist was never explicitly stated to be the Devil, but neither was there ever any alternative explanation for his motivations. In all fairness, perhaps there didn't need to be one.

There are also some similarities between the film script and the third episode of the *Doctor Who* television story 'The Deadly Assassin' (which Baker would start filming in July 1976). Both featured a surreal trek through a scorched Daliesque landscape. Not that there were many other parallels with the style of the television show. Although clearly still *Doctor Who*, the film would certainly have stood somewhat apart from the general themes and structures of the series of the time.

On 10 October, Tom Baker's agent, Jean Diamond at London Management, wrote to Roy Williams at BBC Enterprises to enquire formally into the purchase of the motion picture rights for *Doctor Who*; and it seems that this approach was met with interest. On 14 October, BBC Enterprises replied to Diamond that they were prepared to make a deal for the rights and that they would set about drawing up a draft contract for discussion. The contract would be similar in its terms to the one that had been arranged with Aaru in the '60s, and the earlier paperwork was in fact consulted by BBC Enterprises as they worked on the new deal for Baker.

Baker also spoke about the project to the then-current producer of the *Doctor Who* television series, Philip Hinchcliffe. 'I think, in a way, if it had been a film starring Tom, rather than another actor, I probably would not have been against it,' remembers Hinchcliffe vaguely. 'I ... felt a bit miffed, because, no doubt, there would have been a film producer doing it. Probably the BBC would have secured a role for me as the guardian of the BBC's interests creatively in the project. So I probably would have been involved and that would have appealed to me ... I think it was something that was never really a concrete sort of thought-through proposal.'

---

345 From *Doctor Who Magazine* – Issue 379 (28 February 2007) p.18
346 From *The Doctor Who File* by Peter Haining – W H Allen & Co (1986) p.154

Baker and Marter were aware of Aaru's Dalek films of the previous decade, but didn't particularly seek to emulate them, never having seen them on their original release. 'To boost our morale during one of our frequent bouts of writers' block,' recalled Marter, 'Tom arranged for us to see a private showing of the two Peter Cushing *Doctor Who* films. We emerged from the Wardour Street viewing theatre with our spirits raised. We knew we could do a lot better. No disrespect is intended to Mr Cushing ... but the films were a travesty of the *Doctor Who* ethos. They were crude, vulgar and condescending to the audience.'[347]

Unlike the Dalek films, the plan at this point was to make the new film, as far as was practical, on location. The hiring of stages at Pinewood or the ailing Shepperton would have been costly and the feeling was that a largely location-based picture would help keep budgets low, as location facility fees could be far less daunting than the (invariably fixed) costs of studio hire.

The script was tailored accordingly. There was to be only one 'gigantic finale scene set in the studio,'[348] as Marter recalled. A location somewhere in Scotland was favoured for the earlier parts of the film, and one somewhere on Lanzarote in the Canary Islands was being considered for the second half.

The prehistoric vistas of the Canary Islands had very recently been used by Amicus's Kevin Connor for the filming of *The Land that Time Forgot* in 1974. Lanzarote had also been used some years earlier for Hammer's two dinosaur films, *One Million Years BC* (1966) and *When Dinosaurs Ruled the Earth* (1970)[349]. Marter felt that the island's 'volcanic wasteland would be ideally suited to the story.'[350]

On 25 November, Jean Diamond confirmed with BBC Enterprises that her clients would like to take up the motion picture rights to *Doctor Who* for a period of 18 months under the aegis of James Hill Productions Ltd. This was six months longer than the BBC's initial offer of just one year. A meeting between the relevant parties was soon arranged for after Christmas to discuss the deal further. Meanwhile, consultations were carried out with BBC Copyright and Philip Hinchcliffe in the *Doctor Who* production office.

Hinchcliffe suggested to BBC Enterprises that the BBC should retain some form of final approval over the film's script and should also keep close tabs on the direction in which the production was being taken. This would ensure that the movie complemented, rather than competed with, the television series. Although Hinchcliffe had no problem with the principle of a *Doctor Who* film, he hoped that any production would not go down the

---

[347] From *The Doctor Who File* by Peter Haining – W H Allen & Co (1986) p.154
[348] From *Doctor Who Magazine* – Issue 379 (28 February 2007) p.19
[349] In 1984, Lanzarote would even play host to a *Doctor Who* film crew, who shot parts of that year's 'Planet of Fire' story there, with Peter Davison as the Doctor.
[350] From *Doctor Who Magazine* – Issue 379 (28 February 2007) p.19

Peter Cushing route of a rival reinvention.

'If somebody had come along to me and said, "We love the show. We love what you're doing. We want to do a feature film that is actually bigger and better with more money, but reflects exactly what you're doing," I think I probably would have been for it,' said Hinchcliffe. 'If I'd heard from the BBC bigwigs above me that they had done a deal for some other company to do a *Doctor Who* movie and they were going to use Michael Caine, or some other actor, I don't think that I'd have been happy. Not that I've got anything against Michael Caine. I love him. But, if it hadn't have been a bigger and better version of what we were doing, I personally wouldn't have been happy.'

James Hill and Jean Diamond had their meeting with BBC Enterprises on the morning of 2 January 1976. Hinchcliffe's recommendation that the film should closely tally with what the BBC were currently doing on television fitted with the plans of Baker and Marter anyway, and an agreement was soon reached that *Doctor Who Meets Scratchman* would make every effort to act as a continuation and complement to the BBC's series, rather than a rival. A BBC employee would be attached to the film to ensure that this happened, overseeing the production on behalf of the Corporation. The parties left the meeting confident that a new *Doctor Who* film might be just around the corner.

THE DEVIL RIDES OUT

James Hill began working on a final screenplay for the production, based on the initial draft by Baker and Marter, and hopes were clearly high, although they usually are at the start of any film project. However, to complicate things, Baker had also just signed to play the Doctor in a further series of *Doctor Who* for BBC1, so no movie could possibly begin filming until after recording on that had concluded. This meant that the earliest window of opportunity for Baker to start making his *Scratchman* film would be the middle of February the following year, 1977.

Hill had requested an option on the film for a period of four and a half years, but it still wasn't clear if the BBC would agree to this. On 4 February, Hinchcliffe questioned if the requested timescale was perhaps a little excessive and also raised concerns about the inappropriate inclusion of songs in the film (possibly referring to the script's suggested use of the song 'Yes! We Have No Bananas').

If Hill did get his four and a half years, this would (in theory) give him plenty of time to get a script together and assemble the rest of the necessary finance. However, as studios like Amicus and Hammer were increasingly finding in the mid-'70s, having a good idea for a film wasn't even *half* the battle any more.

Filmmakers in the States were rewriting the rules for escapist cinema productions. As a result, film finance was both more important and yet harder to find than ever before. Baker, Marter and Hill certainly had quite a struggle ahead of them to get together their required funds. And no matter how many years that they had at their disposal, there was no guarantee they'd ever manage it.

GOODBYE SARAH JANE SMITH

Throughout 1976, as cinema audiences thrilled at the simple pleasures of Subotsky and Rosenberg's *At the Earth's Core*, the specifics of Hill's film deal and its projected profit margins were further refined and discussed with Jean Diamond and BBC Enterprises. Meanwhile, Tom Baker and Elisabeth Sladen continued to work with Philip Hinchcliffe on their third television series together for the BBC. Production would start on this series on 2 May 1976 and carry on until 10 February 1977.

Elisabeth Sladen had been a regular in the series since Jon Pertwee's final season in 1973, but had decided that this would be her last year as Sarah Jane Smith. Her commitments to the programme came to an end on 20 July 1976, with a final studio day in TC8 at Television Centre for the story 'The Hand of Fear'. Her last episode would be broadcast a few months later, on 23 October.

With the departure of both Ian Marter and Elisabeth Sladen from *Doctor Who*'s regular television cast, the *Scratchman* script had to be adjusted for a pair of new characters to take their places in the narrative. Marter later explained the revisions: 'It had a character like Harry and a character like Sarah … We were going to set it in the late 1920s to early '30s and it was going to start off in Scotland. The Doctor was going to go off on holiday … The two characters weren't going to be with him at the very beginning. He was going to meet them and strike up a relationship with them. We thought that would be more fun rather than having the format of the people already with him, and it would be nice to have him bump into people and have to get involved with them first, and then get involved in the main situation.'

News of *Doctor Who Meets Scratchman* leaked out to the fanzines in mid-June, with a reports that pre-production could start as early as October, with the cameras set to roll around February/March 1977. This timing would also have coincided with Baker finishing up with the BBC on the then current season.

James Hill met up with Philip Hinchcliffe one evening in September to discuss the latest incarnation of the screenplay, which Hinchcliffe then read. On 16 September, Hinchcliffe wrote to Hill to comment that although the script was far more fantasy orientated than the television series, he nonetheless felt it to be sufficiently in keeping with the series' tone for him not to have any major concerns.

Hinchcliffe's only serious reservations related to the film's intended inclusion of the Daleks and the very Cyberman-like Cybors. The BBC didn't own the entire copyright to either the Daleks or the Cybermen, so if Hill wanted to use them, it was likely to cost him additional rights payments to the copyright holders. Hill sought to allay Hinchcliffe's fears in a letter on 26 September, in which he assured the producer that he had already spoken to Terry Nation about the Dalek rights and was confident of soon reaching an agreement with him concerning their use in the movie.

A close relationship was maintained with the BBC over the course of 1976 and, when Hinchcliffe was replaced as *Doctor Who*'s producer as the year ended, his successor, Graham Williams, continued to maintain an interest in the film's development. On 20 December Williams suggested that he attend a meeting with Hill and his team as their preparations continued.

RICH MAN'S WORLD

Finance was always going to be vital to getting any *Doctor Who* film off the ground and, perhaps predictably, Baker, Marter and Hill didn't have anything like enough of it. 'We just couldn't raise enough enthusiasm and money,' recalled Baker[351].

'I was not directly involved in the financial prospecting,' said Marter, 'but James and Tom worked tirelessly to raise the modest investment our project required. Of course in those days *Doctor Who* had not yet generated the huge and growing following it now enjoys in the United States, so our budget was scaled to recoup costs and hopefully make a profit from its release in the United Kingdom and perhaps countries like Australia where the television show was well known. However, we knew that we could not hope to raise all the capital in the UK. So in addition to the Film Finance Corporation here, approaches were made to organisations like Warner Brothers, Disney, Hammer, Roger Corman, Universal and many others.'[352]

At the time, Universal Studios was going through a bit of a boom period following its 1975 release of Steven Spielberg's *Jaws*. In October, Marter described the studio's interest in the project as 'promising'. However, Baker and Hill were rather keener on attracting British investment to the project – hoping to keep the film, as far as possible, based in the UK. At one point Baker even appears to have sent a copy of the script to Milton Subotsky, who had now left Amicus to work on a number of his own fantasy and horror projects. Sadly, with a gravely ailing British film industry, making any UK-based film wasn't going to be as easy as it might once have been.

---

[351] From *The Doctor Who File* by Peter Haining – W H Allen & Co (1986) p.137
[352] From *The Doctor Who File* by Peter Haining – W H Allen & Co (1986) p.154

'We never, as far as I know, got anywhere near raising the necessary finance,'[353] said Marter.

'I thought it would make a brilliant film,' said Baker. 'Ian liked it too, but, apart from us, very few people did. If it was being mooted now we could probably get the money from America.'[354]

At around this point, the intention appears to have been to start filming in Lanzarote in February 1977, before then travelling on to complete the movie in Scotland.

THE PRICE OF FEAR

By November 1976, the first star name was attached to the film. With an eye on the American market, horror stalwart Vincent Price was being considered for the title role of Scratchman.

Price had made hundreds of film appearances, but specialised in a particular type of lower budget gothic that had already made him a cult figure. Among his better known pictures in this category were *Dragonwyck* (1946), *House of Wax* (1953), *The Fly* (1958), *House on Haunted Hill* (1959), *The Fall of the House of Usher* (1960), *The Pit and the Pendulum* (1961), *The Raven* (1963) and *The Masque of the Red Death* (1964). The last four of these were all produced by B-movie king Roger Corman, one of those whom James Hill approached over possible US financing for the *Scratchman* film.

More recently, Price had been enjoying quite a bit of employment in the UK on a number of small horror pictures. These included the contentiously graphic *Witchfinder General* (1968) and the Shakespearean themed *Theatre of Blood* (1973). He'd also been one of Amicus Films' favoured semi-regulars, appearing for them alongside Peter Cushing in *Scream and Scream Again* (1970) and *Mad House* (1974). Ian Marter had even worked with him personally when they'd appeared together in *The Abominable Dr Phibes* (1971). By 1976, however, Price was largely working on television series in America.

The veteran actor's potential casting was first publicly mentioned by Tom Baker in an interview with the *Daily Mail*'s Martin Jackson for the paper's 25 November edition. Optimistically suggesting that a film could be ready for release as early as December 1977, Baker used the article to voice his frustration over the picture's continuing struggles to find finance: 'It has been a saddening and frustrating experience. The British film industry seems to be closing down, yet here is a film which entails absolutely no risk. With millions of viewers on television each week, we have a guaranteed cinema box-office, and you would have thought the British film industry would have snapped it up. But I couldn't get a single studio interested. We did have an approach from

---

[353] From *Doctor Who Magazine* – Issue 93 (October 1984) p.38
[354] From *Doctor Who Magazine* – Issue 92 (September 1984) p.24

Hollywood, but I wanted this to be a British film. We should have opened our production office a month ago. We have even all offered to work for nothing in an effort to cut costs. But still there have been no takers.'[355]

Next, in a poorly-considered attempt to finally get the money together, Baker went on to tell the *Sun*'s Keith Fisher: 'Maybe *Doctor Who* fans might like to invest a few quid and become shareholders? The budget is around £500,000, which means fans gambling a fiver each.' The remark would unsurprisingly come back to haunt Baker later. On 18 July, the *London Evening Standard* ran a story that claimed: 'Doctor Who has received sacks of mail from his fans and all the letters contained money … Baker was amazed, but when he inquired into the legitimacy of raising money, even inadvertently, in this way, he was told he would have to send the lot back. He was advised that he should have started a company, advertised shares, and promised a dividend.'[356] Baker had received cash from a reported 8,000 people by this point, all hoping to help him get his film off the starting blocks.

Apart from Baker and Price, another name briefly connected with the project was that of the actress Susan George. She was lined up as possible casting for the Doctor's female associate (and Sarah Jane Smith replacement). Known for parts in films as various as *Spring and Port Wine* (1970) and *Straw Dogs* (1971), George wasn't entirely a stranger to *Doctor Who*. She'd been an occasional visitor to the set in the late 1960s when she was the girlfriend of series regular Frazer Hines, and in 1968 she had auditioned for the part of new female companion Zoe Heriot[357].

Another person being very widely touted for the part at the time was model and actress Lesley Hornby, better known to the world as Twiggy. Twiggy was then hoping to establish herself more firmly as an actress following her success in the 1971 musical *The Boy Friend*. Baker said appreciatively that she 'had a zany quality, an "off the ground" quality that would be very good.'[358] As far as Ian Marter remembered, she was interested in the part and 'liked the idea of playing the Doctor's young lady companion.'[359]

Marter also commented on his own replacement casting for the film: 'One American mogul in Los Angeles suggested that Doug McClure would be ideal casting for the young man … Eat your heart out Ian Marter!'[360]

---

[355] From the *Daily Mail* (25 November 1976)

[356] From the *London Evening Standard* (18 July 1977)

[357] Zoe was a regular in *Doctor Who* during the final two years of the 1960s. She was eventually played by Wendy Padbury, who briefly returned to the part in 1983 for a cameo in 'The Five Doctors'.

[358] From *Doctor Who Magazine* – Issue 379 (28 February 2007) p.24

[359] From *The Doctor Who File* by Peter Haining – W H Allen & Co (1986) p.154

[360] From *The Doctor Who File* by Peter Haining – W H Allen & Co (1986) p.154

McClure had only recently finished work for Amicus on *At the Earth's Core*, and he'd have been a popular choice with distributors on both sides of the Atlantic.

OVER THERE

As 1977 arrived, Baker continued to talk up his hopes for the film. In January, while in Northampton filming for the last story of *Doctor Who*'s fourteenth season, 'The Talons of Weng-Chiang', he spoke to local newspapers about his latest plans. The resultant report told expectant Northamptonshire *Doctor Who* fans to 'expect to see that film ... in your favourite cinema around next Christmas.' The article also suggested a 1978 release date, and continued: 'Production will start in February and is scheduled to be completed in September.'[361]

Baker would have a break in his commitments on the television series after studio work on 'The Talons of Weng-Chiang', and the season as a whole, was concluded on 10 February. This was when he hoped to start filming *Scratchman*. He had already signed up for a further season of *Doctor Who*, which he'd start rehearsing in late March and wouldn't finish recording until 16 December, so if the film did not get under way now, he wouldn't be free to work on it again until the end of the year. However, the money still wasn't there. Enough backers hadn't been found and profit margins were still being debated with the BBC. It seemed there would have to be another postponement, and reports soon started percolating through *Doctor Who* fandom that the picture had been pushed back yet another year, with filming now reset to begin around Christmas 1977.

In April, a further report appeared in the *Doctor Who* Appreciation Society journal *TARDIS*, stating: 'Although it was believed that the film had been dropped, it has been heard that despite difficulties, mainly financial, the film will be going ahead. It is believed that financial backing may come from the Universal film studios in America.'[362]

Filming began on *Doctor Who*'s fifteenth television season on 4 May at Ealing film studios, with Tom Baker entering his fourth year as the show's lead. By the summer, *Scratchman* had finally begun to attract some investment interest and Hill was hopeful that Britain's National Film Finance Corporation would now be stumping up half of the budget. By September, they had already officially pledged £250,000 toward the movie, and the BBC had also offered a sum for the television rights. However, Baker's own attempts to get finance from a city bank had proved fruitless when the bank in question were interested only in a three-picture deal. Even

---

[361] From *Doctor Who Magazine* – Issue 379 (28 February 2007) p.25
[362] From *TARDIS* – Vol.2 No.3 (April 1977)

with the new finance , Hill was still £225,000 short of where he wanted to be.

THE RIVALS

Another concern was that there were now other interested parties asking after the *Doctor Who* cinema rights, and the exclusive talks that Hill had been having with the BBC couldn't last forever. As early as August 1976, Philip Hinchcliffe had begun to hear vague rumours that a BBC comedy writer was trying to mount his own film bid. That writer's name was Douglas Adams, and we shall learn more of his wisdom later.

Even following his departure from *Doctor Who* at the start of 1977, Hinchcliffe (now working on the police series *Target*) still found himself being contacted on matters relating to the the the show[363]. On 2 August, he received a transatlantic call at his new office from a lawyer acting on behalf of two producers named Laurence Tetenbaum and Paul Bluhdorn of Cinema Mistrale Inc. Tetenbaum was originally a film editor on small-scale productions including 1969's *Coming Apart*, which starred Rip Torn. However, he'd more recently started to direct and produce a number of higher-profile short films, including the 1975 documentary *Call It Magic* about the making of the 1975 John Huston film *The Man Who Would Be King*. Paul Bluhdorn was the son of Austrian millionaire Charles Bluhdorn, whose company owned Paramount Pictures in America. The two men had read some of the growing range of *Doctor Who* novelisations and were interested in the possibility of acquiring the film rights. As he was no longer working on the show, Hinchcliffe couldn't be of much help, but he did mention the enquiry to his successor in the *Doctor Who* office, Graham Williams, in an internal BBC memo.

Possibly by coincidence, the very next day, 3 August, another film idea was raised, when John Sturges, head of the BBC's business co-productions unit, wrote to Bill Miller at Time Life Films in New York. He asked if Time Life would be interested in co-producing a *Doctor Who* picture with him. They were not. However, the mere fact that Miller felt the idea worth discussing with the American company testifies to *Doctor Who*'s slowly building popularity in the States.

Time Life effectively acted as a distributor for the BBC's programmes in America and in 1972 had been involved in a deal that saw 13 *Doctor Who* stories broadcast over a number of PBS (Public Broadcast Service) television stations.[364] The series wasn't an instant hit, but the episodes continued to be

---

[363] This was possibly due to the fact that the BBC switchboard was (and still is) comically slow to be updated.

[364] This lot of episodes was made up of an almost complete run of the programme's first three colour seasons, all starring Jon Pertwee.

broadcast regularly over PBS networks until 1978. There clearly was a developing market for the show in America.

By October, BBC Enterprises were hopeful that an American producer might possibly be prepared to give them a better (and more lucrative) deal for a *Doctor Who* picture than was currently on the table from Baker and Hill. The deal for *Scratchman* was still far from settled and Enterprises evidently still felt in a position to keep their options open. Representatives from Enterprises were duly dispatched to the States to investigate the American possibilities, with the situation set to be reviewed upon their return on 21 November.

FAR, FAR AWAY

Science fiction filmmaking was about to become very big indeed in America. In 1977, George Lucas, the director of a 1973 college movie called *American Graffiti*, was working on an eccentric new space-opera for 20th Century Fox, and it was attracting a lot of interest. Starring Peter Cushing (among very many others), Lucas's film opened in the US in May and was set to hit a very excited British audience the day after Boxing Day. The film was, of course, *Star Wars*.

'One day, Tom rang to suggest that we go to see the press preview of a new science-fiction blockbuster from America called *Star Wars*,' remembered Marter. 'Next day, we emerged from the Dominion Cinema into the cold, grey wet of Tottenham Court Road feeling utterly dejected. The film we had just seen told us that we were too late. The scale of our project was far too small ... Our project would be a minnow among the whales. Our problem was not that we were asking for too much money, but that we weren't asking for nearly enough.'[365]

It was a feeling mirrored by pretty much every lower-budget sci-fi producer that year. It certainly shook Graham Williams, who had barely started as the new producer of the *Doctor Who* television series, when the film came out.

IT'S THE END

In a piece of endearingly groundless enthusiasm, as 1977 neared its end, the *Doctor Who* Appreciation Society reported: 'The *Doctor Who* film goes into production at Christmas, with some filming being done at the BBC (probably on the TARDIS set). Elisabeth Sladen will not be appearing as one of the Doctor's companions, but a new girl will take her place played by

---

[365] From *The Doctor Who File* by Peter Haining – W H Allen & Co (1986) p.154

Twiggy.'[366]

1978 also began with further hopeful rumours that the movie was on the verge of getting full finance. The latest suggestion was that the Rank Organisation would put up the money along with America's IPC Films and that the film's few studio scenes could be mounted on a stage at Pinewood[367].

At this stage, however, although many agreements had been reached, Jean Diamond was yet to formally sign a contract with the BBC that both parties were happy with. Aware of other approaches from elsewhere, the BBC finally set a deadline by which a final agreement had to be reached, after which time they would look at following up some of the other offers that had been made to them.

Around the end of 1978, America was starting to look like a more likely source of finance and, Tom Baker's reticence about using overseas cash seems to have thinned. PBS had now begun transmitting a run of Tom Baker's first four years in *Doctor Who*, courtesy of Time Life, and Baker's portrayal seemed to strike a chord with American viewers. Although the series was still not a mainstream show in the States, it had begun to acquire something of a significant cult following. It all boded well for the film's potential transatlantic business.

After years of wrangling, James Hill Productions finally acquired its exclusive option on the *Doctor Who* film rights from the BBC on 13 October 1978. Rather ominously, it was Friday 13th.

The clock was now ticking to get a film into production. Hill had the rights for a fixed term of one year. On 1 November 1979, the deal would expire and Hill would lose his chance to make any film at all. Unfortunately, the movie was still short of the necessary finance, and the team already knew that they wouldn't be ready in time for Tom Baker's next window of availability in the first half of 1979.

In February, Baker made a promotional trip to Australia, where the programme had been popular for some time. Australian fan Anthony Howe interviewed him about his hopes for the film, which now appears to have been going under the new working title *Doctor Who and the Big Game*. 'There are two problems,' Baker told Howe. 'One is raising finance, which I don't know will be all that difficult now, and I think the discussions about production money to shoot the exteriors in Australia [are] optimistic … There are a lot of exterior sequences. We wanted to go to Lanzarote because it has that lively, black, shiny moonscape there, but I think it would be better to come to Australia if we could. The second problem is, what time would I

---

[366] From *Doctor Who Magazine* – Issue 379 (28 February 2007) p.26
[367] The Rank Organisation was now running Pinewood Studios, hence the deal to shoot there.

have to do it? If it happens at all, because I can't go on doing this part – the audience should be allowed a change. So it would have to be done in the spring of 1980, starting in January. But before I consider giving someone else a go, I would like to get the film in first!'[368]

Baker had now been playing the Doctor for longer than anyone else in the programme's history. He'd just recently passed the record earlier set by Jon Pertwee. He still very much wanted to make his film, but felt that he could be its star only if he was still performing the same function on television. In short, Baker was staying in the television series, perhaps longer than he intended, in the hope that it would allow him to make a film.

It is telling that around the end of 1978, Baker had even (very informally) resigned from the series in the wake of an argument with Graham Williams. Bridges were mended and Baker stayed on, but it was now clear that leaving the television series was something he was prepared to consider; and it is worth wondering if he might not have done exactly that, were it not for James Hill's hopes for a transfer to the cinema.

By this stage, not only had the title of the script changed, but other plans had altered too. 'We wanted Twiggy to play the girl,' Baker said in 1979, 'now she's had a baby[369] I don't know if we could get her.'[370]

In fact casting problems were the least of his worries as the entire enterprise was now in danger of falling through. Both Hill and Baker had put their own cash into the deal, but there still wasn't quite enough in the pot to fund a whole film. The BBC were made aware of the problem, but didn't feel willing to offer an extension of their original agreement. Baker was due back in the BBC studios playing the Doctor on 19 March 1979 and the BBC would keep him busy on his sixth season for the remainder of the year, past the deadline date for the start of filming on the movie.

On 15 June, as Baker was on location for the BBC's new season opener, 'Destiny of the Daleks', a letter came through to the *Doctor Who* production office. It was from Roger Haskell, who worked for General Aviation in California. He had got wind of the proposed movie and was prepared to offer his company's resources to Baker and Hill if it would help them in the making of their picture. Haskell got a reply from Graham Williams dated 13 July. In it, Williams confirmed that the movie had been 'postponed indefinitely'.[371]

It was over. Hill and Baker had missed the boat.

---

[368] From *Doctor Who Magazine* – Issue 379 (28 February 2007) p.27
[369] Her daughter, Carly, was born in 1978.
[370] From *Doctor Who Magazine* – Issue 379 (28 February 2007) p.27
[371] From *Doctor Who Magazine* – Issue 379 (28 February 2007) p.28

THE FURTHER ADVENTURES OF HARRY SULLIVAN

On 1 March 1980, Ian Marter was a guest at the Who 1 *Doctor Who* convention in Los Angeles. He'd brought with him the script for the *Scratchman* film and spoke of the movie that Baker had first proposed with such high hopes back in the Acton rehearsal rooms in 1974. 'I haven't seen Tom for quite a few months now,' he said. 'As far as I know, it's really died a bit of a death, and it doesn't look as though – at least in the form that we had it there – that it'll be made. Which is a shame, because the original idea was a very wonderful idea and I think it'd make a very good story.'[372]

Had a *Doctor Who* film been suggested in the early 1970s, a few years before Baker joined the show, it probably would have stood a relatively good chance of success. The film industry was stronger in Britain then; *Star Wars* had yet to blow small sci-fi offerings out of the water; and there were still British film companies who were interested in television tie-ins, and more studios in which to make them. In fact, a *Doctor Who* picture starring Jon Pertwee, circa 1972, is a tantalising prospect, and it's only a shame that something like it was never considered at the time.

Unfortunately, Baker, Hill and Marter came just that tiny bit too late to the party. Their ideas, which would have been perfectly reasonable suggestions only five years earlier, were not going to weather the harsher climate of late '70s filmmaking.

Baker continued to play the Doctor on television for two more seasons. He left the show in 1981, shortly after the arrival of new producer John Nathan-Turner, who had bold new plans for the programme.

Marter had enjoyed working on the movie script for *Scratchman* and soon afterwards moved away from acting to concentrate more on a career as a professional writer. In 1977 he began contributing to Target Books' growing range of *Doctor Who* novels. His first of these books, *Doctor Who and the Ark in Space*, was based on a television story that he himself had acted in.

'Actually, it was Tom and a friend of his who suggested the idea [of writing the novels] to me while we were all working on the *Scratchman* script,' recalled Marter. 'To test the idea, firstly for myself and also for the publishers, I wrote a specimen chapter or two. The editor liked them, I was happy with them and I quickly got into the habit.'[373]

He ended up writing a total of nine novelisations based on television scripts from the programme, the last being published posthumously in 1988. He also wrote an original *Doctor Who* novel in 1986. This was *Harry Sullivan's War*, based on the further exploits of the character he had portrayed in the series. Gary Russell described the book in *Doctor Who Magazine* as, 'a

---

[372] From *Doctor Who Magazine* – Issue 379 (28 February 2007) p.28
[373] From *Doctor Who Magazine* – Issue 93 (October 1984) p.38

compelling read. The twists it takes are logical, uncluttered and above all fun – if you want to get totally immersed in a book, then this is the one for you … I really can't praise this enough.'[374]

Marter sent the BBC's production office a proposal for a *Doctor Who* television story in February 1980, although, like *Scratchman*, it was never made. Around 1986, Marter even briefly discussed the possibility of novelising *Doctor Who Meets Scratchman* (again for Target Books).

Marter also wrote novelisations of movies including *Splash!* (1984) and *Tough Guys* (1986) for Star Books, under the name Ian Don[375]. However a series of four books that he wrote for W H Allen featuring characters from Disney's Gummi Bears series were never published due to contractual problems.

Following an illness connected to his diabetes, Ian Marter died on his forty-second birthday in late October 1986.

James Hill continued to direct and write mostly in television, handling episodes of *CATS Eyes* (1985) and Jon Pertwee's *Worzel Gummidge* (1979-1981 and 1987-1989). He died aged 75 on 7 October 1994. His last director's credit was on the 1993 children's series *Alaska Kid*.

For a long time, no copies of any version of the *Scratchman* script were thought to have survived, although Baker believed he had one *somewhere*. However, following the death of *Doctor Who* producer John Nathan-Turner in May 2002, a copy was found among some of his papers. It appears that he had taken the script away with him when the BBC's *Doctor Who* production office was closed in the early 1990s. With the recovery of Nathan-Turner's script, the story could finally be revealed to a wider audience and a synopsis soon appeared in the pages of *Doctor Who Magazine* in early 2007, accompanied by an article about the film and a mock film poster by illustrator Brian Williamson. It was the first time that many fans got to learn about this mythic lost *Doctor Who* film.

---

[374] From *Doctor Who Magazine – Issue 113* (June 1986) p.13
[375] Ian Marter's full name was Ian Don Marter.

Doctor Who Meets Scratchman
(aka Doctor Who And The Big Game)
By
James Hill and Ian Marter
From a story by Tom Baker and Ian Marter

PLOT SYNOPSIS

Two men, Griffin and Potts, are studying a file in the 'Time Lord' section of the futuristic Space Records Bureau in New York. The file is marked 'Dr Who' and speaks of a mysterious time traveller with two hearts. The traveller has no recorded date of birth, but was first sighted in the year 1189 and later at the Battle of Gettysburg. He is even rumoured to have tracked down the Loch Ness Monster[376] to its lair and defeated the Marpeds.

Potts asks his colleague when this traveller is next likely to turn up. Griffin tells him that he's due back today.[377]

The TARDIS materialises behind a hedge, not far from the main runway at London Airport. A crowd of expectant journalists and excited teenagers have assembled on the tarmac to await the arrival of a rock star, due aboard the next Concorde flight. The Doctor believes that the crowd must have gathered to see him. However, the Doctor isn't in the mood to face a gang of fans and tells Sarah and Harry that they'll leave at once.

Instead the Doctor suggests a trip to 1924 Scotland, for a spot of rest and relaxation. He begins to set the TARDIS controls and the three friends

---

[376] This is possibly an allusion to the 1975 *Doctor Who* television story 'Terror of the Zygons', which starred both Tom Baker and Ian Marter. They would almost certainly have been making 'Terror of the Zygons' around the time that they first started work on their film treatment.

[377] At this point in the story a large image of Tom Baker's Doctor was intended to fill the screen, printed by a computer. To illustrate this, an entire page of the script was set aside for a piece of artwork representing Tom Baker in costume as the Doctor.

join in a chorus of 'Yes! We Have No Bananas'[378].

The TARDIS arrives on the windy Scottish island of Mull. A nearby shepherd runs off as the blue box materialises. Still singing, the Doctor and his friends exit the ship and look for a good place on the beach to set up their picnic. Producing a bat and ball from a carpetbag, the Doctor makes a wicket from some driftwood and leads his companions in a game of cricket.

During the game that follows, the ball disappears into the long grass and the Doctor goes off to look for it. Wading through the vegetation, he picks up on a strange noise being carried on the wind – the distant sound of bones being cracked apart. The Doctor finds his lost cricket ball in the hand of scarecrow, standing in a field.

Hearing the kettle boil, the group return to their picnic for some tea, but discover that a heavy vehicle has driven all over their things. Their crockery lays crushed and broken. A little way off, they spot a tractor motoring away into the distance.

The friends 'borrow' an old motorbike and sidecar that they find close by and use it to follow after the tractor. They end up being led to a deserted old barn. As the Doctor, Sarah and Harry quietly approach it, the sound of breaking bones is once again carried toward them on the wind. Inside the barn, all is dark. The three ascend to the hayloft and explore.

Looking through the gaps in the floor, they can see something strange going on in the room beneath. A group of scarecrows seem to be having a party. The scarecrows are tattered and worn, wearing all manner of old clothes and hats. They are tearing into some of bags of fertiliser that are stored into the barn. Using their wooden arms, they scoop out large handfuls of the fertiliser from the bags and rub the powder into their tattered rags. Harry comments that the fertiliser itself seems to be animating the scarecrows and making them live. The Doctor suggests that it is probably just animating the clothes the scarecrows wear, rather than the scarecrows themselves, although the effect is much the same.

The scarecrows spot the Doctor and his friends and chase them from the barn. The travellers only just manage to escape, speeding away on the same motorbike and sidecar that they arrived with – the scarecrows in pursuit.

In time, their transport brings them to a small village. It's quiet and empty. As they walk along the rows of village shops, the Doctor thinks out

---

[378] Originally composed for 1922's *Make It Snappy* musical show, 'Yes! We Have No Bananas' was written by Irving Cohn and Frank Silver and was about a then contemporary shortage of bananas in the shops. It's since appeared in a near countless number of settings and contexts, particularly during World War II and in the 1954 film *Sabrina*.

loud. He concludes that the common moth might be able to help them defeat their scarecrow pursuers. If the Doctor and his friends had a large enough number of moths, they could use the insects to attack the scarecrows. The moths would eat away at the ragged clothes, leaving behind only the lifeless wooden frames and straw. The Doctor suggests they use rapid cell multiplication to ensure they have a sufficient number of moths for the job.

The friends find a load of old clothes piled up in a desolate church hall. Harry searches through the old jackets and jumpers looking for moth larvae. Meanwhile, the Doctor tinkers with some electronics at one of the tables.

Night has drawn in by the time the travellers have finished. The Doctor has completed the construction of an advanced-looking contraption (a High Velocity Moth Machine), built from an old toaster and a tea-urn. And Sarah and Harry have now decanted as many moth larvae as they can into a small box. While Sarah sews together some loose pieces of canvas, Harry is dispatched to the local shop to find some sugar.

As the night darkens outside, a shadowy shape can still be made out in the gloom. It is accompanied by a sinister rasping sound.

Many millions of miles up in space, the village is being monitored. A dark and shapeless creature is addressing a horde of his robotic servants – the Cybors. The shifting shadow of the creature's shape makes it hard for us to get a definite idea of him. He tells the Cybors in a low booming tone: 'We brought movement to men of stick – creatures of bone and tin – gave them breath ... gave them the one ingredient you lack ... life! This was the great experiment. This was our triumph ... but it is being threatened by the meddling of a vile alien ... a monster you all know – a monster that must be eliminated.'[379] Comets explode in the space behind the shadow-man and a clap of thunder rings around the room. Off in deep space the face of the Doctor forms in the lights of the stars.[380]

With the Doctor identified as their enemy, the figure dispatches two Cybors to Earth to destroy him. The robots jump into the void and spin off into space, heading toward Earth.

Harry finally manages to force his way into the village shop, immobilising a scarecrow along the way. He finds a wheelbarrow and loads it up with sugar (and a jar of jelly babies). Menaced by another

[379] From *Doctor Who Magazine* – Issue 379 (28 February 2007) p.18
[380] This forming of the Doctor's face from stars almost exactly mirrors the composition of the *Doctor Who* title sequence during the first half of the 1980s. It's a coincidence, of course, but if you want to see what Tom Baker's face would have looked like forming out of the stars of deep space, just watch the opening of any of the *Doctor Who* television episodes that he made around 1980/1981.

scarecrow with the skull of a sheep for a head, Harry leaves the shop with his supplies.

Out on the beach, the same shepherd who witnessed the arrival of the TARDIS is asleep on the dunes. He is awoken by two Cybors splashing into the ocean in front of him. The sea seems to boil and the Cybors emerge from the water, walking up onto the beach in front of him. The shepherd runs away again.

Harry arrives back at the village hall with his collection of supplies from the shop. The sugar (but not the jelly babies) is poured into an opening in the Doctor's new machine. Drawing power from the old motorbike, the strange apparatus roars into life, much to the delight of the three travellers.

As the machine starts to slow down, the Doctor sends Harry out with a can of petrol to top up the motorbike, but when Harry goes outside, he's confronted by a mob of scarecrows holding burning torches. One even carries an old blunderbuss.

Harry dashes back into the hall to warn his friends. The Doctor grabs his box of incubating moth larvae and heads back to the barn with them. Meanwhile, Sarah is sent off to the TARDIS to fetch something called the P2. Harry causes a distraction among the scarecrows, so that the Doctor and Sarah can get away.

It is daylight by the time Sarah reaches the TARDIS. Inside, she locates the P2 in the cavernous TARDIS workshop, but as she makes to leave, she encounters a large scarecrow in a German army helmet. It has somehow followed her into the TARDIS and is now blocking off her retreat.

The scarecrow chases her through the TARDIS's many corridors and rooms. Finally, they end up inside the workings of a giant clock, which (for some unexplained reason) Sarah finds set into a glass wall. The scarecrow becomes stuck in the mechanism and is smashed between two cogs as the clock chimes.

Sarah leaves the TARDIS with the P2 and meets back up with the Doctor and Harry at the barn. The Doctor connects the device up to his equipment, hoping to use it as a power source. However, in that moment, there is a gigantic explosion and the barn appears to splinter and vaporise around them. As the debris clears, they see two Cybors standing outside. The robots lower their guns and take a hold of a dazed Harry.

Out near the beach, the Cybors' spaceship emerges from beneath the waters. Inside, the Cybor leader receives a report from his ground troops. He tells them that the scarecrow experiment is now at an end and that they have learned all that they wished.

The Doctor, Harry and Sarah are marched off toward the Cybors' ship. However, just as they are about to be taken inside, an alarm bell sounds. The Cybors all pile back into their ship, leaving the Doctor and his companions standing on the beach.

The spaceship quickly takes off, but then explodes only a few thousand feet above the ground. The three friends are bewildered, with even the Doctor unable to figure out what exactly has happened and why.

As the travellers make their way back to the TARDIS, an eerie shadow is cast across the sand behind them. Sarah comments that it has suddenly become very cold. Approaching the TARDIS they find a figure with horns and cloven hooves playing on a set of reed pipes. The figure looks uncannily like the pagan deity Pan.

The Doctor observes that the musical notes the creature is playing actually correspond to a set of galactic co-ordinates. Suddenly, the creature vanishes. The three friends go inside the TARDIS and the Doctor programs the ship to take them to the destination suggested by the tune. As the ship dematerialises, the Pan creature is seen sitting on the roof of the TARDIS.

After a particularly rough journey, the TARDIS finally materialises at its destination – a barren volcanic wilderness of a planet[381]. As they arrive, clambering out of a prone TARDIS, the Doctor Sarah and Harry can still hear the sound of pipe music in the air.

The time travellers follow the source of the music across the rocky landscape until they reach a river. Moored on the banks, seemingly waiting for them, is a small makeshift ferryboat. The Pan creature from earlier is wearing a cloak and standing in the boat. He beckons the travellers toward him.

The Doctor, Sarah and Harry all board the raft and it heads out across the river. However, the crossing is far from smooth, and rapids soon cause their raft to break up. The Pan creature vanishes again and the Doctor only just manages to reach the safety of the shoreline. As the maelstrom subsides, the Doctor realises that Harry and Sarah have disappeared.

Trekking back through the planet's strange rocky vistas, the Doctor sees a dark knight in armour riding on the back of a horse toward him. The knight thunders forward, but the Time Lord manages to jump aside just in time. The Doctor dislodges the knight from his horse with a makeshift bolas, leaving the man stuck in a tree as his horse rides on. When the Doctor goes to lift the knight's helmet, he discovers that the armour is empty. He takes the knight's horse and rides off into the baking wilderness.

After some time, something resembling a giant egg appears on the horizon. A crack splits open the egg and through it the Doctor sees a scarecrow lose its head in a guillotine. The Doctor's horse vanishes.

The Doctor enters the egg to find a plush, oval-shaped office inside.

---

[381] The script not only specifies Lanzarote as a filming location for this wilderness, but also includes two photographs taken on the island as a visual reference.

Several 'men' sit around a desk, all wearing simple pin-stripe suits. Instead of heads, they each have a shiny white orb of light atop their shoulders.[382]

One of the 'headless' men is clearly superior to the others. He sits in the centre of the table, surrounded by telephones, smoking a fat cigar. On the walls of the room, rows of portraits show more blank-headed figures. The 'man' at the centre of the room finally speaks to the Doctor. 'Scratch is the name,' he says in a dark voice. 'Harry Scratch. Occasionally known as Charlie Chaos, Old Clootie, Ahriman.'[383]

The Scratchman tells the Doctor that he has been up to his usual mischief. It was he who manipulated the Cybors into thinking they were controlling the scarecrows, when it was actually he. He gestures to a large tank set into the wall of the office, where a weightless Harry and Sarah are floating in suspension. He asks the Doctor to join him in an alliance, but the Doctor resolutely refuses. The Doctor sees a lift door open across the room. He steps inside and the lift plummets downward at great speed. The lift doors finally open onto the surface of a massive pinball table, where Sarah and Harry await him. A huge glowing image of Scratchman beams at them from a screen at one end. A bell rings and a game begins on the table.

At this scale, the pinball itself is like a gigantic metal boulder, rolling across the floor. The travellers jump aside as the ball rolls toward them and hits various targets. Meanwhile, Scratchman's score accumulates up to millions on the scoreboard and his head glows brighter with each and every hit.

The Doctor comes into play and launches the pinball into a treble play. Sarah and Harry divert the ball and score a hit of five million.

Scratchman strikes back by unleashing a phalanx of Daleks across the table. The Daleks glide out of panels at the sides of the table and move menacingly toward them. However, the Doctor and his companions find that they can deal with the Daleks simply by altering the tilt of the table. The Daleks are rolled off to one side, knocking into each other like skittles.

The Doctor eventually theorises that if they let Scratchman win the game, the onrush of his own pride might just cause him to explode. He pulls back one of the pinball flippers with his scarf and Scratchman gets to score the jackpot. As predicted, Scratchman's globe-like head shatters with an explosion of bright light and splintered crystal.

Back in the office, the travellers find that all of the 'men' in the meeting room are now gone. Only empty suits are left behind. Harry picks up a small lead-coloured ball that rolls out across the floor from inside

---

[382] The script contained another special full-page illustration here of what these 'headless' characters might look like.

[383] From *Doctor Who Magazine* – Issue 379 (28 February 2007) p.21

Scratchman's empty clothes.

Returning to the island of Mull, the Doctor, Sarah and Harry finish their game of cricket. Harry bowls Scratchman's lead-coloured ball and the Doctor hits it with his bat. It smashes into tiny fragments of glass. Inside each one of these tiny fragments, we can see a new Scratchman forming, with a tiny glowing orb for a head. The image is cloudy and indistinct, moving with faint squeaks, as if alive. However, the Doctor and his friends are too busy playing cricket and don't notice. It's a lovely day and they're enjoying their game.

6
Life, the Universe and Everything 'Doctor Who and the Krikkitmen' (1976-1981)

PRIMARY PHASE

Far out in the uncharted backwaters of the unfashionable end of the Western half of London, lies a small unregarded grassy green common. Opposite this, at a distance of roughly 60 feet, is an utterly insignificant little concrete and brick office block.

This is Threshold House, and in 1976 it was the home of the BBC's *Doctor Who* production office. And it was inside this unobtrusive grey office building, not far from Television Centre, that there worked a man called Robert Holmes – script editor of the *Doctor Who* television series. This is not his story.

However, it was on Robert Holmes' desk at Threshold House in 1976 that an unsolicited story idea arrived, written by a comedy writer called Douglas Adams. The story proposal was for a new serial called 'Doctor Who and the Krikkitmen'. And, a few years later, it would very nearly take *Doctor Who* back to the movies.

Douglas Adams had already enjoyed some (though not very much) success as a jobbing scriptwriter on a number of early '70s comedy shows. Some of them were even broadcast. In 1976 he was described in a press release for a play he was directing as 'TV scriptwriter and part-time under-assistant spelling mistake corrector to the Monty Python team.'[384] He'd recently worked with Graham Chapman on a script for the one-off television comedy *Out of the Trees*. Adams had also started on an idea of his own for a new radio series called *The Hitchhiker's Guide to the Galaxy*. However, nobody seemed to like it very much.

Adams had an affection for *Doctor Who* and had submitted a story idea to the show before. In 1974 he had proposed an idea while still finishing his studies at Cambridge University. Sadly, however, it was felt that Adams' story about an 'ark in space' in which a proportion of the Earth's population

---

[384] From *Hitchhiker – A Biography of Douglas Adams* by M J Simpson – Coronet Books (2003) p.79

were sleeping in suspended animation, might just possibly clash with a Robert Holmes script the BBC already had in production called 'The Ark in Space' in which a proportion of the Earth's population were sleeping in suspended animation. Adams' story doesn't seem to have been taken any further.

Two years later, though, when Adams sent in his idea for 'Doctor Who and the Krikkitmen', it got a slightly better reception. Holmes read through the story, which involved xenophobic cricketing robots, and recognised Adams' obvious talent for fantasy. He didn't think the story was quite right for the show, and incoming producer Graham Williams apparently felt it to be 'too silly.'[385] However, Holmes did encourage Adams to send in other ideas. Although it wasn't an entirely discouraging response, a disappointed Adams still summed up the feedback as: 'We'd like to see more evidence of talent than this.'[386]

Adams had also by now started concentrating more on his old idea for a *Hitchhiker's Guide to the Galaxy* radio series and moved away from *Doctor Who* for a time as he got to work on it.

The Hitchhiker's Guide to the Galaxy 'was Douglas's last throw of the dice as a writer,' said Adams' friend, radio producer Geoffrey Perkins. 'He was considering jacking it all in and perhaps taking a job in Hong Kong to become a ship-broker.'[387]

Happily for the sake of world literature (and possibly the Hong Kong shipping industry), on 4 February 1977 producer Simon Brett had a meeting with Adams and asked him to write a pilot episode for his proposed *Hitchhiker* show. A formal commission followed on 3 March. The script was delivered on 4 April and recorded on 28 June. *The Hitchhiker's Guide to the Galaxy* was coming to BBC radio and Adams was delighted. He even borrowed one of the planet names (Bethselamin) from his *Doctor Who* Krikkitmen story for use in the new radio script.

Hopeful that the pilot would lead to a full radio series, but thinking it unlikely to materialise for quite a while, in summer 1977 Adams also started thinking about trying another *Doctor Who* submission.

SECONDARY PHASE

Proud of his first commissioned piece of science fiction writing, Adams sent a copy of the *Hitchhiker* pilot script to Robert Holmes at Threshold

---

[385] From *Don't Panic – The Official Hitch-Hiker's Guide to the Galaxy Companion* by Neil Gaiman – Titan Books (1988) p.95
[386] From *TARDIS* (October 1978)
[387] From *Hitchhiker – A Biography of Douglas Adams* by M J Simpson – Coronet Books (2003) p.91-92

House in around July 1977. However, at this time, Holmes was handing over the script editing reins to a successor, Anthony Read, and it was therefore left to *Doctor Who*'s producer, Graham Williams, to look over Adams' latest work. Williams was very impressed and wanted Adams on board as a writer for *Doctor Who*'s new series. Before the end of the month he had commissioned Adams to write a new four-part *Doctor Who* serial, called 'The Pirate Planet', for the forthcoming season.

'After long periods of intense inactivity, I was suddenly going out of my mind with too much work to do,' said Adams. 'I sat down and wrote four episodes of *Hitchhiker* just like that, four at once, and then took a break off to write four episodes of [*Doctor Who*] ... How did I come to write it? I don't know. I suppose I just got drunk a lot.'[388]

Now he was in, Adams had broader plans for *Doctor Who*. In 1977, he resurrected his old pitch for 'Doctor Who and the Krikkitmen', and wanted to see if he could find anyone interested in developing it as a *Doctor Who* feature film.

Adams wrote a full cinema treatment from his earlier pitch and later, on 3 April 1978, his agent, Jill Foster contacted BBC Copyright about the screen rights to *Doctor Who*. Initially nothing came of this. However, the idea didn't go away.

'Oddly enough, I found *Doctor Who* quite liberating to do,' recalled Adams. 'I did notice one odd thing, which was, I was writing episodes of *Hitchhiker* which all seemed to happen in corridors, and writing episodes of *Doctor Who* which called for huge, enormous, impossibly elaborate sets. I thought, "I've got this the wrong way round".'[389] Oddly this was perhaps also one of the things that made Adams one of the show's strongest writers, and ultimately, in 1978, he was asked to take over from Read as *Doctor Who*'s next script editor. The offer was made to him by producer Graham Williams in the bar at BBC Television Centre. 'I was a bit stunned by that actually,' said Adams. 'I was, well, startled. It was straight out of the blue.'[390]

Adams accepted the offer and worked as script editor from the closing episodes of Season 16 through to the end of Season 17 (1979-80). During that time he wrote or co-wrote two stories himself (one under a pseudonym) and contributed whimsical additions to many others. It was an eclectic time for the series – fantastically witty, yet hamstrung by dwindling budgets during a period of great inflation. Although it wasn't entirely down to Adams, the programme also enjoyed its highest ever

---

[388] From *TARDIS* (October 1978)
[389] From *Book Club* – BBC Radio Four (2 January 2000)
[390] From *Hitchhiker – A Biography of Douglas Adams* by M J Simpson – Coronet Books (2003) p.121

ratings during this period[391].

For all its tensions, Adams enjoyed the job; but when Graham Williams left at the end of the 1979 season, Adams followed suit. 'It was fun to do for a year, but that was quite enough,'[392] he said.

By this time, *The Hitchhiker's Guide to the Galaxy* had become quite astonishingly popular and was taking up a lot of Adams' time. However, he hadn't quite finished with *Doctor Who* altogether. As he packed up his things at Threshold House in late 1979, there was one last *Doctor Who* story he still wanted to give another shot.

He'd tried before without success, but he wanted to try again. He wanted to make a film of 'Doctor Who and the Krikkitmen'.

TERTIARY PHASE

Adams was right. 'Doctor Who and the Krikkitmen' would have made a wonderful film. Compared with the *Scratchman* project, it was clearly the better story. It had all the idiosyncratic humour of late '70s *Doctor Who* but a much broader cinematic scope. It felt like a movie – a big movie – but, importantly, it also still felt like *Doctor Who*.

Like the quickly-aborted film remake of 'The Keys of Marinus' of over a decade before (see Chapter Two), Adams' story had a quest-narrative – a universe-trotting trek through time and space in search an eccentric sci-fi McGuffin that threatened the future of the universe. It had much in common with the similarly-themed 1978 series of *Doctor Who* to which Adams contributed 'The Pirate Planet', although that appears to be mostly a coincidence.

Adams had first conceived the story for television around 1975/1976. At the time, the Doctor's regular travelling companion was Sarah Jane Smith, played by Elisabeth Sladen. Accordingly he had written her into his proposal. However, even if it had been commissioned back then, it would almost certainly have needed to have been rewritten: Sladen left the series in 1976, and by the time Adams' script would have been ready for production, actress Louise Jameson would have taken over as Tom Baker's new co-star. Unlike

---

[391] The top five most watched *Doctor Who* episodes of all time are all episodes that Adams worked on. The highest rated was 'City of Death' part four with 16.1 million viewers. Second was 'City of Death' part three with 15.4 million (both co-written by Adams). 'Destiny of the Daleks' part four is in third place with 14.4 million and part two of 'City of Death' clocks in fourth with 14.1 million. The fifth most watched was part three of 'Destiny of the Daleks', scoring 13.8 million. However, the fact that ITV weren't actually broadcasting any programmes at this time due to industrial action had a lot to do with these exceptional ratings.
[392] From *Hitchhiker – A Biography of Douglas Adams* by M J Simpson – Coronet Books (2003) p.129

Milton Subotsky in the '60s, Adams also went along with Baker and Marter's logic that a *Doctor Who* film should tie directly in to the television series.

When Adams first tried to drum up interest in filming his story in 1977, he'd been unable to get enough people behind the idea, but after a long stint both writing and script-editing the television series itself, perhaps he might now stand a better chance. Tom Baker's own *Scratchman* project had been almost completely written off by 1980, so the way was seemingly clear for another bid to be made to the BBC.

Adams was interested in films. A movie version of *The Hitchhikers' Guide to the Galaxy* was on the cards (well, *his* cards anyway) almost from the start, and his *Doctor Who* proposal could be seen as an extension of this ambition to break into the cinema. It is perhaps surprising, in fact, that having devoted so much time to film projects, Adams never actually had one produced during his own lifetime.

By now, Adams had become acquainted with the film producer Brian Eastman, later to become well-known for his work on television. Eastman was then working in the British movie industry, albeit in quite a small way. In 1978 he had recently formed Picture Partnership Productions with the director Leszek Burzynski.

'I think I went to Douglas,' says Eastman. 'But,it might have been that I went to Douglas about something else and he then said that maybe we should try a *Doctor Who* film ... I think what was in my mind was, "Surely we can recapture the greatness in the show by spending more money on it and making a proper movie." Obviously Douglas had had some of the major ideas for the show, and if we had been allowed to do it, I think that perhaps we would have achieved that.'

The two men's plan was to get the production off the ground with the backing of the giant Paramount Pictures in America, for whom Eastman was then working.

'I remember that I had approached the contracts department at the BBC about getting the rights to make the film,' says Eastman. 'At that time, I was making short films for the cinema, which were funded by Paramount Pictures. They had a programme of making short films in the UK, because in those days there was a government subsidy scheme called the Eady Levy that they wanted to take advantage of; but I think what also happened was the idea that they wanted to help new British talent develop a little bit. When I was working on the *Doctor Who* idea, I thought maybe Paramount would help it as a proper movie and not as a short film.'

In May 1980, Eastman got his opportunity to test the water with Paramount over the *Doctor Who* project. By happy coincidence, an executive from Paramount happened to be coming into London, and Eastman managed to arrange a meeting.

'The executive of Paramount,' says Eastman, 'was a very young Jeffrey

Katzenberg. I had a meeting with Katzenberg in which I proposed the *Doctor Who* idea and he said, "Well, are you sure the rights are okay?" I'd arranged for a person at the BBC to be on the phone to confirm that the BBC were willing to do this. So we rang the person at the BBC, who was on another call. So I had to entertain Jeffrey Katzenberg with other conversation while we waited for this BBC man to become free. So here I was floundering terribly for about 50 minutes trying to keep Jeffrey's interest, because of course, he had a million other things he'd rather be doing, but I didn't want to let the opportunity pass. We did eventually get the BBC chap and he did confirm that they were interested in doing it.'

Still keen to tie in with the television series, then entering its eigtheenth year, Eastman and Adams had Tom Baker firmly in their minds as the film's star. Adams liked Tom Baker – well, most of the time. 'Tom is one of those people who oscillated between being one of the most wonderful, awesome, engaging people you have ever met, to someone you would gladly shove off a cliff,'[393] he later said.

'I do remember meeting with Tom Baker around that time,' says Eastman. 'I expect we were hoping to use him. He was very popular … so it would have been a brave move to think of anyone else at that time.'

Sadly, neither the existing paperwork nor Eastman's memory can shed light on exactly why the Krikkitmen project didn't eventually happen. It's unlikely that it was due to any conflict with *Scratchman*, which was firmly on the rocks by then. It's possible that Adams' increasing commitments to *Hitchhiker* played a part. However, more likely is that it just failed to attract the necessary investment. It wasn't the first *Doctor Who* film proposal to fall at this hurdle and it wouldn't be the last.

'I can't really remember what brought it to a close,' says Eastman. 'One tries different projects in one's life and only a fairly small percentage come to fruition. and you can never quite remember with the ones that didn't work, what brought them to an end … I remember having good times with Douglas and enjoying his company very much and it would have been great to have made something that he had fully written, but things took a different course.'

The failure to set up *Doctor Who and the Krikkitmen* as a motion picture disappointed Adams. He hadn't completely done with the storyline yet, however.

QUANDARY PHASE

1980 was a big year for Douglas Adams. *The Hitchhikers' Guide to the Galaxy* had been a surprise hit on the radio. A second series had started on Radio 4 on 21 January, and had made it to the cover of the *Radio Times*. There was

---

[393] From *Doctor Who Magazine* – Issue 429 (12 January 2011)

a specially-recorded LP and cassette version available in the shops and Adams' novelisations of the scripts from the first two series were soon bestsellers. There was even a stage version. 1980 was also the year that the BBC started work on a highly ambitious television remake. It was a very good year for Adams. And the writer was already in discussions about a new novel too.

The contract for a third *Hitchhiker* novel – this time an original work rather than a novelisation of existing scripts – was signed with Pan Books on 10 July 1981 (for a quite astronomical fee). It would be called *Life, the Universe and Everything* – a reference to a celebrated phrase from the original radio series. And Adams soon set to work writing it. Slowly. Very slowly.

Thankfully, though, he didn't have to come up with a new plot from scratch. There was a rather nice one sitting untouched, all ready and waiting, in his office. For one final time, out came *Doctor Who and the Krikkitmen*. At last it was about to get a public airing. This time it was right, it would work, and no-one would have to distract any American film producers to do it.

Adams was fond of recycling. His very first *Doctor Who* pitch concerning 'the ark in space' eventually ended up being folded into a *Hitchhiker*'s episode, and now the Krikkitmen were going the same way. 'There were good bits in it and I didn't want it to go to waste,'[394] Adams later explained.

'He was jolly good at recycling ideas,' adds Brian Eastman. 'Well, all writers are. You don't want to waste a good idea.'

Despite having his original *Doctor Who* story as a framework, Adams still found the writing of *Life, the Universe and Everything* extraordinarily difficult. The writing coincided with, 'a huge domestic crisis'[395] in his life. His then girlfriend, novelist Sally Emerson, had just left him. 'She went off with this bloke on, to me, the spurious grounds that he was her husband,'[396] he explained. The book was 'written in circumstances I wouldn't want to build a bookcase under, let alone write a book.'[397]

Naturally there were changes to be made to the story in order to transform it into a book. The original *Doctor Who* movie outline had opened at a cricket ground, but Adams' last *Hitchhiker* novel had left his heroes

---

[394] From *Doctor Who Magazine* – Issue 313 (6 February 2002) p.10

[395] From *Don't Panic – The Official Hitch-Hiker's Guide to the Galaxy Companion* by Neil Gaiman – Titan Books (1988) p.96

[396] From *Wish You Were Here – The Biography of Douglas Adams* by Nick Webb – Hodder Headline (2003) p.241

[397] From *Don't Panic – The Official Hitch-Hiker's Guide to the Galaxy Companion* by Neil Gaiman – Titan Books (1988) p.96

marooned on primeval Earth. His rewriting managed to get his characters from primeval Earth to Lord's Cricket Ground in a mere 12 pages of comic wonderfulness that involved a miserable immortal and a flying sofa.

Adams recalled that this opening chapter alone went through 20 drafts. After writing vast reams of material on the hardships and pitfalls of living on prehistoric Earth, Adams eventually edited these drafts down to just one sentence. It ran: 'The regular early morning yell of horror was the sound of Arthur Dent waking up and suddenly remembering where he was.'[398]

Across the novel that followed, most of the Doctor's material was divided up between the *Hitchhiker* characters of Slartibartfast, Tricia (Trillian) McMillan and (in the latter sections) Arthur Dent. The book mainly concentrated and elaborated upon the first half of the *Krikkitmen* film. The second half of the *Doctor Who* story was then condensed into the book's final 30 pages. It would be the first public exposure Adams' *Doctor Who* film ever received.

Published in 1982, the book (of the film of the television serial) was heavily promoted by Pan, and it was another huge hit. 'I assumed, doing this third book, that by now, possibly the interest might have begun to slope off a bit,' said Adams at the time. 'But ... this book has absolutely astonished me, selling much better than the first two, which is something I really wasn't prepared for.'[399]

QUINTESSENTIAL PHASE

Douglas Adams would follow up *Life, the Universe and Everything* with two more *Hitchhiker* books – *So Long and Thanks for All the Fish* (1984) and *Mostly Harmless* (1992). They would form an 'increasingly inaccurately named trilogy'. Adams was thinking about writing a sixth instalment in the saga when in May 2001 he died in America from a heart attack. He was 49. His final unfinished book, *The Salmon of Doubt*, was published in 2002 and featured his other major literary creation, Dirk Gently, the holistic detective[400].

More than three years after his death, and after over a decade in development, a third season (or tertiary phase) of *The Hitchhikers' Guide to the*

---

[398] From *Life, the Universe and Everything* by Douglas Adams – Pan Books Ltd. (1982) p.7

[399] From *Hitchhiker – A Biography of Douglas Adams* by M J Simpson – Coronet Books (2003) p.181

[400] There were two (finished) Dirk Gently novels: *Dirk Gently's Holistic Detective Agency* (1987) and *The Long Dark Tea-Time of the Soul* (1988). The first of these borrowed heavily from Adams' last *Doctor Who* television script, 'Shada', recording on which had been abandoned part-way through due to industrial action at the BBC.

Galaxy radio series finally reached BBC Radio Four in 2004. Featuring most of the original cast, it was a direct dramatisation of the *Life, the Universe and Everything* novel – allowing Adams' Krikkitmen idea finally to be recorded by the BBC, nearly 30 years after it was first rejected by Robert Holmes. It is, to date, the only dramatisation that the story has ever received. This radio series of the book of the film of the television treatment was broadcast in the autumn of 2004.

Brian Eastman would continue to develop his career in the industry, building a considerable reputation on television and earning two BAFTA nominations. His earliest big hit was with the television adaptation of Tom Sharpe's *Blott on the Landscape* (1985), on which he was executive producer. The even more successful *Porterhouse Blue* followed in 1987.

Eastman's Picture Partnership Productions company was rebranded in 1985, when his partner Leszek Burzynski left the business. Carnival Films was set up in 1989 as a result, becoming one of television's most important drama production outfits. Eastman left the company in 2006, following its sale to Australian company Southern Star. In the meantime, however, he'd produced the films *Whoops Apocalypse* in 1988 and *Shadowlands* in 1993. He'd also produced the television version of *Traffik* in 1989. His television adaptation of P G Wodehouse's *Jeeves and Wooster* stories ran from 1990 to 1993 with Hugh Laurie and Stephen Fry. The science fiction series *Crime Traveller* then came in 1997 and *BUGS* from 1995 to 1999. Hs most lasting legacy has probably been an acclaimed run of Agatha Christie's *Poirot* for ITV, starring David Suchet. He acted as its producer from 1989 to 2001. He also co-created another hit ITV series, *Rosemary and Thyme,* which ran between 2003 and 2006. Following his departure from Carnival he moved into theatre production.

Eastman is reflective about his failed *Doctor Who* project. 'Probably, it was almost a bit too soon to suggest the idea, because with it still being on the air … the movie companies probably said, "Oh, I don't really see who would go to the movie." Whereas if I'd waited four or five years when it was off the air completely, I might have had better luck.'

On the surface, Eastman's logic makes sense. However, a *Doctor Who* film wasn't all that much easier to sell, even with the show *off* the air.

Doctor Who and the Krikkitmen
By
Douglas Adams

PLOT SYNOPSIS

The final cricket Test match between England and Australia at Lord's. England are winning and a police box has just materialised in the members' enclosure.

The Doctor and Sarah Jane Smith step out of the TARDIS as the Doctor produces an ancient Lord's membership card, which gets them warily admitted to the grounds. Meanwhile on the pitch, with just three runs needed, England's batsman hits a six and the crowd cheer.

The Ashes are being presented to the captain of the England team when the Doctor walks onto the pitch and asks if anyone would mind if he took them instead. The Doctor nonchalantly explains that the Ashes are actually vital to the future of the cosmos.

Suddenly, a small cricket pavilion appears in the middle of the field. The doors open and eleven robots emerge, wearing cricket whites and carrying cricket bats. With military precision, the padded figures march efficiently onto the pitch. Then, to the horror of the bewildered crowds, the robots attack two indignant officials with their bats and snatch away the Ashes.

Filing back into their pavilion with the urn, the robots use their bats to fire a volley of laser warning-shots above the crowd. As the doors of their strange pavilion close behind them, something resembling a cricket ball is batted into the tea tent. The tent then explodes in a cloud of broken crockery.

As the dust settles, the pavilion disappears as quickly as it had arrived.

The Doctor is still in shock as he picks himself up from the ground. 'I've heard of the Krikkitmen, I used to be frightened with stories of them when I was a child,' he explains 'But 'till now I've never seen them. They were supposed to have been destroyed over two million years ago.'[401]

The Doctor tersely continues to explain that the whole game of cricket is actually the ghost of a traumatic race memory that the English have interpreted as a rather dull and tasteless game (which only they

---

[401] From *Don't Panic – The Official Hitch Hiker's Guide to the Galaxy Companion* by Neil Gaiman – Titan Books (1988) p.174

understand). Breaking from his solemnity, however, the Doctor says that he did enjoy the day's play and asks if he could keep the ball as a memento.

Later, the Doctor argues with the Time Lords about the Krikkitmen robots. During the discussion, Sarah gets to learn a bit more background to the bizarre events at Lord's.

Around two million years ago, on the outer fringes of the galaxy, there was a planet called Krikkit. Over many centuries, the people of Krikkit became a highly sophisticated and technologically advanced civilisation. Only the science of astronomy remained unknown to them, owing to a huge black dust cloud that covered their planet and blotted out the stars.

The galaxy was, at that time, enjoying a period of rare peace and harmony. The symbol of this was the great Wicket Gate – two short horizontal bars, supported by three longer vertical struts. The two bars were made of metal; one of gold (representing wealth) and the other of silver (representing peace). The three struts were made of steel (representing strength), perspex (representing science) and wood (representing nature) respectively. Not that the people of Krikkit knew anything of this, of course.

The Krikkitas knew nothing of the universe at all. Not being able to see any other planets through their inky black atmosphere, it never occurred to them that there *were* any other planets.

Then one day, a wrecked spaceship crash-landed on Krikkit and the entire their way of life was turned upside-down. The sudden knowledge of other worlds and races awakened deep feelings of racialism and xenophobia in the people of Krikkit.

Unable to reconcile themselves with the idea of other life in the cosmos, the Krikkitas soon became a race of cruel and ruthless warmongers who, once they had mastered space travel, began fighting an intergalactic war against the rest of the galaxy. Their only purpose was to destroy all other life, wherever they found it. To help them in their bloody crusade, they built a series of robots called the Krikkitmen.

Under their cricket-cap-like helmets, the Krikkitmen were incredibly advanced killing machines. With laser guns that doubled as clubs and with rocket-packs in their legs, they spread terror wherever they went. Their most terrifying weapons were small red grenades that were primed and targeted with a single strike of their bat-guns.

At long last, after a thousand years of violence, the Krikkit people and their robotic servants were finally defeated. However, the universe was now faced with a great dilemma. The Krikkitas remained unrepentantly genocidal, but that wasn't really their fault; they were just a product of their planet's unfortunate atmospheric conditions. It would be wrong to destroy them and yet impossible to let them continue their fanatical crusade of universal destruction.

The solution was to seal up the whole planet inside a gigantic bubble of 'slow time'. For everyone inside the bubble, time would move almost infinitely slowly, whereas outside, it ran as normal. The only way that anybody was able to gain entry to the imprisoned people of Krikkit was to unlock the great space bubble with a special key, cast in the shape of the mythic Wicket Gate. To modern eyes, the Wicket Gate most closely resembles a set of giant cricket stumps.

Not long after Krikkit had been trapped in its bubble, a group of renegade Krikkitmen had attempted to steal the Wicket Gate. However, they had merely succeeded in blowing it apart into fragments that then fell into the space-time vortex. Since then, the Time Lords have closely monitored the location of the shattered pieces. The sport of cricket, which is practised only on Earth, is just a subtle re-enactment of the Krikkit myth. The rest of the universe views it as all rather tasteless.

On Gallifrey, the Doctor and Sarah attempt to find out what they can about the Krikkitmen and the Wicket Gate. However, they are obstructed by the grinding bureaucracy of the Time Lords. They eventually discover that the Ashes are really part of the remains of the central 'stump' of the original Wicket Gate key and that the rogue Krikkitmen have stolen these ashes in order to release their masters from the spatial bubble around Krikkit.

The mystery of where these rogue Krikkitmen came from is eventually explained by one of the Time Lords, who reveals that since they were partly sentient, they couldn't legally be destroyed (according to the conventions of war). Therefore, they were instead kept in suspended animation in a secret location within the space-time vortex. Clearly, they seem to have escaped.

With the arrival of news that the perspex stump has now also been stolen, the Time Lords are forced to concede the seriousness of the situation and give the Doctor details of the locations of the other Wicket Gate pieces, so that he can find them and put a stop to the Krikkitmen's plan.

The Doctor and Sarah soon discover that they are too late to stop the theft of the steel 'stump' and the golden 'bail'. So, they decide to go after the silver 'bail'. Their quest takes them to the distant world of Bethselamin, where the vital fragment of the key is worshipped by the natives as a holy relic. The TARDIS materialises in the heart of their main temple and the Doctor proceeds to remove the 'Wicket' segment from where it is kept. Naturally, the people of Bethselamin – the Bethselamini – are angry at the Doctor's theft. However, as he leaves the temple, he hopes to smooth over the offence by giving them a humble bow. It turns out to be fortuitous, for as he bows his head, a Krikkit bat is swung into the vacant space by a Krikkitman, just arrived on the scene.

Hordes of Krikkitmen pour into the temple and a battle breaks out between the robots and the Bethselamini (who feel forced to side with the Doctor, despite his crime). Amidst the clamour, the Doctor manages to fight his way into the Krikkitmen's pavilion. Inside, he is faced with more

Krikkitmen, bent on his destruction. However, as he stumbles back from a swinging bat, he falls against a control lever, and all the Krikkitmen suddenly slump down – limp and inanimate. Quite by accident, the Doctor has fallen against their off-switch. Outside, all the robots are similarly lifeless and still. The battle is over.

Picking through the devastation, the Doctor finds a strangely dazed Sarah, staring into the motionless face of one of the inert Krikkitmen. It quickly becomes apparent that she has been somehow hypnotised, but the Doctor doesn't seem to have noticed yet.

Dismantling one of the Krikkitmen, the Doctor discovers that the Time Lords were wrong about the creatures. They are not semi-sentient androids at all. They are just robots – mere machines, with no capacity for individual thought or will. As such, there wasn't really any reason for them to have been preserved following the war. The Lime Lords would have been quite within their rights to have simply turned them off and had them destroyed. The universe would have been a lot safer too.

The Doctor and Sarah are about to leave in the TARDIS, but before they go, Sarah suggests that they take the inactive robots back to Gallifrey, along with their pavilion. She observes that it would be safer than leaving them on Bethselamin. Once on Gallifrey, they could then be destroyed. Sarah further suggests that she take the pavilion machine to Gallifrey herself while the Doctor deals with whatever other Krikkitmen are still kept prisoner by the Time Lords. She will then wait for him to join her there.

The Doctor agrees and pre-sets the pavilion's controls for Sarah's journey. However, while he isn't looking, Sarah quietly operates some of the TARDIS's controls. We see a strange alien quality in her eyes. She then obscures one of the control panels with her hat.

The Doctor leaves Sarah to make her journey alone and returns to the TARDIS to make his. He notices that the controls are not quite as he left them, but he seems to dismiss it with a slight frown. Meanwhile, inside the pavilion, Sarah resets the controls for an entirely different destination.

The Doctor's journey in the TARDIS to the supposed last resting-place of the sleeping Krikkitmen is a complex one, and he soon calls on the assistance of the Time Lords to get him there. When he finally arrives, he finds one of many chambers full of coffin-shaped life-support machines. Leaving the TARDIS, he fails to notice a bright warning light twinkling under Sarah's hat.

After the Doctor has gone, Sarah appears from nowhere and picks up her hat from the console. We see that the display underneath reads: 'SCREENS BREACHED: INTRUDER IN TARDIS.'

Sarah quietly follows after the Doctor, and once outside (still unseen by him) she operates a control panel set into one of the walls. A group of Krikkitmen emerge from the TARDIS behind her.

The Doctor is examining one of the preserved Krikkitmen in its life-support unit when one of the vats behind him slowly opens. Suddenly he hears Sarah's voice and he looks up to see her standing in front of him. The room is swarming with Krikkitmen. One of the robots hits the Doctor on the back of the head and he falls to the floor.

The Doctor recovers consciousness in the TARDIS, surrounded by Krikkitmen. He notices the flashing control panel and realises what must have happened. He pushes a button and one of the TARDIS's internal walls falls away, revealing the concealed pavilion behind it.

The entire five million-strong army of Krikkitmen has now been revived, and the Doctor is ordered to take them to an asteroid near Krikkit, where the great slow-time bubble can be unlocked. The hypnotised Sarah holds a knife to her own throat. If the Doctor refuses, she will kill herself.

Once the TARDIS has arrived on the asteroid, Sarah slumps to the floor. The influence of the Krikkitmen has left her. She remembers nothing after the battle on Bethselamin.

The Krikkitmen have now reconstructed the Wicket Gate, and they carry it out to a large altar that has risen out of the planet's surface. The Wicket Gate is slotted into a perspex support and lights begin to glow and twinkle in the structure. The planet of Krikkit, which has remained invisible for two million years, slowly fades back into view, together with its single star.

As the Krikkitmen chant, the Doctor and Sarah make a run for the TARDIS, leaving the robots behind on the asteroid.

Realising that it's too late to stop the Krikkitmen, the Doctor reluctantly decides that the only course of action is to travel to the planet Krikkit itself and try to change the minds of the Krikkit people – to tempt them away from committing genocide.

The TARDIS takes the Doctor and Sarah to one of the Krikkit cities. After they have picked their way through the back streets, they accidentally stumble into one of the main city squares. They are confronted by shocked and angry Krikkitas, who pursue them through the city. They hide down an alley, but find themselves taken by surprise and are knocked out.

The Doctor and Sarah eventually awake and escape their captors, before being recaptured and then escaping again. During the course of their adventures on Krikkit, they discover that the real reason behind the Krikkitas' great wars wasn't natural xenophobia at all. It was all down to an erratic supercomputer.

Long ago, a powerful supercomputer had been built by the original (long gone) people of Krikkit to help them with their warmongering. The computer's main job was to create a bomb ('a very small bomb') that would, at the touch of a button, destroy all other life in the universe.

However, the computer didn't quite do what it was supposed to. It instead built a harmless dummy bomb. Naturally, its creators weren't terribly pleased about this and had the computer destroyed – atomising it into a cloud of dust. It is this opaque dust cloud that now encircles Krikkit, cutting out all daylight around the planet.

Despite being just a cloud of dust particles, the computer is still able to function, although not as effectively as it once did, and its 'consciousness' lives on. The Doctor and Sarah speak to it, and it reveals to them that it created the wrecked spaceship that crashed into Krikkit and inspired the inhabitants' xenophobia in the first place. Its intention was to ensure that they became every bit as warlike as its original creators. When the slow time bubble was erected, however, the computer's mind control over the people of Krikkit subsided.

Finally, the Doctor and Sarah manage to collect the components of the Wicket Gate. They arrive back on Earth only moments after the robots' attack on Lord's, and return the Ashes.

7
A New Hope
'Doctor Who – The Movie'
(1985-1987)

AXED

On 26 February 1985 the news broke[402] that the BBC had cancelled *Doctor Who*. A new season had been due to go into production that spring for transmission from early January 1986.

Despite maintaining fairly healthy ratings and a still-devoted following, *Doctor Who* was unpopular with many of the people who ran the BBC in the mid-1980s. Controller of BBC1 Michael Grade later commented: 'I thought it was rubbish. I thought it was pathetic … I think it was a waste of the licence-payers' money.'[403] Jonathan Powell, the BBC's Head of Series and Serials (the department responsible for *Doctor Who*), had little time for it either, and the general feeling circulating around the sixth floor offices at Television Centre was that it was *not* the sort of thing the BBC should be spending its time and money on.

As it turned out, the cancellation was only a temporary suspension. Following a public outcry, the BBC announced that the programme would in fact be returning to BBC1 in September 1986 – some nine months later than originally scheduled. However, during that brief period in the wilderness, plans began to be laid for an altogether different future for the Doctor, away from television screens entirely.

Almost as soon as the BBC confirmed *Doctor Who*'s hiatus in early 1985, BBC Enterprises received an approach from a pair of independent filmmakers, Peter Litten and George Dugdale, concerning the film rights to the series.

Litten had been an effects assistant at the BBC Visual Effects Department for a few years in the early 1980s, working under various effects supervisors, including *Doctor Who*'s K-9 operator Mat Irvine. He'd since gone on to become a freelance special effects artist. Dugdale was a writer/director

---

[402] In that day's London *Evening Standard*.
[403] From *Room 101* prod. Victoria Payne – BBC2 (8 April 2002)

specialising in horror films, who had just been involved in the production of a one-off television movie entitled *Max Headroom: 20 Minutes into the Future*, based on the computer-generated Max Headroom character featured in a.contemporary Channel 4 pop music series.

Litten and Dugdale had recently started working together on their first full-length feature-film, *Slaughter High* (which had yet to be released), when they first approached the BBC with their proposal for a *Doctor Who* film in February 1985.

'We said, "Well, this [hiatus] is crazy,"' remembers Litten. '[The show had] got a good following in the States and we felt that it would make a great movie. So, we approached the BBC.'

Litten and Dugdale gained the support of John Humphreys, a colleague from *Max Headroom*. Litten and Humphreys had known each other for some time, having met through work in the theatre. When Litten left the BBC Visual Effects Department, he started working with Humphreys at Coast to Coast Productions, an independent visual effects business, undertaking contract work for film and television.

'We did a lot of stuff for the BBC,' says Humphreys, 'including lots of stuff for *Doctor Who*[404] and other TV programmes: *The Young Ones*, *The Two Ronnies* – all this sort of stuff. Plus, Peter and I had designed Max Headroom for Channel Four and we were doing quite well with that. We worked on some films as well, of course.'

It was at Humphreys' Coast to Coast Productions that the three aspiring filmmakers first started developing ideas for a *Doctor Who* picture. The trio would eventually form a separate limited company specifically for their *Who* project.[405] That company's trading name, Daltenreys, was made up from their respective surnames (Dugdale, Litten and Humphreys).

'John Humphreys ... was involved in a financial capacity and ultimately he would have been doing a lot of the creature designs,' explains Litten. 'Until the production actually started (which of course, it never did) he was kind of involved on the edge rather than at first-hand ... I was originally going to be co-directing it, with my then partner George Dugdale, and we were much ... involved in the storyline and narrative.'

The company also brought in fellow filmmaker Mark Ezra, a writer/producer with whom they had previously worked on *Slaughter High*. Together, Litten, Dugdale, Humphreys and Ezra embarked on getting

---

[404] Humphreys recalls working on the realisation of a character called Sil for the 1985 story 'Vengeance on Varos'. This work would have been carried out under the BBC's visual effects supervisor on that story, Charles Jeanes.

[405] Coast to Coast Productions didn't officially become a limited company until 1987. However, Daltenreys still used Coast to Coast as its main imprint, and that was the name that headed its letters to the BBC as early as 1985.

permission from the BBC to proceed with their *Doctor Who* film.

'Peter and I had worked for several years at that point on various other films,' recalls Ezra. 'We were hoping to do *Doctor Who* as a sort of climax to that relationship ... I went with Peter Litten and George Dugdale to meet with a woman (whose name escapes me) at BBC Worldwide[406] [sic] and we made an offer at that time of, I think, £100,000 for the rights. I was part of the pitch. At that stage, I think I was going to be co-producer with them and also write the script.'

WHO ART ...

Among the first people to be approached about working on the proposed film was the prolific concept artist and illustrator, Rodney Matthews. Matthews had been behind album covers for the group Thin Lizzy and the Mountain Records label and was also a regular illustrator for the novels of Michael Moorcock. His poster art was very popular in the 1970s and '80s.

Matthews was approached by Litten early in 1985, on behalf of Coast to Coast Productions, and was asked to handle the concept design on their *Doctor Who* film. 'If I remember correctly,' the artist recalls, 'the film was something to do with an inter-galactic romp that centred around Stonehenge. Stonehenge was used as some star-gate type of thing for dragging enemy craft onto planet Earth.'

At this stage, Dugdale's and Litten's story ideas for the film (fleshed out with Mark Ezra) centred on a villainous cyborg called Varnax. Matthews remembers that the character was to 'travel in some kind of levitating cage, a bit like the Mekon from *Dan Dare.*'

Matthews continues: 'I went up to their offices in London, several times. I attended several meetings and they told me that I would be in charge of the entire conceptual art for the film ... I did go as far as to produce an illustration – an orangey thing – a huge mantis creature and some sort of science fiction-looking characters in the foreground ... The TARDIS was actually floating in the central part of the picture.'

By the autumn of 1985, Coast to Coast had made their initial pitch to the BBC and were pursuing a deal with them. Their first offer was not accepted. However, they soon revised it and submitted a second (more expensive) proposal to the BBC around September/October.

Much to Matthews' 'bitter disappointment', his involvement with the project didn't go beyond this point. 'The way it was put to me was, "Oh everything's in the bag". I've heard it so many times before and since. I've had such a lot of this stuff.'

---

[406] BBC Enterprises only changed its name to BBC Worldwide in 1995, following extensive restructuring at the Corporation.

In September 1985, Matthews used his *Doctor Who* concept art as an illustration in his first art anthology book, *In Search of Forever*. He painted out his image of the TARDIS first, though, to avoid any copyright infringement. 'I can't remember getting paid anything for this, which is why I felt justified in using the illustration in one of my books,' he says.

HIGH HOPES

By November 1985, nine months on from their initial approach to the BBC, and with *Doctor Who* still away from the nation's television screens, negotiations for Coast to Coast's feature film were still ongoing.

By this stage, John Keeble, Director of Business Administration (and effective Chairman) at BBC Enterprises, had become involved. On 20 November, he wrote to Coast to Coast, asking for more information about their proposal.

Peter Litten wrote back later that week. He explained that since the BBC were asking for more money, Coast to Coast felt forced to increase the scale of their proposed production. To this end, some funding for the project appears to have been promised to them by the Sun Alliance insurance company.

No actual storyline was outlined to the BBC at this stage, but Litten did cite the names of a number of people who had 'agreed' to take part in the prospective film. The names included actors Caroline Munro[407], Denholm Elliott, Steven Berkoff, Tim Curry and even Laurence Olivier[408].

Composer Mike Oldfield was said to have agreed to take on the film's incidental music (including a rearrangement on the existing *Doctor Who* theme). Christopher Tucker, make-up artist on *The Elephant Man* (1980) and *The Company of Wolves* (1984), was reported to be handling the creation of various prosthetic creature designs and John Stears, late of *Star Wars*, was down to direct some of the visual effects shots.

Both Anton Furst[409] – who had also worked on *The Company of Wolves* – and Rodney Matthews were said to be handling the costume and production design, despite the fact that Matthews, at this time, understood his involvement in the project to have already come to an end.

How many of these people actually had *confirmed* their agreement is

---

[407] Munro agreed to work on the film early on and stayed with the project throughout all its many incarnations.

[408] Lord Olivier had already been invited to play a small part in the *Doctor Who* television series, in the 1984 story 'Revelation of the Daleks'. However, perhaps unsurprisingly, the offer to play a hideously deformed mutant living in a frozen pond didn't appeal very much to the world's most famous theatrical actor.

[409] Later to receive great plaudits for his work on Tim Burton's first *Batman* film in 1989.

possibly open to question. Many of them had certainly been approached, but others were, in practical terms, just on Coast to Coast's wishlist.

'A lot of it was hopeful speculation,' admits Litten. 'I mean, obviously, at that stage of developing ... there was nothing in writing. There can't be anything in writing until you get the rights anyway. So a lot of it was speculative – really to give [the BBC] a sense of the kind of thing that we were looking to do.'

Perhaps most encouragingly of all, Litten's letter also confirmed that Robert Holmes would be writing the screenplay for the movie, with Douglas Adams having agreed to act as script editor. By this time, Holmes was the most prolific and probably the most respected of all *Doctor Who* writers. He had first contributed scripts to the series in 1968. Following a number of well-received stories across the early '70s, he had then worked as the show's script editor from 1974 to 1977 (see Chapter Six). In 1984, he returned to *Doctor Who* after a few years away, and enjoyed great plaudits for his 'The Caves of Androzani'[410] teleplay. In 1985, he had just written a story ('The Two Doctors') for the recently-aired twenty-second season and had already been pencilled in to write for the twenty-third, just prior to its temporary cancellation. He was a very good choice for the film.

Douglas Adams had spoken to Litten early on about acting as script editor on the production, with some consideration even being given to Adams writing the film's screenplay itself. Adams' *Krikkitmen* project was fresh in his mind and he still had hopes of breaking into Hollywood with a big screen version of *The Hitchhiker's Guide to The Galaxy*.

'[Adams] was quite up for writing it,' says Litten. 'I can't remember why he didn't. Other commitments or something at the time ... Maybe he was just too expensive or something. I wouldn't be surprised.'

Given his reputation for being catastrophically bad at sticking to deadlines, it's unclear exactly how much help Adams would have actually been able to give the film anyway. In 1985, he was embarking on a new novel – *Dirk Gently's Holistic Detective Agency* – which was to take up a great deal of his time over the coming year, as he listened to the sound of deadlines whooshing over his head, one after the other.

Litten's letter to BBC Enterprises also spoke of his hopes that Richard Lester would direct the new picture. Lester was arguably Britain's most successful director then working in Hollywood. He had been behind *A Hard Day's Night* (1964), *Help!* (1965), *The Three Musketeers* (1973), *The Four Musketeers* (1973/4), *Robin and Marian* (1976) and the two most recent *Superman* films. Coast to Coast were aiming very high indeed.

On 22 November, John Keeble forwarded Litten's latest plans to Jonathan

---

[410] In 2009, 'The Caves of Androzani' was voted the best *Doctor Who* story of all time in a poll of nearly 7,000 viewers and fans.

Powell. Never one of *Doctor Who*'s greatest fans at the best of times, Powell shared none of Keeble's cautious enthusiasm for the Coast to Coast bid. On 2 December, he wrote back to Keeble via an internal BBC memo and was scathing in his criticism of the proposal, pouring scorn on Litten's entire enterprise and dismissing his ideas as fantasies. Even casting doubt over the truthfulness of Litten's letter, he stated his belief that none of the cited actors was actually likely to have agreed to take part in the film at all – certainly not without seeing a script. He also thought it unlikely that any of the technical crew would have given their backing to it without production dates. He particularly made reference to the proposed hiring of Richard Lester, stating that although lots of people may *want* Lester to work on their film, hoping he'd be interested didn't actually mean anything.

Overall, Powell believed Coast to Coast's words and promises to be nonsense. His advice was that the BBC should hold onto its cinematic rights in *Doctor Who* and make absolutely certain of the credentials of any interested parties before leasing them out. Never having heard of Peter 'Litton' [sic] before, he had great doubts over Coast to Coast's ability to successfully mount a production like this at all.

'[Powell] was a bit of a problem. I remember that,' says Litten. 'We did a meeting with him in the end or something, to try and win him over … I remember meeting him.'

Powell was also decidedly unimpressed with the choice of Robert Holmes as writer. Despite Holmes's considerable reputation, Powell was not a fan of his work on the series and shared little of the audience's great enthusiasm for him. In January 1986, when Holmes delivered his first scripts for the (much-delayed) new *Doctor Who* season, Powell ordered extensive rewrites to them, in spite of protests from the show's own production team. Holmes felt hurt by Powell's criticisms of him and embarked on the rewrites with reluctance.

Holmes was then battling terminal illness. He died in hospital of liver failure on 24 May 1986. His final scripts for the new *Doctor Who* season remained unfinished.

FIRST DRAFT

The meeting that Litten and Dugdale had with Jonathan Powell seems to have been enough to talk him round from his outright opposition to their film. In 1986, after many months' negotiation, Keeble finally agreed a deal with the filmmakers over the cinematic rights to *Doctor Who*. Daltenreys was officially registered as a limited company on 24 April 1986 and the attempt to make a feature film adaptation of *Doctor Who* formally began.

The finished contract did not give Daltenreys access to all of the rights pertaining to *Doctor Who* and explicitly excluded certain recurring characters and concepts, which the BBC were unable and/or unwilling to lease to them. These included the Daleks, the Cybermen[411] and the Doctor's robot dog, K-9[412]. The dramatic rights to the first were jointly held by the BBC and Terry Nation, and for the latter two, in common with almost every monster created for the show, by outside parties. The contract was, nevertheless, fairly generous in what it afforded the producers to work with and appears to have also included some (possibly informal) options for further films if Daltenreys/Coast to Coast[413] wished to pursue those in the future. The filmmakers' obligations to the BBC were largely concerned with maintaining the character and good-standing of the *Doctor Who* concept.

The rights were for a fixed term (about two or three years) and could be used only during that period. They could however be renewed; and there was every expectation that Coast to Coast would want to do this at least once, in order to give them enough time to get their project into production.

'When we signed that deal,' says Peter Litten, 'a lot of elements were done on a gentleman's handshake, which is sort of how the BBC used to be run. We, on our side, promised to protect the integrity of the *Doctor Who* brand. In other words, and this was never written, we'd always be honest to the spirit of *Doctor Who*.'

As part of the deal, Daltenreys paid an undisclosed sum to the BBC in exchange for the exclusive cinematic rights. The exact amount was never officially divulged, but reports have cited it to have been anywhere between £46,000 ($74,000) and £380,000 ($620,000). George Ezra even recalls, 'The BBC raised the purchase price to £400,000 plus VAT (which was, at that stage, 15%). So [the producers] had to find 460 grand.'

On 3 February 1987, Coast to Coast Productions was formally registered as a limited company and work on the film's pre-production began in earnest. There was a lot to do. Money had to be found (an estimated £1.5 million initially); stories and characters settled upon; and cast and crew approached. As early as July 1987, negotiations had apparently begun with Warner Chappell over the rights to use Ron Grainer's famed *Doctor Who* theme music. And all this work had to be done at a time when the British film industry was increasingly less subsidised. It was clear that none of it would be easy.

The team certainly had an eye on Hollywood and there was never any

---

[411] Although the BBC owned certain design aspects, the copyright to the overall character and concept of the Cybermen was owned by the two writers who first created them, Dr Kit Pedler and Gerry Davis.
[412] Writers Bob Baker and Dave Martin created K-9 and still held the copyright to the character. Only the design of the robot dog was BBC intellectual property.
[413] Although Daltenreys was their official company name, Coast to Coast was the banner under which the film was publicly promoted.

question that the picture would be anything other than a big-budget blockbuster. 'At that time, I'd just written a script for a chap called Robert Watts, who wanted to produce it,' says Mark Ezra. 'He was the actual guy who produced *Raiders [of the Lost Ark]* with Steven Spielberg, working for George Lucas. So, I was working with him at Thorn EMI, who were like the second studio in those days. So, I had access to funds and very good contacts with people who were interested in doing a big-budget film – big budgets at that time being around 15 million.'

With Robert Holmes' illness and subsequent death, it seems that there was never sufficient time for any serious consideration of his writing the screenplay to Coast to Coast's film. The earliest script to be attached to the project was one written by Ezra, based on ideas from Dugdale and Litten. This was written while negotiations with the BBC where still ongoing. 'In order to raise the money,' says Ezra, 'people want to know that there's a script that will work. So, we put our heads together and I did a draft.'

Ezra's script was an expansive fantasy epic, which although straying far from the tone of the original television series, was nonetheless designed to be a continuation of the same saga. In his story, the Doctor was to come up against a power-mad cyborg called Varnax (a Litten and Dugdale idea) who plans to invade Earth. Varnax needs to gather together a number of special 'transporter crystals' in order to summon his army to Earth via a gateway at Stonehenge. The Doctor goes on an intergalactic quest to find the crystals before Varnax can get to them[414]. It was an early version of this idea that Rodney Matthews saw when working on his concept art.

The script made use of a number of concepts and characters lifted directly from the television series, including the Doctor's old friend Brigadier Alastair Gordon Lethbridge-Stewart[415] and K-9[416]. However, it diverged radically from the television series in the way it dealt with the Doctor's background. In Ezra's telling, the Doctor effectively lives on the planet Gallifrey and is a part of the establishment there (albeit a reluctant one). He has friends there and clearly spends a lot of his time there, obeying instructions issued to him by the Time Lords. This is, needless to say, very

---

[414] Waiting for Varnax to arrive and then hitting him on the head with something heavy, although more logical, would probably have made for a rather short film.

[415] Played by actor Nicholas Courtney and created by Mervyn Haisman and Henry Lincoln (see Chapter Four), Brigadier Lethbridge-Stewart was the longest serving of all the television series' supporting characters. He first appeared in 1968 and last in 2008. The series killed off the character in 2011, shortly after the death of Courtney. In 1985, when Ezra wrote his script, Lethbridge-Stewart was a semi-regular guest-star in the series. He'd last appeared on screen in 1983 and would next return in 1989.

[416] As mentioned, Coast to Coast didn't actually have the rights to use K-9, as they would probably have found out in due course had the script progressed further.

different from the premise of the television series, where the Doctor is a renegade who shuns his own people in order to wander the universe, 'cut off … without friends or protection.'[417]

Surprisingly, and probably coincidentally, Ezra's script also bears some passing similarity to Douglas Adams' *Krikkitmen* pitch of a few years before – similarly making use of the 'quest' narrative as an excuse to throw the Doctor around an assortment of different times and places. Overall, it is perhaps closest in tone to films like *Masters of the Universe* (1987), which was also in pre-production at around this time. It also, quite deliberately, makes several nods in the direction of George Lucas's *Star Wars* trilogy, which had only recently been 'completed' with the release of *The Return of the Jedi* in 1983.

'*Doctor Who* had gone a bit downhill,' considers Ezra. 'Our approach, at that stage, was to sort of do something that was going to be slightly more of a *Raiders of the Lost Ark* type of film, but using time travel as well.'

Ezra's script remained in semi-active pre-production until at least August 1987, being used to help with the difficult task of touting for potential investment. However, by this point Ezra himself had effectively moved away from the project.

'I did a draft and, I think, half a second draft – at which point things sort of got a bit tricky,' he says. 'I went off and made a film in Africa – quite a big feature film … We didn't fall out or anything like that … I went off and did other things, as one does in life.'

Even though Ezra was off the project, Lytten and Dugdale still continued with their plans for a *Doctor Who* film. However, events relating to the television series were fast catching up with them …

---

[417] From *Doctor Who* – '100,000 BC': 'An Unearthly Child' – BBC1 (23 November 1963)

Doctor Who – The Movie[418]
Draft One
By
Mark Ezra
From a story by George Dugdale and Peter Litten

PLOT SYNOPSIS

A vast warship is orbiting high above the planet Trufador. The ship belongs to the powerful warlord Zargon. On board, Zargon is issuing a final ultimatum to the defeated people of Trufador. They must surrender to him or die. As Zargon finishes his speech, we see a familiar blue police box standing nearby. Meanwhile, a chained figure is dragged into the room – his face obscured by a hood. It is the Doctor.

The Doctor's time rotor has been stolen by Zargon and the warlord is keeping him as his prisoner. He orders that the hood be removed from the Doctor's head, so that he might witness the destruction of the planet below. Zargon proposes to fire a powerful 'Doomsday Weapon' at Trufador. It will kill all life on the surface.

However, just as Zargon makes ready to fire, the Doctor miraculously breaks free from his handcuffs and snatches back his time rotor. Although it is against the laws of the Time Lords, the Doctor uses the reclaimed time rotor to create a black hole, and Zargon's Doomsday Weapon is sucked into the void.

The Doctor arrives back on Gallifrey in the TARDIS and is immediately arrested by the Time Lords.

Meanwhile, many millions of miles away, the barren planet of Centros faces an imminent apocalypse, as a bloated and dying sun slowly expands towards it. And yet, the world of Centros is not quite uninhabited. Walking across its scorching surface are two lone figures.

Centros is the last resting place of the Voyager space-probe, and when our two figures discover its wreckage, they take it back to their leader Varnax. Still

---

[418] Ezra's script was initially untitled, although numerous titles were attached to the production as the film progressed through development.

visible on the wrecked probe is a plaque showing Earth's astronomical position in the galaxy. It is this plaque that the two scavengers hope will be of interest to Varnax.

Varnax *is* interested, but not in the probe's two salvagers. He orders the men killed and charges his two associates, the glamorous Morgana and the brutish cyborg Neglos[419], with carrying out the job.

Varnax himself is a cyborg – no longer entirely organic, nor entirely robotic either. He is 'a vile travesty of a human being – more machine than man; his deformed, twisted frame is supported by a complex arrangement of tubes, cables and pistons that give life to his otherwise useless body.'[420]

Elsewhere on the bleak surface of Centros, two young rebels, Onyx and Kalcis, plot an attack on Varnax's base with explosives.

Within his base, Varnax rallies his followers, promising them that he will soon lead them back to their rightful home again. Back to Gallifrey.

Unknown to Onyx, Kalcis and the other rebels, Varnax knows all about their plans to destroy him, but is hoping to use their plot to his own advantage. He realises that they are likely to seek support for their insurrection from the Time Lords. They hope to capture a cosmic transmitter and broadcast a message to Gallifrey. This will play into Varnax's hands however, luring the Time Lords to Centros and directly into a trap.

Heavily armed, the rebels succeed in reaching Varnax's transmitter (as planned), but Kalcis is killed in an act of self-sacrifice, helping his comrades to escape from the castle.

Back on Gallifrey, the Doctor is standing trial, charged with breaking the strict laws of non-intervention laid down by the Time Lords.[421]

The Time Lords squabble amongst themselves over what the Doctor's fate should be. They all agree about the severity of his crimes. The Doctor argues that the laws should be changed and that Time Lords have a moral duty to use their powers to fight evil in the cosmos. His rhetoric falls largely on deaf ears and the Time Lords pass a guilty verdict anyway.

Meanwhile, Neglos and his followers are hunting Onyx and the other rebels with a pack of savage multi-eyed tracking animals. Onyx manages to reach the rebel encampment (a cavern) and is reunited with Lois – another of the rebel fighters. Onyx has brought with him the captured transmitter and uses it to send a distress signal to Gallifrey. He has only just finished sending

---

[419] Neglos is not to be confused with Meglos, the villain of a 1980 *Doctor Who* television story of the same name.

[420] All quotes taken from *The Nth Doctor* by Jean-Marc and Randy Lofficier – iUniverse Books (2003) p.15

[421] This would be the third time that the Doctor had faced such charges. The Time Lords of the television series had him in the dock on two separate occasions: in 'The War Games' (1969) and 'The Trial of a Time Lord' (1986). In both instances, his defence was similar to that which he gives here.

his message when Neglos and his retinue burst into the rebels' hideout. All of the rebels manage to escape, with the single exception of Onyx, who stays behind with a small furry creature called Pog.

Before being taken prisoner, Onyx attaches a small device to Pog's collar – containing a recording of his story. On Gallifrey, the Doctor finds his TARDIS in the docking bay. Its time rotor is being removed by a hard-nosed mechanic called Cora. The TARDIS is being decommissioned, prior to being sent onto the 'Museum of Primitive Transport'.

The Doctor notices Onyx's incoming SOS on the TARDIS's instruments and manages to cajole Cora into letting him set course for the planet Centros. Cora is decidedly reluctant to leave Gallifrey (having never left before), but the Doctor enthuses her with the idea of a 'vacation'.

The TARDIS lands the Doctor and Cora deep in the wilderness of Centros. Once there, the pair almost immediately encounter something called a Woog – an apparently sweet and cuddly creature that suddenly transforms into a ferocious monster without warning. Overcoming the creature, they are then captured by Varnax's henchman and taken to his fortress.

Inside the citadel's subterranean foundry, Varnax is attending to the final repairs of his own TARDIS – a sinister black model. Brought before the warlord, the Doctor immediately recognises Varnax as a figure from Gallifrey's past. It emerges that the renegade Varnax has used up all of his natural regenerations and is now in his thirteenth and final incarnation. Varnax plans to cannibalise the time rotor from the Doctor's TARDIS to use in his own craft. He will then leave Centros for good.

A chained Onyx is dragged in by Neglos. However, in that moment and to everybody's great surprise, what appears to be a clone of the Doctor, looking only a little older, suddenly bursts onto the scene and rescues Onyx. Moments later, a confused Onyx then pops back into existence in the middle of the room – reappearing out of thin air.

With nobody able to give any explanation for this brief series of events, Neglos throws Onyx into a cryogenic capsule, freezes him and has his body launched into deep space, where he will slowly drift away into Centros's dying sun. The Doctor and Cora are chained to the ground to await a flow of molten metal, which will eventually incinerate them. Varnax and Morgana depart in Varnax's re-energised TARDIS, together with the Doctor's stolen time rotor.

The Doctor and Cora are then unexpectedly rescued by Pog, who diverts the flow of molten metal away from the two Gallifreyans. As they escape, the foundry collapses behind them.

While the Doctor fends off Neglos, Cora throws together a makeshift time rotor from assorted bits of machinery left behind by Varnax[422]. The pair then depart in the TARDIS, taking Pog with them.

---

[422] It does beg the question why Varnax himself didn't do this.

Once on their way, the Doctor notices the recording device clipped to Pog's collar and plays back Onyx's message. Onyx explains the plight of his people and Varnax's plans to colonise Earth. Varnax has discovered the location of three powerful 'transporter crystals' that will enable his army to descend on Earth in vast numbers. Unless the Doctor can prevent it, humanity will suffer the same desolation as Onyx and his people. The message then cuts out before it is finished.

The Doctor pilots the TARDIS toward the expanding sun of Centros to rescue Onxy from the cryogenic pod. After a dangerous chase through the vortex, in which both the Doctor and Cora noticeably age, they finally manage to bring the pod on board. However, they are too late. Inside, they find that Onyx is dead.

However, still desperate to discover the rest of his message, the Doctor decides to take the TARDIS to a point in time just before Onyx was placed in the pod. He does this, arriving back in the foundry just as we saw him do earlier on.

Onyx tells the Doctor that the transporter site is located at Stonehenge. He also gives the Doctor a part of a map, detailing the location of the other crystals. Onyx asks the Doctor to reveal to him if he survives his jettisoning into space. The Doctor tells him that he does not. Onyx returns to the foundry anyway. Going to his certain death, he is hopeful that his people might live on.

The Doctor, Cora and Pog next travel on to the Smithsonian Institute in Washington DC in the present day. One of the interns working there is Mike Bradley, a 16-year-old comic-book fan, who is being victimised by one of his colleagues, Gilbert Chubley. As Varnax's warriors burst into the museum, the Doctor and Cora run into Mike and pull him out of their way.

The Doctor soon determines that the missing fragment of Onyx's map – which Varnax's people have also come looking for – is probably being kept in the Smithsonian's archives. Proceeding to the vaults, they bump into Chubley, who tries to stop them taking the Smithsonian's fragment of the map. During a tussle, the fragment is ripped and a small piece is left in Chubley's hand. Chubley passes out. Varnax and his cronies enter the room and take the torn fragment from Chubley.

The Doctor and Cora have hidden the TARDIS in a Victorian exhibition[423] and return there with Mike. All three depart in the ship. The Doctor sets the co-ordinates for Victorian England.

---

[423] Quite how the TARDIS was meant to be any less incongruous here is a bit puzzling. Even if we accept the presence of an exhibition dedicated to Victorian Britain in an American museum, there's still no reason for there to be a police box there. Police Boxes didn't start appearing in the UK until the 1920s and the first of the MacKenzie Trench-designed boxes (on which the TARDIS shape is based) didn't arrive until 1929.

Leaving Pog behind in the TARDIS, the three travellers arrive at the Tower of London. Neglos and his men are also on the scene, preparing to steal the crown jewels. The Doctor tries to warn the captain of the guard and almost succeeds in convincing him that he is actually Sherlock Holmes. But it's too late. Neglos already has both the crown and the sceptre. The Doctor and Mike pursue the alien across the battlements. Neglos gets away, but not before the Doctor manages to wrest the sceptre from him

Meanwhile, back in the TARDIS, Pog is exploring the ship's sprawling interior and accidentally activates the Doctor's slumbering robot dog K-9.

The Doctor attempts to set off for their next destination, but Pog has damaged the time rotor in his enthusiasm and the TARDIS crash-lands on board Christopher Columbus's ship, the *Santa Maria*, in 1492.

Cora fixes the TARDIS's controls and they travel on to Peru in 1572, where Spanish Conquistadors led by Captain Mendoza capture them in the jungle around Machu Picchu. The Conquistadors are here to loot gold from the Incas. While Cora fends off the advances of a group of lusty Spaniards, the Doctor and Mike are taken to an Incan Temple, where they see a giant crystal skull[424] atop a statue. The crystal skull is one of the transporter crystals that they've been looking for.

The Doctor and Mike manage to get hold of the crystal skull, but are then recaptured. However, by now Cora has freed a number of the Inca and a battle breaks out between them and the Conquistadors. During the commotion, Varnax arrives and fights with the Doctor over the crystal skull. Varnax uses his time rotor to slow down time in a bid to get hold of the crystal, but fails to snatch it before the Doctor.

The Doctor and his friends leave with the crystal, the sight of which frightens Pog. Following Varnax's timestream, the Doctor's next stop is an arid future Earth of dust and sand. They find Varnax's TARDIS, but it is deserted and there is no sign of the missing third crystal that they seek.

Leaving Varnax's ship, the trio are captured by insectoid robots called Sandroids and taken to a woman named Axis, the Queen of Aquatia. Aquatia is a city built around an oasis in the desert. Its people offer the travellers some water, but recognising how desperately low their supplies are, Cora declines. Axis then takes the Doctor down to the city's great Ice Chamber,

---

[424] Despite what legend (and Indiana Jones) tells us, there's no conclusive evidence that crystal skulls were ever manufactured in ancient South America. The oldest crystal skull ever to be authenticated is a 19th Century European fake. Today, the whole idea of the pre-Columbian crystal skulls is believed to be largely a Victorian myth. However, even if it were true, it would still be unusual to find one in an Incan setting (as here). Most crystal skull myths are either Mayan or Aztec in origin. Ezra's script could be seen as somewhat prophetic, though, as in 1992 an unattributed crystal skull was donated to the Smithsonian Institute, where the Doctor and Mike first meet in this story.

where the rest of its population have been frozen in suspended animation. Among the frozen bodies is that of Axis's husband, the founder of the colony. The next transporter crystal is held in his hands. Without warning, Cora suddenly runs forward and smashes through the glass covering the body. She snatches away the crystal before the Doctor can intervene. There is a struggle and Cora's face is torn away, revealing that she is actually a robot. The Sandroids try to stop the robot Cora, but at that moment Varnax's TARDIS appears and spirits her and the crystal away.

Inside Varnax's ship, the real, flesh and blood Cora is being kept prisoner by Varnax, who now has all of the various crystals he needs.

Escaping from pursuing Sandroids, the Doctor and Mike take the TARDIS to 20th Century Earth. They arrive on an English golf course, where the Doctor's old friend Brigadier Alastair Gordon Lethbridge-Stewart is playing golf with his wife Dorothy[425] and some of their friends. The game is interrupted when the Doctor turns up, asking for the Brigadier's help.

Cora is lashed to one of the standing stones of Stonehenge, while Varnax lays out his transporter crystals. Some distance away, the Brigadier has arranged for the site to be surrounded by an armed taskforce.

As the sun rises, light streams through the crystals, creating a forcefield around the stone circle. The Brigadier asks the Doctor wearily, 'Don't you know any alien creatures who aren't immune to shell fire?'[426]

Unable to break the forcefield, the Doctor and Mike crawl underneath it. The Doctor unties Cora, while Mike uses the Brigadier's gun to fend off Varnax's lackeys. The Doctor disables the forcefield by deflecting the light beams with some mirrors, and the Brigadier gives the order to advance. Varnax tries to attack the Doctor with the crystal skull, but it shatters. Varnax then leaves in his TARDIS with Morgana. Alien energy swirls about Stonehenge, and Neglos is sucked up into the sky.

The storm of energy finally subsides and Cora is found lying dead, but one of Pog's tears brings her back to life. The three crystals have vanished – restored to their proper places in space and time – and the Doctor travels to Centros to rescue Onyx's people from their doomed planet. When he returns to Gallifrey, he finds that Varnax is holding the Time Lords to ransom,

---

[425] At the time this script was written, the Brigadier's wife had not appeared in the *Doctor Who* television series. However, in 1989, the series contradicted Ezra's Dorothy character when it introduced a different wife for the Brigadier in a story called 'Battlefield'. This was Doris (played by Angela Douglas), who had been previously mentioned as an old flame of the Brigadier's in the 1974 story 'Planet of the Spiders'. Behind the scenes, Brigadier actor Nicholas Courtney held the view that Doris was the character's second wife, and that his first was called Fiona.

[426] This is an almost exact retread of one of the Brigadier's lines from the 1974/5 *Doctor Who* television story 'Robot': 'You know, just once I'd like to meet an alien menace that wasn't immune to bullets.'

threatening to destroy their world. He voluntarily gives himself up to Varnax and surrenders his TARDIS in order to save Gallifrey.

Varnax has Morgana use a mind probe[427] on the Doctor to obtain the secrets of the 'Time Warp' – a source of unimaginable power that can transport whole armies through time and space.

The Doctor says that Varnax can access the Time Warp by a simple adjustment of the time rotor. Varnax does so and the great black void of the Time Warp opens up before them. However, what Varnax doesn't know is that the Doctor has used the Time Warp to store Zargon's ultimate weapon (from the start of the film). Zargon's missile comes barrelling out of the void towards them.

The Doctor has somehow managed to get hold of one of Varnax's transporter crystals and uses it to transport himself out of harm's way before the missile hits. Varnax and Morgana are left behind to meet their deaths.

[427] Another hang-over from the television series, mind probes had previously appeared in 'Day of the Daleks' (1972), 'Frontier in Space' (1973) and 'The Five Doctors' (1983).

8
The Motionless Picture
'Doctor Who – The Movie'
(1987-1992)

TRYING TIMES

By the time full development on Coast to Coast's film began in 1987, *Doctor Who* had weathered the storm of Michael Grade's 'almost cancellation' of 1985 and had once again returned to BBC1 as a weekly television series. However, it was not quite the same show it had once been.

Production of the 1986 season (the twenty-third) had been a chaotic and miserable experience for those involved. Originally scheduled (and partly scripted) as a series of 13 x 45 minute episodes, it was radically rethought when the series was taken off the air, with a number of stories abandoned before production even began. When a twenty-third series finally was given the go-ahead it was with a signficantly reduced allocation of only 14 x 25 minute episodes – more than a 50 percent cut in the usual annual airtime. To add to the difficulties, the season's lead writer Robert Holmes died before finishing his work on it, and script editor Eric Saward resigned following a very public falling-out with producer John Nathan-Turner. Saward's script for the final episode (based on a Holmes idea), had to be scrapped when Saward refused to allow his friend's original ending to be rewritten, and an eleventh-hour replacement had to be commissioned from writers, Pip and Jane Baker, who had no knowledge of how the season-spanning story arc was originally intended to end[428]. Pretty much anything that could have gone wrong for *Doctor Who* in 1986 did go wrong.

Perhaps understandably, the season was not very well received, and ratings plummeted from an average of 7.12 million for the 1985 season to an average of 4.80 million for 1986. Perplexingly, rather than appoint a new producer or make other changes in the *Doctor Who* office, BBC executives then took the decision to sack lead actor Colin Baker, to whom Nathan-Turner was reluctantly obliged to give the bad news in October 1986.

---

[428] For copyright reasons, the Bakers were not allowed to see any of Saward's original script for the final episode. A BBC lawyer attended production meetings to make sure this did not happen.

The *Doctor Who* television series reached a low ebb. The budget and episode count had been slashed. One of its leading writers had died. The script editor had resigned. The lead actor had been sacked. The ratings had slumped

Tasked with picking up the pieces for the 1987 season, Nathan-Turner recruited a new script editor, Andrew Cartmel, and a new lead actor in the form of Sylvester McCoy. Cartmel arrived with an enthusiastic 'masterplan' for the series' future and an entirely new writing team slowly nursed the ailing show back to something resembling good health, at least as considered by some of the show's remaining fans. However, the show was scheduled in a 'graveyard' slot opposite ITV's hugely popular soap opera 'Coronation Street' and given minimal promotion, and its ratings failed to stage a significant recovery. Not when *Coronation Street* had the excitement of Hilda Ogden falling victim to a violent robbery and Gail Tilsley sleeping with her husband's Australian cousin.

It was against this grim background that Daltenreys attempted to mount their *Doctor Who* feature film. With the show's public profile at an all-time low, it certainly wasn't the best of climates in which to do so. And with a target release date of summer 1989, there was still a lot that needed to be decided upon – not least of all, a replacement for Mark Ezra's script.

A NEW START

On 29 May 1987 there was another name change for Daltenreys, with the registration of Dr Who – The Movie Limited as the company's new official trading name. Although this was barely used in any public capacity – Coast to Coast Productions continued to be the company's public identity – the reformatting of the name coincided with a fresh push to get the film into full pre-production.

'One of the problems,' says Litten, 'was that although *Doctor Who* had a very significant fanbase in the States, it certainly wasn't widely known. It was only playing off PBS[429]. It wasn't a no-brainer in terms of why people would go to see it. That made it a more complex sell.'

However, by autumn 1987, news of the project had at least *reached* America, with a report in the *Oklahoman* newspaper, quoting the producers' intentions 'to produce the big budget film for Coast to Coast Productions.'[430] Of course, despite the publicity, there was still no concrete backing from the USA.

---

[429] *Doctor Who* was then being shown in rotation on a large number of small PBS channels. By 1986, American viewers were enjoying regular repeats (some edited) of all of the full stories that had been produced between 1970 and 1985. There were also broadcasts of some 22 black and white stories from the 1960s.
[430] From the *Oklahoman* (11 September 1987)

Vital to securing investment would be a workable script to arouse studio interest. Following Mark Ezra's departure from the project, the producers turned to experienced television writer Johnny Byrne. Then working on the BBC's *One By One*, a light-hearted drama series set in a zoo, Byrne was still best known for his work as a writer on the hit Sunday night drama *All Creatures Great and Small*. Originally run between 1978 and 1983, it had recently been resurrected for a 1985 Christmas special, with. Byrne just about to take over as the programme's full-time story consultant on a new season of episodes. More relevantly, Byrne had also written three *Doctor Who* television stories[431] in the early 1980s – 'The Keeper of Traken' (1981), 'Arc of Infinity' (1983) and 'Warriors of the Deep' (1984). Although not among the best received stories, neither were they among the worst, and Byrne's work on the show had come to an end only following his falling out with the then script editor Eric Saward. As an additional qualification, Byrne had also worked on the glossy ITV science fiction series *Space: 1999* (1975).

'After the first draft, George and Peter felt they needed someone who could project a certain kind of character-driven drama,' remembered Byrne. 'Apparently they contacted the agencies, and when my CV eventually flopped through the letter box, George said "Let's talk to that guy."'[432]

'Mark Ezra wrote a very early draft,' says Litten. 'Johnny Byrne came on the scene somewhat later and he was involved on a number of drafts … He was the primary writer on it.'

Byrne recalled that Litten, Dugdale and he 'worked very closely. We restructured the whole thing and a completely new concept evolved.'[433]

Between 1988 and 1991, there were at least four substantially different *Doctor Who* movie scripts, all written by Johnny Byrne. The title attached to Byrne's earliest treatment was *The Time Lord*. However, later drafts were known as *Last of the Time Lords*[434] or *The Last Time Lord*. And Daltenreys' own favoured title for the film was *Doctor Who – Last of the Time Lords*.

Byrne's early drafts for the movie took most of their basic ideas from Ezra's script as a starting point, but reworked them. Remaining virtually unchanged was Varnax – the power-mad central villain, originally created by Dugdale and Litten back in 1985. He was clearly a character Daltenreys were keen to retain. A number of other supporting characters and settings were brought over from the earlier script as well.

---

[431] Byrne did start work on a fourth *Doctor Who* story, 'The Guardians of Prophecy', intended for the programme's 1985 series, but it was ultimately abandoned. Eventually it re-emerged as a straight-to-CD audio drama in 2012.

[432] From *DWB (Dream Watch Bulletin)* – Issue 72 (December 1989) p.13

[433] From *DWB (Dream Watch Bulletin)* – Issue 72 (December 1989) p.13

[434] In 2007, 'Last of the Time Lords' was used as the title for the final episode of that year's *Doctor Who* television series. Russell T Davies wrote the episode.

Byrne's scripts for the film are also not too dissimilar in tone from Mark Ezra's. Again they translated *Doctor Who* into the space epic format more familiar to viewers of the *Star Wars* franchise and the Doctor is far more a part of established society on Gallifrey than he ever was on television. In the *Doctor Who* television series, the Doctor's home planet is the main setting of only four full stories. For the series' new movie incarnation however, it was always going to be a key part of the Doctor's life.

Byrne's re-versioning saw Varnax out to collect a series of 'fusion crystals' that will make him immortal. The crystals are scattered about various different planets throughout time and space. Once Varnax has collected them all together, he plans to detonate a planet in order that his transformation into an immortal should be made permanent.

'Central to the *Doctor Who* format is the nature of the conflict,' explained Byrne, 'a struggle between good and evil; the Doctor taking sides with the weak, the innocent, the threatened, against the forces of the strong, the powerful, the downright evil. This kind of epic conflict is the crux of *Doctor Who*. Every story has pretty much been a variation on this theme, a theme that has been considerably amplified in the script for the first movie ... personified in a way that we have never seen before, simply because it was not possible to do so in the context of the TV [show].'[435]

Considering Byrne's experience on the television series it is perhaps surprising how far his vision for the *Doctor Who* movie strayed from what had been previously established. In Byrne's script, not only does the Doctor have a planetary 'home', but we are also introduced to a woman with whom he once had an intimate relationship. And finally, perhaps most un-*Doctor Who*-like of all, the Doctor and his friends are seen to be directly responsible for the sometimes gruesome deaths of a number of their enemies, with the Doctor shooting several guards and the Doctor's niece, Cora, slicing off some poor unfortunate's head.

Byrne admitted he had 'taken liberties with some aspect of the traditional format', but justified these by arguing that they were 'not at variance with our understanding of the character and his universe – they have, at the very least, extended the formidable corpus of knowledge that already exists concerning *Doctor Who*.'[436]

Byrne's scripts retained much less obvious continuity with the television series than Ezra's. In terms of established supporting characters, K-9 had now been removed from the story and only the Brigadier remained from Ezra's draft. However, the society of the Time Lords can be seen to have been drawn from Byrne's previous Gallifrey-based teleplay for 1983's 'Arc of Infinity'. Although the similarity to Douglas Adams' *Krikkitmen* pitch was

---

[435] From *DWB (Dream Watch Bulletin)* – Issue 72 (December 1989) p.13
[436] From *DWB (Dream Watch Bulletin)* – Issue 72 (December 1989) p.13

now even more noticeable than with Ezra's version, as before this was almost certainly just a coincidence.

Of Byrne's new characters, probably the most prominent creation was that of the Doctor's new best friend, Gonjii. Byrne saw Gonjii as 'A tragic heroic figure, a mature character who is on a level with the Doctor in terms of respect and abilities. We need someone like this to reveal new aspects of the Doctor's character, aspects that are difficult to explore in his traditional interaction with the companion/s, which has, by its nature, tended to be overly paternal. A character like this – Hans Solo [sic] in *Star Wars* is another – can provide a vital bridge in movie sequels of this kind. As to whether this particular character will return in a second story though is still an open question at this point.'

Very dark, quite violent, and revealing far more about the 'mysteries' of the Doctor than we were ever allowed on television, Byrne's reworking of Ezra's script was deliberately designed for an audience who had never heard of *Doctor Who*, and it justified the jettisoning of much of the show's mythos on those grounds. Whether it replaced that mythos with something better or worse is debateable, but it certainly made the film a far more 'Hollywood' kind of production. And it was to Hollywood that Dugdale and Litten soon travelled in search of distribution and co-production deals. In December 1987, the BBC even gave them a full set of videocassettes of the programme's most recently concluded run of episodes (Season 24), in order to give potential US investors an idea of its nature.

'You can't make a big budget film and not be utterly driven by what the American market will do,' says Litten.

However, as 1988 arrived, Daltenreys and Coast to Coast were still no closer to getting together enough finance to produce their film, even with a summer '89 premiere still being touted. And increasing public pressure wasn't helping.

In March 1988, press rumours even suggested that the film had actually entered active production. Of course, it hadn't. In fact, no director had even been attached to the project, although Litten and Dugdale had, by this stage, decided not to direct the film themselves, as they had at one point considered.

Even with no director at the helm, Daltenreys had approached other crew members, partly to assist in pitching idea to the States. One of the first of these to be publicly named was visual effects artist Paul Catling.

'I was involved … on a creature design basis for a while,' recalls Catling. 'I even went to the States with George and Peter for a short while. I think they were having meetings there. I was doing some drawings for a couple of months – something like that.'

Dugdale, Litten and Catling hawked the project around a number of American studios. No deals were actually settled, but the new script wasn't entirely unsuccessful in attracting interest. However, some of the suggestions being made by certain studios were, to say the least, unusual.

'We turned down a number of offers we had from Paramount,' says Litten. 'One, believe it or not, was for Michael Jackson to play the Doctor, and the other was for Bill Cosby to play the Doctor. On both counts, we turned down those deals – very lucrative deals they would have been too ...'

TARDIS CREW

Around summer '88, Litten and Dugdale were back in America, meeting with three or four major distributors.

In July, press rumours reported back that '*Doctor Who – The Movie*' could be in cinemas by either autumn or Christmas 1989. The June 1988 edition of fan magazine *DWB* (*Doctor Who Bulletin*) asserted: 'The final draft of the script was completed in mid-June and the financing of the film is in place ... Pre-production commences in September-October with shooting starting in January or February 1989.'[437] Needless to say, all these rumours were, at best, massively optimistic.

Meanwhile, still without a director, Daltenreys pressed on, approaching various potential crew members about becoming involved. Many were excited at the proposition of taking the Doctor to the big screen.

By August, Daltenreys had asked Allan Cameron to become production designer on the picture. Cameron had carved out a prestigious career for himself since moving to film work in the early '80s, having previously gained impressive television credits on *The Naked Civil Servant* (1975), produced by Verity Lambert. On film, he'd been art director on *The French Lieutenant's Woman* (1981) and production designer on *Nineteen Eighty-Four* (1984), *Highlander* (1986), *The Fourth Protocol* (1987) and (most recently) *Willow* (1988).

'We were very keen for him to design it,' asserts Litten. 'He did quite a lot of preliminary work with us. He certainly came out to Thailand on all the recces we did there. We were also working on another picture with him as well, simultaneously ... He was a very fine designer.'

'I was doing another project, which didn't go through,' remembers Cameron. 'I was in Thailand and places like that with them and they were talking about the *Doctor Who* film to me then ... I can remember sitting in a hotel somewhere in Thailand and discussing it with them ... Then the project I was on in Thailand fell through and I didn't hear from them again.'

In August, news broke that Mike Southon[438] had been approached to be

---

437 From *DWB* (*Doctor Who Bulletin*) – Issue 55 (June 1988) p.1
438 Southon would finally get a job as director of photography for *Doctor Who* on the television series in 2012.

director of photography on the film. However, nearly 25 years on, Southon can only 'vaguely remember one meeting' with Daltenreys, and the offer wasn't followed up any further.

Also reported around this time was the bringing on board of special effects artist Bill Pearson to look after the movie's extensive miniature work. Having worked on both *Alien* (1979) and *Flash Gordon* (1980), Pearson was an obvious choice and was also known to Litten from his time working at the BBC Visual Effects Department. Ultimately, however, it was not Pearson who was chosen by Daltenreys to handle the modelwork, but another effects man, Ron Thornton, who produced a number of pieces of work to help with the difficult job of selling the picture to distributors. Thornton's movie CV included *Critters* (1986) and *Spaceballs* (1987), but he had also worked for the BBC on both *Doctor Who* and *Blake's 7* (1977-1981), which was where he'd met Litten. 'He did a lot of early modelmaking for us,' says Litten. 'I was at the BBC with him. At the time we were all at Visual Effects together.'

As the year drew to a close, there was still no firm sign of production starting, and the originally pencilled-in filming dates were looking increasingly unlikely. To be fair, none of this was terribly unusual in filmmaking at a time when movies routinely took several years to reach the cinema. However, with the extra scrutiny that a *Doctor Who* film attracted from many sections of the press, the public were getting impatient to see the long-touted production move out of the development hell it seemed to be stuck in.

The rumour-mill continued to churn unabated over December 1988 as *Witch Mountain* (1975-1978) and *Biggles* (1986) director John Hough was (wrongly) touted as the film's latest director. In spite of the speculation, as 1988 ended there was still no concrete confirmation of either a distributor or a director. Similarly, casting for the picture was still described as 'up in the air.'[439]

THE REEL McCOY?

The possible identity of the actor who would star as the Doctor in Daltenreys' film was a constant feature of almost all the press reports . With the series' concept allowing for its central character to be played by literally *any* actor, the speculation over who the next actor might be has always been intense. 'We never stopped thinking and talking to people about it,' says Litten. 'Across the period of time, we spoke to a good number of people.'

Casting was the focus of one of the very first stories to appear relating to the film, when certain tabloids suggested that Tim Curry was in the running for the lead. Some even reported the rumour that Curry had already turned

---

[439] From *Doctor Who Magazine* – Issue 135 (April 1988) p.7

down the part. Unlike a lot of the subsequent speculation, this rumour (possibly by accident) did actually have some grounding in fact.

The very first person to be officially proposed as the Doctor had indeed been Tim Curry. That was way back in November 1985, when Coast to Coast were still trying to persuade BBC Enterprises to sell them the rights. 'That was very early stages,' remembers Litten. 'I thought he could have been really good actually – the younger version of Tim Curry.'

In 1988, Sylvester McCoy was happily getting ready for his third television season as the Doctor, with no indication that he'd be leaving any time soon. However, as in the mid-'60s, it seems that no serious consideration was ever given to retaining the BBC's own Doctor for the big-screen adaptation, and Daltenreys were keen to have their own man – and it was a *male* actor they were looking for – in the job.

The decision not to use McCoy disappointed John Nathan-Turner, who was then producing *Doctor Who*'s twenty-fifth television season and celebrating its silver anniversary by invading Greenwich gasworks with a fleet of Cybermen[440].

He commented: '[I am] very keen that Sylvester should appear as the Doctor, because it is misleading to have one person on the television and someone quite different in the cinema'[441]

'Basically, when the licence was drawn up,' the producer explained, ' I wasn't invited to put in any additional clauses, because [BBC] Enterprises reckoned by the time it came to fruition, I'd be gone from the programme. I would have attempted to persuade George and Peter to use the current Doctor.'[442]

'The problem is,' he continued, 'we shoot our episodes all through the summer, and the filmmakers want to shoot in April to June for a November release.'

August 1988 brought with it an announcement that a big-screen Doctor had finally been cast. However, Daltenreys remained 'intent on keeping his identity secret.'[443] Who this person was, was never actually made clear, and nobody ever owned up to being the actor in question. However, a variety of newspapers and media outlets were, of course, ready with the names of a whole host of possible candidates – some more likely than others.

American newspaper columnist Marilyn Beck reported rumours that either John Cleese or Albert Finney was lined up to play the Doctor in a film

---

[440] For the location recording of the three-part anniversary story *Silver Nemesis* (1988).
[441] From *Doctor Who – 25 Glorious Years* by Peter Haining – W H Allen & Co.(1988) p.70
[442] From *Doctor Who Magazine* – Issue 141 (October 1988) p.9
[443] From *DWB (Doctor Who Bulletin)* – Issue 57 (August 1988) p.4

to be directed by Canadian Bob Clark[444], based in Washington. The Washington connection had some foundation in the filmmakers' then current plans, but the rest appears to have been conjecture.

Jon Pertwee, who had played the Doctor between 1969 and 1974 (with a brief return in 1983), aired his desperation at the constant speculation over the film on 11 December 1988, remarking: '[The project has] been going on for bloody years. We [television Doctors] were all very disappointed that they were not going to consider any of us for it, but they obviously wanted an international name. When I heard John Cleese was apparently going to play it, I thought it was a bad idea, but he could have carried it off. Then I heard the rumour about Dudley Moore and I abandoned ship altogether.'[445]

A 1989 edition of the *Daily Express* even made the phenomenally unlikely suggestion of Sylvester Stallone for the part.

One of the most 'interesting' pieces concerning the film appeared in Scotland's *Daily Record* newspaper. Under the sober strapline 'NOW IT'S THE SEXY BOOZY DR WHO', the piece reported (if 'reported' is the right word):

TV's favourite Time Lord Dr Who is to be turned into a James Bond-style hero in a new multi-million pound feature film. Canadian actor Donald Sutherland has been given the task of turning the all-British time traveller into a modern American-style macho man. US movie makers Pathe films will make the children's favourite:
CARRY a high-tec gun to zap baddies
BRAWL in bar rooms with weird aliens
AND BONK his beautiful assistant – Britain's former 3-2-1 star Caroline Munroe.
Sutherland landed the role of Tardis Man in the £20 million blockbuster despite stiff competition from British actors. The role had been linked with John Cleese, Dudley Moore, Bob Hoskins and the current TV Doc, Sylvester McCoy. An insider said yesterday: 'The Doctor will be more of a James Bond type character, sent on missions to save the universe.
'The movie will be very like *Star Wars*, promising a whole host of spectacular space battles along the way. It's a far cry from the TV series, which is now considered tame.'
Many of the country's Dr Who fans are expected to be outraged. But veteran Dr Who writer Johnny Byrne – who has written the new movie – said: 'It will definitely take the Doctor into the nineties'. The filmmakers hope the picture will revive interest in

---

[444] Then best known as the writer/producer/director of the 1982 film, *Porky's*.
[445] From *DWB (Dream Watch Bulletin)* – Issue 64 (April 1989) p.8

the time traveller whose BBC TV series may be axed after disastrous ratings.'[446]

Obviously, the piece was quite blindingly inaccurate on a number of levels, but surprisingly it did get *some* things right. Who the quoted 'insider' was remains a mystery, although Daltenreys suspected the rumours (which were strenuously denied) had originated in some gossip at Liverpool's *Nebula* science fiction convention earlier that year.

The November 1989 edition of *Starburst* Magazine also picked up on the paper's 'erroneous'[447] linking of Donald Sutherland to the film.

In a statement, Daltenreys stated: 'Recent press reports claiming that Donald Sutherland has been cast as the film Doctor are totally fictitious. Coast to Coast would like to clarify that no-one can be cast until a deal has been finalised with a studio to actually make the film.' However, they also went on to concede: 'Although no-one has formally been approached to play the lead, several actors are being considered and Donald Sutherland does appeal.'[448]

In reality, there was some truth to the Sutherland rumour. 'Donald Sutherland we were actually very keen on,' admits Litten. 'We had discussions with him.'

'My preference has been for Donald Sutherland ever since his name was floated for the role,' commented Johnny Byrne as early as October 1989. 'He has worked with the very best American and European directors and he understands and is in tune with European rhythms of filmmaking. So it will not be a complete culture shock for the Doctor, traditionally English, to be played by someone like Sutherland. He is, I believe, a man for all seasons, a universal actor, one that would immeasurably enhance the character.'[449]

Another piece of casting that the *Daily Record* got right was (a misspelled) Caroline Munro. Although this had never really been a secret anyway. Since playing a part in Amicus's *At the Earth's Core* in 1976, Munro's career had been doing quite well. She'd had a prominent supporting role in Roger Moore's third James Bond film, *The Spy Who Loved Me* (1977), and had also taken the lead in 1978's aptly named *Star Wars* cash-in *Starcrash*. She'd first worked with George Dugdale and Peter Litten in 1985, whe playing the lead in their first feature, *Slaughter High*. Dugdale and Munro became very close and later, in 1990, they married. Munro was always going to be somewhere in the *Doctor Who* movie cast, and both Ezra's and Byrne's scripts had characters written in for her to play.

---

[446] From The *Daily Record* (November 1989)
[447] From *DWB (Dream Watch Bulletin)* – Issue 72 (December 1989) p.4
[448] From *DWB (Dream Watch Bulletin)* – Issue 72 (December 1989) p.4
[449] From *DWB (Dream Watch Bulletin)* – Issue 72 (December 1989) p.13

'Caroline Munro was a great friend of mine over many years,' says Litten. 'She was very much involved on a first-hand basis with the whole project ... She was playing one of the evil villains, called Morgana[450], I seem to remember. She was an alien.'

The part was essentially that of number two villain, after Varnax. Her character was most fleshed out by Byrne, who wrote her to be an old flame of the Doctor's.

'It would be untrue to say that a role was specifically written for Caroline,' explained Byrne. 'I have nothing to do with the casting, but I know that an actress of Caroline Munro's looks, talents and experience uniquely qualify her for this role.'[451]

Munro was the only confirmed member of the cast ever to be publicly announced by Daltenreys, and she went along with Litten, Dugdale and Byrne when they made their first public appearance together to promote the film at the PanoptiCon IX *Doctor Who* convention on 18 September 1988.

It was at this convention that various bits of information concerning the film were confirmed for the first time. The movie was now reportedly due either for Christmas 1989 or summer 1990 and the producers spoke of the creation of some 147 new 'creatures' to populate it. The production's repeated delays were put down to the filmmakers' reluctance to 'lose artistic control, in order to ensure that it will neither ignore nor corrupt the *Who* concept.'[452]

The group also announced that both the TARDIS's police box exterior and Ron Grainer's theme music would survive the translation to the cinema screen. The projected budget was confirmed to be £12 million ($19 million).

Projected budgets are often somewhat fluid in films that are touting for investment. Ask for too little money and the project risks not being taken seriously. Tom Baker argued that his *Scratchman* project perhaps fell victim to this. However, studios are obviously going to be wary of any 'big-budget' projects that don't have some proven likelihood of recouping their expenditure. The solution to this problem is that producers usually try pitching and re-pitching their projects to various studios – each time with a different budget. If they fail to get finance for a small budget film, they suggest making a big budget one instead. Daltenreys' film had already gone from a very small-budget project to a very big one and then back to somewhere in the middle. Projected figures would, at one point, peak as high as £25 million ($40 million).

'When you're setting a film up, the budget seems to move anywhere from kind of a few million, up to tens and tens and tens of millions,' Litten

---

[450] Referred to as Zilla in some of Byrne's drafts.
[451] From *DWB (Dream Watch Bulletin)* – Issue 72 (December 1989) p.13
[452] From *DWB (Doctor Who Bulletin)* – *Issue 59* (October 1988) p.8

comments. 'That shift occurs above the line of who the stars are and who is directing. So, one ends up looking at every option in the whole world.'

The budget was also being partly dictated by how much money the BBC wanted. When the film had been first pitched in 1985, Daltenreys had not anticipated the BBC asking for as much money for the rights as they did, so the project was deliberately scaled up in the hope that a larger-scale production would stand a better chance of recouping the company's high spending in that area.

Unfortunately this also made the film more difficult to set up, and the longer it took, the longer Daltenreys would have to wait to make their money back. Then, in June 1989, their option on the *Doctor Who* movie rights expired.

In order to renew the option, Daltenreys had to sign a new contract with BBC Enterprises, giving them another few years to develop a film. Naturally, there was another hefty price tag attached. Each time Daltenreys renewed their rights, the black hole in their finances only increased – with no immediate sign of anything coming along to fill it.

'We basically had three [successive] options on the rights from the BBC for two years each, or something like that,' remembers Litten. 'I think the BBC made, in options alone, over a million and a quarter pounds [from us].'

With the BBC itself then investing very little money into the production of *Doctor Who* on television, Daltenreys' cash doubtless seemed very welcome to them – particularly as it came from a property that they had very little interest in doing anything with themselves.

However, as 1989 wore on, prospects were still not looking too strong for Daltenreys, and without a director on board, things were even harder. In June 1989, rumours had even surfaced that controversial English director Ken Russell had been approached to take on the project.

'As I understand it, there was a second-hand, but not direct, interest by Ken Russell in directing ... a much earlier version of the script,'[453] explained Johnny Byrne.

In September, Daltenreys got yet another alias, when they changed the name of their production company to Green Light Productions. The Coast to Coast Productions brand was finally retired. It was to be the start of a slight change of direction for the company, who were planning to make another 'possibly final' concerted push to exploit their recently-renewed *Doctor Who* movie rights. There was to be both a revised pitch and a new script.

However, as Green Light was born, back at the BBC, something very special died.

On 6 December 1989, BBC1 broadcast the last episode of *Doctor Who*'s twenty-sixth television season. As the closing credits played out, there was

---

[453] From *DWB (Dream Watch Bulletin)* – Issue 72 (December 1989) p.13

no announcement that the series would be returning in the new year. Quietly, behind closed-doors and with few people even noticing it, *Doctor Who* had been cancelled.

Plans for a twenty-seventh season for the end of 1990 remained unrealised. The *Doctor Who* production office was discreetly wound down and the powers-that-be attempted to mollify fans with a simple promise that the show would (one day) return. The official line was that it was taking a 'rest' and production would resume (probably with an independent production company) before too long. Most people were citing 1991 as a likely return date for the show. In reality, however, nobody in any position of authority at the BBC actually had any intention of making this happen. *Doctor Who*'s future was merely described as 'secure', which technically it was – securely non-existent.

Even with the effective shutdown of the television series, Daltenreys did continue to keep John Nathan-Turner, still nominally in place as *Doctor Who*'s BBC producer, in the loop as to their plans – out of courtesy, if not contractual obligation. In July, Nathan-Turner told the press: 'I've seen the script and it's excellent. It will make a very good film.' In late 1988 he added: 'I think the producers of the movie are as keen to preserve the idea of *Doctor Who* not being a special effects show as I am. It's a big budget movie, but they don't intend to replace strong narrative storylines with 20-minute space battles. I think the film can do nothing but good for the telly series, provided it is good.'[454]

'I worked for him for a number of years when I was at the BBC and after I left the BBC,' remembers Litten. 'He wasn't involved in any way in the project, but, out of courtesy, I certainly always let him know what we were doing and gave him copies of the script.'

'Peter Litten and George Dugdale... asked me whether I'd like to be creative consultant,' explained Nathan-Turner. 'Basically they come to me for advice, which they use or disregard. I have no veto.'[455]

From 1990, however, Nathan-Turner's involvement in *Doctor Who* was largely peripheral. To all practical intents and purposes, *Doctor Who* was dead as a continuing television series. It certainly seemed that whatever future *Doctor Who* might have would be on the big screen ... Or would it?

GREEN LIGHT AT THE END OF THE TUNNEL

With confidence in the *Doctor Who* concept at its lowest ever ebb, both on television and in the cinema, Johnny Byrne defended the Daltenreys project in an interview for *DWB* magazine.

---

[454] From *Doctor Who Magazine* – Issue 141 (October 1988) p.9
[455] From *Doctor Who Magazine* – Issue 141 (October 1988) p.9

'Clearly, if all the finance had been in place from day one, then the process would be that much further along the road,' he explained. 'But that's not how things work in filmmaking.' He added hopefully: 'The ideal order of events would be for the movie to come out before *Doctor Who* reappears in 1991. This would give the new producers the opportunity to benefit from changes that have evolved during the translation to the big screen.'[456]

As a new decade dawned, however, *Doctor Who*'s prospects on the big screen weren't looking all that much more positive than they were on the small screen. In 1990, Litten was forced to deny speculation that the project was being backed by Pathé Films. Although hopeful that another studio *would* be backing the project, nothing was certain. And the bank balance wasn't looking too good either. Company accounts show that on 2 February 1990, the business registered a mortgage taken out to free up funds.

ALL CHANGE

Around the start of 1990, Peter Litten was reported suggesting that the projected budget for the film would now be a (comparatively modest) £10 million to £30 million (or around $15 million to $40 million). The eventual figure was actually around $31 million. Press reports meanwhile suggested that the film's new TARDIS interior set was to be built at a cost of £150,000.

'Quite frankly I think all of us feel that if we had the best deal on the table a year and a half ago, we would have been making the wrong film,' ran a Daltenreys statement. 'We're now relying less on the grandiose sets and creatures; now you have 90 instead of 150. It [will] still [look] good on screen, but the reductions [give] us room to really enhance the character development.'[457]

With the production now being more comfortably targeted as a 'mid-budget' picture, various ways of economising were under active consideration. One way to keep the costs down would have been to shoot overseas, in a territory with generous tax breaks (like the UK used to have, but didn't anymore). 'If you shot it in Yugoslavia, then you could do it at 10% of the cost that you could if you shot it at Pinewood,' recalls Litten. 'But obviously, certain directors think twice about shooting in less comfortable environments. It's horses for courses. We looked at all kinds of options across the Earth, to try and make it happen.'

With a number of overseas recces conducted by Daltenreys, it does seem that at this stage an overseas-based production was by far the most practical option. It was an increasingly popular option too. In July 1988, producers Cubby Broccoli and Michael G Wilson ended a near 30 year relationship

---

[456] From *DWB (Dream Watch Bulletin)* – Issue 72 (December 1989) p.13
[457] *DWB (Dream Watch Bulletin)* – Issue 72 (December 1989) p.4

with Pinewood Studios when they filmed their latest James Bond movie, *Licence to Kill*, at Mexico City's Churubusco Studios in South America. Again, the reason was to cut costs and make possible an otherwise uneconomical picture.

Still hoping to push the production forward with a major distributor, Daltenreys continued to promote their project throughout 1990. Notably, to coincide with the MIFED Film Festival in October, Green Light unveiled an attractive colour poster promoting *Doctor Who – The Last of the Time Lords*. The tagline at the top read: 'The Man. The Myth. The Movie'.

By March 1991, Rutger Hauer had become the press's latest piece of 'star-casting' rumoured for the film's lead. However, some wondered if Hauer's involvement in a series of then popular Guinness commercials might jeopardise his chances.

Also in 1991, Byrne completed an extensive redraft of his script for the production. Having had little luck with the earlier 'Varnax' storylines from Ezra and Byrne, it seems that there was a feeling that a change of tack might help the production attract its much longed-for international finance. With this in mind, the final incarnation of Byrne's script was essentially an entirely new story. The writer scrapped virtually all that had gone before and started from scratch.

Apparently never completed and running to just 75 pages, this script went by the title *Chameleon* and had little input from either Dugdale or Litten. In the new script, the Doctor was depicted as being 'elderly, quirky, eccentric',[458] and once more based on Gallifrey.

It is on Gallifrey that the Doctor is targeted by a renegade Time Lord, whose identity is initially unknown. The Doctor's own time-stream has been manipulated, leaving him weak and vulnerable. False evidence, planted by the Doctor's hidden nemesis, leads the Time Lords to imprison the Doctor on charges of time meddling (again). The Doctor manages to escape to New York and attempts literally to put his life back together. However, in attempting to fix his own time-stream, he gets something badly wrong and brings a younger version of himself forward through time and into the present day.

The younger Doctor and the older one don't get on too well, but the pair are physically dependent on one another. If one dies, the other will cease to exist. A hired assassin known as Chameleon is brought in to kill one of the Doctors (it doesn't matter which) and the Doctors must put things right before he finds them. Along the way, the two Doctors meet Mallie Jordan. Young and terribly well-organised, Mallie falls a little bit in love with the Doctor in both his guises. She is particularly attracted to the more

[458] From *The Nth Doctor* by Jean-Marc and Randy Lofficier – iUniverse Books (2003) p.113

'handsome' younger Doctor.

Inadvertently sharing some DNA with Milton Subotsky's earlier 'two Doctors' movie idea from the 1980s, the film would also have brought to mind other 'multi-Doctor' stories from the original television series – 'The Three Doctors' (1972), 'The Five Doctors' (1983) and 'The Two Doctors' (1985) – similarly trading on the friction between different incarnations of the same person. However, like the previous versions of the script, it seems there would have been few other similarities to the original television series.

As it turned out, Byrne's latest idea didn't find favour with Daltenreys and no final draft was ever actually completed. Soon after, Byrne left the project altogether, eventually to be replaced by another writer.

'It happens,' said Byrne stoically. 'Writers are rolled aside and their work taken in hand by other writers – it did, after all, happen with me and Mark Ezra. Obviously, if someone else could produce a better screenplay, then George and Peter would be duty bound to set him to work.'[459]

MAKING MOVIES (IN DIRE STRAITS)

As 1991 came to an end, Byrne was not the only person to step away from the film. Six years on from the movie's initial pitch, production wasn't any closer to starting, and even some of those at Daltenreys itself had understandably become a little jaded about its prospects.

On 31 December 1991, Peter Litten moved a little back from the project when he formally ceased to serve as a company director for the group and moved across to the post of company secretary instead. That same day, chartered accountants Stephen Garbutta and Ronald Michael Harris from the firm Harris & Trotter LLP joined Daltenreys as company directors, as did musician John Illsley, guitarist with the pop group Dire Straits.

'In essence,' says Illsley, 'I suppose I was … one of the financial backers for it. The script needed funding and the process needed funding and, at that particular point in time, I was interested in looking at different sorts of projects to get involved in and this came forward.'

Illsley was then travelling with Dire Straits on their On Every Street tour, playing around 200 concerts between August 1991 and October 1992. 'I was a bit sort of preoccupied,' he remembers. 'I was playing five nights a week. So, I had plenty of stuff on my plate and I couldn't really concentrate on it, but I had a certain amount of money invested in the project. I can't remember how much, but it was certainly six figures.'

'When other directors come on board, studios and all the rest of it,' says Litten, 'it gets rewritten and rewritten. So, one had far less say frankly. I think it could have made a very good picture. Was it the one I myself would

---

[459] From DWB (Dream Watch Bulletin) – Issue 72 (December 1989) p.13

have made? Possibly not. Whether that would have been better or worse, who knows?'

The following year, there were further changes. On 23 September 1992, John Humphreys ceased to be a company director, leaving only George Dugdale from the original group still remaining.

Doctor Who – The Movie Draft Two By Johnny Byrne From a story by George Dugdale and Peter Litten

PLOT SYNOPSIS

London – 1932.

Jack the Ripper, returned to London 45 years after he first terrorised the city, stalks a prostitute through the East End smog. Suddenly the woman turns to face the Ripper and we see that she isn't a woman at all. She is, instead, 'a fit, striking looking man, keen-eyed, sharp-witted and deceptively subtle.'[460] It is the Doctor.

The 'Ripper', actually an alien Weazll[461], lashes out. But the Doctor is quicker and produces a small torch-like instrument that dissolves the creature's flesh. It swells up like a balloon before finally bursting.

Policemen chase the Doctor from the scene.

Once back inside his TARDIS, the Doctor activates his time rotor with a palm-print scanner and the ship dematerialises.

As the Doctor settles down to try to fix the TARDIS's faulty chameleon circuit, he receives an incoming message from Cora – a communications expert on Gallifrey, and also the Doctor's niece. Cora tells him that an old friend of his called Gonjii[462] has been trying to get in touch.

The Doctor takes the TARDIS to Raqetz, a run-down shanty-town on the planet Demos. It is the year 98349.01. He makes his way to the Palace of Profit, a faded wreck of a night-spot cum casino. On his way there, he passes an overweight, sedan chair-borne alien called Mother Cajage[463], who

---

[460] From Byrne's original script, as quoted in *DWB (Dream Watch Bulletin)* – Issue 97 (January 1992) p.14

[461] In certain drafts of the script, the Weazll appears elsewhere in the story and in a different context – aboard the TARDIS of a renegade Time Lord, where it attacks the Doctor.

[462] In some drafts, Gonjii has the surname 'Iboritrix'.

[463] A corruption of 'Mother Courage' from the play by Bertolt Brecht, perhaps?

recognises the Doctor with dismay.

Inside the Palace of Profit, an alien Marlene Dietrich lookalike with green skin sings 'Falling in Love Again' as various species try their luck at the gambling tables. Gonjii sits in a raised chair overlooking the room, his little pet 'Pog' at his side. He used to be the commander of one of Gallifrey's Time Battalions, but that was a long time ago. He's a mercenary now. He's summoned the Doctor here because he thinks he's seen a time rotor for sale at a local auction house.

After throwing out a rowdy customer, Gonjii goes with the Doctor to the auction that has been organised by Mother Cajage. The auction room is packed with 'discarded Cybermen, trashed Daleks, a truncated K-9 and other TV *Doctor Who* metallic creatures and artefacts.'

The Doctor gives a writ to Mother Cajage, ordering her to withdraw the time rotor from the auction, but she refuses. The time rotor is eventually sold to a mysterious figure in a cloak. The Doctor and Gonjii follow the figure as he exits the auction house and observe him as he cuts the throat of a mugger who accosts him in the street.

High above the city of Raqetz, a vast ancient spaceship, the *Creator*, sits in orbit around the planet. Inside, there is a crew of two: Morgana and Varnax. The darkly beautiful Morgana is essentially human in appearance, except for a snake of thick plastic tubing that seems to emerge from her back. Varnax, on the other hand, has a much bulkier frame. His actual body is almost invisible, buried deep beneath a massive mechanical exoskeleton. The pair eagerly watch events on the planet's surface, via a monitor screen. Observing the shadowy cloaked figure, Varnax gives the order to land the ship on the surface of Demos.

The Doctor stops the cloaked figure in the street and attempts to deliver his writ of seizure for the time rotor. The figure suddenly throws back its cloak, revealing itself to be a seven foot high armoured cyborg. This is Neglos, a once-handsome humanoid now misshapen and distorted with shining metal implants and a towering robotic exoskeleton.

Gonjii manages to stop Neglos from killing the Doctor, but is nearly killed himself when Neglos turns an in-built flame-thrower on him. The Doctor saves Gonjii by tearing at the fuel lines on Neglos's arm. However, when the *Creator* appears overhead, both Gonjii and the Doctor are too late to stop Neglos from jumping aboard and being carried to safety, the spaceship lifting off through the atmosphere.

The Doctor tells Gonjii gravely that he recognised Neglos and that if Neglos is still alive, then Morgana and Varnax are unlikely to be very far behind. The revelation horrifies Gonjii. It was Varnax who destroyed

Gonjii's home planet[464].

It emerges that a thousand years ago, Varnax offered the Time Lords a source of unimaginable power: the great 'time-fusion crystals'[465]. However, afraid that the crystals would threaten the natural order of the cosmos, the Time Lords sent the Doctor to kill Varnax. Although badly injured, Varnax has somehow survived, and he intends to use the fusion crystals to regenerate himself and his followers[466].

The first of the fusion crystals is hidden on the planet Kernos. The Time Lords order the Doctor to travel there, find Varnax and stop him getting to it. Cora and Gonjii go with the Doctor on his mission.

Arriving on Kernos, the Doctor, Cora and Gonjii are soon captured by cannibal natives and placed in a cage. The natives worship a 'Singing God'. This is actually a statue, which holds a Varlian Radioprobe in one of its hands. The natives refer to it 'singing' because when the Radioprobe comes into contact with sunlight, it produces the sound of a 1930s radio transmission.

The natives are about to kill the Doctor and his companions when Neglos and five of his warriors[467] burst into the room. Gonjii kills one of the warriors, while two more are crushed by the falling arm of the statue and another is decapitated by Cora. In the commotion, Neglos escapes with the Radioprobe. As furious natives pour into the chamber, the Doctor summons the TARDIS by remote control[468] and he and his friends escape.

Aboard the *Creator*, the Radioprobe is revealed to be the first crystal, and Varnax installs it in his 'Crucible' – a large structure housed deep in the bowels of his ship. Varnax now has his first crystal: the White Crystal. However, there are still more to be found. Varnax sets off after the next one: the Dark Crystal.

The TARDIS next takes the Doctor and his companions to a London museum. The Doctor locates the Dark Crystal hidden in one of the

---

[464] Some drafts of the script actually showed the devastation of the planet Demos right at the start of the film. In these drafts, we witness it engulfed in flame. These events happen in the year 9889999E78.03 AR.

[465] The time-fusion crystals are referred to as 'matrix crystals' in some drafts of the script and appear to have originated on Gallifrey.

[466] Again, some drafts of the script have these events actually depicted at the start of the film, rather than just being mentioned in retrospect. Some drafts showed Varnax disperse the crystals throughout time and space after he's used them to devastate Demos. Varnax is then caught up in an explosion on the *Creator* that leaves him an emaciated wreck.

[467] These warriors are referred to as the Mordread in some drafts.

[468] The idea of the TARDIS having a remote control was first introduced in the 1985 television story 'The Two Doctors', in which Patrick Troughton's Doctor uses one to summon his TARDIS.

museum's cabinets. He is just picking the lock when he becomes aware that Varnax has arrived in the *Creator*. Varnax's warriors cut off their exit, so the Doctor and his friends head off in the opposite direction. They wind up in the Gents toilets, where an Irish-American student called Shane O'Neill[469] is hiding.

Shane helps the Doctor's party to the fire exit, with Neglos hot on their heels. The group are almost back at the TARDIS when a massive explosion rocks the museum, wounding Shane. The Doctor, Cora and Gonjii finally manage to escape in the TARDIS, bringing the injured Shane along with them.

The Doctor's TARDIS is pursued through the time vortex by the *Creator*. The Doctor attempts to evade Varnax, but his plan fails and he is left dramatically aged by the forces of the vortex. Neglos and his warriors board the TARDIS and force the Doctor to surrender by holding a knife to Cora's throat.

Morgana is revealed to be an old flame of the Doctor's. He once claimed to love her, but betrayed her when she sided with Varnax. Their reunion is a tense one. Noticing the thick cluster of tubes that trails down Morgana's back, the Doctor asks her what has happened to the immortality Varnax promised her. Varnax enters, swearing that the Doctor will pay for the painful years he has had to spend in a life-support suit.

Varnax hopes to use the fusion crystals to compress billions of years of evolution into just a few seconds. This will make him a genetically perfect and immortal superbeing. Varnax will need to destroy an entire planet in order for fusion to take place. He orders the Doctor be dragged away to join his friends in a nearby cell.

However, Gonjii, Cora and Shane have already escaped from their cell. Shane managed to snatch the key from the guard. They now burst into the room. Gonjii overcomes Morgana and demands that she tell them which planet Varnax is planning to destroy to activate his fusion device. Gonjii tugs at Morgana's life-support pipes and visibly weakens her, but still she does not reveal the name of the planet, and soon she escapes through a secret exit.

The Doctor and his friends beat a path to the bridge, where they come under heavy fire from Varnax and Morgana. At this point it is discovered that, by unlikely coincidence, Shane is the distant relative of an ancient Irish warrior who was once close friends with the Doctor.

The Doctor realises that Varnax is planning to activate his fusion device on Earth, devastating the planet in the process. He is unable to find out the precise location, but explains that Varnax will need weapons-grade nuclear waste in order to activate his crystals. As Varnax, Neglos and Morgana

---

[469] In some drafts Shane is nicknamed Spanish (for no immediately obvious reason).

continue their attack, the Doctor and his companions escape in the TARDIS.

The TARDIS has been badly damaged by its experiences in the vortex and makes a forced landing on Christopher Columbus's sailing ship, which is on its way to the New World. On board, Cora is mistaken for a vision of the Virgin Mary and Shane leaves behind a map of America for Columbus.

Following their brief adventure with Columbus, the Doctor next takes the TARDIS back to the museum where they first met Shane. There he should be able to repair the TARDIS using one of the museum exhibits.

Meanwhile, the *Creator* materialises above a large security complex built on a desolate North of England moor[470]. It is a top-secret nuclear waste dump. Neglos and his warriors kill the guards and take a lift down to an underground nuclear waste silo.

Using a nearby payphone, the Doctor gets in touch with his old friend Brigadier Alastair Gordon Lethbridge-Stewart, who is observing penguins in the Falklands. The Brigadier realises that Varnax is most likely to be headed to the Rogarth Fell nuclear facility and tells the Doctor where to find it.

Outside the museum, a team of engineers from the phone company are replacing old public phone boxes. Unseen by the Doctor, they take the Doctor's TARDIS away on the back of their lorry, replacing it with a new phone kiosk.

At Rogarth Fell, Neglos watches as a set of heavy Gallium rods are lowered into the nuclear waste silo.

With the TARDIS gone, the Doctor's party are forced to travel to Rogarth Fell by train and walk the rest of the way across the moor. Posing as an amorous couple, the Doctor and Cora trick Varnax's cronies and manage to get into the complex, on the way killing a number of guards (with their own weapons).

As the Doctor attempts to activate the complex's failsafe, he explains that the Gallium and the radioactive waste will cause the planet to explode. The resultant energy will charge Varnax's crystals.

Neglos stabs Gonjii from behind, but an enraged Shane exacts revenge by pushing the cyborg into a vat of radioactive slurry, killing him.

The Doctor enters the Crucible – the heart of Varnax's masterplan. The whole area has been transformed into a lush and verdant garden, with limpid pools and lush foliage. There he sees the shrivelled forms of Varnax and Morgana lying in a small pavilion. They are regenerating. Morgana is now as young and beautiful as she was when the Doctor first fell in love with her.Varnax is now ready to withdraw the Gallium rods from the nuclear waste, making his transformation complete. However, this will, of

---

[470] In some drafts this last act takes place on Demos. There is also a trip to the planet Centros, described by Johnny Byrne as 'inhabited by ferocious hallucinating warrior monks.'

course, also destroy the Earth. Morgana asks the Doctor to join them, but he refuses.

The Doctor fires his gun directly into the crystal helix in the centre of the room. It shatters into liquid flame. The garden is devastated as Morgana screams. The explosion leaves Morgana dead, but a part of the crystal (the dark part) still survives and Varnax still lives off its energy. Leaving Morgana's corpse behind him, Varnax makes ready to elevate the Gallium rods and destroy the planet.

However, at that moment, Cora succeeds in reactivating the complex's failsafe mechanisms and the computer begins to seal off the base.

For some reason, an enraged Varnax now turns into a winged demon and flies after the Doctor. The Doctor manages to outrun the flying Varnax and escapes from the *Crucible*, just as the door seals shut behind him. Varnax is left trapped inside.

Pilotless, the *Creator* crashes into the Rogarth Fell complex, as the nuclear silos are sealed. Before they leave, Cora and Shane show the Doctor, the body of Gonjii. The Doctor pays his respects by performing a death rite with Gonjii's Demosian amulet.

Later, the Doctor, Shane and Cora are walking along one of the desolate roads near Rogarth Fell, trying to hitchhike back to civilisation. They're not having much luck. Finally, Cora manages to hail a passing car. It is a battered Ford Cortina. The young driver welcomes them aboard and the car drives off. As the vehicle pulls away, it momentarily morphs back into the shape of a police box, before dematerialising off into time and space.

9

The End of Time
'A Doctor Who Film'
(1992-1994)

ROUND THREE

On 18 September 1992, a new producer, Felice Arden, joined Daltenreys as a company director with fresh hopes of finally pushing the *Doctor Who* project forward into production before their rights expired in 1994.

Arden had come out of the world of magazine publishing, working in the States on the highly regarded feminist journal *Ms.* (1977-1983) and later on US music magazine *Spin* (1984-1988). She had also previously worked as unit co-ordinator on the 1990 horror film *Living Doll*[471]. The picture had featured a number of Daltenreys' prospective *Doctor Who* team. Co-directed by Peter Litten and George Dugdale, it also had a script by Mark Ezra and included some visual effects work from John Humphreys and Paul Catling.

It was off the back of *Living Doll* that Arden joined the *Doctor Who* project, taking over some of the responsibilities that had previously been Peter Litten's. She also took on the dual job titles of producer and company financial director.

'I kind of moved out of the day to day business of it towards the end,' explains Litten, who had now all but left the film project he had helped instigate seven years earlier.

Between September and December 1992, Arden was reportedly scouting out American distributors armed with videotapes of old *Doctor Who* television stories such as 'Pyramids of Mars'[472] (1975) and 'Earthshock'[473]

---

[471] *Living Doll*'s production manager Kevan Van Thompson also had a *Doctor Who* connection. He'd worked on four episodes of Colin Baker's last season and in 1993 was assigned to *Doctor Who*'s (ultimately never made) thirtieth anniversary special 'Lost in the Dark Dimension'.

[472] This 1975 *Doctor Who* serial was then commercially available as an edited VHS cassette from BBC Video. It had been released in the UK in February 1985 and in America in 1988.

[473] This 1982 *Doctor Who* serial had recently been released commercially in the UK on VHS cassette by BBC Video in September 1992. It was not yet on sale in the US.

(1982) with which to pique their interest. Her hope was that one last fresh push would finally gain the production its much-needed studio backer.

While in the States, Arden also took the opportunity to speak to some US-based fans and attended an American convention to talk about a project, which *DWB* magazine was now describing cynically as *Doctor Who – The Motionless Picture.*

'It's unfortunate that we've received so much press attention,' said Arden. 'People don't seem to understand that it takes time to put together even the biggest feature film. It doesn't happen overnight ... People expected a film in two or three years.'[474]

Arden described the company's ambition to 'make this a classy film ... We could have made it sooner, but we would have been cheating the fans. It would have been a parody of the Doctor.'[475]

THIRTY YEARS IN THE TARDIS

1993 was a big year for *Doctor Who*. The programme was 30 years old that November. However, as the new year arrived there was still little sign of either a new series on television or a film. Numerous independent production companies had made pitches to take on the running of the programme, but all had been turned away.

Despite this, even its critics couldn't ignore the show's thirtieth anniversary. It was remarkable if for no other reason than it demonstrated that nearly four years on from cancellation, the programme was still very popular. The Doctor's adventures continued both in a burgeoning range of original novels from Virgin Publishing and in a continuing comic strip in Marvel Comics' *Doctor Who Magazine*. To celebrate the show's birthday, August and September saw the broadcast of a new radio serial, 'The Paradise of Death', written by Barry Letts and starring Jon Pertwee, Nicholas Courtney and Elisabeth Sladen, on BBC Radio 5.

However, despite promises of a brand new all-film television special from BBC Enterprises and BBC1 – the eventually cancelled 'Lost in the Dark Dimension' – the BBC's television celebrations were minimal at best. The chief attraction was the two-part, 15 minute 'Dimensions in Time', produced in 3D to coincide with the BBC's *Children in Need* telethon, also featuring the cast of the BBC1's *EastEnders*. It seemed that BBC executives were little more in love with *Doctor Who* than they had been in the late '80s. The one hope of a lasting reprieve for the ailing Doctor still seemed to lie solely with Daltenreys/Green Light.

However, with the expiry date on the company's BBC rights option

---

[474] From *DWB (Dream Watch Bulletin)* – Issue 106 (October 1992) p.5
[475] From *DWB (Dream Watch Bulletin)* – Issue 106 (October 1992) p.5

looming, things were looking far from optimistic at Daltenreys, and on 9 June and 5 August another two mortgages were taken out by the company to ease their sluggish cash-flow.

By mid-1993, *DWB* magazine was reporting that sufficient funds to allow the movie's go-ahead had finally been raised. 'Dire Straits bass player John Ilsley is said to be involved [in raising finance]'[476], the magazine reported. Meanwhile, actor and comedian Robin Williams was the latest rumoured casting suggestion for the film's lead.

'We seemed to be beating our heads against a brick wall trying to get this thing made,' recalls John Illsley, who was now struggling to get another film project off the ground[477]. 'Various people we contacted seemed to be interested, but … it didn't really get going.'

Daltenreys were now almost completely out of both time and money. If they didn't find a financially viable production partner right now, it seemed the whole enterprise would end in ruin for the entire company. Such a collapse would also take many of the company directors down with it.

It was therefore much to the relief of all concerned when, in 1993, a studio was finally brought on board.

LET THERE BE LIGHT

Arden's contacts and Litten's and Dugdale's persistence finally bore fruit when, at long last, Daltenreys entered into an agreement with the French-based Lumiere Pictures.

Lumiere (whose name is the French word for light[478]) already owned the rights to the two Peter Cushing Dalek films (see Chapter Three) and were one of the largest businesses of their kind in Europe. They certainly had the funds to finance a picture of this type and welcomed the opportunity to make another *Doctor Who* film to add to their stable. However, in exchange for their backing, there were strings attached.

Lumiere wanted near total control of the production – leasing the rights from Daltenreys and, in the process, making the film a Lumiere production rather than a Green Light one. There seems to have been no intention to use either Ezra's or Byrne's scripts, nor any appreciable part thereof. The film would be starting from scratch, with less than a year to go until the BBC rights option expired. Nevertheless, relieved finally to have a viable deal on the table, Daltenreys agreed to the terms.

---

[476] From *DWB (Dream Watch Bulletin)* – Issue 113 (May 1993) p.3
[477] Around this time, Illsley was also helping television director Charles Sturridge to mount a film based on Robert O' Connor's 1993 novel *Buffalo Soldiers*. The film was eventually made by another director, Gregor Jordan, in 2001.
[478] And also the surname of the inventors of modern cinema.

News of the Lumiere deal soon percolated into the press. The short-lived *Today* newspaper took the news as an opportunity to speculate (without foundation) that Jane Seymour would be playing the Doctor – an idea that was probably a lot more controversial then than it would be now. Other sections of the media meanwhile mentioned Michael Crawford's name. And on 12 April 1994, the *Daily Star* touted David Hassellhoff as the Doctor with Pamela Anderson as his co-star.

In fact, the production's real first choice to play the Doctor – favoured by both Lumiere and Daltenreys – was Alan Rickman, considered by Litten to be the right kind of 'well known cult superstar' needed for the part.

TO BOLDLY GO

Work on another script had to start very quickly indeed before the rights lapsed, and Lumiere looked to America for their new writer, choosing Nicholas Meyer, a popular writer/director who had recently worked on the big-budget *Star Trek* movie franchise for Paramount Pictures.[479] Meyer unfortunately wasn't interested in getting involved in another science fiction movie, but he did suggest that Lumiere approach his co-writer on his last *Star Trek* film, Denny Martin Flinn.

A multi-talented Californian, Flinn had been raised in both San Francisco and Los Angeles before moving to New York to perform in a number of Broadway shows. His stage work included a 1972/3 *Some Like it Hot* adaptation called *Sugar* and revivals of *Hello, Dolly!*, *Pal Joey* and *Fiddler on the Roof*. Following 18 months spent with a national tour of *A Chorus Line*, he wrote and directed *Groucho*, a play that premiered Off-Broadway and toured for two years.

As a choreographer, Flinn worked on *The Deceivers* (1988) and the Patrick Swayze hit *Ghost* (1990). It was while on the former that he first collaborated with director Nicholas Meyer. And it was his relationship with Meyer that then lead to the pair co-writing the script for 1991's *Star Trek VI – The Undiscovered Country*, which Meyer directed. The script was later nominated for a Saturn Award in Best Writing from the Academy of Science Fiction, Fantasy & Horror Film, and it had clearly caught the attention of Lumiere.

Star Trek and *Doctor Who* have never actually had all that much in common, either in theme or content. In many ways, they sit at opposite ends of the science fiction spectrum. However, to Lumiere, the linking up with a property that had already spawned its own successful series of spin-off films was a logical connection and did no harm to the reputation of the project

---

[479] Paramount had of course previously expressed an interest in a Daltenreys' *Doctor Who* project themselves, and had been approached by Brian Eastman with the Douglas Adams pitch in the '70s.

within the industry. Flinn was a sensible choice of writer, and he readily accepted Lumiere's offer.

Although it retained the notion of the Doctor as a part of Time Lord society and the idea of a quest narrative driven by a powerful nemesis, Flinn's eventual movie script was quite different from what Daltenreys had been previously working with. It was an intentionally fresh start.

Flinn's story told of a renegade Time Lord called Mandrake and his attempts to achieve immortality by recombining the disparate sections of the Key to Time. In theme, it was similar to Ezra's and Byrne's treatments, but there all similarity ended. The new script drew heavily on elements from the television show's past, but Flinn re-engineered the Doctor's backstory, with much of the established continuity either reshaped or thrown out of the window altogether. 'I thought of it as a sort of genesis story, in which many people would learn about the Doctor,' said Flinn. 'I wanted to show who he was and where he came from.'[480]

One idea that Flinn played with went back to the very origins of *Doctor Who* in the 1960s. In his script, real historical characters were brought into the plot to meet up with the Doctor and his friends. Although a popular conceit during William Hartnell's time, it was something that lost currency in the television series from about 1967 onwards, and by 1979 was expressly forbidden in its writer's guidelines (as drawn up by Douglas Adams).

Flinn's story had the Doctor meet up with Amelia Earhardt, William Shakespeare, Kit Marlowe and a few others. Most important was a scene in which the playwright Marlowe was murdered in a tavern.

'I did some historical research to ensure that I didn't have any inaccuracies,' said Flinn. 'The only thing that I cheated with was that group of writers who meet in the tavern. I cheated with their ages, by making them all about the same age, when in reality, one of them would have been, like nine and the other, say, 45 ... Everything else is pretty accurate ... In fact, in the British tavern scene, the poets say things they did say in real life, although I made up some of their dialogue, obviously. Marlowe's death remains somewhat of a mystery, one that has never been solved satisfactorily. Yes, I took some artistic licence with the facts, but we do know that he was attacked by an assassin and died in a duel in a tavern.'[481]

Despite the script's fairly major revisionism, there were still quite a lot of elements drawn from the original television show too, mostly from 1970s stories – although not all of these would necessarily have been ultimately useable for rights reasons.

---

[480] From *The Nth Doctor* by Jean-Marc and Randy Lofficier – iUniverse Books (2003) p.162

[481] From *The Nth Doctor* by Jean-Marc and Randy Lofficier – iUniverse Books (2003) p.161-2

The most signficant of these elements was the character of the Master, who had been introduced as the Doctor's arch-enemy in the television series in 1971, and to whom the BBC still owned the rights. Flinn initially planned to use the Master as the film's lead foe, and wrote an early draft with him. However, when objections were raised, the script was revised and the character renamed as Mandrake.

'When I started plotting the story, he was the Master,' admitted Flinn. 'Then someone, the BBC or the producers, I don't recall, told me that we couldn't use any villains from the television series, so we decided to start from scratch and come up with a new villain, which in many ways suited me much better ... [However] Mandrake is taken from the image of the Master.'[482]

The producers also expressed some reservations over Flinn's writing of K-9 into the script, feeling the writer hadn't given the character a sufficient amount of action to justify his inclusion[483]. However, this was something that Flinn began to rectify in later drafts, developing another scene for the dog toward the end of the film. 'I put K-9 in the script because, honestly, I like him and I always wanted him in there,' said Flinn. 'Then, when I wrote the first draft, I didn't come up with anything for him to do.'[484]

Perhaps most surprising of all was Flinn's writing in of another incarnation of the Doctor, which he hoped could be played by Tom Baker – not as left-field a suggestion as it might initially seem. Baker had already been approached twice that year to take part in special *Doctor Who* episodes for the BBC and was the actor by far most readily associated with the programme to American audiences. How Baker's cameo was to fit into the movie's altered history for the Doctor is not entirely clear however.

'I had watched a lot of Tom Baker episodes,' said Flinn. 'When I found, by watching the [*Tom*] *Baker Years* tape[485] that he was not only still alive but very much working, I decided that I had to find a way to use him in the film. I thought of the 1970s and of his virtual identification with that decade, and that it would be a nice touch to place him there. It would be something the

---

[482] From *The Nth Doctor* by Jean-Marc and Randy Lofficier – iUniverse Books (2003) p.161

[483] Daltenreys' deal with the BBC didn't actually give them any rights to use K-9. Neither the filmmakers nor the BBC seem to have realised this at the time. However, it seems likely that the issue would have eventually come up.

[484] From *The Nth Doctor* by Jean-Marc and Randy Lofficier – iUniverse Books (2003) p.161

[485] *The Tom Baker Years* was a special compilation video featuring newly-recorded material of Tom Baker reminiscing about his stories as the Doctor. It was produced by former television series producer John Nathan-Turner for BBC Video and was commercially released in the UK in September 1992. It came out in America in March 1993, which was presumably when Flinn watched it.

fans would enjoy.'[486]

'The BBC had overall approval of everything we did,' continued Flinn. 'For example, one argument we had that frustrated me greatly was about a scene that takes place in the 1960s, when the villain slips the Doctor some LSD. The BBC nixed that scene because they felt it besmirched the image of the Doctor to take drugs. We argued that he did not take drugs, it was the villain who fed them to him, but they wouldn't budge, so I had to rewrite that scene, which I felt was a great shame because it was a very visual, very photogenic sequence. I was surprised to see how nervous they were about that sort of thing, but I couldn't do a thing about it, because they had that total approval power.'[487]

John Illsley, who was still part-financing the project at this point, remembers being impressed with some of the ideas in Flinn's script. 'There were a couple of scripts that came through that I thought were very interesting,' he says. 'Because it's a time travel idea, one of the great ones that came back was that he essentially meets himself by travelling back in time ... which I thought could have been developed as a really good idea.'

With a script in progress, Lumiere's attention very quickly turned to a director, and the studio saw the attachment of a respected name as essential for the film's prospects. With Nicholas Meyer having turned the job down, it was another *Star Trek* luminary that they next contacted.

'Shortly after I had written the first draft, Tim Van Rellim, a talented line producer, and I had breakfast with the producer of the film,' remembered Flinn. 'We urged that offers go out to director Leonard Nimoy, with whom I had been much impressed, not only by my own experience in the *Star Trek* world, but by his dramatic film *The Good Mother* (1988).'[488]

As well as being world-famous for his role as the Vulcan Spock in *Star Trek*, Nimoy was at that time gaining a not inconsiderable reputation for his work behind the camera. His work as director on two *Star Trek* films, *Star Trek III – The Search for Spock* (1984) and *Star Trek IV – The Voyage Home* (1986), had led to him helming other Hollywood pictures, including the comedies *3 Men and a Baby* (1987) and *Funny About Love* (1990). He was, at the time of Lumiere's approach, directing another comedy, *Holy Matrimony*, for PolyGram.

Nimoy evidently had sufficient stature in the industry to attract investment and was also eager to accept the film.

---

[486] From *The Nth Doctor* by Jean-Marc and Randy Lofficier – iUniverse Books (2003) p.160
[487] From *The Nth Doctor* by Jean-Marc and Randy Lofficier – iUniverse Books (2003) p.160
[488] From *The Nth Doctor* by Jean-Marc and Randy Lofficier – iUniverse Books (2003) p.128

According to the terms of their contract with the BBC, the film had to begin shooting by 6 April 1994, or the producers would lose their rights to make any film at all. It would, of course, have been practically impossible to complete the film by that time, nor mount a production of any significant scale. However, according to the contract, they didn't have to *finish* the film by 6 April, they just had to *start* it.

A simple solution to the problem was eventually devised with the help of Denny Martin Flinn. Flinn had already created a small flashback section for his script that would recount a little of the Doctor's past. By its nature, this wouldn't actually have to feature any of the main cast. A relatively little-known actor could quite comfortably be cast as a younger version of the Doctor. Coupled with some smaller-scale set-pieces, the flashback could be filmed at a fraction of the cost of the rest of the picture. Work could conceivably be started on this material much sooner than would have been possible for any of the film's other scenes. With this in mind, Flinn was asked to expand on his 'young Doctor' sequence, to create something simple and manageable on which filming could be started right away, before the rights lapsed. Once the cameras started rolling, Lumiere then had as much time as they needed to finish the movie.

'Lumiere asked me to expand that scene, because they needed to start principal photography sooner, in order to not lose their option,' confirmed Flinn. 'The idea ... would involve the Doctor, and yet at the same time, not require any stars.'[489]

Lumiere reportedly booked a crew to begin filming Flinn's new material 'as early as October 1993, with a shooting schedule projected to commence on 6 April 1994 [the very day the rights expired].'[490]

However, there were clouds gathering quickly on the horizon. A long time had passed since the film had been first mooted and *Doctor Who*'s status as a property at the BBC had subtly changed during that period. With only a few months to go until cameras rolled, there were other forces coming into play in the *Doctor Who* world. After nearly a decade of development, these forces would finally derail Daltenreys' film altogether.

JOURNEY'S END

During 1993, faint whispers began to circulate that *Doctor Who* might be resurrected as a television series. The BBC management still had no intention of entirely funding a production themselves, but they had begun to respond positively to certain approaches for an Anglo-American co-

---

[489] From *The Nth Doctor* by Jean-Marc and Randy Lofficier – iUniverse Books (2003) p.162
[490] From *Doctor Who Magazine* – Issue 213 (8 June 1994) p.4

production from a producer named Philip David Segal. Although brought up in England, Segal was now working with Steven Speilberg's Amblin company in Hollywood. His initial proposal was for a three-way co-production deal between BBC Enterprises, Amblin and Universal Television for a new *Doctor Who* series to be made in the States. Certain figures at the top of the BBC and within BBC Enterprises started to become quite excited at this prospect. There was just one niggling problem in the way. The film rights to *Doctor Who* were with Daltenreys and Lumiere – and there was serious concern that if their movie went ahead, it could scotch any chances of the BBC's prestigious partnership with Spielberg's Amblin.

'I was actually on tour, I think, with Dire Straits,' remembers John Illsley. 'While I was away on tour, I got a phone call from somebody at the production office … [saying] that Spielberg had done some kind of another deal with the BBC and he was going to make a three-part or a four-part … series in America.'

'At the time, they were talking to Spielberg's company and all the rest of it,' confirms Peter Litten. 'They were all getting very excited and so they basically wanted to remove us from the field.'

It was an open secret and had been for some time. In 1993, incoming BBC1 Controller Alan Yentob had spoken cagily about the negotiations when interviewed by director Kevin Davies for the *30 Years in the TARDIS* documentary (see Chapter Three), and by 15 April 1994 even *GMTV* had begun to report on the Amblin talks.

Illsley recalls: 'It was Amblin, but the whole press thing was, "Oh, it's Spielberg, it's Spielberg," although he probably didn't have anything to do with it at all.'

Daltenreys had cause for concern. They had been pursuing their project for nearly a decade without much luck. The patience of many, particularly at the BBC, had now gone, and most of the friendlier faces with whom they had made their deal in the 1980s, including John Keeble, had now left to be replaced by other, less accommodating colleagues.

Sensing that their film might be unlikely to ever reach fruition, Illsley suggested a possible way out to Felice Arden at the Green Light office. 'What I said,' he remembers, 'was, if Spielberg or Spielberg's company … are interested in *Doctor Who* …, why don't we do some kind of a deal with [them], saying: "We've got the film rights for the world. Do you want to buy those?" Because there's no point us taking on somebody like Amblin … I thought it was crazy. We're beating our heads against a brick wall trying to get the thing made. We can't. Now Spielberg or his company has stepped into the frame somewhere and want to go along with this, but they don't have the film rights. They only have TV rights. My point was that if Amblin come to us for the film rights, then they'll probably make something out of it. They'll probably make a film out of it. We didn't seem to be getting anywhere with the project. I think that's what my feelings were ... I had a certain amount of money invested in the project ... and I thought that this was probably quite a good way of clawing some of it back, to be brutally honest ... [Felice Arden] was quite a character, I have to say ... She didn't budge on that one.' Illsley's idea never came to pass.

The BBC now effectively felt forced to choose between Daltenreys and the much shinier and more attractive name of Steven Spielberg's Amblin. What happened next was perhaps inevitable, but still came as a bitter and devastating blow to the team at Daltenreys.

The June 1994 edition of *Doctor Who Magazine* reported that Lumiere's film crew, booked back in October, had since been cancelled and (inaccurately) 'that Lumiere have lost their rights to make the film in a bidding war against Steven Spielberg's Amblin Entertainment.'[491]

After nearly ten long years, the spending of staggering sums of money and the drafting of at least three principal scripts, Daltenreys' bid to make a *Doctor Who* film came to an abrupt end.

'[BBC Enterprises] had a change of personnel and the new personnel didn't want us to proceed,' says John Humphreys. 'I'm not saying that it was the BBC's plan to do this, but somebody there decided to run us into the ground ... We were just ready to go [into production], that's the [frustrating] thing. They just didn't want us to go ahead with it. They just didn't want us to. If they'd just said to us, "Can we sit down? Our previous people shouldn't really have given you the rights. Can we buy them back?" we'd have looked at that. We'd have realised that if they didn't want us to make it, there was no point in trying. We were bright enough to realise that if somebody doesn't want you to do something, you might as well not bother. But we never had that opportunity.'

'We were on the cusp of starting production,' says Litten. 'After a very rocky road ... we were ready to go into production and the BBC withdrew our rights. We were still within our window and everything. They withdrew it on a technicality – a ludicrous technicality.'

'As I understand it, and I may be wrong,' says original writer Mark Ezra, 'they had a [clause in their] deal with the BBC that they could not license or assign the rights to anybody else without the BBC's approval.'

Of course, this was exactly what Daltenreys had done when they assigned the rights to Lumiere, and consequently the BBC argued that they were in breach of their agreement.

'Something went wrong,' continues Ezra. 'I don't know if Peter and George assigned it without getting the BBC's approval, or if something else went wrong, but essentially, they lost the rights. The BBC clawed them back ... I believe that ... [Litten] did make a small error at some stage, which

---

[491] From *Doctor Who Magazine* – Issue 213 (8 June 1994) p.4

allowed some smart lawyer at the BBC to say, "Ah, you're in breach of this and we're having the rights back." I don't think that their investors were that thrilled.'

'[The BBC's] behaviour was absolutely appalling,' says Litten. 'Basically, they took the money and got out of the deal on a technicality, in order to do other things with the rights.'

The BBC stood firm by their legal arguments, and treated the agreement as void. With the project clearly unlikely ever to resurface, John Illsley took the opportunity to cut his losses. 'I was getting a bit frustrated with the production company,' he says. 'I suppose I was suffering from a certain amount of naivety … It never really got going, and after several sort of frustrating meetings, I sort of gave up on the project, to be honest.'

Illsley left the company as a director on 1 February 1994. He had recouped none of the money he'd put into Daltenreys' business.

'[I] probably had a bit of spare cash in the bank,' he says, 'so it wasn't hurting too much, but it certainly cured me, I think, … of any other involvement in the film business.'

'Across the period of the few years we were setting it up, the BBC very much changed its remit,' says Litten. 'They moved from being a kind of gentlemanly organisation, where things were done on handshakes, to being like any other kind of corporation … If it's not in the contract, it's not part of the deal … The people that we did the deal with moved on. New people came in, and it was the new people that were the ones who shafted us.'

Daltenreys never made another film. The company was financially ruined. 'About three and half million of development went down the drain,' estimates Litten. (The exact figure is unclear.)

With the company's finances crippled, on 16 December 1994 there was another change of company directors. Nobody realistically expected the business ever to recover.

TRIAL OF A TIME LORD

In the end, the BBC's deal with Amblin fell through when Philp David Segal left the company, taking the *Doctor Who* series proposal with him. However, Segal's efforts did eventually bear some fruit. Working with the BBC, he steered his pet project through numerous set-backs. It was rejected by various parties, including CBS, Paramount (yet again passing on a *Doctor Who* proposal) and Fox. Eventually, though, a 90-minute one-off TV movie was made as a co-production between the BBC and Universal, with Fox also contributing to the budget. This was not formally a pilot for a television series, but rather a 'backdoor' pilot that could still potentially lead to one if it was well received.

The TV movie was the single most expensive *Doctor Who* episode ever produced. It showed off the largest TARDIS set ever constructed (to date) and went to great pains to tie directly into the BBC's own series. Picking up where the series had left off with Sylvester McCoy in 1989, it also gave us a new actor in the role of the Doctor, Paul McGann.

When broadcast on BBC1 on 27 May 1996, the new Anglo-American production was a tremendous hit with British audiences, pulling in over 9 million viewers – *Doctor Who*'s highest rated episode since 1982. McGann's Doctor was instantly popular, the production values and direction of British director Geoffrey Sax were much lauded and, for many, *Doctor Who* was back, and it was 'about time too'.[492]

Sadly, the TV movie did not lead to any further episodes being made, and the transatlantic experiment ended almost as soon as it had begun. Although the UK ratings had been very good, American figures had been (perhaps predicatbly) less impressive. Unfortunate scheduling meant most Stateside viewers spent the night instead watching a key episode of the popular sitcom *Roseanne* ('Heart & Soul'), which had been extensively promoted.[493] Executives at Universal and Fox had pet projects of their own that were favoured over Segal's.

The BBC, for their part, were also still unwilling to invest in a wholly in-house revival of *Doctor Who*, perhaps afraid that the show's galactic scale would be too much for a BBC budget ever to shoulder without outside investment.

Daltenreys were naturally unimpressed that their own bid to make *Doctor Who* had been invalidated for the sake of such a seemingly fleeting experiment. 'They sold us the feature film rights to make three films and then they went ahead and made a TV film' says John Humphreys. 'They had a TV series that they were bringing to an end and we bought the feature film rights to do something, because they were not interested in doing anything on TV with it. So, we buy the feature film rights and they go ahead, and our investors are looking at us and saying, "What's going on?" So, you go to the BBC and say, "Hold on a minute. You're actually undermining our project here, by doing this." … They just didn't care. It was just terrible really … We were astonished at the attitude we were having to deal with … I didn't see it coming at all.'

In their final set of accounts, Daltenreys revealed a total of £1,878 in the bank, but £961,363 in debt.[494] With the company on the verge of bankruptcy, they had no intention of going down without a fight.

On 31 January 1996, some three months before the Paul McGann TV

---

[492] 'He's back – and it's about time' was the slogan used to promote the TV movie.
[493] The episode featured one of the lead characters, Roseanne's husband Dan, suffering a near-fatal heart attack.
[494] These accounts, covering 1996, were submitted on 16 January 1997.

movie was transmitted, the *Otago Daily Times* in New Zealand reported the earliest rumblings of a possible legal challenge from Daltenreys against BBC Worldwide (previously known as BBC Enterprises). Under the headline 'Pop artists to sue BBC', the newspaper article focused on a relatively small investment that the singer Bryan Ferry had put into the project as well as the more extensive involvement of John Illsley:

'While Ferry has lost "only a few thousand", Illsley has lost more than $155,000. The three founders of Daltenreys ... claim they have been nearly bankrupted ... Ferry, according to a friend, had long been a fan of *Doctor Who*. "Bryan's always watched it, which is why he was interested, but it wasn't a huge investment, only a dabble really."'[495]

The article also made mention of the hoped-for casting of Alan Rickman as the Doctor, before going on to quote Illsley as saying: 'I'd be staggered if the BBC does not do the decent thing and compensate the company. When they started talking to Spielberg, it totally pulled the rug from under us.'[496]

A spokeswoman from BBC Worldwide responded to the paper's article by stating simply: 'The rights were licensed ... for a specific period. Unfortunately, the production did not get off the ground within an extended license time and the rights reverted to the BBC ... If legal proceedings were to be issued they would be vigorously contested.'[497]

Only a few days earlier, on 10 January, the London *Evening Standard* also carried a two page exposé on the problems that had beset the film project.

Over a year later, on 14 February 1997, Litten, Dugdale and Humphreys issued BBC Worldwide with a writ in the High Court. This sought £15 million in compensation, to recoup £1 million of pre-production costs and an additional £14 million to cover the lost profits of a projected film trilogy. Humphreys was reportedly 'devastated', claiming that Worldwide had 'obstructed and delayed' the project and finally 'breached the undertaking'[498] that they had made with Daltenreys.

In response, BBC Worldwide's Mary Collins[499] only reiterated the company's previous position, telling *Doctor Who Magazine*: 'We have received a writ. It's content is currently being considered – but it will be contested vigorously.'[500]

As the story reached the national news, Daltenreys' lawyer Stuart Lockyear, from the firm Stephens Innocent Ltd, commented in *The Times* that

---

[495] From the *Otago Daily Times* (31 January 1996)
[496] From the *Otago Daily Times* (31 January 1996)
[497] From the *Otago Daily Times* (31 January 1996)
[498] From *Doctor Who Magazine* – Issue 250 (9 April 1997) p.4
[499] Head of international communications at BBC Worldwide (1993-2005).
[500] From *Doctor Who Magazine* – Issue 250 (9 April 1997) p.4

the BBC's actions had 'caused financially great hardship [for Daltenreys].'[501]

'We will take this as far as we need to,' Lockyear told the *Independent* the same day. 'You don't start legal proceeding unless you want to go to court – however long it takes. My clients say it is a breach of contract because the BBC set about preventing them making the film. They mortgaged their homes to make this film and it is only down to the sympathy of NatWest bank that they are still in them.'[502]

'It cost me very, very dearly,' recalls Humphreys. 'I nearly lost my home over it. It caused me a great deal of distress and family upheavals and I'm very angry about it, to this day … My wife had just given birth to twins when it all started going belly up. Even now, when I think about it, it makes my blood boil, but what can I do?'

At the time, an angry Humphreys told the *Independent*: 'The simple fact is that we have been ruined by the BBC. They have behaved in a way that even now we find unbelievable.'[503]

On 31 December 1997 Daltenreys met with their creditors, and on 12 January 1998 they issued a notice of voluntary liquidation. The company's lawyers then continued trying to save the owners' personal finances through the courts.

'We had some of the top lawyers in the country fighting it for a number of years afterwards on a "no win, no fee" basis,' recalls Litten. 'We had no more money. Fortunately, a very prominent set of lawyers [Stephens Innocent] agreed to fight it on [that] basis, because our case was so strong. They did [so] for a number of years, but ultimately, the BBC had the funds to throw more money and more lawyers [at it] than we could possibly muster up.'

'I'd never been to court with anyone and I didn't realise that it was just like playing poker,' says Humphreys. 'The way it works when you go to court against someone like the BBC is that they … will bring in an army of lawyers and that army of lawyers has to be paid. So, what they do is they go to court and they ask the judge for security of costs, which means basically that they want a pot of money putting together from both sides that's put down on the table. That way, if someone wins, they get their costs covered. The loser loses everything. You might think that's fair enough, but the trouble is that if you're just a small outfit, working against an organisation like the BBC, you can't compete with the security of costs. You put a hundred grand down. They come to court with a QC and god knows what. After a very short length of time, that money's been spent. They then ask for a further security of costs and a further security of costs.'

---

[501] From *The Times* (15 February 1997)
[502] From the *Independent* (15 February 1997)
[503] From the *Independent* (15 February 1997)

The legal struggle rumbled on across another year, returning to the papers on 24 August 1998 with a further article in *The Times*. John Humphreys was quoted as saying: 'This has taken its toll on us ... Some [have lost] a few thousand, others everything. When you're dealing with the BBC, you expect absolute honour. You wouldn't think you'd have a situation like this. Just before we started filming, the BBC wrote us a letter pulling the rights, saying we'd broken the agreement.'[504]

In 1998 Daltenreys reduced their claim to £8 million in damages as Humphreys suggested to *The Times* that the BBC had only 'belatedly realised the commercial potential' of *Doctor Who* when Spielberg's name was first mooted. The crux of the BBC's argument against Daltenreys was still their assigning of the *Doctor Who* rights to a finance company (with the Lumiere bid), however Humphreys maintained that his company, 'had told the BBC, which raised no objection. It was perfectly straightforward. They leapt upon this at the eleventh hour in order to justify their claim.'[505]

'You're asking your backers to give you more money to fight the case,' remembers Humphreys. 'And in the end they shrug their shoulders and say, "We can't go on anymore." You just have to walk away from the table. You just can't play the game anymore. And that's what happened to us.'

Daltenreys didn't win their fight. 'It became untenable basically,' recalls Litten. 'The BBC had all the money in the world to throw at lawyers, and they did. After x number of years of fighting it, there's a point where one can't go any further. It left a very bad taste in our mouths.'

On 9 June 2001 there was one final meeting of Daltenreys' creditors. A notice of the company's final dissolution was issued a few months later, on 25 September 2001. Daltenreys, Coast to Coast, Green Light and Dr Who – The Movie Limited were all dissolved.

'At least two people's lives were pretty much ruined,' says Litten. 'My defence against it was to forget all about it. Unfortunately, other people didn't weather so well out of it.'

'We were young and naïve,' says Humphreys. 'I've learnt a hard lesson since. I always say to anyone, if you sign a contract with anyone, it's not worth anything unless you can financially enforce it.'

'The trouble is,' says John Illsley, 'these iconic TV programmes are quite difficult to take into a different medium, I suppose. I think that's probably what the problem was ... You'd think that somebody should be able to make a movie of the bloody thing, but God, there you are ... Some things are obviously best left alone.'

Asked if he'd ever considered attempting to return to the *Doctor Who* brand, Litten is adamant: 'I'd sooner stick pins in my eyes then get involved

---

[504] From *The Times* (24 August 1998)
[505] From *The Times* (24 August 1998)

in a film of *Doctor Who* again, or the BBC for that matter.'

POSTSCRIPT

Following the revoking of the *Doctor Who* deal in 1994, Peter Litten went on to direct that year's *To Die For* (aka *Heaven's A Drag*), a film about a man who is haunted by the ghost of his recently deceased partner. He worked on the script with Johnny Byrne.

Byrne himself remained as a writer on *All Creatures Great and Small* through until the series' end in 1990, and in 1992 he helped to develop *Heartbeat* for ITV, writing 23 of its episodes, the last in 2005. He died on 2 April 2008, aged 72.

Mark Ezra continued writing and directing on a number of low- to mid-budget features, including the 1996 thriller *Savage Hearts*. In 2000 he worked with former *Doctor Who* script editor Andrew Cartmel and *Doctor Who* writer Ben Aaronovitch on Channel 5's *Dark Knight* series.

John Humphreys stayed in special effects for some time, also working on Litten and Byrne's *To Die For*. He was a sculptor on Oliver Stone's *Alexander* epic in 2004 and on Tim Burton's *Charlie and the Chocolate Factory* remake in 2005. Having been a student at the Royal Academy in his youth, he later returned to the world of art, working on a series of realist and surrealist sculptures from his workshop on the South coast.

Denny Martin Flinn never had another film produced after his Hollywood success on the sixth *Star Trek* movie in 1991, although he did write various books, including a number of detective novels. He also adapted his friend Nicholas Meyer's novel *The Seven Percent Solution* for BBC Radio 4 as a 90 minute play starring Simon Callow as Sherlock Holmes and Ian Hogg as Dr Watson. On 24 August 2007 he died aged 59 at his home in the Woodland Hills, California. He had been suffering from throat cancer. His last two books, *The Great American Book Musical – A Manual, a Manifesto, a Monograph* and *Ready for my Close-Up!: Great Movie Speeches*, were published posthumously.

George Dugdale hasn't acted as a producer on any film since the collapse of the *Doctor Who* movie. However in 2003 his wife (and prospective co-star in the movie) Caroline Munro appeared in the *Doctor Who* audio drama 'Omega', starring Peter Davison and Ian Collier. Speaking at the recording of the play, she reflected on her husband's doomed project. 'Sadly, that wasn't to be,' she said. 'But it's nice to be in the fold now.'[506]

Lumiere Pictures didn't get the opportunity to renew their bid for the *Doctor Who* rights, but they did retain their control over Aaru's 1960s Dalek films and in 1995 produced the straight-to-video *Dalekmania* documentary

---

[506] From *Doctor Who Magazine* – Issue 334 (September 2003) p45

(see Chapter Three).

For the rest of the decade (and indeed the century) the BBC largely continued to maintain its argument that any future *Doctor Who* production would have to be in association with an independent company. However, despite this assertion, no independent company would ever again successfully lease any of the screen rights to the programme from the corporation. Daltenreys was the last.

In fact, in the wake of the 1996 TV movie, much of the *Doctor Who* brand was brought back under the BBC's own in-house umbrella. Publishing rights were pulled back from Virgin Books and objections were raised against independent producers such as BBV regarding some of their unlicensed *Doctor Who* spin-offs (see Appendix A). As the century ended, the BBC perhaps came some way toward a reconciliation with its long-spurned offspring.

A Doctor Who Film[507]
By Denny Martin Flinn

PLOT SYNOPSIS

'A cosmos without the Doctor scarcely bears thinking about.'[508]

The Death Zone[509] on Gallifrey: A Middle-Eastern man called Rachmed staggers through a sandstorm, dodging scarlet laser blasts that rain down from the sky. On his way, he encounters rock creatures and two-headed snakes with tusks, before he finally reaches his destination, the craggy stone tomb of the great Time Lord Rassilon: the infamous Dark Tower.[510]

Inside the tower, Rachmed passes floors made of quicksand and invisible electric barriers, before entering the tomb of Rassilon itself. There is a carved stone sarcophagus in the centre of the room. A stone relief of Rassilon shows the great man wearing a large jewelled ring on his finger.[511]

Wrenching off the heavy stone lid, Rachmed is suddenly bathed in a cold, unnatural light, which spills out from inside the sarcophagus. He staggers stiffly about the room, wracked with pain. He tries to cry out, but can't. Slowly, Rachmed's features darken as his flesh turns to stone.

Bread Street, England, 1593. The Doctor enters the Mermaid tavern,

---

[507] Flinn seems never to have given his script a title, beyond the designation *A Doctor Who Film*.

[508] This quotation was to appear as an opening caption at the start of the film. It is taken from 'The Five Doctors', a 1983 *Doctor Who* television story written by Terrance Dicks.

[509] Another hangover from 'The Five Doctors', in which the Death Zone was also the central setting.

[510] The aerial laser fire is consistent with what we saw of the Death Zone in the BBC's original television production of 'The Five Doctors'. The Dark Tower, containing Rassilon's tomb, is also much the same. However, the dust storm is something new. On television, the BBC had to make do with filming at Carreg Y Foel Gron quarry near Ffestiniog in North Wales for their realisation of the Death Zone. This Death Zone didn't have any sandstorms – just a lot of mist (and a little rain).

[511] The ring on Rassilon's finger is another direct lift from 'The Five Doctors' – where it was used to grant the 'gift' of immortality.

dressed as a nobleman. At a table sit William Shakespeare[512], Robert Greene[513], Christopher Marlowe[514], Francis Beaumont and John Fletcher. The five famous writers are arguing about the public reaction to Shakespeare's *Romeo and Juliet*. Overhearing their conversation, the Doctor butts in, raving about Shakespeare's qualities and about his great place in future history.

The writers try to question the Doctor over his outlandish predictions, but there isn't time. Suddenly, a man with a neatly trimmed beard calling himself Mandrake bursts in and deliberately knocks over Shakespeare's drink. Following an argument the bearded man challenges Shakespeare to a duel. Marlowe accepts on Shakespeare's behalf. The Doctor tries to dissuade Marlowe, but the writer is insistent. A sword-fight ensues, in which Mandrake kills Marlowe. Mandrake then turns on Shakespeare, but before he can run him through, the Doctor intervenes, producing a blade of his own and fending off Mandrake. Shakespeare profusely thanks the Doctor, who then leaves in his TARDIS.

The inside of the Doctor's TARDIS is full of 'the most futuristic materials with mechanical and art deco designs … It is laden with artefacts from many times and places throughout the universe.'[515]

The Doctor is talking to K-9 when a message comes in from the Celestial Intervention Agency[516], ordering him to return to Gallifrey – specifically to the Dark Tower. The Doctor obeys the summons and sets the ship's controls accordingly.

When he arrives, the Time Lords ask the Doctor's opinion on the calcified remains of Rachmed, which they have found standing next to the

[512] This isn't the first time that Shakespeare crops in the context of a *Doctor Who* story and it won't be the last. Shakespeare first appeared in *Doctor Who* via a small cameo in the 1965 television story 'The Chase'. Later, in 2002, he had a more substantial role in the audio play 'The Time of the Daleks'. He finally got to meet the Doctor in a television story in the 2007 episode 'The Shakespeare Code'. He is also a prominent character in the 1995 *Doctor Who* novel *The Empire of Glass* by Andy Lane. The television series also had the Doctor mentioning meeting Shakespeare on other (unscreened) occasions – notably in 1979's 'City of Death'.
[513] Robert Greene (a jealous rival of Shakespeare's) would go on to be one of the central characters in the 2005/6 *Doctor Who* comic strip *A Groatsworth of Wit*, published in *Doctor Who Magazine*.
[514] Christopher (Kit) Marlowe was another of the real historical characters used by Andy Lane in his 1995 *Doctor Who* novel *The Empire of Glass*.
[515] All quotes taken from *The Nth Doctor* by Jean-Marc and Randy Lofficier – iUniverse Books (2003) p.130
[516] The Celestial Invention Agency (CIA) featured prominently in only one *Doctor Who* television story, 'The Deadly Assassin' (1976). However, they also play an extensive rôle in a number of *Doctor Who* novels (e.g. *Alien Bodies* (1997)) and audio dramas (e.g. 'Neverland' (2002)).

tomb of Rassilon. Unbeknownst to the Doctor, as he examines the strange corpse, he is observed by Mandrake hiding in the shadows.

A world away (literally), a Lockheed Electra light aircraft is flying through the clear blue skies above the Pacific Ocean. It is a beautiful day (in 1937). Without warning, suddenly everything changes. The clouds darken and swell and a violent storm begins to buffet the little aeroplane. Waves crash and the sky turns an inky black. Mandrake has created the storm, using a magical golden jewel (stolen from the Great Pyramid in Giza) to manipulate the elements. As its instruments go wild, the small plane loses control.

The Doctor has left Gallifrey, hoping to get to the bottom of the mystery of the stone man. He observes the events above the Pacific from his TARDIS and comes up with a plan to save the little plane and its pilot. He tells K-9: 'If we ... rematerialise around the co-ordinates of the flying device, we could bring it aboard by opening the zero room[517] in the same time frame.'

The Doctor soon puts his plan into operation. He and K-9 help to extinguish the flaming plane as it stands in the zero room. The pilot gets out of the cockpit. It is the famous American aviator Amelia Earhardt (but that isn't made clear as yet and, for the moment, she is referred to only as Amy).

The Doctor eventually manages to explain to 'Amy' the nature of her rescue, although she is understandably difficult to convince. She eventually concludes that she has been abducted by aliens (well, one alien and a dog).

Meanwhile on an unnamed alien planet, Mandrake is visiting a nightclub called the Androsterone Strain. One of the belly-dancers at the club is an alien called Milky Waye. Embedded in her costume is a bright red jewel, similar to the golden one that endangered Amy's plane. Mandrake has come looking for this. He cons his way into Milky Waye's dressing room, kills her and steals the jewel. As Mandrake brings the red jewel close to the golden one, there is a disturbance in the timestream (which is soon felt by the Doctor and Amy in the TARDIS).

The Doctor and Amy travel to Egypt in around 2500 BC. While there, they bump into an Egyptian peasant called Aman, who is stealing from some of the local merchants. Aman explains that Rachmed is his brother and has been missing for days. The Doctor notices that Aman is wearing a digital wristwatch. Aman explains that he stole the watch from Mandrake,

---

[517] The zero room was a special room aboard the TARDIS that appeared in the 1982 television story 'Castrovalva'. It was designed to be used by Time Lords for rest and recuperation. The room was destroyed during the course of this, its first and only story.

who had hired his brother as a guide before he went missing.

The Doctor and Amy persuade Aman to take them to the last place he saw his brother and Mandrake together. He takes them to the Great Pyramid at Giza. The Doctor soon works out that Mandrake must have arrived in Giza, with his TARDIS disguised as a stone-block. He then hired Rachmed to steal Rassilon's great ring of immortality. The Doctor tells Aman that his brother is dead.

Saying that he wishes to avenge Rachmed's death, Aman goes along with the Doctor and Amy. They travel forward to the year 1900 and explore the King's Chamber inside the Great Pyramid. The bodies of two grave robbers (whom Mandrake used to steal the golden jewel for him) lie on the floor. In the hands of one of them is a small metal button, which comes from Eastern Europe in the 15th Century. The three travellers decide to make that their next port of call. As they leave, they tell Aman not to steal any gold from the tomb.

The Doctor realises that Mandrake is behind everything that's been going on. He explains to his companions that Mandrake is a fellow Time Lord and a contemporary. Across a series of flashbacks, we get to find out more about the joint history of the Doctor and Mandrake.

The Doctor's very first journey into time was with Mandrake at his side. It was a trip to the Ottoman Empire in the 13th Century. Both the Doctor and Mandrake were still young then. Whilst there, they watched as an innocent man had his hands cut off as a punishment for a crime he did not commit. When a physically sickened Doctor complained to Mandrake of the needless severity of the punishment, Mandrake was unmoved, dismissing the victim's innocence as merely 'a minor detail.'

Following their experiences in the 13th Century, the Doctor and Mandrake didn't meet again for some time. The Doctor eventually abandoned Gallifrey altogether, and began travelling as a freelance adventurer in a stolen TARDIS.

The pair were finally reunited late one night in 1912, aboard the *Titanic*. The Doctor was aboard with a young travelling companion named Victoria[518]. The friends were enjoying the general atmosphere on board when the ship struck an iceberg and started to sink. All had been somehow arranged by Mandrake. It was never 'meant' to happen at all. The Doctor tried to get people to the lifeboats, but could do only so much. When he asked Mandrake why he had engineered the sinking, Mandrake only gave

---

[518] This was presumably intended to be an entirely new and original character, not to be confused with Victoria Waterfield, a regular in the *Doctor Who* television series between 1967 and 1968, played by Deborah Watling. In fact, at the time Flinn wrote this script, no *Doctor Who* episodes featuring Victoria Waterfield had yet been broadcast in America.

an evil grin and said simply: 'Because I can!'

Thrown over the side of the ship, the Doctor had been left by Mandrake to 'die' in the freezing waters of the Atlantic Ocean. Floating in the sea, the Doctor's body had regenerated for the very first time[519].

Following the trauma of his metamorphosis, this 'new' Doctor spent some time resting and recuperating in the 19th Century Lake District. It was during this retreat that he met another Time Lord known only as the Monk[520]. The Doctor and the Monk chatted and reminisced for a while before the conversation eventually turned to Mandrake. The Monk mentioned that Mandrake's escapades had started to become of some concern to the Time Lords, and he even suggested enlisting the Doctor's help in dealing with Mandrake. 'The Time Lords would not care to see Mandrake do harm,' commented the Monk.

Back in the 'present day', with the Doctor finished recounting the backstory, we return to the immediate problem of Mandrake's latest masterplan.

The Doctor explains that Mandrake is planning to reassemble the Key to Time[521], a pan-dimensional device of great power. The 'jewels' that he has been collecting are all components of the Key to Time. Mandrake is hoping to track down all of the other components in order to have a complete Key. Naturally, the Doctor plans on stopping him.

Following a trip to an Earth of the far-flung future that is swarming with cockroaches, the Doctor finally traces Mandrake, and he and his companions set a trap for him. They deposit one of the jewels that Mandrake is searching for in a crystal shop on Earth and hope to use it as bait to draw the villain out into the open.

At this point, another incarnation of the Doctor enters the story (played

---

[519] This directly contradicts the Doctor's history as laid out in the BBC television series, where the Doctor's first regeneration came in the 1966 serial 'The Tenth Planet'.

[520] Again, there was also a character called the Monk in the original *Doctor Who* television series. He was one of the Doctor's own people, and appeared in 'The Time Meddler' (1965) and 'The Daleks' Master Plan' (1966). However, he was a very different character from the one we see here. As with Victoria Waterfield, no television episodes featuring the Monk had been broadcast in America at this point.

[521] The Key to Time is another concept 'borrowed' from the television version of *Doctor Who*. In the series, the Key is (as here) a device of unimaginable power that can control the very nature of the universe. It was a recurring plot-point during *Doctor Who*'s sixteenth television season (1978-79).

by Tom Baker[522], if all went to plan). This alternate Doctor helps safely deposit one of the crystals in the shop before spending a brief moment chatting with his other self about old times (and new).

'I have so much to ask you,' says the other Doctor. 'Did you ever run into those frightful Daleks again? Are the Time Lords giving you a hard time? And what of the Cybermen?' Before they part, the Doctor warns his earlier self to be wary of Logopolis[523].

Meanwhile, Amy and Aman go off to a café on the other side of the street, where the Doctor (their Doctor) soon joins them to wait for the arrival of Mandrake.

Mandrake eventually turns up. However, entering the crystal shop, he runs into the other Doctor, who is about to leave. Mandrake attacks him and renders him unconscious. 'Our' Doctor arrives to survey the shattered crystal and general chaos of the shop. Aman soon joins them, but is brutally batted away by Mandrake. Amy hits Mandrake on the head with a hookah, but the evil Time Lord is unharmed and takes her hostage, telling the Doctor that he will only allow her to go free in exchange for the last jewel.

The two incarnations of the Doctor depart amicably and 'our' Doctor goes with the injured Aman to chase after Mandrake and Amy.

The TARDIS takes them to a San Francisco rock concert in the 1960s, where The Who are performing later that day. The Doctor and Aman find Mandrake and Amy and manage to rescue the girl, before escaping in the general commotion of the concert. However, unknown to them, Amy has been hypnotised by Mandrake.

The Doctor releases Amy from Mandrake's mind-control by kissing her. However, it turns out that various members of the crowd have also been hypnotised by Mandrake and have been handing out drinks laced with LSD. Amidst the resulting chaos, Mandrake is able to snatch his final jewel and escape in his ship.

Using his telepathic powers to probe his nemesis's mind, the Doctor discovers that Mandrake's secret base is located in a city on a distant asteroid drifting through deep space. The travellers go there and face Mandrake once again. Mandrake reveals he has run out of regenerations and is hoping to begin a whole new life-cycle by stealing Rassilon's ring of immortality. However, before he can put his plan into operation, he first

[522] In the BBC series, Tom Baker was the fourth incarnation of the Doctor. However, with this film's alternate continuity, that isn't necessarily the case here. The Doctor's first two incarnations (at least) are quite different from their television equivalents, so there's no reason to suppose the fourth isn't as well.

[523] Logopolis was the setting (and title) of Tom Baker's final *Doctor Who* television story in 1981. It's not clear how this fits in with the film's 'reboot' of *Doctor Who* continuity. It is perhaps best seen as just a subtle nod or in-joke,

needs to stop time itself, and to do that he needs the Key to Time.

'I have no more lives left to me,' explains Mandrake. 'When I die, I will be forgotten. Unlike your precious William Shakespeare ... You see why I despise him so? His work will make him immortal. My last hope is to stop time.'

Mandrake then 'reaches to his chin and slowly peels off his handsome, bearded, if sinister, face and exposes the real one underneath: chilling, collapsed, ancient with harsh age lines.'

As the decrepit Time Lord assembles the Key to Time, reality itself starts to unravel. Native Americans from the 19th Century appear on the streets of New York over a century later. Spaceships from different time periods pop into sudden existence throughout history. The time continuum rips apart and the vortex starts to collapse in on itself.

The Doctor and his friends launch a desperate attack on Mandrake and his army of headless zombies. In the struggle, Aman briefly gets hold of the Key to Time, but he is blasted away by a bolt of electricity from Mandrake's hand. The Doctor defeats the headless soldiers, but he's too late to stop Amy and Mandrake falling through a widening hole in the time vortex.

Amy holds onto the lip of the chasm by her finger-tips, but Mandrake is clinging to her waist, pulling her down into the swirling vortex. Amy finally lets go, sacrificing herself in order to rid the universe of Mandrake. The Doctor is left clutching her scarf as she tumbles deep into the void. The Doctor and Aman then leave the scene of the devastation in the TARDIS.

Later, we return to the Elizabethan tavern from the start of the film. All is exactly the same as it was before, except that now Aman is in the bar too. This time round, the Doctor does not disarm Mandrake. Instead they fight a sabre duel. During the fight, Mandrake trips and falls onto his own dagger. Having reached the end of his regeneration-cycle, Mandrake finally dies and crumbles away to dust.

Aman decides to stay with the Doctor on his travels, and the pair collect Amy from 1937 – an Amy who has no memory of the Doctor nor their adventures with Mandrake. 'I'm in the middle of a round-the-world flight,' protests Amy. 'I don't have time for this.'

'On the contrary, we have all the time in the world,' replies the Doctor[524].

---

[524] The sixth movie in the James Bond series, *On Her Majesty's Secret Service*, also used this line as a closer.

10
Back Home
BBC Films (1998-2003)

ONE BBC

In 2002, BBC Director General Greg Dyke spoke publicly of his vision for 'One BBC'. A BBC working together as a unit, rather than competing within itself. Outside the BBC, many perhaps assumed that it was already like that. There is still talk of 'the BBC is doing this' or 'the BBC is doing that', as if 'the BBC' were a single and united entity. Of course, as with any reasonably large organisation, the BBC isn't really like that and probably never has been.

The BBC is a group of individual people, all with widely differing views and opinions. Just like the rest of human society in fact. So, when in the '80s and '90s it was said that 'the BBC' didn't like *Doctor Who* and didn't want to make it anymore, that wasn't strictly true. There were just *some* people at the BBC who didn't like *Doctor Who*. And there probably still are. There were also however lots of others who absolutely loved the show and really wanted to make another series and/or movie. Unfortunately for *Doctor Who*, at least in the '80s and '90s, those in charge were largely the people who *didn't* like it.

However, by the dawning of the new millennium, things were starting to change. Most of those people who'd killed off *Doctor Who* in 1989 were no longer at the BBC. Some had left to pursue jobs elsewhere. Others had retired. With a rosta of new faces beginning to dominate BBC management, attitudes to certain programmes had started to change, and *Doctor Who* was no longer considered to be quite the embarrassment it once had been.

WORLDWIDE

The BBC's commercial arm, BBC Worldwide, exists in an almost unique relationship to the BBC itself. It is an independent and limited company. However, it is also entirely owned by the BBC. It is both a part of the BBC and yet not exclusively accountable to it.

A comment in the BBC's staff newspaper *Ariel*, a few years after Greg Dyke's 'One BBC' speech summed up the relationship as follows: 'We are One BBC. And they are another One BBC'. The statement neatly illustrated the tension that can sometimes exist between the two bodies.

It was BBC Worldwide that dissolved Daltenreys' *Doctor Who* contract in 1994. However, it wasn't BBC Worldwide that Daltenreys had originally dealt with back in 1985.

In the early 1960s, the commercial exploitation of the BBC's television programming had been handled by an internal television promotions department called BBC Exploitation (actually run by just one man). Radio was similarly (from 1965) handled by a radio promotions department. In 1969, the two departments were merged and a new BBC Enterprises department was formed. There was also a separate department, BBC Records and Tapes, handling audio releases. Eventually, in 1979, all these disparate areas and groups were pulled together into a wholly owned BBC subsidiary company called BBC Enterprises Ltd. This was responsible for marketing BBC programmes on video, audio and later (from 1986) in print. And it was *this* incarnation of BBC Enterprises that dealt with much of the *Scratchman*, *Krikkitmen* and Daltenreys *Doctor Who* projects.

Friction between the BBC proper and its commercial arm was perhaps inevitable. When in 1993 BBC Enterprises had commissioned a straight-to-video *Doctor Who* special, 'Lost in the Dark Dimension', to celebrate the show's thirtieth anniversary (see Chapter Nine), certain people within the BBC Drama Department had been less than pleased by the idea, seeing it as *their* job to make drama and Enterprises' job just to exploit their output. Bridges were mended only when BBC1 agreed to give the special a television screening. Although, as it turned out, the project foundered for other reasons anyway and never happened at all.

Finally, in 1995, following substantial reorganisation at the BBC, BBC Enterprises became more independent still, and was rebranded as BBC Worldwide.

BBC Worldwide, as well as looking after the exploitation in all media of the output of BBC Television, also had an exciting new responsibility. It now made films too.

BBC FILMS

BBC Films came into existence at around the same time BBC Worldwide arose from the ashes of the old BBC Enterprises. As its name suggests, it was there to make cinema features – something the BBC had never really done before.

Outfits like Euston Films had been making pictures in conjunction with commercial television for some time. However, the BBC's output had been (pretty much) exclusively for broadcast, until now. The cinema was largely uncharted territory. And with an incredibly weak British film industry, nobody could be really sure if BBC Films was ever going to work. Happily for the future of both the BBC and the British film industry however, it did work, and it worked very well indeed.

BBC Films was run, essentially as an independent company, by David Thompson, whose full job title was Head of Film and Single Drama. Thompson had been working at the BBC for well over a decade. He'd been a producer on such things as the *Everyman* documentary series (1979-1986), the *Screen One* (1991) and *Screen Two* (1987-1995) drama strands and 1985's television version of *Shadowlands*.

Although also producing an eclectic range of made-for-television projects, BBC Films was quick to break into the cinema. Early co-productions, under Thompson's stewardship, included 1992's *Sarafina!* with Whoopi Goldberg and Jimmy McGovern's *Go Now* (1995). Later there would be *Jude*, a film based on Thomas Hardy's *Jude the Obscure* (1895), starring Christopher Eccleston.

In just a few years, BBC Films proved itself to be a worthwhile enterprise for the BBC, and as the century neared its end, Thompson was keen to capitalise on his early successes with more adventurous productions. It was with this in mind that in 1998 Thompson attended the Cannes Film Festival to make a small and, so he thought at the time, innocuous little announcement that created a great deal more publicity than he was probably expecting. He announced that he wanted to make a *Doctor Who* film.

ON THE SLATE

It was almost 33 years to the day since *Doctor Who* had last featured in reports from the Cannes Film Festival, during the promotion for *Dr. Who and the Daleks*, way back in 1965.

It was therefore something of a bolt from a blue when on 18 May 1998 David Thompson told a panel at the Cannes Film Festival of his hopes to develop a *Doctor Who* feature-film for his forthcoming production slate. Indicating a possible budget of around £6 million, he spoke of a 'lavish reincarnation … without the wobbly cardboard sets of old. There is obviously a great movie to be made from *Doctor Who*.'[525]

'It was always fascinating,' says Thompson. 'We'd make sort of ten announcements about all the very exciting films we were making, but the one thing the press always wanted to focus on was *Doctor Who*. We'd be inundated with missives from the *Doctor Who* society.'

Excited but wary about Thompson's news, *Doctor Who Magazine* asked a BBC source for more information. They were told there were 'absolutely no concrete plans for a *Doctor Who* movie' and that 'no such project is actually in development.'[526]

Of course, no 'concrete' plans didn't mean no plans at all, and the idea was quickly seized on by sections of the press as very big news indeed. And, as

[525] From *Doctor Who Magazine* – Issue 266 (1 July 1998) p.4
[526] From *Doctor Who Magazine* – Issue 266 (1 July 1998) p.4

was now usually the way, the first thing everyone seemed to want to know was, who would be playing the Doctor?

A few days later, the staff of the BBC News website obligingly reported: 'The question of who should be Who is one of the crunch issues.'[527] Among those the BBC News site interviewed was Christopher H Bidmead, who had written and script-edited for the *Doctor Who* television series in the early 1980s. Bidmead said: 'Every time it has been taken out of the rickety old BBC studios it seems to go wrong. Even when they put the great Peter Cushing in the role he became not Dr Who but someone different.'

The writers of ITV's Teletext soon jumped on board, deciding, for reasons best known to themselves, that the real story was the possibility of a *woman* being cast as the Doctor. And they saw this as a good opportunity to host a phone-in survey to establish the 'people's choice' casting for a new female Doctor. They probably weren't expecting the 1,155 responses that came through their switchboards.

When the Teletext votes were counted, Honor Blackman[528] came out top with 23% of the vote. Second place was taken by Helen Mirren with 19%, and joint third were Helen Baxendale and Kate Winslet with 14% each. Emma Thompson[529] attracted 9%, while both Liz Hurley and the Duchess of York appeared toward the bottom of the poll.

In response to the increasingly fevered casting speculation, David Thompson commented: 'We could cast a man or a woman. That's possible, although we haven't decided yet.'[530] Needless to say, regardless of his intentions, that statement only acted to drastically raise the temperature of the speculation.

In reality, Thompson didn't yet have anyone of either gender in the frame to play the Doctor. He didn't even have a script. It was probably unreasonable to expect that he would. He had done no more than air an intention to *try* to pursue a *Doctor Who* film; everything else that had followed had merely been supposition and gossip.

Hoping to put matters more realistically into perspective, *SFX* magazine asked for a comment from Alan Ayres, spokesman for BBC Drama. 'It's a piece of wild speculation,' asserted Ayres with refreshing bluntness. 'It was never a statement – it was just an aside in a conversation blown into something it isn't. Anything you may read about casting or budget is total

---

[527] From *BBC News Website* (21 May 1998)

[528] Honor Blackman had appeared in *Doctor Who* before. She'd played Professor Laskey in four episodes of the 1986 serial 'The Trial of a Time Lord', starring Colin Baker.

[529] Emma Thompson had never appeared in *Doctor Who*. However, her father Eric Thompson had. He featured in the 1966 television serial 'The Massacre of St Bartholomew's Eve', alongside William Hartnell.

[530] From BBC News website (21 May 1998)

bollocks … It's simply a gleam in the eye. I wouldn't put it any stronger than that. We have had preliminary discussions with a distributor, but I can't reveal who that is at the moment.'[531]

By July, *Variety* were telling their American readers that Hal Films, the London offshoot of the US distribution giant Miramax, were in talks with BBC Films over the new *Doctor Who* picture. They also quoted David Thompson stating that the opportunity to work on a *Doctor Who* feature had come up only a week prior to his 'announcement' at Cannes.

The Hal Films rumour was further reinforced when the July edition of *Doctor Who Magazine* reported that its own sources suggested that talks with Miramax had taken place as early as the end of February. The magazine went on to urge its readers 'not to lobby BBC Films, Hal Films or Miramax with *Doctor Who* related queries.'[532] Naturally, this didn't stop many people from doing exactly that, as they had been doing since May.

In June, Tim Collins, the Conservative MP for Westmoreland and Lonsdale, who just happened also to be a *Doctor Who* fan, contacted Thompson at BBC Films to clarify his position on the future of a *Doctor Who* movie. A now weary Thompson replied on 4 June, 'It is true that *Doctor Who* was mentioned in Cannes as one of a number of possible films that we are exploring making – the coverage that we received was out of proportion to what was said. However, together with co-production partners, we are examining the possibility of a feature film; but there are, as yet, no definite plans to go into production.'[533]

'It raises quite strong feelings in some people and some people thought we were mad to even attempt it,' recalls Thompson. '"You can't do this" and "You'll ruin it". We got all that kind of stuff. They're a very vociferous lot and I think people might feel they'd be attacked if they embarked on this and people didn't like it … they might have to go into hiding … You're dealing with something sacred to people. So people were very wary of it. And it is a very difficult thing to pull off as a movie. It's a very big leap.'

Despite the downplaying by Thompson and Ayres, the question of a possible *Doctor Who* movie refused to go away, being posed in all sorts of unlikely corners over the summer of 1998.

On 14 July, Millbank Tower in Westminster was the venue for the launch of the BBC's Annual Report and Accounts, held before an assorted mix of government politicians and their aides. Somewhat to the surprise of the assembled executives, Ian Garrard on behalf of *Doctor Who Magazine* took this opportunity to broach the subject of the film with the BBC's Director of Television (and occasional champion of *Doctor Who*), Alan Yentob. Although

---

[531] From *SFX Magazine* – Issue 41 (June 1998)
[532] From *Doctor Who Magazine* – Issue 267 (29 July 1998) p.4
[533] From *Doctor Who Magazine* – Issue 268 (26 August 1998) p.5

effectively ruling out a solely BBC-produced series for television, Yentob remained optimistic about a co-production for the cinema; something that Director General John Birt also confirmed.

As the summer wore on, much to the relief of Thompson and his team at BBC Films, the press maelstrom slowly began to die down and the company were able finally to begin looking at the actual feasibility of making a *Doctor Who* picture.

MEN IN BLACK

Thompson had been considering the possibility of a *Doctor Who* film for some time. Ever since the revocation of the Daltenreys contract in 1994, the BBC and BBC Worldwide had held onto the cinematic rights to the show. Initially the hope seems to have been that a suitably sized (probably American) production company would make an acceptable offer for them. However, with the successful establishment of Thompson's BBC Films, the idea of the BBC making (or co-producing) the film themselves was suddenly possible in a way it had never been before.

'We were always looking at the possibility of turning TV gems into films,' remembers Thompson. 'In the past [however], the received wisdom was that the transition from television to film was usually disastrous. The [example] that was always quoted to me was *On the Buses*.'

Certainly there hadn't been a great boom in television-based movies in Britain since the 1970s, when Hammer Studios produced a raft of sitcom tie-ins. Recently, the team behind Channel Four's much-praised *Drop the Dead Donkey*[534] had failed to get a movie of their series into cinemas. Doug Naylor, the co-writer of the BBC's *Red Dwarf* series, was also failing to attract sufficient investment in a film version of his programme[535]. The late '90s, it seems, was no better a time to be making a big-screen translation of *Doctor Who* than the late '80s had proven to be. However, Thompson was still prepared to give it a try. After all, in the years it would take to get any such film off the ground, the climate in the industry might change.

After a number of different distributors were approached about backing a proposed feature, thoughts soon turned to exactly what sort of film might be made out of *Doctor Who*. And the answers proved just as tricky to pin down as they had always been.

---

[534] The *Drop the Dead Donkey* film was worked upon between 1994 and 1996, but was cancelled during production.
[535] Work on mounting a film of *Red Dwarf* really got under way in about 1999, but had been an idea that Naylor had been keen to pursue at least as early as 1997. Only a few minutes of special effects footage was ever filmed for the aborted production.

'What we struggled with I suppose was, how do you introduce that world to someone in just one movie?' says Thompson. 'That's the challenge for whoever's going to make the movie, to do that ... That was the challenge, which we didn't succeed in overcoming ... A lot of discussion was had about it and various concepts with it, but, particularly in those days, it was a very old brand. It hadn't been revitalised.'

Unlike Daltenreys' proposed film, which went through various drafts over its long gestation period, BBC Films' one didn't have a script at this stage. In fact, it didn't even have a story. In all fairness, it was probably less important for the BBC, who owned the show anyway, than it had been for an independent project touting for support. However, even though BBC Films hadn't commissioned a script, they had thought about possible writers. Top of Thompson's list was American screenwriter Ed Solomon.

Solomon was a not entirely illogical choice, having co-written the two *Bill and Ted*[536] time-travel movies in 1989 and 1991, in which two friends travel through the history of Earth in a phone box. He had also recently scored a very big hit with 1997's *Men in Black,* starring Will Smith and Tommy Lee Jones. In 1998, Solomon was much in demand and had already started working on a big-budget Hollywood remake of the US television series *Charlie's Angels,* finally to reach cinema screens in 1999.

'We did have lots and lots of discussions with a number of writers, recalls Thompson, 'but the most serious one was the meeting we had in America with the writer of *Men in Black* ... I can vividly remember an extremely nice breakfast with him in Los Angeles, to talk about it ... He had a very interesting idea ... He never in fact wrote a script. We never got that far, but we talked ideas and things – outlines and things.'

Bearing in mind his work on *Bill and Ted,* it's perhaps not unreasonable to think that Solomon might have been interested. By the 1990s, *Doctor Who* had become something of a niche cult in the US, mostly thanks to its regular circulation on PBS television. Tom Baker's incarnation of the Doctor would even appear as an occasional guest character in America's hit animation series *The Simpsons*[537]. Solomon certainly knew of *Doctor Who.*

'For a time ... [he] was going to do it,' remembers Thompson. 'But it's quite a daunting task for a writer. More daunting then, because *Doctor Who* hadn't been revived into the success that it is today. We were more wary of it then. We're wary of it now too ... He felt that he didn't want to take it on, in the end

---

[536] *Bill and Ted's Excellent Adventure* (1989) and *Bill and Ted's Bogus Journey* (1991) also spawned two short television series, *Bill and Ted's Excellent Adventures* (1990, 1992).

[537] At the time of writing, the Doctor has appeared as a background character in *The Simpsons* on three separate occasions: in November 1995, December 1998 and October 1999.

... I think he felt, understandably, that it wasn't for him.'

Elsewhere, as 1998 neared its end, the BBC's News website marked *Doctor Who*'s thirty-fifth anniversary (one day late) with a report that quoted a misinformed spokesman as saying: 'We're in talks about a possible feature film for the cinema ... Scripts have been prepared, but the film will be at least two or three years away if we decide to go ahead with it.'[538]

Who this 'spokesman' is wasn't stipulated, which was just as well, as the statement was completely false. No *Doctor Who* script was ever commissioned in any form by BBC Films.

CHAOS THEORY

With the movie rights to *Doctor Who* having reverted to the BBC in the wake of the death of Daltenreys and with no continuing *Doctor Who* series on television to tread on his toes, Thompson had the brand largely to himself in the late 1990s. However, prospective bids to return *Doctor Who* to full time production had never really gone away, and there were additional interests both inside and outside the BBC working on other possible reinventions, either for television or the cinema.

As early as December 1996, Philip Segal, the man responsible for getting that year's *Doctor Who* TV movie off the ground, told *Doctor Who Magazine* of his hopes for his own revival project. He commented that when Universal Television's option on *Doctor Who* came to an end in late 1997, 'the field is then open for anyone to negotiate ... Let's just say, I'm waiting in the wings.'[539] Later, on 5 February 1998, Segal confirmed to the Outpost Gallifrey *Doctor Who* web site that he was soon to meet with the BBC concerning the film rights to *Doctor Who*. In April, he told *Doctor Who Magazine* that his discussions were ongoing. However, by this time Thompson had already started on his BBC Films project and Segal does not appear to have taken his attempts to make a film any further.

Others were not so easily discouraged. In fact, the next rival attempt to mount a *Doctor Who* movie had made headlines within days of Thompson's own announcement at Cannes. On 26 May 1998, independent producer, Mitchell (Mitch) Henderson officially registered the formation of his new Chaos Films Ltd production company. Based in the Devon area, Henderson had recently been working on a movie called *Chaos*, from which his company took its name. The production starred Danish actress Sara-Marie Maltha (later to appear in hit DR1 series *Forbrydelsen*[540]) and German actor Erich Redman. It

[538] From BBC News website (24 November 1998)

[539] From *Doctor Who Magazine* – Issue 263 (8 April 1998) p.4

[540] Maltha appeared in the third and final series of this internationally successful Danish television thriller, which was retitled *The Killing* when broadcast in Britain.

had a very low budget and did not gain a general release. However Henderson was happy enough with the end result to set up his own company off the back of it with fellow producer Martin Clifford Cahill. The partial aim of this company was to make a new *Doctor Who* feature film. This would have been in direct competition with BBC Films' own project; although, in fairness, Henderson probably didn't know about BBC Films' intentions when he first started making his plans.

As the BBC themselves currently held the exclusive rights to the *Doctor Who* brand, it appears that Henderson's hope was somehow to exploit the rights that had originally been assigned to Aaru productions for their two Dalek pictures in the 1960s. It was even suggested that Henderson's project would, in fact, be a final realisation of Milton Subotsky's failed *Doctor Who's Greatest Adventure* picture from the 1980s (see Chapter Three).

In hindsight, it is extremely difficult to see how Henderson ever thought he might be allowed to mount such a production, considering the steps the BBC had taken to thwart Daltenreys only a few years earlier. However, the 1983 release of *Never Say Never Again*, a James Bond film made outside and in competition with the established franchise, has at least shown that it can be done if you have enough lawyers and enough money to pay them with.

Following Subotsky's idea for *Doctor Who's Greatest Adventure*, Henderson's plans seem to have involved two incarnations of the Doctor, one of whom would be older than the other. The person that Henderson had in mind for his 'older' Doctor was actor Michael Sheard.

Michael Sheard had been a recurring guest actor in the *Doctor Who* television series between 1966 and 1988[541]. In that time, he'd acted alongside William Hartnell, Jon Pertwee, Tom Baker, Peter Davison and Sylvester McCoy. However, Sheard was probably best known for playing Herr Grunwald in the first series of *Auf Wiedersehn Pet* in 1983 and Mr Bronson in *Grange Hill* from 1985 to 1989. He was also notably choked to death by Darth Vader in the second *Star Wars* picture, *The Empire Strikes Back* (1980), and played Adolf Hitler in *Indiana Jones and the Last Crusade* (1989). His professionalism as an actor had earned him the nick-name 'one take Mike'.

Sheard told *SFX Magazine*: 'I received a telephone call from this person who said they were pushing hard to get the rights to the script and, if they were successful, would I be interested in playing Doctor Who? Of course I would be.'[542]

In late May, Sheard chose to announce publicly his involvement in the

---

[541] Sheard appeared in the following stories: 'The Ark' (1966), 'The Mind of Evil' (1971), 'Pyramids of Mars' (1975), 'The Invisible Enemy' (1977), 'Castrovalva' (1982) and 'Remembrance of the Daleks' (1988). He also appeared in the *Doctor Who* audio drama 'The Stones of Venice', released in 2001.

[542] From *SFX Collection – Doctor Who No.1 – Special Edition 20* (February 2005) p.24

production at the Frontier in Mann *Doctor Who* convention in America. His unexpected statement was relayed as a news story in the July issue of *Doctor Who Magazine* (Issue 267). A notice had also now been placed by Henderson in the *New Producers' Alliance* newsletter, asking for an 'established producer or business partner'[543] to help him further develop and pursue the Subotsky rights and present a proposal to the BBC for either a feature film or a pilot for a US television series.

Sheard optimistically told readers of *SFX* magazine that the production was 'very much a case of watch this space.'[544] Unfortunately no film from Chaos Productions ever materialised. The entire project is still shrouded in some degree of mystery over exactly what happened. The family of Milton Subotsky certainly do not recall ever hearing from Henderson concerning the rights to use any elements of the aborted *Doctor Who's Greatest Adventure* script, which appears to have formed the cornerstone of the Chaos project.

After his brief dalliance with *Doctor Who*, Mitchell Henderson appears not to have remained in the film business for very long in any publicly active capacity. Ann Margaret Sleigh-Henderson (believed to be Henderson's mother) joined Chaos Productions as a company secretary on 1 April 1999. Later that year, on 3 June, Martin Clifford Cahill left the partnership. The company's annual returns continued to be officially filed until 4 May 2000, via the Stevens and Willey chartered accountancy firm in Devon, but the business was finally dissolved on 13 May 2009.

What happened to Henderson and his plans for *Doctor Who* is still uncertain. Erich Redman, who appeared in Henderson's early *Chaos* feature, lost touch with him early in the new century and no longer knows where he is. Neither have any of his other Chaos colleagues been able to provide any information. Final reports of Henderson place him in either Bideford, North Devon or St Austell, Cornwall.

RESIDENT EVIL

There were however other, perhaps more credible, approaches being made for a *Doctor Who* film at this time. In the summer of 1999, news broke in the pages of *Total Film* that British director Paul (W S)[545] Anderson had also expressed an active interest in directing such a project.

Anderson had recently scored a more than moderate hit with the movie adaptation of popular videogame *Mortal Kombat* (1995), and even more

---

[543] From *Doctor Who Magazine* – Issue 267 (29 July 1998)
[544] From *SFX Collection* – *Doctor Who No.1* – *Special Edition 20* (February 2005) p.24
[545] From about 2002, Paul Anderson started to be credited as Paul W S Anderson, apparently to avoid confusion with the American film director Paul Thomas Anderson (who made *Boogie Nights* (1997) and *The Master* (2012)).

recently had helmed the somewhat less successful sci-fi picture *Event Horizon* (1997). Both these films were collaborations with producer Jeremy Bolt, with whom Anderson had formed a production company called Impact Pictures in 1992. And it was both Bolt and Anderson who were hoping to make a *Doctor Who* film through Impact Pictures. Bolt's involvement in the enterprise was later confirmed in Issue 285 of *Doctor Who Magazine*.

In August, *SFX* magazine quoted a BBC spokesperson on the approach that had been made to them by Bolt and Anderson. The spokesperson said: 'We can confirm that we are at a very early stage of development on this. At present we have no announcements to make regarding the writer or director on this project.'[546]

Media casting speculation was, predictably, soon re-ignited. The Film Culture section of the *Independent on Sunday* ran a refreshingly measured article on 29 August in which writer Matthew Sweet raised the possibility that Denzel Washington might be cast in the lead. Depressingly, other publications saw the colour of the actor's skin as almost as controversial an issue as the possibility of a woman being cast in the role.

Sweet's article also quoted a statement from Mike Phillips at BBC Worldwide, stating: 'Paul [W S Anderson] wrote an interesting treatment ... and we thought he had a good take on the material, and that it might be a saleable mainstream film. So we made a deal with Paul and Jeremy, and they're in LA talking to studios about making a *Doctor Who* movie ... *Doctor Who* is one of those iconic properties that always presents opportunities ... But it needs a new approach. It needs to be updated and made relevant for today's audiences ...'[547]

'*Doctor Who* needs to be reinvented for a global audience,' said Jeremy Bolt. 'That means casting an international name in the lead ... What about Laurence Fishburne? Or Anthony Hopkins?'[548]

Prophetically, the article also commented: 'The fast progress on *Doctor Who: the Movie* has scuppered plans by the BBC's Drama Department for a domestic, small-screen revival of the series. Only a few months ago, Russell T Davies – the talented writer-producer of the Channel Four drama series *Queer as Folk* – was invited to develop a new series for broadcast on BBC1. Davies is a long-time fan of the programme ... Channel Four even altered the production schedule for an imminent *Queer as Folk* special to allow Davies time to set up the series, tentatively titled *Doctor Who 2000*. Now that Impact is poised to take the Doctor into the cinema, however, these plans have been abandoned.'[549]

Issue 282 of *Doctor Who Magazine* fanned the flames of speculation when it

---

[546] From *SFX Collection – Doctor Who No.1 – Special Edition 20* (February 2005) p.25
[547] From the *Independent on Sunday* (29 August 1999) p.4
[548] From the *Independent on Sunday* (29 August 1999) p.4
[549] From the *Independent on Sunday* (29 August 1999) p.4

mentioned that Gary Oldman, Linus Roache and Sean Pertwee had all also been suggested by 'sources', as possible movie Doctors. The magazine commented: 'To date, news of the film has been classified "above top secret" in BBC circles.'[550]

Gary Oldman told *TV Times* that he would be happy to join any future *Doctor Who* film 'if the money and the script were right.'[551] Meanwhile, Neil Morrissey said he'd happily to do it for a shandy and a Mars bar.

The following month, *The Sunday Times* reported Bolt and Anderson to have been in discussions with Artisan Studios, who had recently worked on the low-budget cult horror *The Blair Witch Project*. 'We intend to make this bigger than Bond,'[552] asserted Bolt. The usual 'BBC insider' meanwhile tried to allay fears of a possible Americanisation of the programme by commenting: 'The script will be witty, suspenseful and very English.'[553] There was still no comment from the very Welsh Russell T Davies about his own project.

In October, bizarre reports appeared in Scotland's *Herald* newspaper, claiming that Hollywood visual effects company Arc/Haven had been spotted in the Glasgow area taking measurements from some of Britain's few surviving police boxes. The suggestion was that they'd been commissioned to work on a new TARDIS for the film. However, the BBC's refreshingly blunt Alan Ayres poured cold water on the idea, telling *SFX Magazine*: 'It's complete baloney. Why on Earth would an American FX company come all the way to Scotland to measure police boxes when we have no script and no director. It's almost as ludicrous as a report that ran recently saying that Richard Briers and Francesca Annis[554] had been spotted filming a new story ... It's too premature to talk about casting ... I'm wary of talking about the film before the deal is done, simply because *Doctor Who* always arouses such passion and interest. At the moment we have no distributor, and with no distributor we have no finance for the film.'[555]

Meanwhile, Russell T Davies (temporarily) withdrew, stating simply: 'Both ideas – film and TV series – were being discussed, and for the moment they've gone for the film option.'[556]

As November rolled round, the production was still 'looking at getting American finance,' as Bolt told *SFX* magazine. 'It will be new and contemporary without patronising either the new or the old audience,' he continued. 'There will be a large time travel element to it ... and I can say that

[550] From *Doctor Who Magazine* – Issue 282 (22 September 1999) p.4
[551] From *SFX Collection – Doctor Who No.1 – Special Edition 20* (February 2005) p.25
[552] From *SFX Collection – Doctor Who No.1 – Special Edition 20* (February 2005) p.25
[553] From *SFX Collection – Doctor Who No.1 – Special Edition 20* (February 2005) p.25
[554] Francesca Annis and Richard Briers didn't actually work together on any projects in 1999.
[555] From *SFX Collection – Doctor Who No.1 – Special Edition 20* (February 2005) p.25
[556] From *SFX Collection – Doctor Who No.1 – Special Edition 20* (February 2005) p.25

the Master will be there in one form or another.'[557]

Around Christmastime, expectations were once again high for a forthcoming *Doctor Who* film production.Then, however, just as had happened many times before, the brakes were suddenly slammed on hard again, knocking Bolt and Anderson out of the running.

Doctor Who Magazine Issue 286 quoted Bolt saying with some evident bitterness: 'Artisan Entertainment and ourselves have parted company with the BBC. They decided not to go with it ... It'll take the BBC god knows how long to sort something else out.'[558]

That month, *SFX Magazine* ran their own interview with Bolt under the headline 'Boo Who'. In the interview, Bolt continued, 'What can you do? I worked for six months on this, brought the BBC the most exciting film company in the world, and they decide not to go with it. To say that I am happy would not be the case.'[559]

MILLENNIUM

The intense fan and press interest in a *Doctor Who* film failed to abate as a new century arrived, even though nobody had yet officially announced any such project to be going ahead. In December 2000, BBC Films claimed that it was still 'early days'[560] for their own project.

'Everybody seized on it,' recalls David Thompson, who was then still batting away journalists from his desk at BBC Films. 'That's what happened to me. I used to do press-conferences ... We'd have a number of journalists there. We'd talk about 30 things and you'd make a throwaway remark about *Doctor Who* and that would be the headline. "BBC to make *Doctor Who* film!" It was always quite amusing. Each year they'd come back and say, "What happened to your *Doctor Who* film?" We once made a similar announcement over a *Buffy* film we were doing – *Buffy the Vampire Slayer*. The nature of the film business is that you have a lot of ideas and you talk about them, sometimes too early when they're in development. Or sometimes you talk about them early in order to attract attention, because you want to get funding for the development or something, or you want to stop somebody else doing it. It's a very fickle business ... It's a long, long process. The average time for a movie is something like seven or eight years from start to finish ... It's very tempting for all of us to shoot our mouths off about what we're doing and it sometimes comes back to haunt you.'

In June, the *Sun* claimed that Stephen Fry had been cast as the Doctor. Not

[557] From *SFX Collection – Doctor Who No.1 – Special Edition 20* (February 2005) p.25
[558] From *Doctor Who Magazine* – Issue 286 (12 January 2000) p.4
[559] From *SFX Collection – Doctor Who No.1 – Special Edition 20* (February 2005) p.25-6
[560] From *Doctor Who Magazine* – Issue 300 (7 February 2001) p.44

to be outdone, a few days later the *News of the World* claimed it to be Tom Selleck. The *Mirror* said Sean Bean in January 2001, with Tara Fitzgerald as his co-star. And *SFX* misread the *Men in Black* rumour to suggest either Kevin Kline or Will Smith, under the auspices of director Barry Sonnenfeld. In November, *Bella* magazine heralded Alan Cumming[561].

Bookmakers Ladbrokes at one point even opened bets on the Doctor's casting. Stephen Fry came out top at 4/5, Alan Davies was at 4/1 and Gary Lineker at 100/1. Naturally, none of this had any foundation in what BBC Films were really doing at the time.

Still without the backing of a major distributor, the project seemed no closer to fruition at the end of July 2002, when Alan Yentob, now the BBC's Director of Drama and Entertainment, tried to remain optimistic. He said during a webchat with BBC staff: 'We're developing … with a prominent writer, a feature film of *Doctor Who* – but who knows if it will happen. We get *Doctor Who* enthusiasts asking to give it another go, so I don't rule anything out.'[562]

Four or five years, seen in the context of other major blockbuster films, wasn't really all that long a period of time for the *Doctor Who* project to have spent in development. However, few other projects had to endure such close and public scrutiny at such an early stage. And by the early noughties, the patience of many even within the BBC itself was wearing thin.

Between 1998 and 2003, quite a few parties had expressed an interest in developing new *Doctor Who*, but the BBC felt forced to turn most of them away, on the grounds that a project was already in development with Thompson at BBC Films. However, with no film forthcoming, BBC Films were not going to be allowed to sit on their project forever. If BBC Films weren't going to make their movie, the feeling was that perhaps somebody else should be given a chance.

Frictions between BBC Films and the main body of the BBC itself had always existed, and there were some within the BBC Drama Department who felt particularly annoyed. Their argument was that the ongoing BBC Films project was getting in the way of them possibly bringing *Doctor Who* back as a television series.

In fact, the early 2000s were something of a tense period for the relationship between BBC Drama and BBC Films in general. Another source of friction was BBC Films' *Murder Rooms: The Dark Beginnings of Sherlock Holmes*, a series of films based on the life of Sir Arthur Conan Doyle, then pulling in

---

[561] Alan Cumming had no previous *Doctor Who* credits. However, he had appeared in the 1993 drama *The Airzone Solution*, which had a strong *Doctor Who* flavour (see Appendix A). In 2004, he was also very nearly cast as the Doctor in an aborted *Doctor Who* drama planned for BBC South West.
[562] From *Doctor Who Magazine* – Issue 321 (18 September 2002) p.9

rapturous audiences on BBC1. It was much to the surprise of many that this series was never re-commissioned. One of its writers, Stephen Gallagher, explained that the show's demise was 'the outcome of a silent turf war between BBC Drama and BBC Films. The word went around that the show had been "too successful for the wrong department."'[563]

Conflicts such as this are illustrative of the way the BBC was run at the time, and feelings of annoyance over BBC Films' work on *Doctor Who* were just another example of it. However, this wasn't just a petty demarcation dispute. BBC Drama did have a point. For the first time in a very long while, there were people at the BBC who genuinely wanted to make a new series of *Doctor Who* for television. And BBC Films' project was seen to be getting in the way.

Russell T Davies had been asked to help develop a new series even before the new century had begun; and in 2001 there was a further pitch, from writers Mark Gatiss, Gareth Roberts and Clayton Hickman. The will was finally there to put *Doctor Who* back into production as a continuing television series. But only if there was no conflict with BBC Films.

One person who was very keen to see *Doctor Who* back on television was BBC1's Controller Lorraine Heggessey. However, as BBC Films had been working on the *Doctor Who* movie for a very long time, she had agreed not jeopardise their plans by setting up a television series in competition with them … at least for the time being.

REGENERATION

In 2003, *Doctor Who* was celebrating its fortieth anniversary. However, unlike with the muted fanfare of 1993, there was actually something *to* celebrate this time around. Following the show's effective cancellation in 1989, other things had grown up to fill the void left in fan's lives by its absence from the Saturday evening schedules. An already-successful range of continuing *Doctor Who* novels had grown larger than anyone could ever have realistically predicted, recently becoming the longest continuing series of printed stories anywhere in world literature. In 1999, the independent company Big Finish Productions had started work on a series of full-cast *Doctor Who* audio dramas starring Peter Davison, Colin Baker, Sylvester McCoy and (from 2001) Paul McGann. There were increasingly sophisticated comic strips and spin-off videos, stage plays, cartoons and novellas. There were, in fact, more *Doctor Who* stories in continuous production now than there ever had been when the show was on the air. But, of course, the one thing fans didn't have was a television series.

By 2003, most had come to the conclusion that it was best to just give up

---

[563] From *http://brooligan.blogspot.co.uk/search?q=murder+rooms* (3 January 2012)

hope of *Doctor Who* ever returning to the medium that spawned it. As *SFX* put it, fans felt 'battered by seven years of false dawns, beaten senseless by endless misinformation, our optimism left bloodied and smashed on the floor.'[564]

In his introduction to a book on the series, journalist and fan Mark Campbell even went so far as to say '*Doctor Who* is dead and buried ... If it was something the BBC wanted to continue making, don't you think we'd have more than one 90-minute TV movie to show for a whole decade? Of course we would ... *Doctor Who* just doesn't seem to fit in with today's current multichannel, multi-rubbish world.'[565]

As late as 15 October 2003, *Doctor Who Magazine* was still to be found quoting sources claiming: '[BBC Films is] currently developing a *Doctor Who* movie for theatrical release.'[566] Nothing, it seemed, had changed. Few anymore believed that anything ever *could* change. However, this time, defying all expectations to the contrary, they were wrong.

In 2003, BBC Films' attempts to make a *Doctor Who* movie were finally abandoned. 'We put it all on hold,' remembers David Thompson. 'Everyone thought that the best thing was to hold back on further progress on the film.'

Then, through one of those small television miracles that hardly ever happen, something very surprising occurred.

At the autumn 2003 Edinburgh TV Festival, Controller of BBC1 Lorraine Heggessey reaffirmed her hopes to resurrect *Doctor Who* as a Saturday evening television series. Of course now, as with the boy who cried wolf, few people believed her.

Rumours concerning the show's return had been circulating in certain circles within the BBC for a little while, but then rumours had been doing that for as long as most people could remember. Except, this time the rumours were true. With the BBC Films project now formally dropped, Lorraine Heggessey had decided to commission a new series of *Doctor Who* for BBC television.

'[BBC Films] has now agreed that, as they haven't made the film and I've been waiting for two years,' said Heggessey, 'it's only right that BBC1 should have a crack at making a series.'[567]

A few months later she explained: 'Eventually, I just lost my patience. I said, "Look, it's ridiculous! You keep saying you need these rights to make a movie, but you haven't made a movie." I said, "I've been waiting for quite a long time now. You said you wanted to do it, but you haven't! Surely BBC1, who started the whole project, should take back the rights to make it on

---

[564] From *SFX Collection – Doctor Who No.1 – Special Edition 20* (February 2005) p.27
[565] From *The Pocket Essential Doctor Who* by Mark Campbell – Pocket Essentials (2000) p.7
[566] From *Doctor Who Magazine* – Issue 335 (15 October 2003) p.4
[567] From *Doctor Who Magazine* – Issue 336 (12 November 2003) p.5

television?"'[568]

The seemingly impossible had finally happened. And once it had happened, few could any longer remember why it had seemed so impossible in the first place. In 2005, *Doctor Who* returned to BBC1 as a prime-time show, and it was popular too. Very, very popular. Every bit as popular as it ever had been before and more.

Of course, film rumours still resurfaced from time to time, but there was an awful lot less riding on them with a regular series being beamed across television sets all over the world.

THE FUTURE?

BBC Films carried on making movies. It co-produced *Iris* (2001), *Match Point* (2005), *Mrs Henderson Presents* (2005), *Miss Potter* (2006), *Becoming Jane* (2006), *An Education* (2009), *We Need to Talk About Kevin* (2011) and many more too numerous to mention.

'In the end, we moved on and did lots of other films,' says David Thompson. 'Essentially, whenever I spoke about anything at Cannes, we got loads of articles [saying], you know, "BBC to make *Doctor Who* film!" Every year, we were asked about it, and we'd obviously made 70 or 80 other films during that period. It holds a complete fascination for people. Who knows? Maybe a film will be made … It would be wonderful if it was, I'm sure … It's probably a good time to make it now. A better time now than then, because the brand is more known now and has been modernised, and I think people have got a clear idea about how to do the transition.'

In 2007, a restructuring saw Thompson leave BBC Films, with the company becoming much more closely integrated as part of the BBC itself, taking up new offices at BBC Television Centre. Thompson left to form Origin Pictures, who, working closely with the BBC, were behind the 2011 television series *The Crimson Petal and the White*.

---

[568] From *Doctor Who Magazine* – Issue 356 (25 May 2005) p.9

11
The End?

Brian Eastman, who tried and failed to make his own *Doctor Who* film in 1980 with Douglas Adams, reflects: 'You could hardly imagine a movie now, because, of course, the telly really make movies, don't they? On a Saturday night, they are almost as good as you could ever imagine in the cinema. So, I'm sure somebody probably *is* proposing a *Doctor Who* movie, but they'd be hard pressed to do it as well as they do it on television.'

In the early 1990s, it seemed that the only future *Doctor Who* could possibly ever have would be in the cinema. The only prospect for a television series would be from an independent production company, maybe even through a commercial broadcaster. Whatever future there might be would, it seemed, have to be far away from its original home as a weekly BBC1 television series, produced in-house for a family audience on a Saturday teatime. Of course, the irony is that in 2005, that was precisely what *Doctor Who* returned to being.

The Doctor didn't need to be played by a big movie star like Alan Rickman, Donald Sutherland, Bill Cosby or even Michael Jackson in order to make the show popular again. It just needed good character actors like Christopher Eccleston, David Tennant and Matt Smith. In fact, exactly the same kind of good character actors who had made the Doctor so great to watch in the first place.

It didn't need a Hollywood studio either. It could do just as well with the BBC's own facilities on its own soil. The show didn't *need* the cinema, after all.

And of course, it begs the question. After half a century of failed attempts to take *Doctor Who* to the movies, perhaps television is simply the best place for it to be.

Appendices

APPENDIX A

STRAIGHT-TO-VIDEO MOVIES

This book is about *Doctor Who*'s difficult relationship with the cinema. As such, it has not included any significant mention of the plethora of independently produced feature-length *Doctor Who* spin-off movies that exploded onto the market in the 1990s. Following the BBC's cancellation of *Doctor Who* as a continuing series, a number of small independent production companies (principally Reeltime Pictures and BBV) obtained the rights to use various *Doctor Who* characters and concepts in order to produce spin-off movies centred around them. Although produced outside of the BBC, these officially-endorsed spin-offs often featured members of the series' original cast and crew. These straight-to-video (or DVD) offerings were never designed primarily for either cinema release or television broadcast, although most were produced to broadcast quality. Despite this, however, they were a legitimate continuation of the *Doctor Who* story and were very important to fans during those years when the show was off the air.

These productions were as follows ...

WARTIME (1987) (Revisited 1997 and 2015)
Reeltime Pictures Ltd
30 mins approx. (1987 Version)
35 mins approx. (1997 Version)
35 mins approx. (2015 Version)

Written by Andy Lane and Helen Stirling
Produced and directed by Keith Barnfather
Music by Mark Ayres

CAST:

BENTON	John Levene
FATHER	Michael Wisher
MOTHER	Mary Greenhalgh
PAUL	Chris Greenhalgh
JOHNNIE	Steven Stanley
PRIVATE WILLIAMS	Peter Noad
LETHBRIDGE-STEWART	Nicholas Courtney (1997 Version)
SOLDIER	Nicholas Briggs

STORY:

During a routine mission, Benton revisits an old childhood home and is haunted by ghosts from his past.

NOTES:

This story features Benton (John Levene), a semi-regular character in the *Doctor Who* television series between 1968 and 1975. The 1997 re-edited version of this movie also credits a cameo from Nicholas Courtney (he was also in the original 1987 version), who played Alistair Gordon Lethbridge-Stewart between 1968 and 2008. This was the only independent *Doctor Who* video spin-off to be produced while the series was still on the air. It was also one of the first dramas to be scored by musician and sound engineer Mark Ayres. Ayres would join the *Doctor Who* television series as a composer the following year. Nicholas Briggs (Soldier) would later go on to provide the voices of the Daleks and the Cybermen (among others) for *Doctor Who* following its BBC relaunch in 2005.

The 2015 version is the same as the 1997 release, but with improved picture quality and digital effects.

P.R.O.B.E. – THE ZERO IMPERATIVE (1994)
BBV 90 mins approx.

Written by Mark Gatiss
Produced and directed by Bill Baggs
Music by Mark Ayres

CAST:

LIZ SHAW	Caroline John
PATRICIA HAGGARD	Louise Jameson
PETER RUSSELL	Colin Baker
DR O'KANE	Jon Pertwee
DR DOVE	Sylvester McCoy
LOUISE BAYLISS	Linda Lusardi
DR BRUFFIN	Mark Gatiss
PATIENT ZERO	David Terence
DR HEARST	Nicola Fulljames
DR GILCHRIST	Patricia Merrick
CUMMINGS	Jonathan Rigby
PR OFFICER	Sophie Aldred
ORDERLY	Simon Messingham
ORDERLY	Alexander Kirk
PATIENT ONE	Peter Davison
BOY	Daniel Mills

STORY:
Liz Shaw and the Preternatural Research Bureau investigate a series of bizarre deaths at a psychiatric hospital.

NOTES:
Liz Shaw (Caroline John) was a regular character in *Doctor Who*'s seventh television season in 1970. She is the only character from the original series to feature in this movie. However, most of her fellow cast members also have a *Doctor Who* connection. Colin Baker played the Doctor on television between 1984 and 1986, Jon Pertwee did the same between 1969 and 1974 and Sylvester McCoy between 1987 and 1996. Sophie Aldred played the character Ace in the series from 1987 and Peter Davison, who makes a brief cameo appearance at the end, was the Doctor from 1981 to 1984. Louise Jameson played Leela, alongside Tom Baker's Doctor between 1977 and 1978. This was Mark Gatiss's first teleplay, but he has since written for and acted in *Doctor Who* on many occasions, on television, radio and in print. Simon Messingham has also written a number of *Doctor Who* novels and short stories for the *Doctor Who* books range.

SHAKEDOWN – RETURN OF THE SONTARANS (1994)
Dreamwatch Media
55 mins approx

Written by Terrance Dicks
Produced by Mark Ayres, Kevin Davies and Jason Haigh-Ellery
Directed by Kevin Davies
Music by Mark Ayres

CAST:

CAPTAIN DERANNE	Jan Chappell
KURT	Brian Croucher
ZORELLE	Carole Ann Ford
ROBAR	Michael Wisher
MARI	Sophie Aldred
NIKOS	Rory O'Donnell
STEG	Toby Aspin
VARN	Tom Finnis
TROOPERS	Jonathan Saville
	Keith Dunne
	Derek Handley
	Julian Jones
	Stephen Mansfield

STORY:
A space yacht is boarded by a platoon of Sontarans. Something is loose aboard the ship and the Sontarans intend to find it.

NOTES:
Nearly a decade on from their last appearance in the *Doctor Who* television series, the warmongering alien Sontarans take centre-stage in this one-off feature from the director of the Dalek docudrama *Dalekmania* (see Chapter Three). The script was written by Terrance Dicks, one of *Doctor Who*'s most prolific writers, who had also been the show's script editor between 1968 and 1974. Most of the actors taking part in the production had earlier appeared in episodes of either *Doctor Who* or *Blake's 7*. Carole Ann Ford had played the Doctor's granddaughter Susan during the first two years of *Doctor Who*. Michael Wisher was a regular guest-actor on the programme throughout the 1970s, most notably playing Davros in 1975's 'Genesis of the Daleks'. Sophie Aldred also clocked up another spin-off appearance here as Mari. Visual effects on the production were supervised by Ian Scoones, who had worked on the effects for a number of *Doctor Who* television serials in the 1960s and 1970s. The video also called on the services and facilities of effects man Clifford Culley at Pinewood Studios, who had previously worked for the BBC on three *Doctor Who* serials in the early 1970s. *Shakedown* was later novelised by Terrance Dicks for Virgin Publishing's range of continuing *Doctor Who* novels in 1995. The book expanded on the video to include the character of the Doctor.

P.R.O.B.E. – THE DEVIL OF WINTERBOURNE (1995)
BBV
82 mins approx

Written by Mark Gatiss
Produced and directed by Bill Baggs
Music by Mark Ayres

CAST:

LIZ SHAW	Caroline John
PATRICIA HAGGARD	Louise Jameson
CUMMINGS	Jonathan Rigby
GAVIN PURCELL	Peter Davison
INSPECTOR BURKE	Terry Molloy
BRIAN RUTHERFORD	Geoffrey Beevers
BARBARA TAPLOE	Charmian May
GEORGIE	Mark Gatiss
CHRISTIAN	Daniel Matthews

ANDREW POWELL   Reece Shearsmith
LUKE   Stephen Dolomore

STORY:
Satanic rites at a Winterbourne school bring Liz Shaw and her team to investigate the gruesome murder of the school's headmaster.

NOTES:
Caroline John returns as Liz Shaw for the second entry in the *P.R.O.B.E.* series (see above). Louise Jameson also returns, as does Peter Davison. The script is again by Mark Gatiss. Terry Molloy played Davros in the *Doctor Who* television series between 1984 and 1988. Geoffrey Beevers, as well as being Caroline John's husband, also played the Master in the 1981 *Doctor Who* serial 'The Keeper of Traken'. This movie was originally released in two volumes.

DOWNTIME (1995)
Reeltime Pictures/Tropicana Holdings/Dominitemporal Services
70 mins approx

Original Story and Screenplay by Marc Platt
Produced by Keith Barnfather
Associate Producers: Ian Levine, Paul Cuthbert-Brown, Andrew Beech
Directed by Christopher Barry
Music by Ian Levine, Nigel Stock and Erwin Keiles

CAST:
BRIGADIER LETHBRIDGE-STEWART   Nicholas Courtney
SARAH-JANE SMITH   Elisabeth Sladen
VICTORIA WATERFIELD   Deborah Watling
PROFESSOR TRAVERS   Jack Watling
KATE LETHBRIDGE-STEWART   Beverley Cressman
DANIEL HINTON   Mark Trotman
HARRODS   Geoffrey Beevers
CHRISTOPHER RICE   Peter Silverleaf
ANTHONY   John Leeson
CAPTAIN CAVENDISH   Miles Richardson
LAMA   James Bree
RECEPTIONIST   Kathy Coulter
GORDON LETHBRIDGE-STEWART   Alexander Landen
CHILLY 1   Jonathan Clarkson
CHILLY 2   Miles Cherry
LEAD YETI   Richard Landen

YETI	David J Howe
	Tony Clark
	Conrad Turner
UNIT SOLDIERS	Stephen Bradshaw
	Keith Brooks
	Mark Moore
	Gabriel Mykaj
	John Reddington

STORY:
A quarter of a century after its last invasion of Earth, the Great Intelligence returns and some of the Doctor's oldest friends must defeat the menace.

NOTES:
Downtime probably has more direct links with the *Doctor Who* television series than any other spin-off. Its heroes are Brigadier Alistair Gordon Lethbridge-Stewart and Sarah Jane Smith. The Great Intelligence and its robotic servants, the Yeti, return from the programme's fifth season (see Chapter Four) and we also get to meet up with both Professor Travers and Victoria Waterfield from the same period. All these characters are played by the same actors who created the parts for television. In addition to this, the script comes from one of the *Doctor Who* series' own scriptwriters, Marc Platt, who wrote 'Ghost Light' for the twenty-sixth season in 1989. The production is directed by one of *Doctor Who*'s most oft-used television directors, Christopher Barry, who returns to *Doctor Who* for the first time since 1979. Actors John Leeson, James Bree and Geoffrey Beevers had all appeared in *Doctor Who* before, with Leeson best known for providing the voice of the Doctor's robot dog K-9. *Downtime* was novelised by Platt in 1996 for Virgin Publishing's range of *Doctor Who* books. Finally, *Downtime*'s Kate Lethbridge-Stewart, here played by Beverley Cressman, crossed over into the *Doctor Who* television series in 2012. Now played by Jemma Redgrave, she appeared in that year's episode 'The Power of Three'. She then returned for the show's fiftieth anniversary story in 2013.

P.R.O.B.E. – UNNATURAL SELECTION (1996)
BBV
47 mins approx

Written by Mark Gatiss
Produced and directed by Bill Baggs
Music by Mark Ayres

CAST:

LIZ SHAW	Caroline John
PATRICIA HAGGARD	Louise Jameson
BRIAN RUTHERFORD	Geoffrey Beevers
JULIUS QUILTER	Charles Kay
ALFRED EMERSON	Mark Gatiss
COLONEL ACKROYD	Alexander Kirk
DR GILCHRIST	Patricia Merrick
CLARE	Zoe Randall
ANGELA	Kathryn Rayner
CUMMINGS	Jonathan Rigby
DR DENNIS LANCASTER	Simon Wolfe
SECURITY GUARD	George Murphy
SOLDIERS	Stephen Bradshaw
	Keith Brooks
	Mark Moore
	Gabriel Mykaj

STORY:
The discovery of a number of horrifically mutated human bodies brings about the reopening of a file on a secret government project.

NOTES:
John, Jameson, Beevers and Gatiss all return for the third of Bill Baggs' *P.R.O.B.E.* videos. Although an independent production, this particular movie called on the services of Mike Tucker of the BBC's own Visual Effects Department to supervise a number of special effects shots. Tucker had worked as a visual effects assistant on several *Doctor Who* television stories and associated productions in the late 1980s and early 1990s. Later, when the show returned to television, he headed up the BBC Model Unit, who worked on a number of episodes between 2004 and 2006. The Model Unit split from the BBC in 2006 and became an independent company, next working on the *Doctor Who* television series in 2012, providing effects shots for an episode called 'Cold War' (2013).

P.R.O.B.E. – GHOSTS OF WINTERBOURNE (1996)
BBV
42 mins approx

Written by Mark Gatiss
Produced and directed by Bill Baggs
Music by Mark Ayres

CAST:

LIZ SHAW	Caroline John
PATRICIA HAGGARD	Louise Jameson
GAVIN PURCELL	Peter Davison
MARGARET WYNDHAM	Charmian May
CHRISTIAN	Daniel Matthews
ANDREW POWELL	Reece Shearsmith
MAX	David Hankinson
IAN	Nathan Hamlett
LIBRARIAN	Alan Nicholas

STORY:
When a body goes missing and book on black magic is stolen from a museum, Liz Shaw's team are forced to return to an old case.

NOTES:
Peter Davison rejoins John and Jameson for Baggs' and Gatiss's final *P.R.O.B.E.* movie – a sequel to the earlier *Devil of Winterbourne*. The production again turned to the BBC Visual Effects Department to achieve certain effects shots.

AUTON (1997)
BBV
56 mins approx

Written and directed by Nicholas Briggs
Produced by Bill Baggs
Music by Alistair Lock

CAST:

LOCKWOOD	Michael Wade
WINSLET	George Telfer
DR SALLY ARNOLD	Bryonie Pritchard
JANICE	Verona Chard
DANIEL MATTHEWS	Reece Shearsmith
RAMSAY	Andrew Fettes
SOLDIERS	Richard Smith
	Gabriel Mykaj
	Mike Parry
	David Ringwood
AUTONS	John Ainsworth
	Gareth Baggs
	Blaine Coughlan

STORY:
A long-dormant alien menace is brought back to life at a military storage facility.

NOTES:
This was the first spin-off video not to feature any members of the cast of the BBC television series. It was originally planned as a follow-up to *Downtime*, with actor Nicholas Courtney set to reprise his role as Brigadier Lethbridge-Stewart. However, when Courtney became suddenly unavailable due to illness just weeks before the studio recording, the script had to be hastily rewritten for a new lead character, Lockwood. The principal connection between this production and *Doctor Who* was its use of the alien Nestenes and their plastic Auton servants, which had appeared in two *Doctor Who* television serials in the early 1970s: 'Spearhead From Space' (1970) and 'Terror of the Autons' (1971). This pre-dated the Autons' reintroduction to the show in the 2005 episode 'Rose'.

AUTON 2 – SENTINEL (1998)
BBV
57 mins approx

Written and directed by Nicholas Briggs
Produced by Bill Baggs
Music by Alistair Lock

CAST:

LOCKWOOD	Michael Wade
WINSLET	George Telfer
NATASHA ALEXANDER	Jo Castleton
DR. SALLY ARNOLD	Bryonie Pritchard
RAMSAY	Andrew Fettes
WILSON	John Wadmore
DARON	Warren Howard
CHARLOTTE	Patricia Merrick
DAVE	David Rowston
MIKE	Nicholas Briggs
HARDGRAVES	John Hawkins
DAVIS	John Hansell
SOLDIERS	Mark Moore
	Gabriel Mykaj
	Blaine Coughlan

STORY:
Two years on from the Auton incursion at UNIT's warehouse facility, the Nestenes resurface on the isolated Sentinel Island.

NOTES:
A sequel to the previous year's *Auton*, again featuring the Nestenes and Autons. This is the first spin-off to make substantial use of computer generated imagery and the first to feature an entirely computer generated character in the shape of a Nestene creature. As with the original *Auton* spin-off, design concepts for the Autons and their energy spheres were borrowed from the *Doctor Who* television series. In contrast to *Auton*, this sequel was recorded almost entirely on location.

LUST IN SPACE (1998)
Reeltime Pictures
55 mins approx

Written and directed by Roger Stevens
Produced by Keith Barnfather

CAST:

JUDGE	Nicholas Courtney
THE DEFENCE	James Bree
PROSECUTION	Mark Strickson
CLERK	Steve Nankervis

STORY:
Was *Doctor Who* ever guilty of sexism? The series is put on trial.

NOTES:
This 1998 documentary is not really a spin-off movie as such, and it makes no attempt to continue or pick up on the *Doctor Who* story. However, it does feature a number of dramatised scenes, in which the *Doctor Who* television show is brought before a fictional courtroom to defend itself against charges of sexism.

MINDGAME (1998)
Reeltime Pictures
30 mins approx

Written by Terrance Dicks
Produced and directed by Keith Barnfather

CAST:

HUMAN	Sophie Aldred
SONTARAN	Toby Aspin
DRACONIAN	Miles Richardson
ALIEN	Bryan Robson

STORY:
A human, a Sontaran and a Draconian all find themselves trapped together in a cell on an unknown planetoid.

NOTES:
The second spin-off to be written by former *Doctor Who* script editor and writer Terrance Dicks. The only two aspects of this story directly tied to the television series are the use of a Draconian, whose race appeared in a 1973 serial 'Frontier in Space', and a lone Sontaran. Although the character played by Sophie Aldred is never named, it is clearly suggested that she is Ace, the Doctor's former travelling companion from the late 1980s television episodes of *Doctor Who*. The unnamed Sontaran is later identified as Sarg in *Mindgame Trilogy*, a sequel to this first story.

AUTON 3 – THE AWAKENING (1999)
BBV
57 mins approx

Written by Nicholas Briggs (writing as Arthur Wallis) and Paul Ebbs
Produced by Bill Baggs
Directed by Bill Baggs and Patricia Merrick
Music by Alistair Lock

CAST:

NATASHA ALEXANDER	Jo Castleton
LOCKWOOD	Michael Wade
DR. SALLY ARNOLD	Bryonie Pritchard
WINSLET	George Telfer
ROSS PALMER	Graeme Du Fresne
RAMSAY	Andrew Fettes
NURSE	Helen Baggs
DALBY	Peter Trapani
AUTONS	Steve Johnson
	Blaine Coughlan

STORY:
Lockwood has gone missing. UNIT set up a team to track him down before

the Nestenes can use his mind as a means to take over the planet.

NOTES:
The conclusion to the *Auton* trilogy and the only one of the series not to be directed (nor solely written) by Nicholas Briggs. *Auton 3*'s co-director Patricia Merrick had previously been Briggs's second assistant director on *Auton 2*.

MINDGAME TRILOGY (1999)
Reeltime Pictures
80 mins approx

Written by Terrance Dicks, Miles Richardson and Roger Stevens
Produced and directed by Keith Barnfather
Music by Nicholas Briggs

CAST:

HUMAN	Sophie Aldred
DRACONIAN	Miles Richardson
SONTARAN	John Wadmore

STORY:
A Draconian ponders his future in a prison cell, a Sontaran warrior prepares to meet death on the battlefield and a lone human drifts through the void in her spaceship.

NOTES:
A sequel to *Mindgame* that picks up on that movie's three lead characters. The production is a portmanteau anthology picture, telling three quite distinct individual stories. Each story had a different writer. Actor Miles Richardson had to fly back to Britain from France (where he was filming on the US television series *Highlander: The Raven*) specially so that he could shoot his scenes as the Draconian in the segment he had written. The material was shot in a single day on a tiny studio set in London, then Richardson flew back to France again. The Sontaran was originally played by Toby Aspin in *Mindgame*. However, here he is recast as John Wadmore.

CYBERON (2000)
BBV
62 mins approx

Written by Lance Parkin
Produced and directed by Bill Baggs

Music by Mike Neilson

CAST:

LAUREN ANDERSON	Jo Castleton
GEORGE COOPER	Oliver Bradshaw
RAY	David Roecliffe
TOM MORDLEY	P J Ochran
DENISE	Camilla Aitken
BOUNCER	Mark Donovan
PATHOLOGIST	Glenn Supple
WAITER	Chris Bell
LAWYER	Jennifer Wagner
DETECTIVE	Nigel Fairs
CYBERON (Voices)	Steve Johnson

STORY:
A new wonder-drug called Cyberon offers hope to a group of patients with severe brain injuries. However, it has another, more sinister purpose too.

NOTES:
Cyberon probably has the most tenuous link to the *Doctor Who* television series of any spin-off. It features no cast, crew or characters from the actual BBC programme at all, although the script was written by a *Doctor Who* novelist. The story instead revolves around a race of cyborgs. The true nature of this mysterious alien race is never really explained. However, it is made fairly clear that they are meant to be some form of extension of the Cybermen, who first appeared in the *Doctor Who* television series in 1966. The producers of *Cyberon* did not have any permission to use the Cybermen in their movie, so the word 'Cybermen' is not used in the production at any point. However, the Cyberons are obviously based on the Cybermen in both concept and design. The movie's central character, Lauren Anderson, would appear in *Zygon*, another *Doctor Who* spin-off, a few years later (see below).

DO YOU HAVE A LICENCE TO SAVE THIS PLANET (2001)
BBV
30 mins approx

Written by Paul Ebbs and Gareth Preston
Produced and directed by Bill Baggs
Music by

CAST:

THE FOOT DOCTOR	Sylvester McCoy

APPENDIX A

MARK DONOVAN	The Salesman
NIGEL FAIRS	The Licensor
GLORIA	Jo Castleton
RASSILON	Nigel Peever
DELIVERY MAN	Gareth Preston
SONTARAN	Rupert Booth
AUTON	Philip Robinson
CYBERON	Paul Griggs
CYBERON (Voice)	Paul Ebbs

STORY:
A mysterious traveller called the Foot Doctor attempts to thwart a plan by the Cyberons and the Autons to invade Earth.

NOTES:
A *Doctor Who*-related comedy featuring the Sontarans and Autons from the original BBC series and the Cyberons from *Cyberon* (see above) – making use of costumes that BBV Productions had left in storage from earlier video dramas. Sylvester McCoy plays a character who is deliberately similar to the Doctor as he portrayed him in *Doctor Who*, and the production makes some humorous play of its entirely unofficial status. Rupert Booth, who plays a Sontaran, had earlier played the Doctor in his own completely unlicensed fan video series.

THE MEGÈVE EXPERIMENT (2003)
Reeltime Pictures
50 mins approx

Written by David J Howe
Produced and directed by Keith Barnfather

CAST:
ACE	Sophie Aldred
VICTORIA	Deborah Watling

STORY:
The Doctor's former travelling companions, Ace and Victoria, meet one another for the first time.

NOTES:
Perhaps stretching things a little here, as this documentary from 2003 never purported to be a drama. However the video features a short dramatised scene featuring two of *Doctor Who*'s original cast members. For that reason

284

and no other, it is included here.

DAEMOS RISING (2004)
Reeltime Pictures
53 mins approx

Written by David J Howe
Produced and directed by Keith Barnfather
Music by Alistair Lock

CAST:

KATE	Beverley Cressman
CAVENDISH	Miles Richardson
GHOST	Andrew Wisher
TIME SENSITIVE	Amanda Evans
DAEMON	Alistair Lock
NARRATOR	Ian Richardson
PRIESTS	Andy Delafield
	Christian James
	Stefano Rossini
	Bevis Taylor

STORY:
When ghosts start haunting an isolated cottage, it presages the return of an ancient supernatural menace, long thought destroyed.

NOTES:
A sequel to both the *Doctor Who* television story 'The Daemons' (1971) and the earlier independent spin-off movie *Downtime* (1995) – and also a tie-in to Telos Publishing's range of *Time Hunter* novellas, a literary *Doctor Who* spin-off. Something of a family affair, *Daemos Rising* features husband and wife actors Miles Richardson and Beverley Cressman (from *Downtime*) and also Miles Richardson's father Ian Richardson – probably the starriest piece of casting ever to be attracted to any *Doctor Who* spin-off. Ian Richardson also owned the cottage in Devon where much of the movie was shot. The production was originally intended to feature the Sea Devils, a race of amphibious reptiles who had earlier featured in two *Doctor Who* television serials, 'The Sea Devils' (1972) and 'Warriors of the Deep' (1984). However, when Reeltime Pictures failed to gain copyright permission to use them, the script was rethought. Actor Andrew Wisher was the son of Michael Wisher, a regular guest in the *Doctor Who* television series who also cropped up in *Dalekmania* (see Chapter Three). David J Howe scripted a sequel to *Daemos Rising*, called *Face of the Fendahl*, but it was never made. The scripts for both

Daemos Rising and *Face of the Fendahl* can be found in Howe's collection of short fiction *talespinning* (Telos Publishing, 2011).

ZYGON (2008)
BBV
58 mins approx

Written by Jonathan Blum (uncredited) and Bill Baggs
Based on an idea by Lance Parkin (uncredited)
Produced and directed by Bill Baggs
Music by Alistair Lock

CAST:

LAUREN ANDERSON	Jo Castleton
MICHAEL KIRKWOOD	Daniel Harcourt
BOB CALHOUN	Keith Drinkel
RAY	Daniel Roecliffe
JOANNA	Becky Pennick
SAMMS	Alistair Lock
ZYGON	Nigel Peever
WEALTHY MAN	Matt Montgomery
WEALTHY WIFE	Lucy Lockly
INSPECTOR	Georgina Windsor

STORY:
Stranded on planet Earth for two decades, a Zygon commander loses himself in the assumed identity of a human named Michael Kirkwood.

NOTES:
Production on *Zygon* was suspended in early 2004, one day away from completion. In July 2007, producer/director Bill Baggs called his cast and crew back together to finish it. The movie was originally intended as a 90-minute science-fiction thriller featuring the Zygons, an alien race that had first appeared in the 1975 *Doctor Who* serial 'Terror of the Zygons'. The story was also a sequel to the earlier BBV production *Cyberon* and saw the return of Jo Castleton's Lauren Anderson from that story. Early (unusued) drafts of the script were written by Lance Parkin and later (partially used) ones by Jonathan Blum, both of whom were *Doctor Who* novelists. During production, Baggs decided to rewrite large sections of the script, inserting a number of scenes of full-frontal nudity. It was Baggs' hope that these revisions would help the video appeal to a wider audience. To facilitate this, around half an hour of finished footage was also cut by Baggs during editing. Parkin and Blum were both very unhappy with the changes and

asked not to be credited. In fact, the final production does not credit any writer at all. Although made entirely independently, *Zygon* was partly shot at the BBC's own television studios in Southampton. It is the only *Doctor Who*-related drama to receive an 18 certificate from the BBFC.

WHITE WITCH OF DEVIL'S END (TBR)
Reeltime Pictures
90 mins approx

Written by Sam Stone, David J Howe, Jan Edwards, Raven Dane, Debbie Bennett and Suzanne J Barbieri.
Producer: Keith Barnfather
Director: Anastasia Stylianou

CAST:
OLIVE HAWTHORNE   Damaris Hayman

STORY:
In her cottage, Olive Hawthorne, White Witch of Devil's End, thinks back over and remembers key events from her life, events that shaped her and her role as Guardian of the village.

NOTES:
Designed as a 'Talking Heads' style production, this production presented actress Damaris Hayman recreating her role as Olive Hawthorne from the 1971 *Doctor Who* story 'The Daemons'. The script was outlined by Sam Stone, and then several writers, including Stone herself, contributed the individual stories which tell of different times and adventures in her life.

The production was unreleased at the time of publication of this book.

DOCTOR WHO-RELATED PRODUCTIONS

Both BBV and Reeltime Pictures are perhaps best known for their catalogue of *Doctor Who* spin-off dramas. However, they were also behind a number of other *Doctor Who*-related productions. These included a large number of documentaries from Reeltime Pictures and a variety of audio dramas from BBV. In addition, both companies were involved in the production of a handful of independent video dramas that sit outside the *Doctor Who* canon. These independent movies are of interest to *Doctor Who* fans as they often feature cast members from the television series and sit in a similar genre. The best known of these videos are ...

THE STRANGER SERIES (1991-1995)

BBV's first productions comprised this six-part video drama series starring Colin Baker, Nicola Bryant and David Troughton. The series followed the story of a mysterious individual known only as the Stranger, played by Colin Baker, and his friend Miss Brown, played by Nicola Bryant. *Doctor Who* fans were attracted to the movies because of their intentional similarity to the mid-1980s *Doctor Who* television series. It was initially hinted that Colin Baker was essentially playing a version of his Doctor and Nicola Bryant essentially a version of Peri Brown, the *Doctor Who* companion character she had portrayed between 1984 and 1986. As it progressed, however, the *Stranger* seriesevolved into more straightforward science fiction thrillers, and it was eventually made explicitly clear that the lead character was *not* the Doctor. However, for a time, in the early 1990s, it was very much seen as *Doctor Who* by-any-other-name. The six videos in the series were: *Summoned by Shadows* (1991), *More Than a Messiah* (1992), *In Memory Alone* (1993), *The Terror Game* (1994), *Breach of the Peace* (1994) and *Eye of the Beholder* (1995). A small number of audio dramas were also produced to tie in with these movies.

THE AIRZONE SOLUTION (1993)

In 1993, when the BBC's own plans to celebrate *Doctor Who*'s thirtieth anniversary with the multi-Doctor drama 'Lost in the Dark Dimension' fell through (see Chapter Nine), BBV's Bill Baggs saw a gap in the market. He consequently produced his own video drama, *The Airzone Solution*. The story has no direct links to *Doctor Who* whatsoever. It is an entirely standalone environmental thriller. However, Baggs did manage to get together a very large number of *Doctor Who* actors to star in his production, including Jon Pertwee, Peter Davison, Colin Baker and Sylvester McCoy, all of whom had, of course, previously played the Doctor. The production was written by Nicholas Briggs and also featured Nicola Bryant, Alan Cumming, Michael Wisher and Gary Russell.

APPENDIX B

DR. WHO AND THE DALEKS (1965)

Cast and Crew

CAST

Dr Who	Peter Cushing
Ian	Roy Castle
Barbara	Jennie Linden
Susie/Susan	Roberta Tovey
Alydon	Barrie Ingham
Dyoni	Yvonne Antrobus
Antodus	John Bown
Temmosus	Geoffrey Toone
Ganatus	Michael Coles
Elyon	Mark Petersen
Thals	Gary Wyler
	Jane Lumb
	Sharon Young
	Ken Garady
	Jack Waters
	Nicholas Head
	Michael Lennox
	Virginia Tyler
	Martin Grace
	Bruce Wells
	Mike Reid
Daleks (Operators)	Robert Jewell (Credited as Robert Jewel)
	Kevin Manser
	Gerald Taylor
	Bruno Castagnoli
	Michael Dillon
	Bryan Hands
	Eric McKay
	Len Saunders
Daleks (Voices)	David Graham
	Peter Hawkins

CREW

Story	Terry Nation
Screenplay	Milton Subotsky
	David Whitaker
Director	Gordon Flemyng
Assistant Director	Anthony Waye
Producers	Milton Subotsky
	Max J Rosenberg
Executive Producer	Joe Vegoda
Production Manager	Ted Lloyd
Director of Photography	John Wilcox
Camera Operator	David Harcourt
Camera Grip	Ray Jones
Art Director	Bill Constable
Assistant Art Director	Ken Ryan
Construction Manager	Bill Waldron
Set Decorator	Scott Slimon
Film Editor	Oswald Hafenrichter
Sound Supervisor	John Cox
Sound Editors	Ted Priestley
	Roy Hyde
Sound Recordist	Buster Ambler
Effects Supervisor	Ted Samuels
Effects Assistant	Allan Bryce
Effects Cameraman	Peter Harman
Matte Painter	Gerald Larn
Electronic Effects	Les Hillman
Music	Malcolm Lockyer
Electronic Music	Barry Gray
Continuity	Pamela Davies
Wardrobe Supervisor	Jackie Cummins
Make-Up	Jill Carpenter
Hairdresser	Henry Montsash

APPENDIX C

DALEKS – INVASION EARTH: 2150 AD (1966)

Cast and Crew

CAST

Dr Who	Peter Cushing
PC Tom Campbell	Bernard Cribbins
Louise	Jill Curzon
Susie/Susan	Roberta Tovey
David	Ray Brooks
Wyler	Andrew Keir
Brockley	Philip Madoc
Wells	Roger Avon
Dortmun	Godfrey Quigley
Conway	Keith Marsh
Thompson	Eddie Powell
Craddock	Kenneth Watson
Young woman	Sheila Staefel
Old woman	Eileen Way
Burglar	John Wreford
Man on bicycle	Peter Reynolds
Man with bag	Bernard Spear
Lead Dalek (Operator)	Robert Jewell
Daleks (Voices)	David Graham
	Peter Hawkins
Robomen	Steve Peters
	Geoffrey Cheshire
Stunt artists	Eddie Powell
	Joe Powell
	Jackie Cooper
	Gerry Crampton
	Paddy Ryan

CREW

Story	Terry Nation
Screenplay	Milton Subotsky
	David Whitaker
Director	Gordon Flemyng
Assistant Director	Anthony Waye
Producers	Milton Subotsky
	Max J Rosenberg
Executive Producer	Joe Vegoda
Production Manager	Ted Wallis
Unit Manager	Tony Wallis
Director of Photography	John Wilcox
Camera Operator	David Harcourt
Camera Grip	Ray Jones
Art Director	George Provis
Construction Manager	Bill Waldron
Set Decorator	Maurice Pelling
Film Editor	Alan Chegwidden
Sound Supervisor	John Cox
Sound Editor	John Poyner
Sound Recordist	Buster Ambler
Effects Supervisor	Ted Samuels
Effects Assistant	Allan Bryce
Effects Cameraman	Peter Harman
Matte Painter	Gerald Larn
Music	Bill McGuffie
Electronic Music	Barry Gray
Continuity	Pamela Davies
Wardrobe Supervisor	Jackie Cummins
Make-Up	Bunty Phillips
Hairdresser	Bobbie Smith

APPENDIX D

DALEKMANIA (1995)

Cast and Crew

CAST

Boy	Josh Maguire
Girl	Natalie Jarrett
Mother	Anastasia Mulrooney
Commissionaire	Michael Wisher
Robomen	Steve Arnott
	Tony Aspin
	Dave Hicks
	Stephen Mansfield
Dalek	Mick Hall

CREW

Director	Kevin Davies
Producer	John Farbrother
Executive Producers	Colin Higgs
	Colin T Webb
	Ashley Morgan
Lighting Cameramen	Terry Doe
	Dave Hicks
	Robin Lee
Video Editor	Nick Elborough
Dubbing Editor	Mark Ayres
Productions Assistant	Katherine Barnes
Floor Assistants	Roger Diley
	Peter Gilman
Programme Consultants	Andrew Pixley
	Marcus Hearn
Set Decorator	Tony Clark
Props	Steve Allen
	Mick Hall
	Julian Vince
Modeller	Dave Brian
Make Up	Michelle Daniels

	Helen Colthart
Music	Malcolm Lockyer
	Bill McGuffie
Electronic Music	Barry Gray
Sound	Gerard Abeille
	James Mastroianni

BIBLIOGRAPHY

BOOKS

Douglas Adams – *The Hitchhiker's Guide to the Galaxy* – Pan Books Ltd (1979)
Douglas Adams – *Life, the Universe and Everything* – Pan Books Ltd (1982)
Anon – *Dr. Who and the Daleks – Campaign Book* (June 1965)
Tom Baker – *Who On Earth Is Tom Baker* – Harper Collins (1997)
Allan Bryce ed – *Amicus – The Studio That Dripped Blood* – Stray Cat Publishing (2000)
Mark Campbell – *The Pocket Essential Carry On Films* – Pocket Essentials (2002)
Mark Campbell – *The Pocket Essential Doctor Who* – Pocket Essentials (2000)
Paul Cornell, Martin Day and Keith Topping – *The Avengers Dossier* – Virgin Publishing (1998)
Sir Arthur Conan Doyle – *The Lost World and Other Stories* – Wordsworth Classics (1995)
Jeff Evan – *The Penguin TV Companion* – Penguin Books (2006)
Roger Fulton – *Encyclopaedia of TV Science Fiction* – Boxtree Books (2000)
Neil Gaiman – *Don't Panic – The Official Hitchhiker's Guide to the Galaxy Companion* – Titan Books (1988)
Peter Haining – *Doctor Who – 25 Glorious Years XXV* – WH Allen & Co (1988)
Peter Haining – *Doctor Who – A Celebration* – WH Allen & Co (1983)
Peter Haining – *The Doctor Who File* – W.H. Allen & Co (1986)
Marcus Hearn – *Dalekmania – Doctor Who at the Cinema* – Lumiere (1995)
Sally Hibbin – *The New Official James Bond Movie Book* – Hamlyn Publishing (1989)
Sally Hibbin and Nina Hibbin – *What a Carry On –The Official Story of the Carry On Film Series* – Hamlyn Publishing (1988)
David J Howe, Mark Stammers and Stephen James Walker – *Doctor Who – The Sixties* – Virgin Publishing (1993)
David J Howe, Mark Stammers and Stephen James Walker – *Doctor Who – The Seventies* – Virgin Publishing (1994)
David J Howe – *Doctor Who – Timeframe – The Illustrated History* – Virgin Publishing (1993)
David J Howe – *Doctor Who – A Book of Monsters* – BBC Books (1997)
Alan Hume and Gareth Owen – *Memoirs of a Film Cameraman – A Life Through The Lens* – McFarland and Company (2004)
Wayne Kinsey – *Hammer Films – The Bray Studios Years* – Reynolds and Hearn (2002)
Andy Lane – *Doctor Who – The Missing Adventures – The Empire of Glass* – Virgin Publishing (1995)
Jon E Lewis and Penny Stempel – *Cult TV – The Essential Critical Guide* –

Pavilion Books (1993)

Jean-Marc Lofficier – *The Doctor Who Programme Guide – Volume 1 – The Programmes* – WH Allen & Co (1981)

Jean-Marc Lofficier – *The Terrestrial Index* – Virgin Publishing (1991)

Jean-Marc and Randy Lofficier – *The Nth Doctor* – iUniverse Books (2003)

Tom Milne ed – *The Time Out Film Guide* – Penguin Books (1989)

Richard Molesworth – *Wiped! – Doctor Who's Missing Episodes* – Telos Publishing (2010)

George Perry – *Movies From The Mansion – A History of Pinewood Studios* – Pavilion Books (1986)

Andrew Pixley, Stephen James Walker, Gary Gillatt and Gary Russell – *Doctor Who Yearbook* – Marvel Comics UK (1995)

Tony Reeves – *The Worldwide Guide to Movie Locations* – Titan Books (2003)

Justin Richards and Andrew Martin – *Doctor Who – The Book of Lists* – BBC Books (1997)

M J Simpson - *Hitchhiker – A Biography of Douglas Adams* – Coronet Books (2003)

Daniel Stashower – *Teller of Tales – The Life of Arthur Conan Doyle* – Penguin Books (1999)

Mike Tucker and Sophie Aldred – *Ace – The Inside Story of the End of an Era* – Virgin Publishing (1996)

Tise Vahimagi – *British Television – An Illustrated Guide* – Oxford University Press (1996)

John Walker ed – *Halliwell's Film & Video Guide 2003* – Harper Collins (2002)

Patricia Warren – *British Film Studios – An Illustrated History* – B T Batsford (1995)

Nick Webb – *Wish You Were Here – The Biography of Douglas Adams* – Hodder Headline (2003)

VIDEO / AUDIO

A History of Horror with Mark Gatiss dir. John Das – BBC Four (18 October 2010)

At The Earth's Core dir. Kevin Connor – Amicus Productions / AIP (1976)

A Whole Scene Going prod. Elizabeth Cowley – BBC Television (16 March 1966)

Book Club – BBC Radio Four (2 January 2000)

The Curse of the Crimson Altar dir. Vernon Sewell – AIP / Tigon British Film Productions (1968)

Daleks – The Early Years prod. John Nathan-Turner – BBC Video (1992)

Daleks – Invasion Earth: 2150 AD dir. Gordon Flemyng – Aaru / Amicus Productions (1966)

Dalekmania dir. Kevin Davies – Lumiere Video (1995)

Doctor Who – Death to the Daleks (*Special Features*) – BBC DVD (2012)

Doctor Who – The Beginning (*The Daleks* – Special Features) – BBC DVD (2006)

Dr. Who and the Daleks dir. Gordon Flemyng – Aaru / Amicus Productions (1965)
The Hitchhikers' Guide to the Galaxy – BBC Radio Four (March 1978 – June 2005)
ITN Nine O'Clock News – ITV (11 August 1994)
The Land that Time Forgot dir. Kevin Connor - Amicus Productions / AIP (1975)
LBC Radio – The Bob Harris Phone-In Show (15 May 1988)
More Than 30 Years in the TARDIS dir. Kevin Davies – BBC Video (1994)
The One Show (26 June 2008)
Room 101 prod. Victoria Payne – BBC2 (8 April 2002)

PERIODICALS

The Australian Women's Weekly (31 August 1977)
The Berkshire Chronicle (6 August 1965)
The Chicago Tribune (3 January 1965)
The *Daily Cinema* (25 June 1965)
The *Daily Cinema* (8 July 1966)
The *Daily Express* (June 1965)
The *Daily Mail* (13 March 1965)
The *Daily Mail* (5 August 1965)
The *Daily Mail* (July 1966)
The *Daily Mail* (25 November 1976)
The *Daily Record* (November 1989)
The *Daily Record* (24 December 2009)
The *Daily Sketch* (5 March 1965)
The *Daily Sketch* (23 June 1965)
The *Daily Telegraph* (25 June 1965)
The *Daily Telegraph* (27 June 1965)
The *Daily Worker* (26 June 1965)
DWB (Doctor Who Bulletin) – *Issue 55* (June 1988)
DWB (Doctor Who Bulletin) – *Issue 57* (August 1988)
DWB (Doctor Who Bulletin) – *Issue 59* (October 1988)
DWB (Dream Watch Bulletin) – *Issue 64* (April 1989)
DWB (Dream Watch Bulletin) – *Issue 72* (December 1989)
DWB (Dream Watch Bulletin) – *Issue 81* (September 1990)
DWB (Dream Watch Bulletin) – *Issue 97* (January 1992)
DWB (Dream Watch Bulletin) – *Issue 106* (October 1992)
DWB (Dream Watch Bulletin) – *Issue 113* (May 1993)
Doctor Who Magazine – *Issue 92* (September 1984)
Doctor Who Magazine – *Issue 93* (October 1984)
Doctor Who Magazine – *Issue 113* (June 1986)
Doctor Who Magazine – *Issue 135* (April 1988)

Doctor Who Magazine – Issue 141 (October 1988)
Doctor Who Magazine – Issue 197 (17 March 1993)
Doctor Who Magazine – Issue 213 (8 June 1994)
Doctor Who Magazine – Issue 218 (26 October 1994)
Doctor Who Magazine – Issue 250 (9 April 1997)
Doctor Who Magazine – Issue 263 (8 April 1998)
Doctor Who Magazine – Issue 266 (1 July 1998)
Doctor Who Magazine – Issue 267 (29 July 1998)
Doctor Who Magazine – Issue 268 (26 August 1998)
Doctor Who Magazine – Issue 282 (22 September 1999)
Doctor Who Magazine – Issue 286 (12 January 2000)
Doctor Who Magazine – Issue 300 (7 February 2001)
Doctor Who Magazine – Issue 313 (6 February 2002)
Doctor Who Magazine – Issue 321 (18 September 2002)
Doctor Who Magazine – Issue 326 (5 February 2003)
Doctor Who Magazine – Issue 332 (23 July 2003)
Doctor Who Magazine – Issue 334 (8 September 2003)
Doctor Who Magazine – Issue 335 (15 October 2003)
Doctor Who Magazine – Issue 336 (12 November 2003)
Doctor Who Magazine – Issue 349 (10 November 2004)
Doctor Who Magazine – Issue 353 (2 March 2005)
Doctor Who Magazine – Issue 356 (25 May 2005)
Doctor Who Magazine – Issue 379 (28 February 2007)
Doctor Who Magazine – Issue 390 (9 January 2008)
Doctor Who Magazine – Issue 429 (12 January 2011)
Doctor Who Magazine – Spring Special (February 1996)
Doctor Who Monthly – Issue 84 (January 1984)
The (Glasgow) *Evening Citizen* (22 July 1966)
Evening Standard (20 July 1966)
Evening Standard (18 July 1977)
Everywoman (August 1965)
Film Review (June 1965)
Film Review (July 1966)
Film Review (August 1966)
Films and Filming (August 1965)
Films and Filming (August 1966)
The Financial Times (22 July 1966)
The Frame – Issue 10 (May 1989)
The Guardian (13 February 2009)
The Independent (15 February 1997)
The Independent On Sunday (29 August 1999)
Kinematograph Weekly (April 1965)
Kinematograph Weekly (24 June 1965)

London Evening News (February 1966)
Monthly Film Bulletin – Vol. 43 No.510 (July 1976)
Morning Star (23 July 1966)
New Reveille (31 May 1974)
The Oklahoman (11 September 1987)
Otago Daily Times (31 January 1996)
The People (June 1965)
SFX – Issue 1 (June 1996)
SFX – Issue 41 (June 1998)
SFX Collection – Doctor Who No.1 – Special Edition 20 (February 2005)
The South London Advertiser (12 August 1966)
The Star (26 June 1965)
The Sun (11 February 1965)
The Sun (21 July 1966)
TARDIS – Vol.2 No.3 (April 1977)
TARDIS (October 1978)
The Times (21 July 1966)
The Times (29 October 1966)
The Times (23 July 1980)
The Times (20 September 1991)
The Times (15 February 1997)
The Times (24 August 1998)
The Times (21 June 2004)
TV Century 21 – Issue 28 (31 July 1965)
Variety (10 August 1965)
What's On (25 June 1965)
Yorkshire Evening Post (20 August 1966)

INTERNET

www.bbc.co.uk/news – BBC News Website (21 May 1998)
www.bbc.co.uk/news – BBC News Website (24 November 1998)
brooligan.blogspot.co.uk/search?q=murder+rooms (3 January 2012)
www.galeon.com/artinmovies/GeraldLarn/Gerald_Larn.htm
flickfeast.co.uk/spotlight/interview-kevin-connor/ (10 August 2012)
www.filmflausen.de/Seiten/interview7.htm
www.heyuguys.co.uk/2012/08/07/the-studio-that-time-forgot-an-interview-with-amicus-director-kevin-connor/ (7 August 2012)
lovehorror.co.uk/amicus-interview-with-director-kevin-connor (8 August 2012)
www.tvstudiohistory.co.uk/ (20 December 2012)

INTERVIEWS

I am indebted to the following individuals who kindly gave me so much of
their time to talk about their own personal involvement in *Doctor Who* at the
cinema. Also listed are the dates these interviews took place:

David Thompson (09/02/12)*
Allan Cameron (29/02/12)*
Peter Litten (01/03/12)*, (07/03/12)*, (13/08/12) and (18/09/12)
Kevin Davies (31/07/12), (02/08/12) and (22/10/12)
Marcus Hearn (12/08/12)
Paul Catling (13/08/12)
Dr Fiona Subotsky (13/08/12)
Rodney Matthews (15/08/12)
Brian Eastman (17/08/12)
Colin Higgs (17/08/12)
Ashley Morgan (25/08/12)
Vic Simpson (27/08/12)
Paul Magrs (27/08/12)
Philip Hinchcliffe (02/09/12)
Mark Ezra (16/09/12)
John Illsley (01/10/12)
Ian Wingrove (08/10/12)
Paul Tams (09/10/12)
John Humphreys (14/10/12)

---

* David Thompson, Allan Cameron and Peter Litten were all originally interviewed
as part of the research for a magazine article called *The Doctor Who Films That Never
Were*, written for the 11 April 2012 edition of *Sci Fi Now* magazine.

INDEX

16386603R00168

Printed in Great Britain
by Amazon